Coping with Complexity
in the International System

Pew Studies in Economics and Security
Series Editors
Craufurd D. Goodwin
and Jim Leitzel, Duke University

Coping with Complexity
in the International System,
edited by Jack Snyder and Robert Jervis

The Macroeconomic Dimensions
of Arms Reduction,
edited by F. Gerard Adams

Power, Economics, and Security:
The United States and Japan in Focus,
edited by Henry Bienen

FORTHCOMING

Economics and National Security,
edited by Jim Leitzel

Incentives in Procurement Contracting,
edited by Jim Leitzel and Jean Tirole

Funded by
The Pew Charitable Trusts
Through the Program for
Integrating Economics and National Security

Coping with Complexity in the International System

EDITED BY

Jack Snyder
and Robert Jervis

Westview Press

BOULDER • SAN FRANCISCO • OXFORD

Pew Studies in Economics and Security

Published in 1993 in the United States of America by Westview Press, Inc., 5500 Central Avenue, Boulder, Colorado 80301-2877, and in the United Kingdom by Westview Press, 36 Lonsdale Road, Summertown, Oxford OX2 7EW

Library of Congress Cataloging-in-Publication Data
Coping with complexity in the international system / edited by Jack
    Snyder and Robert Jervis.
        p.   cm. — (Pew studies in economics and security)
    Includes bibliographical references and index.
    ISBN 0-8133-8607-1
    1. International relations—Philosophy.   2. International economic
relations—Philosophy.   3. World politics—20th century.
I. Snyder, Jack L.   II. Jervis, Robert, 1940–   .   III. Series.
JX1391.C665   1993
327'.01—dc20   92-26066
                                                                                CIP

Printed and bound in the United States of America

 The paper used in this publication meets the requirements
of the American National Standard for Permanence of Paper
for Printed Library Materials Z39.48-1984.

10   9   8   7   6   5   4   3   2   1

Contents

Acknowledgments

This volume's basic concepts were drawn from Robert Jervis's forthcoming book on systems effects and from the preliminary statement of his ideas in his chapter "Systems and Interaction Effects," in Richard Zeckhauser, ed., *Strategy and Choice*. We are grateful to MIT Press for permission to publish a revised version as Chapter 2 in this volume. Contributors to the volume have attempted to show how their ongoing research illuminates this approach to systems theory in international relations.

These ideas were discussed and elaborated in a series of workshops and meetings at the Institute of War and Peace Studies, Columbia University, during 1991. In addition to the authors of chapters in the volume, Mary Barker, Samuel Barkin, Mlada Bukovansky, James Davis, James McAllister, Biagio Manieri, Ren Yue, Alan Rousso, George Shambaugh, Tami Stukey, and Patricia Weitsman played an active role in these discussions and made a significant impact on several of the published essays. Several of the workshop participants and chapter writers wrote detailed memoranda which helped with the conceptualization of the project. Other specific contributions are cited in the notes to individual essays.

Teresa Pelton Johnson and Miriam Avins went far beyond the efforts of normal copyediting in working with chapter authors on conceptual, organizational, and expository problems. Working with them on a manuscript means getting an intensive course on how to write and think effectively. Not only is this book much better for their efforts but the impact of their tutoring is sure to improve our future efforts as well.

We are especially grateful to Joseph DePiro, Jennifer Dharamsey, and the staff of the Institute of War and Peace Studies, who provided efficient and congenial organizational support for the project and its workshops, and to James Davis, who prepared the index.

The book was made possible by a grant from the program on economics and security of the Pew Charitable Trusts.

Jack Snyder
Robert Jervis

1

Introduction: New Thinking About the New International System

Jack Snyder

By almost any criterion, the international system has undergone fundamental changes since Mikhail Gorbachev came to power. Most of these changes are making the world a more complex place than it was during the era of the bipolar nuclear stalemate. Political actions and reactions in that world, though often tense, followed a comparatively predictable pattern. Indeed, during the Brezhnev era, our eyes glazed over from the tedious sameness of East-West relations.

Mirroring that reality, scholars' theories of the international system were simple, parsimonious, and static. By far the most important attempt to portray the Cold War international system theoretically was Kenneth Waltz's *Theory of International Politics*.[1] His deductive scheme was driven entirely by one constant factor, the absence of supranational authority above states, and one variable, the number of great powers in the system. The theory of stable nuclear deterrence, sometimes adjoined to Waltz's theory as an explanation for the main features of Cold War politics, was likewise simple, static, and inattentive to the social, economic, and intellectual undercurrents that undid the Cold War system.[2]

Though these theories were not necessarily refuted by the way that the Cold War ended, they did little to illuminate that process.[3] Nor are they likely to be sufficient as guides to the more complex relationships that are currently emerging in the new international system. Preliminary attempts to use Waltzian systems theory and nuclear deterrence theory to predict or prescribe for the future have been inattentive to the manifold changes in world politics. John Mearsheimer, for example, acknowledges that the new multipolar distribution of power will create greater complexities and

1

uncertainties, but relying only on ideas about polarity and deterrence, his solution is to eliminate those uncertainties by recreating some of the features of the Cold War stalemate through nuclear proliferation.[4]

Richer, more flexible ways of understanding systems effects in international politics will be needed to cope with the complex interrelationships of the coming era. At the same time, the quest for parsimony cannot be abandoned lest scholars' arguments become as complex and opaque as the reality that they are trying to make comprehensible. The contributions to this volume are intended to demonstrate the feasibility of a flexible yet orderly approach to analyzing systemic interactions.

The second chapter in this volume, Robert Jervis's "Systems and Interaction Effects," serves as the touchstone for the other contributions. He analyzes the multifarious interconnections of complex systems, such as the international system, which confound diplomats and lead their projects astray. Most of the remaining chapters present case studies which show how these systems dynamics affected the management of international security and the international economy in the multipolar period from the late eighteenth century to 1945. The chapters by Richard Betts, Jeffry Frieden, and Kathleen McNamara discuss the importance of systems effects in understanding contemporary security and economic issues. A concluding chapter by Thomas Christensen presents an innovative interpretation of the requirements of systemic stability, drawing on the arguments of all of the contributors.

While the contributors take a variety of approaches, a few central themes stand out. The stability of the international system depends in part on how well powerful actors understand the system in which they are operating. As Christensen argues, a sophisticated comprehension of systemic effects should lead diplomats to adopt strategies to reduce the vulnerabilities of important actors in the system. These efforts should focus especially on reinsuring the security of the weakest of those actors, whose recklessness might be able to bring down the system. This means shoring up the position of the most vulnerable of the great powers. Crafting such a strategy will require an understanding not only of military security in the balance-of-power system but also of economic security in the world market. Insights from parsimonious balance-of-power theories can serve as a useful starting point for such analysis, but interactions with international economic, domestic, and transnational social systems cannot be ignored.

Increasing Complexity After the Cold War

Sidney Verba, a specialist in comparative politics not burdened by prevailing preconceptions in the field of international politics, has produced a commonsense list of recent changes in "the international system." He begins where more parsimonious theorists also begin, with changes in the distribution of power. Thus, the bipolar system has become either unipolar or multipolar, depending on which criteria are used, reflecting shifts in the power resources of major states. But then he notes a series of additional developments whose importance is evident but which fit awkwardly into parsimonious systems theories: the easing of great-power confrontation, the adoption of democratic forms of government in many more states, the strengthening of some supranational institutions, the renegotiation of some national frontiers, claims for statehood by new entities, and demands by international actors that states adhere to international human rights standards.[5] He might also have mentioned the spreading of market-based forms of economic organization.

The first reaction of a parsimonious systems theorist to such a list would probably be to deny by definition that this profusion of domestic, intellectual, institutional, and economic changes is a systemic phenomenon.[6] If everything is included as part of the system, the clutter of details will mask the underlying pattern. Thus, it is better in this view to focus on the bare structure of the system—for example, the distribution of power among its units—and treat other elements as residual factors, perhaps causally important in episodic ways but not part of the system's basic structure.

Though understandable on the laudable grounds of parsimony, this viewpoint unacceptably ignores the tight connections that many commentators see among the elements of Verba's list. The collapse of the Soviet domestic political economy triggered the change in the distribution of power among the major states, as well as the border disputes and the new claims for statehood. As part of the same process, the intellectual discrediting of the old Soviet political economy gave rise to liberal democratic aspirations among many key groups in the former Soviet empire, spurring regime changes and collaborative relations with the West in support of the liberalization. Demands for improved human rights, an ideological tenet and functional necessity of contemporary liberalism, go along with these domestic changes and the new East-West economic relationship. Finally, the strengthening of supranational institutions, which have been found essential for managing the high levels of interdependence among liberal but sovereign states, was not caused by the Gorbachev revolution, but it might nonetheless be seen as part of the same trend toward a liberal, interdependent pattern of world politics.[7]

Even if only part of the foregoing characterization is correct, it suggests that the analysis of systemic interactions cannot be confined to the balance-of-power minuet among states. Domestic, economic, and intellectual processes are tightly connected with each other and with the balance-of-power game. Causal impetus seems to run in every direction, including reciprocal feedback between domestic change and international behavior, as well as between military and economic strategy. Moreover, all of the major issues of concern to parsimonious systems theorists are arguably affected by these interconnections, including the military and alliance behavior of states. Relegating some of these factors to a residual category means *a priori* deciding that these interconnections are of secondary causal importance.

Recognizing the untenability of an arbitrary stand in favor of theoretical simplicity, parsimonious systems theorists tend to accept some of these interconnections but argue that the primary lines of causation flow from the structure of the state system to the resulting domestic, economic, and intellectual outcomes. In one variant of this view, Gorbachev's reforms are portrayed mostly as an attempt to redress an increasingly untenable international power gap by emulating more successful states. But proponents of international explanations for the Gorbachev reforms sometimes make the opposite argument: Russia could afford to dismantle its garrison state and liberalize because stable nuclear deterrence provides a virtually absolute security guarantee and makes power disparities irrelevant. Just as insularity gave the U.S. and Britain the necessary security to adopt liberal institutions, now nuclear deterrence is doing the same for Russia.[8]

Less persuasively, some proponents of international-level explanations also argue that West European economic interdependence and even West European democracy were Cold War artifacts that came with the American nuclear umbrella and the Soviet threat that overrode fears of each other. These luxuries consequently are predicted to collapse under the uncertainties of multipolar anarchy.[9] In such ways, domestic, economic, and intellectual changes are subsumed as by-products of military power relations. Though not fully convincing, this approach at least acknowledges that the question of systemic interconnections between the distribution of military power and other variables is an empirically contestable issue, not a definitional matter.

In contrast to ultraparsimonious systems theorists, the contributors to this volume are more flexible in adapting systems theory to the complex realities of international politics. Many of them do this by adding variables to overly parsimonious theories in order to generate more determinate predictions of the behavior that is to be expected in a given situation. These additions are not made indiscriminately but with an eye toward parsimony and toward consistency with the logic of the initial theory. For example, Waltz's method of simply counting the number of great powers yields indeterminate predictions about alliance choices in multipolarity: rational states may choose either to ride free on the balancing efforts of others, or they may in opposite fashion tie themselves unconditionally to their vulnerable allies. In the present volume, Randall Schweller, by the simple method of considering not only the number of poles but also their relative size, makes the predictions of balance-of-power theory more determinate.

Many of the contributors add to the richness and realism of simple structural theories by focusing on how the actors understand the system that they are in. Some older theories of the balance of power held that in order to achieve a stable balance, at least some actors had to understand the nature of the balancing system and act with the goal of creating a balance. Inis Claude called this the "manually operated" version of balance-of-power theory.[10] Recent theories have discarded this allegedly primitive notion in favor of the "automatic" version, wherein balances of power (though not necessarily stable ones) occur entirely through the myopic actions of self-seeking states. Many of our contributors, in contrast, go back to the earlier idea that systemic stability depends on the actors' understanding the way the system works. The chapters by Paul Schroeder and William Daugherty are particularly explicit in making this case.

An underlying assumption of the volume is that complex systems like the international political system are hard to understand. Many actors, consequently, think only about the direct effects of their behavior, overlooking feedback and indirect effects. Such failures to think in terms of systemic interconnections produce unintended consequences, many of which exacerbate conflict. Susan Peterson's chapter, for example, shows how Russian diplomacy on the eve of the Crimean War backfired by provoking unforeseen reverberations in British domestic politics. Likewise, Kathleen McNamara traces the unforeseen contradictions between the European Monetary System and the European Community's method of financing its Common Agricultural Policy.

Thus, one reason to improve understanding of systems effects is to help actors to anticipate which measures will help stabilize the system and which will have the opposite effect. Another, exemplified by the chapter on reputation by Jonathan Mercer, is to explode erroneous ideas about systems effects that impede cooperation. Conversely, two of the chapters—by Richard Betts on collective security and by Anne Uchitel on economic interdependence—warn about the danger of facile cooperation schemes which misunderstand systems effects. Yet another purpose of studying complex systems is to help actors understand which norms or institutions will help to overcome some of the systems effects that hinder cooperation in an anarchic environment. In contrast, proponents of ultraparsimonious systems theory often reject norms and institutions as irrelevant distractions from underlying structural forces.

In the remainder of this introduction I will try to place our approach to understanding the international system in the context of other literature on systems effects. First, I will explore some traditional and some novel ways of applying general systems theory to international politics. Second, since many students of international politics have come to accept Kenneth Waltz's highly restrictive definition of what may be legitimately included in an analysis of the structure of the international system, I will try to justify our own, quite different view. Pursuing this, I will discuss ways to relax the excessive parsimony of Waltz's systems theory. Third, I will discuss the problem of unintended consequences due to a failure to understand systems effects. Finally, I will take up the manipulation or management of systems effects. Readers should bear in mind that the case studies were written in response to Jervis's essay, not to my own theoretical arguments, which were written after the case studies were completed.

A Fresh Look at the Tool of General Systems Theory

Scholars studying international politics have become accustomed to a very narrow understanding of systems effects. For the most part, because of Kenneth Waltz's compelling reformulation of balance-of-power theory, they think of systems effects almost entirely in terms of the consequences of the distribution of power across states for alliance choices and international stability. Such ideas are indeed a fruitful starting place for understanding systems effects. Several of the contributors to this volume accept this point of departure, either explicitly or implicitly. Nonetheless, the perspective of general systems theory suggests that there is no necessity to adopt such a restrictive usage.

A system is commonly defined as "an arrangement of certain components so interrelated as to form a whole," or as "sets of elements standing in interaction."[11] There is no requirement that to be usefully studied as a system these components need to be tightly interacting or closed off from outside influences. As long as the mutual juxtaposition of these components significantly affects their characteristics or behavior, it will make sense to consider the ensemble as a system.

The general systems approach identifies a number of dimensions along which systems may vary: stable/unstable, closed/open, simple/complex, organized/unorganized, loosely/tightly coupled. Overall, the contributors to this volume portray the international system as open, complex, semiorganized, coupled in varying and conditional ways, and varying in its stability depending on the arrangement of its parts. Each of these dimensions merits brief discussion. Together, they help explain why we adopt a less restrictive definition of international systems dynamics than do other recent approaches.

Stable Versus Unstable Systems

Most students of international systems seek to learn which systemic configurations are likely to be stable, and which are likely to be unstable. Stability is thus the main dependent variable of international systems theory, though it is not the only reason to understand systems dynamics. For example, aggressors who care nothing about stability need to understand systems effects in order to decide how to exploit other states without provoking the formation of an overwhelming hostile coalition. Indeed, aggressors probably have a greater need for a nuanced understanding of systems effects because the general line of their policy runs counter to the natural forces at work in a balance-of-power system. They need to know the precise conditions under which expansion will not trigger balancing reactions and the precise limits that their aggressive maneuvers can reach at any given point. As the "Bolshevik operation code" might put it, they need a good systems theory to "know when to stop."[12]

Most scholars, however, are especially interested in the conditions that promote stability. For them, the first task is to define what stability means. In general systems theory, "the system is stable if it returns ultimately to its initial equilibrium point after a perturbation has been introduced." Conversely, it is unstable "if the perturbation response does not die away" but increases over time.[13]

In studies of the balance-of-power system, it is commonly argued that the system tends toward stability because aggression gives rise to balancing reactions which reestablish an equilibrium of power. If bandwagoning reactions to aggression were more common than balancing responses (which they are not), then the international system would be unstable.[14] Each power would vie to be more offensive than the next in order to promote its own bandwagon, and one of these contending powers would quickly establish a global hegemony.

Of course, most scholars have somewhat more restrictive standards in mind when they seek to learn whether a system is stable or unstable. They want to know not just that balances recurrently form or that in the long run balancing is more common than bandwagoning. Scholars and state leaders want to know whether the particular states they care about will survive the balancing process and at what cost. We are not satisfied to label 1914 and 1939 as stable systems simply because the aggressors failed in their bids for hegemony. Consequently, we need to know which systems are more stable than others in the sense that the balancing mechanism operates at lower cost, and how the existing system can be made more stable.

Waltz's own hypothesis is that bipolar systems are more stable than multipolar systems. Even if this is true, this knowledge is of limited practical value since the polarity of the system is difficult to manipulate. Realizing this, Waltz and Mearsheimer pay great attention to the spread of nuclear weapons, a nonsystemic element according to Waltz's definition, as a purportedly stabilizing influence.[15] Other scholars look to still other mechanisms for enhancing the stability of the balancing system: the construction of institutions and norms that promote international cooperation; the adoption of defensive force postures; the encouragement of economic interdependence; the promotion of democratic change; the exploding of bandwagon myths.[16]

Whether such measures would actually foster international stability is open to debate. Anne Uchitel's chapter in this volume, for example, shows that some forms of economic interdependence have been a major source of offensive military strategies, which endanger the balance of power. But even to evaluate such questions, we need a broader definition of the international system. Such a definition should direct attention to the interactions among various subsystems— military, economic, domestic political, and intellectual—of the broader international system.

Closed Versus Open Systems

In terms of the independent variables, systems may first be classified as closed or open—that is, as entirely self-contained, or as receiving inputs from and creating outputs to their environment. In the case of very open systems, the designation of the boundary between the system and its environment may be essentially arbitrary. In the case of partially open systems, locating the boundary is less arbitrary. The boundary will fall at the gradient where mutually constraining interactions among the components fall off sharply—e.g., the national boundaries of a highly protectionist economy without a convertible currency.[17]

Waltz's theory, notwithstanding its imagery of tightly interacting parts behaving according to a systemically generated logic, in fact portrays a very open system. States in his system seek at a minimum to survive but at the maximum to "conquer the world."[18] Waltz makes no claim to be able to predict the extent of a state's goals from its structural position in the international system. The state's relative power undoubtedly affects, but does not determine its goals except within a very wide range. Thus, the variation in state goals must be largely explained by forces that lie outside the boundaries of Waltz's system. Moreover, the workings of the balance-of-power system are set in motion precisely by states who seek to conquer the world, or a substantial part of it. In that sense, the fundamental dynamic of Waltz's system is driven by inputs from outside the boundaries of the system, as he defines those boundaries. Finally, changes in the distribution of power, the key variable affecting the stability of the system for Waltz, are largely exogenous to Waltz's system insofar as they depend on uneven economic growth or technological change within individual states. In short, Waltz posits a very open system whose boundaries have been drawn in a way that leaves much of the consequential activity taking place offstage.

Simple Versus Complex Systems

Systems also vary along the dimension of complexity. Complexity can in part be defined in objective terms: complex systems are those that have many components, many feedback loops among those components, and multiple interconnections among subsystems. Conversely, simple systems have mainly linear causal sequences with few feedback loops and largely self-contained subsystems.

Many systems theorists, such as Charles Perrow, also define complexity in subjective terms: because of their complex interconnections and multiple feedback channels, complex systems involve "unfamiliar sequences, or unplanned and unexpected sequences, either not visible or not immediately comprehensible."[19] Likewise, Herbert Simon defines a complex system as one in which, "given the properties of the parts and the laws of their interaction, it is not a trivial matter to infer the properties of the whole."[20] Thus, systems theory is so fundamentally concerned with the difficulty of understanding the workings of complex systems that it builds intellectual opacity into the definition of complexity itself. Thus, by focusing on the unintended consequences of action in hard-to-understand systems, the contributors to this volume are working squarely in the mainstream of the general systems tradition.

One of the themes of our approach is the stress on the complex interactions of the various subsystems of the international system. Uchitel, for example, examines the interaction between the military balance-of-power system and the international economic system; Peterson, McNamara, Frieden, and McNeil explore the interactions between international economic systems and domestic political systems. As our contributors tell the story, these interactions are complex in both the objective and subjective senses of the term. Objectively, the feedback connections among these subsystems are multiple and complicated; subjectively, they are hard to understand in part because the specialized knowledge of scholars and practitioners often focuses only on one of these subsystems at a time. Both cognitive and organization theory note the strong tendency to make complex, interactive problems more manageable by factoring them into discrete parts, which can ostensibly be solved separately.[21] Though resorting to this expedient is to some extent unavoidable, it is the task of a systems approach to try to put the pieces back together again in an effort to rediscover the interaction effects that have been ignored.

Organized Versus Disorganized Complexity

Another important distinction differentiates between systems of organized and disorganized complexity. In disorganized complexity, according to Warren Weaver, "the number of variables is very large," and "each of the many variables has a behavior which is individually erratic, or perhaps totally unknown." Nonetheless, "the system as a whole possesses certain certain orderly and analyzable [features]."[22] Heated gas molecules in a container exemplify a system of disorganized complexity. Another example might be firms in a perfectly competitive market, acting on average "as if" they were rational.[23] Despite the lack of determinate predictions about any given component, statistical and probabilistic techniques can yield precise predictions about the behavior of the system as a whole.

Conversely, says Weaver, systems of organized complexity involve "a sizable number of factors which are interrelated into an organic whole." The behavior of an individual component is not random but is determined by its position in the organized ensemble. Systems analysis, not statistical or probabilistic analysis, is the appropriate method for understanding the behavior of the whole and its parts.

Which is the better way to conceive of the international system? Waltz's scheme portrays it as a system of disorganized complexity in two senses.[24] First, the system is an anarchy. The parts are interrelated, but more in the manner of pinging gas molecules than as parts of an "organic" whole in which different organs carry out different functions for the organism. Second, the behavior of individual components is at best probabilistic. The formation of balancing alliances against threats is statistically more common than joining the bandwagon of a threatening power. However, individual strategic choices remain highly indeterminate. In multipolarity, states can avoid making alliance commitments to contain a rising threat, passing the buck to others, or they can chain themselves tightly to reckless states in unconditional balancing alliances. The logic of multipolarity leads to each of these opposite behaviors; multipolarity alone cannot predict which course will be adopted. Similarly, in bipolarity Waltz's arguments imply that the state can shun alliance commitments in the periphery on the grounds that small powers do not affect the balance, or the state can overcommit itself in the periphery on the grounds that there is no one else who can contain the opponent's expansion. In this way, Waltz's system has the worst of both worlds: it is a system of disorganized complexity, but with a small number of units in the system. Thus, successful predictions can be made neither by statistical means nor through knowledge of the position of the unit in relation to the whole.

In part this problem may be intractable, insofar as it reflects the reality of the international system. In part, however, Waltz creates the problem of indeterminacy by leaving those elements that create organized complexity out of his definition of the system. States, the units in his system, may operate in a disorganized anarchy when facing states abroad, but they are part of a hierarchical, organized system when facing their own societies. States, therefore, are part of a system of organized complexity in terms of domestic politics, and this may make their behavior less unpredictable even in their foreign relations, which are influenced by their position in the domestic system. Beyond this, even the interstate sphere might be at least partially considered an organized complexity—organized by transnational norms, supranational or multilateral institutions, or cartel-like agreements among oligopolistic competitors. Most of the contributors to this volume conceive of the international system as organized complexity in at least one of these senses. This is true explicitly for Schroeder and Daugherty, implicitly for McNamara and Frieden, for example.

This perspective also calls into question a particularly faddish idea about the international system. Chaos theory, suddenly popular among social scientists by virtue of its success in understanding the hidden order in complex physical systems, has been developed for analyzing systems of disorganized complexity with large numbers of components. Applying it to systems of organized complexity such as the interacting systems and subsystems of world politics is a questionable enterprise.[25]

Tight Versus Loose Coupling

In tightly coupled systems, changes in one part of the system necessarily and quickly trigger changes throughout the system. Changes may even be amplified in a tightly coupled system such that small changes produce big effects in other parts of the system. In more loosely coupled systems, some parts of the system may be partially or completely buffered from the effects of changes elsewhere; changes are dampened, not amplified.

The instinct of most international relations specialists is probably to view tightly coupled systems as destabilizing and dangerous. For example, the domino theory, which spurs states to intervene recklessly abroad, posits a tightly coupled international system in which small defeats in far-flung corners of the globe might quickly erode power and credibility in core areas.[26] The Schlieffen Plan likewise created tight coupling before 1914, whereby any small Balkan quarrel could quickly produce a world war.[27] Similarly, in the strategic nuclear sphere, counterforce doctrines and launch-on-warning procedures create tight coupling of the most dangerous sort.[28] Thus, enlightened scholars look for ways to introduce buffers into tightly coupled systems. They will breathe a sigh of relief when they read Jonathan Mercer's chapter, which argues that Thomas Schelling's argument about the tight interdependence of commitments is a myth.[29]

But loosely coupled systems have their own dangers. Though the alliance system in 1914 was so tightly coupled that its stability was hostage to the most reckless power, the alliance system of the 1930s had the opposite flaw. Would-be allies were so loosely coupled that aggressors could expect to pick off their victims one by one. What determines stability is not simply whether the system is tightly or loosely coupled, but the way it is coupled. Bismarck's conditional, defensive alliances of the 1880s, for example, stipulated that coupling would be tight in defense of an ally who was attacked but that the commitment would be loose, or nonexistent, if the ally was the aggressor.

In summary, there are several strong reasons why it is necessary and legitimate to relax the ultraparsimonious criteria that prevail in contemporary international systems theory. These include the increased complexity of the post-Cold War international system; the practical need for more fine-grained hypotheses about the conditions for system stability; and the specific character of the international system as open, complex, partially organized, and coupled in complex, conditional ways. For these reasons, systems theories which vary in only one dimension, the number of great powers, will yield indeterminate predictions of limited practical value. Thus, the question is, how can excessive parsimony be relaxed without starting a slide down the slippery slope toward ad hoc description?

Ways of Relaxing the Criterion of Parsimony

The contributions to this volume illustrate four ways in which the parsimony of international systems theory can be eased in order to allow more determinate predictions and more useful insights into interconnections in world politics. These are (1) adding variables while remaining inside the deductive logic of structural balance-of-power theory; (2) adding variables from different, but complementary theories; (3) adding a second system or subsystem, such as the domestic political system, which interacts with the international-level system to codetermine the characteristics of the overall system; and (4) reconceptualizing the international system, at least partially, as a socially constructed system organized around norms and intersubjective understandings.[30]

Adding Further Structural Variables

Waltz counts only the number of poles in the balancing system and consequently produces weak, indeterminate predictions. In this volume, Randall Schweller stays within the Waltzian framework but permits himself a small reduction in parsimony by measuring the relative size of the poles. This allows him to make more determinate predictions about the strategic choices of states. It also leads him to reclassify the supposedly multipolar period on the eve of World War II as an instance of tripolarity. Thus, a very small retreat from parsimony leads to a novel, more determinate, and more persuasive interpretation of a major event in the history of balance-of-power politics.[31] All the while, Schweller remains firmly inside the fundamental logic of Waltz's deductive scheme.

In an earlier article, Thomas Christensen and I made a similar attempt to make the alliance predictions of Waltz's theory more determinate by adding a single, structural variable.[32] Since Christensen draws on those arguments in the conclusions to the present volume, it is pertinent to review them here. We argued that, for Waltz, bipolarity is more stable than multipolarity because the vulnerability of each of the two poles is less than in large-number systems. This invulnerability obviates the need for the two poles to chain themselves recklessly to allies to uphold the balance of power. At the same time, the poles' invulnerability also makes buck-passing less consequential for the overall power balance. For this reason, we proposed that adding a variable from Robert Jervis's theory of the security dilemma, which likewise focuses on the consequences of states' vulnerability, would in no way violate the coherence of Waltz's deductive scheme. Given Europe's checkerboard multipolarity, we deduced that when offensive military technology has the advantage, states will balance unconditionally (what we called chain-ganging); but when the defender has the advantage, states will pass the burden of resisting the aggressor onto others (buck-passing). Adding this one variable allowed us to explain fairly well the alliance choices of all the great powers in 1914 and 1938, with one caveat. That is, since decisionmakers misperceived the realities of offensive and defensive advantage, we had to add a perceptual adjunct from outside structural theory to achieve successful explanations. But even if the structural theory did not suffice on its own to explain the outcome, its parsimony and deductive logic allowed us to focus our question in a productive way. In the concluding chapter, Christensen again focuses on the variable of vulnerability in developing hypotheses about systemic stability.[33]

Adding Variables from Complementary Theories

A less parsimonious approach is to supplement ultraparsimonious structural systems theory with variables from other kinds of theories. In this approach, the deductive framework of a parsimonious structural theory of the international system, like balance-of-power theory or hegemonic stability theory, serves as a Christmas tree on which variables from other theories are hung. These alter the predictions of the basic structural theory, making them more determinate and a better approximation of reality. At the same time, however, the advantages of structural theory—its deductive character, parsimony, and focus on fundamentals—are largely retained. In this volume, for example, Mercer uses psychological theory to amend the predictions of theories of alliance commitment.

Interacting Systems and Subsystems

Another approach attempts to add not just individual variables to the core systems theory but posits additional systems or subsystems that interact with the core system. Included in this are some of the studies that portray world politics as a "two-level game" in which state organizations mediate between the demands of competition in the international-level game and the requirements of political success in the domestic-level game. Robert Putnam has provided a label for this approach through his seminal article on two-level bargaining games.[34] Despite the increased complexity of analyzing two games simultaneously, Putnam retains theoretical coherence by making commensurate assumptions about the games at both levels. That is, both games assume rational actors seeking to maximize their goals given the coalition possibilities allowed by the structure of the game; central concepts like "win sets" apply in both domains. The games at both levels are each taking place in systems with a distinctive structural dynamic. A true systems approach to two-level games should specify how systems effects constrain the win-sets of the bargainers, the domestic ratification procedures, and other game parameters.[35]

Other two-level analyses also study systems dynamics at both levels. Some of these operate entirely within the realm of structural rational-choice theories. Ronald Rogowski, for example, examines the interaction of domestic political cleavages with changing price levels in world markets in a theory that conceptualizes both systems in terms of neoclassical economic theory.[36] In this volume, the chapters by Frieden and McNeil trace the mutual interaction between the international monetary system and the domestic systems of key states.[37]

The interacting subsystems approach, in addition to studying international-domestic interactions, can also illuminate the reciprocal effects of the international military and international economic subsystems. As Uchitel's chapter shows, some of these interaction effects can be quite surprising. Finally, some theories may attempt to analyze simultaneously the interactions of several subsystems—military, economic, and domestic—as a unified, interdependent process. Christensen's concluding essay offers some thoughts along these lines.[38]

Systems as Social or Normative Constructions

An even more radical approach relaxes the assumption that system structures can be taken as objective given facts of nature. Instead, they can be viewed as social constructions rooted in intersubjective understandings about the norms and social purposes that establish a structure for social interactions. This can help in explaining where particular structures come from and by implication what might cause them to change. By conceiving of an international society as a complex system organized around its characteristic norms and institutions, systems theorists might make their predictions more determinate. Considerations of power alone may be compatible with a variety of strategic options, but power plus social purpose may narrow the range of predicted choices.

Michael Doyle's theory about the international relations of democratic states offers a highly successful example of this approach.[39] He shows that democratic states never fight each other because they share a normative framework that makes it difficult to legitimate aggression and hard to visualize mutual threats. At the same time, the clash of normative frameworks between democratic and nondemocratic states makes unrestrained warfare between them more likely than a realist theory would predict.

Sometimes approaches that stress the social construction of systemic structures imply that people create norms out of thin air and intersubjectively agree to treat the arbitrary system as real. This is not a useful notion. As Marx said, people make their own history, but not just as they please. John Ruggie's essay on laissez-faire versus "embedded" liberalism shows, for example, that a particular constellation of norms and social purposes emerges not only from a cultural and intellectual climate but also from underlying economic and political circumstances.[40] Social consensus emerges around particular ideas because they serve specific social functions and because specific social constituencies promote them effectively. With the rise of universal suffrage, political leaders came to understand that markets would have to be regulated by certain norms and political processes lest the politically active masses seek refuge from cruel market forces in fascist regimes. These ideas have affected the way politics and economics have been structured since 1945, both domestically and internationally. Ideas thus give rise to system structures, but at the same time ideas are also embedded in preexisting, underlying social relationships.

Similarly, the post-Cold War era might be characterized as one of "embedded realism."[41] That is, the international system may still be an anarchy composed of states that look ultimately to their own devices to provide for security in a potentially dangerous world. Nonetheless, the balance-of-power game may be played very differently than it has been in past multipolar periods because the game is now embedded in a very different set of contextual variables, e.g., democratic great powers with nuclear weapons holding changed ideas about the ethical standing of large-scale warfare.

The contributors to this volume who stress the socially constructed character of international systems are Schroeder and Daugherty. Both show that behavior in a balance-of-power system is decisively influenced by the social purposes of the actors, by the ability of the actors to think consciously about the requirements of systemic stability, and by the emergence of shared norms that regulate strategic interactions in the system.

In summary, the contributors to this volume explore four methods to enhance the usefulness of overly parsimonious systems theories by adapting them to the realities of the open, complex, semiorganized international system. These include adding variables within the logic of the core structural theory, adding variables from complementary theories, exploring interactions between the core system and other subsystems, and examining socially constructed norms underlying the system's structure and dynamics. The goal of these theoretical efforts is to improve understanding of systems effects so that actors can better anticipate the consequences of their strategies. In the next section I discuss why system effects are so hard to understand, and what can be done to mitigate this problem.

Intellectual Problems
in Understanding System Effects

Several of the contributors to the volume argue that the stability of the international system hinges on actors' ability to understand system dynamics and to use that knowledge to act in ways that promote stability. Schroeder and Christensen argue that the key is to understand how to locate the points of greatest vulnerability in the system and to design strategies for shoring up these systemic Achilles' heels. Jervis shows more generally that actors commonly fail to anticipate the indirect and feedback effects of their behavior. In short, actions in complex systems are likely to produce unintended consequences, which confound actors' efforts to achieve their goals. Moreover, as Richard Betts's chapter on collective security shows, attempts to stabilize the balance-of-power system may themselves cause instability if they are based on a misunderstanding of how the balancing system works.

Why are systems effects so hard to understand, and in what ways might this be remediable? One reason is that systems effects may be indeterminate, or at any rate indeterminate within a very broad range of possible outcomes. In Waltz's depiction of multipolarity, for example, states may respond to threats by forming tight balancing alliances or by the opposite strategy of buck-passing. Such indeterminacy may be an inherent feature of the reality itself because of the random behavior of some components, the large effects on outputs of minuscule variations in initial conditions, or self-conscious adaptive behavior of actors within the system.[42] However, insofar as indeterminacy is the result of a poorly specified or overly parsimonious theory, this can be fixed by improving the theory.

Another barrier to understanding is the sheer difficulty of tracing all the multifarious causal chains, including their complex feedback effects, that a hypothetical action might set in motion. Even if in principle these effects could be calculated, thinking up all the possible consequences, gathering data on the initial conditions of the variables to be affected, and testing hypotheses about predicted effects would constitute a daunting intellectual burden. To make the task manageable, the actor needs a fairly parsimonious theory to suggest where to look for the most important consequences, what data about initial conditions must be gathered, and which effects an action is likely to produce.

But theories can be part of the problem as well as part of the solution. Unintended consequences often occur because an actor's worldview creates a blind spot for certain kinds of effects. Sometimes this is a function of a specialized focus of attention. Generalists may miss the effects of their proposals on the domestic politics of other states, whereas area specialists will miss broader systemic effects. Likewise, military and economic specialists may overlook interaction effects with each other's issue areas.

Even more fundamentally, it is possible that human beings are intellectually hard-wired in ways that systematically hinder the understanding of systems effects. Some studies suggest that the bias for cognitive simplicity leads most people to leave feedback loops out of their causal "cognitive maps" of reality.[43] Jonathan Mercer suggests in his chapter, however, that at least one kind of cognitive bias leads people to exaggerate the systemic interconnectedness of alliance commitments. If so, this is partially good news: it means that people can understand systems effects if only they learn to discriminate the real ones from the imaginary.

Blind spots about systems effects can also occur for political and ideological reasons. I have argued that proponents of strategies of imperial expansion spread the myths that the balance of power does not work and that dominoes fall.[44] Insofar as such myths are persuasive, they may not only mislead the targets of the propaganda but they may also politically constrain the perpetrators to act as if they believed the myths. When subsequent generations of elites become socialized to the strategic ideology, the ability to distinguish tactical argumentation from strategic reality may be lost entirely. Thus, improvements in systems thinking can come not only from inventing better systems theories but also from exposing extremely bad ones that are being sold in the public marketplace of ideas.

Finally, the most pernicious systems effects are those that actors understand perfectly well, and precisely for that reason, they are condemned to take actions that leave everyone worse off. An example from Thomas Schelling is the reciprocal fear of surprise attack in a system where vulnerable strategic forces create irresistible incentives for a preemptive first strike.[45] In such cases of inherently unstable systems, a better understanding of systems effects can promote stability only if it leads to a redesigning of the systemic constraints.

Manipulating, Managing, and Remaking Systems Effects

A better understanding of systems effects can help actors to achieve their goals while avoiding the destabilization of the system. Beyond this, improved systems thinking can also help actors design institutions and promote norms that may overcome some of the perverse systems effects of competition in anarchy.

Some of the chapters in this volume show how leaders can avoid self-defeating policies by improving their understanding of feedback processes and indirect consequences of acting in a complex system. Jervis reminds us of the dynamics of conflict spirals and the self-defeating aspects of many coercive strategies.[46] Mercer points out that standing firm in an international showdown for the sake of future reputation is probably unnecessary. Peterson shows the importance of broadening the scope theories of deterrence and coercive diplomacy to take into account their indirect effects on domestic politics. As the West ponders a "grand bargain" to promote Soviet economic reform, McNeil recalls the unintended consequences of the Dawes and Young plans for the political stability of the Weimar Republic.

Some of these missteps could have been corrected easily if the actors had learned how to calculate better the implications of systems effects for their own short-run selfish interests. Deeper problems, however, may require leaders to learn to think consciously in terms of the long-run requirements of the stability of the system as a whole. For example, Bismarck, in my view, came to understand that German national interests could be achieved only if he promoted a system of conditional, defensive alliances which would stabilize the European balance-of-power system as a whole. Schroeder and Christensen argue that enlightened systems thinking should compel the strongest states to act in ways that reduce the vulnerability of the weakest great powers.

The deepest problems, however, may require more than enlightened policy change. If anarchy and the security dilemma really do create strong incentives for competitive behavior, states will not be able to decide simply to be more cooperative. They will have to create an objective basis for such cooperation by fashioning institutions that ensure that cooperation will pay off and not be exploited. Betts's chapter, however, warns that naive tinkering with institutional forms may, if it leaves underlying structural dilemmas unchanged, produce unintended consequences that will undermine the system's stability.

This volume does not offer a new theory of the international system. It does, however, offer suggestions and illustrations for thinking in new ways about international systems effects. Especially in the increasingly complex, interdependent, multipolar world that is currently emerging, parsimonious systems theory needs to open itself up to the analysis of complex interactions among military, economic, and domestic subsystems. Only by doing so can systems approaches help scholars advise leaders on the complex choices they face and the complex criteria that should guide the construction of a new world order.

Notes

1. Kenneth Waltz, *Theory of International Politics* (Reading, Mass.: Addison-Wesley, 1979).

2. Kenneth Waltz, *The Spread of Nuclear Weapons: More May Be Better* (London: International Institute of Strategic Studies, Adelphi paper no. 171, 1981); John Lewis Gaddis, *The Long Peace* (New York: Oxford, 1987), ch. 8; Robert Jervis, *The Meaning of the Nuclear Revolution* (Ithaca: Cornell, 1989).

3. For a balanced and comprehensive discussion, see Daniel Deudney and G. John Ikenberry, "The International Sources of Soviet Change," *International Security* 16:3 (Winter 1991–92), 74–118.

4. John Mearsheimer, "Back to the Future: Instability in Europe after the Cold War," *International Security* 15:1 (Summer 1990), 5–56.

5. Sidney Verba, unpublished memorandum presented to the Committee

on International Conflict and Cooperation of the National Academy of Sciences, September 1991.

6. See Waltz's criticism of what he considers pseudo-systemic theories in *Theory of International Politics*, ch. 2–4.

7. For several attempts to place the Soviet changes in the context of the broader pattern of international relations, see Sean Lynn-Jones, ed., *The Cold War and After* (Cambridge: MIT, 1991); Robert Jervis and Seweryn Bialer, eds., *Soviet-American Relations after the Cold War* (Durham: Duke, 1991); Kenneth Oye, Robert Lieber, and Donald Rothchild, eds., *Eagle in a New World* (New York: HarperCollins, 1991); Richard Ned Lebow and Thomas Risse-Kappen, eds., *The Gorbachev Revolution*, forthcoming; and Robert Jervis, "The Future of World Politics: Will It Look Like the Past?" *International Security* 16:3 (Winter 1991–92), 39–73.

8. An effective argument along these lines is made by Kenneth Oye, "Explaining the End of the Cold War: Morphological and Behavioral Adaptations to the Nuclear Peace," in Lebow and Risse-Kappen, *The Gorbachev Revolution*. Evidence for this view can be found in Vitalii Zhurkin, Andrei Kortunov, and Sergei Karaganov, "Vyzovy bezopasnosti," *Kommunist* No. 1 (January 1988).

9. Mearsheimer, "Back to the Future."

10. Inis Claude, *Power and International Relations* (New York: Random House, 1962), 48–50. See also Edward V. Gulick, *Europe's Classical Balance of Power* (Ithaca: Cornell, 1955).

11. George Klir, "The Polyphonic General Systems Theory," in Klir, ed., *Trends in General Systems Theory* (New York: Wiley-Interscience, 1972), 1; Ludwig von Bertalanffy, *General System Theory: Foundations, Development, Applications* (New York: George Braziller, 1968), 38; citations from Randall Schweller.

12. Alexander George, "The 'Operational Code': A Neglected Approach to the Study of Political Leaders and Decisionmaking," *International Studies Quarterly* 13 (June 1969), 190–222.

13. J.H. Milsum, "Mathematical Introduction to General System Dynamics," in Milsum, ed., *Positive Feedback: a General Systems Approach to Positive/Negative Feedback and Mutual Causality* (Oxford: Pergamon, 1968), 46–7. Thanks to Randall Schweller for these quotations.

14. Stephen Walt, *The Origins of Alliances* (Ithaca: Cornell, 1987).

15. Kenneth Waltz, "The Emerging Structure of International Politics," paper presented at the annual meeting of the American Political Science Association, August 1990.

16. For example, Robert Keohane, *After Hegemony* (Princeton: Princeton, 1984); Robert Keohane and Joseph Nye, *Power and Interdependence* (Boston: Little, Brown, 1977); Robert Jervis, "Cooperation under the Security Dilemma," *World Politics* 30 (Janaury 1978), 167–214, and other works cited elsewhere.

17. On open and closed systems, see Floyd H. Allport, *Theories of Perception and the Concept of Structure* (New York: Wiley, 1955), 469–484;

Ludwig von Bertalanffy, *General System Theory: Foundations, Development, Applications* (New York: George Braziller, 1968), 11–41, chapter 5; Ervin Laszlo, *The Systems View of the World: The Natural Philosophy of the New Developments in the Sciences* (New York: George Braziller, 1972), 36–40; John W. Sutherland, *A General Systems Philosophy for the Social and Behavioral Sciences* (New York: George Braziller, 1973), 36–51; Paul A. Weiss, "The Living System: Determinism Stratified," in Arthur Koestler and J. R. Smithies, *Beyond Reductionism: New Perspectives in the Life Sciences* (New York: Macmillan, 1969), 3–55, esp. 16–17. Samuel Barkin and Randall Schweller provided assistance on these points.

18. Waltz, *Theory of International Politics*, 91; also, 118.

19. Charles Perrow, *Normal Accidents* (New York: Basic, 1984), 78, also 88.

20. Herbert Simon, *The Sciences of the Artificial* 2d ed. (Cambridge, Mass.: MIT, 1981; orig. ed. 1969), 195. Randall Schweller provided both quotations.

21. John Steinbruner, *The Cybernetic Theory of Decision* (Princeton: Princeton University Press, 1974.

22. Warren Weaver, "Science and Complexity," *American Scientist* 36 (October 1948), 538–9.

23. Of course, both these systems need some entity, a lab technician or a political system, to "organize" the scientific experiment or to create the market's legal and institutional framework.

24. Waltz, *Theory of International Politics*, 59, argues that "international politics lacks the articulated order and the hierarchic arrangement that would make a general-systems approach appropriate."

25. Writers enamored of chaos theory include John Lewis Gaddis, "Forecasting in International Relations: The End of the Cold War as a Case Study," *International Security* (forthcoming); and James Rosenau, *Turbulence in World Politics* (Princeton: Princeton, 1990).

26. Robert Jervis and Jack Snyder, eds., *Dominoes and Bandwagons* (New York: Oxford, 1991).

27. Stephen Van Evera, "The Cult of the Offensive and the Origins of the First World War," *International Security* 9:1 (Summer 1984), 58–107.

28. Paul Bracken, *The Command and Control of Nuclear Forces* (New Haven: Yale, 1983).

29. Thomas Schelling, *Arms and Influence* (New Haven: Yale, 1966), 55–62.

30. The following sections draw in part on an unpublished memorandum by Thomas Christensen, June 5, 1991.

31. In addition to adding measurement of the size of the poles, Schweller also includes a distinction between revisionist and status quo poles. The latter is not really an additional complication of Waltz's theory, however, since Waltz himself recognizes that states' goals vary on this dimension. States, he says, "at a minimum, seek their own preservation and, at a maximum, drive for universal domination." Like Schweller, Waltz does not attempt to explain this variation in goals in terms of the states' structural position in the system. *Theory of International Politics*, 118.

32. Thomas Christensen and Jack Snyder, "Chain Gangs and Passed

Bucks: Predicting Alliance Patterns in Multipolarity," *International Organization* 44:2 (Spring 1990), 137–168.

33. Waltz's theory is not the only parsimonious structural theory that can serve as the basis for analyses of this type. Hegemonic stability theory and the more general theory of collective action, on which it is largely based, can serve as a parsimonious deductive foundation to which related structural variables can be added. For example, David Lake's theory of the role of middle powers as supporters or spoilers of a stable system is a parsimonious, fruitful amendment to hegemonic theory, much like Schweller's amendment to Waltz. David Lake, "International Economic Structures and American Foreign Economic Policy, 1887–1934," *World Politics* 35:4 (July 1983), 517–43.

34. Robert Putnam, "Diplomacy and Domestic Politics: The Logic of Two-Level Games," *International Organization* 42:3 (Summer 1988), 427–460.

35. For a very rough attempt to do this for one application of Putnam's theory, see Jack Snyder, "East-West Bargaining over Germany: The Search for Synergy in a Two-Level Game," in Robert Putnam, Peter Evans, and Harold Jacobson, eds., *Double-Edged Diplomacy: International Bargaining and Domestic Politics* (Berkeley: University of California, forthcoming); see also Andrew Moravcsik's introduction to that volume.

36. Ronald Rogowski, *Commerce and Coalitions* (Princeton: Princeton, 1989).

37. My own attempt to study the interaction of international and domestic systems is Jack Snyder, *Myths of Empire: Domestic Politics and International Ambition* (Ithaca: Cornell, 1991).

38. Other works that attempt to theorize across multiple subsystems are Immanuel Wallerstein, *The Modern World System* (New York: Academic, 1974), and James Kurth, "The Political Consequences of the Product Cycle," *International Organization* 33:1 (Winter 1979), 1–34.

39. Michael Doyle, "Liberalism in World Politics," *American Political Science Review* 80:4 (December 1986), 1151–1169.

40. John Ruggie, "International Regimes, Transactions, and Change: Embedded Liberalism in the Postwar Economic Order," *International Organization* 36:2 (Spring 1982), 379–416.

41. Robert Jervis coined the term.

42. For a comprehensive discussion of the failure to anticipate recent changes in the international system, see Gaddis, "Forecasting."

43. For example, Stuart Ross, "Complexity and the Presidency: Gouverneur Morris in the Constitutional Convention," in Robert Axelrod, ed., *The Structure of Decision* (Princeton: Princeton Univeristy Press, 1976), 104.

44. Snyder, *Myths of Empire*, ch. 2.

45. Thomas Schelling, *The Strategy of Conflict* (Cambridge: Harvard, 1960), ch. 9.

46. Robert Jervis, *Perception and Misperception in International Politics* (Princeton: Princeton, 1976), ch. 3; also ch. 2 in the present volume.

2

Systems and Interaction Effects

Robert Jervis

When you pick up one piece of this planet, you find that, one way or another, it's attached to everything else—if you jiggle over here, something is going to wiggle over there . . . We need this sense of the continuing interconnectedness of the system as part of the common knowledge, so that politicians feel it and believe it, and so that voters feel it and believe it, and so that kids feel it and believe it, so that they will grow up with an ethic. Because what we do—or not do—now will be an inheritance for all time. . . .

[To minimize oil spills] we should . . . mandate double-hulled vessels and compartments in tankers.

—Dr. Sylvia Earle
Leading marine biologist and ecologist

Although they are familiar, the basic ideas of systems and interactions go against the grain of instinctive ways of thinking and so are often ignored.[1] We fail to realize that many outcomes result from complex interactions of forces and behaviors. The world would be easier to understand if its relationships were straightforward, one-way, linear, and additive. During the Cold War, it was often sufficient to understand how the structure of the system influenced national behavior;[2] in the current era it is particularly important to pay heed to the range of dynamics that can be at work.

A few definitions are in order before we proceed:

- A straightforward effect is one whose direction accords with common sense. That is, a straightforward effect of giving foreign aid to a country would be to benefit it; providing incentives for a person to behave in a certain way would make her more likely to do so; a policy of deterrence would decrease the

25

probability that the target country would take the proscribed
action.

- In a one-way relationship, independent and dependent variables
can be clearly distinguished.
- In linear relationships, variable A influences B in direct
proportion to the magnitude of A.
- By additive I mean that the combined effect of A and B on C can
be estimated by summing the separate impacts of A and B. The
same method can be used backward to determine the impact of
any particular variable on a known outcome. That is, in
conformity with the standard scientific method, one can see what
role a given variable is playing by comparing situations identical
except for the difference in the variable under consideration.

I do not want to suggest that these assumptions and ways of proceeding
are always misguided, let alone foolish. But they are not adequate for
catching systems effects.

In a system, behavior may have consequences that are not linear,
additive, and straightforward.[3] A force may change the environment
in which it operates such that amplifying or counterbalancing forces
are called up; the kind as well as the degree of the effect may depend
on the magnitude of the stimulus; and the combination of several
factors may produce an effect that cannot be deduced from their
independent influences. Indeed, the language of independent and
dependent variables, actions and responses, and separate factors and
forces may be misleading when we are dealing with a system. Because
the impact of a change may be indirect and mediated, it may be quite
different from what our first impressions suggest.

Consider the epigraph at the head of this chapter. It seems obvious
that if tankers had double hulls, there would be fewer oilspills. But
because of interconnections, the obvious and immediate effect might
not be the dominant one. The straightforward argument compares two
worlds, one with single-hulled tankers and one with double-hulled
ones, holding everything else constant. But while this assumption is
analytically simple, the world is so interconnected that the
assumption is not only incorrect but misleading. In many cases, even the
most careful study could not predict all the consequences of an action
(and the predictions themselves could change some of the effects).
Indeed, I would conjecture that no major human endeavor has had all
the effects and only the effects that were expected and intended.

. We can nevertheless suggest that requiring oil tankers to have
double hulls might not decrease—and indeed might even increase—
the amount of oil that was spilled. Shipping companies forced to

purchase more expensive tankers might cut expenditures on other safety measures, perhaps believing such economies were justified by the greater protection supplied by the double hulls. The relative cost of alternative means of transporting oil would decrease, perhaps shifting the incidence of spills from the ocean to the areas traversed by new pipelines. But even tankers' spills might not decrease. Captains, knowing that their ships were safer, might go faster, take more chances, and get into more accidents than they did before. The current trade-off between costs and spills may reflect the preferences of shippers and captains who could adjust to the new constraints to return to something like the old equilibrium. Let's take an example from a different context. Society might try to compensate for weaknesses in the family by asking schools to provide more support and nurturance for children; this approach would not be effective if parents reacted to the schools' greater efforts to help their children by reducing their own efforts so that they could use the liberated time and energy for other purposes.

This reasoning may seem farfetched, but it is consistent with the basic insights of economics and systems theories. Some studies of automobile safety indicate that laws requiring the use of seat belts and better braking systems did not decrease injuries and deaths. Rather, drivers took advantage of the fact that they were more likely to survive an accident to drive faster or more recklessly. In effect, rather than saving lives, laws requiring seat belt use led to drivers choosing to save time spent on the road.[4]

Two Qualifications

Many actions do have straightforward and expected consequences, of course, for not everything in the world is connected to everything else. The way I behave toward my wife has very little impact on the price of cement, and vice versa. Even in the international system, many interconnections are weak enough to be ignored. Furthermore, some cases of apparent systems effects really are instances of actors either reacting to the same objective situation or being driven by internally generated impulses. Thus countries involved in an "arms race" may be responding primarily to domestic pressures rather than to each other.[5] In other cases, the interconnections may be understood by the actors and, as I will discuss below, can be used to reach desired goals.

Furthermore, as Albert Hirschman has stressed, straightforward effects are common, and unexpected consequences can reinforce rather than undermine the expected ones.[6] Indeed, if unexpected and undesired consequences dominated, it would be hard to see how society or stable human interaction could have developed. Action often does work: seat belts may not always decrease fatalities, but many safety measures have been effective. Even if it is true—which is highly debatable—that some welfare measures have increased rather than decreased poverty, government food stamps ended most extreme hunger; public health measures have controlled diseases; the federal highways program has vastly increased commerce and travel throughout the United States, albeit at the expense of a number of undesired and at least initially unexpected side effects.

Systems: The Example of Deterrence

Some of the ways in which systems produce indirect and unintended effects can be seen in the operation of deterrence; some of the failures to appreciate these system dynamics can be seen in weaknesses in some versions of deterrence theory. Although the idea of deterrence is built on the fundamental understanding that one side's behavior does affect the other and that the latter's responses affect the first side, many analyses are excessively static. They do not appreciate the alternative possibilities for the other's behavior and assume that the nature of the adversary, its beliefs and its preferences, remain unchanged throughout the encounter. In fact, threats can set off spirals of counterthreats; the state's attempt to increase its security can decrease it; the effort to contain an adversary can create an enemy; the effort to reduce the other side's opportunity to expand can increase the incentives it feels to do so.[7] These processes are well known to scholars, if not to decisionmakers, although the conditions under which they are likely to occur are less well understood.

Less familiar changes can be at least as disturbing for deterrence. First, success with deterrence may make later deterrence more difficult by increasing the challenger's dissatisfaction with the status quo and therefore the strength of its motivation for change. By blocking the most obvious paths by which the adversary could reach its goal, the state also inadvertently gives the other strong incentives to develop alternative means to reach the desired ends. In the years after the 1967 war, for example, Israel's air superiority kept Egypt from launching attacks across the Suez Canal. But this very fact drove the Egyptians to discover ways of nullifying this advantage, which they did by developing an effective antiaircraft system. Second, a challenger can learn and adapt to the tactics that permitted successful deterrence in the past. For example, if the defender prevailed by using the tactic of commitment—i.e., staking its reputation on standing firm[8]—the challenger might learn that next time it must act before the defender can become committed. Third, the challenger may change its beliefs about the defender in ways that alter the effect of the latter's policy. For example, it may react to a policy based on the "rationality of irrationality"[9] by concluding that the defender is so irrational that a war is inevitable. Or it may come to see the defender as a state that seeks to overturn rather than uphold the status quo.

Systems processes also operate when actors physically clash with each other. When the United States introduced combat forces into Vietnam, its leaders correctly estimated that it would be able to defeat the enemy's large military formations which were threatening to conquer the country. But they believed that this military victory would defeat the other side. Overlooked was the possibility that the enemy would revert from what Mao had called "stage III" (large-unit warfare) to the preceding phase of insurgency, with which the army was not prepared to cope.[10] A systems approach also questions the standard account of the late 1950s in which the American advisers in South Vietnam erred by worrying about a conventional attack from the North and so trained the South Vietnamese army to meet a fictitious danger.[11] It is at least possible that Diem's enemies turned to guerrilla warfare precisely because the South Vietnamese had foreclosed the option of conventional warfare. The American policy did not protect its client, but it may not have been foolish from the start.

Identification of a System with Its Parts

Common sense suggests that a system must share the characteristics of its parts. If a lawn is to be green, the component blades of grass must be green as well. But when the units interact rather than accumulate, this may not be true. According to Margaret Thatcher, "You get a responsible society when you get responsible individuals."[12] According to Charles Kindleberger, "For the world economy to be stabilized, there has to be a stabilizer."[13] It is frequently argued that for the balance of power to work, one country must be a balancer, or that restraint in international politics is possible only if the individual nations restrain themselves. But it is a mistake to identify the state of the system with that of its parts. A geometrical figure can be symmetrical even though—or because—each of its components is asymmetrical.

As the theory of collective goods makes clear, the fact that all actors desire a certain common goal does not mean that it will be attained. Thus even if everyone wants the system to be stable, no one may have incentives to contribute to that end. To turn Thatcher's quote on its head, even if individuals are responsible, the society may not be. Conversely, the system characteristic could result from the unintended by-products of individual actions taken for other reasons. Thus Thatcher seems to deny the basic argument of the *Wealth of Nations*, although she is a follower of Adam Smith in so many respects. Similarly, while Kindleberger's position is supported by arguments about the illogic of collective action, we cannot dismiss the possibility that stability could arise even if no stabilizer set out to produce this result; the externalities of individual behavior can be positive as well as negative.[14] The balance of power may similarly not require a balancer. Indeed, the mistaken argument (often advanced in international politics texts) that Great Britain stabilized the system by "holding the balance" in the nineteenth century seems plausible largely because of the tendency to equate the characteristics of systems with those of their parts.

Closely related is the propensity to treat systems as though they could be understood by summing the characteristics of the parts or adding up the bilateral relations between pairs of actors. One student of international politics maintains that "a system of merely growth seeking actors will obviously be unstable; there would be no provision for balancing or restraint."[15] Other scholars have argued that international systems will be moderate when the conflicts of interest between powerful pairs of states are relatively limited.[16] This commonsense position may be correct for certain historical periods.[17] But if we are dealing with a system, then immoderation, instability, and conflict can result even if the countries are peaceful and most bilateral relations are relatively good; similarly, stability and perhaps peace can result even if each state is dissatisfied with the status quo and wants to expand.

Indeed, the most careful version of balance-of-power theory argues that stability results not from the fact that any state desires this outcome but from the competitive interaction among states' conflicting desires.[18] Each state's attempt to expand can check the expansionist tendencies of others. The other side of this coin is that even if states follow moderate foreign policies and bilateral conflicts are relatively mild, large wars are possible. This is one reading of World War I. The states' goals were generally limited—even Germany did not want to overthrow the system—and the bilateral conflicts were relatively slight. France's desire to regain Alsace-Lorraine was muted to say the least; the Anglo-German trade rivalry was not a strong incentive for armed conflict; even the Russo-Austrian rivalry in the Balkans was much less intense than other conflicts that did not burst into flame. But the concatenation of elements, including other factors such as states' needs for allies and beliefs about military technology, produced the outcome.

Outcomes Do Not Follow from
Intentions—Indirect Effects

The previous paragraphs are linked to the most obvious characteristic of systems: the outcomes may not correspond with the intentions of any of the actors, even the most powerful ones.[19] This point is sufficiently obvious. I bring it up only because people—even those who write about systems dynamics—are prone to ask instinctively about any result of human action, "Who sought that?" Thus a sophisticated reporter analyzed the 1988 elections in these terms: "The electorate covered its bets . . . almost as if they had read their James Madison so carefully that they set off to the polls wearing buttons that read 'Checks and Balances Now!'"[20] But while many voters split their tickets, none may have wanted divided government. Similarly, in the closing years of World War II many analysts argued that because Stalin needed peace to rebuild his country, he would cultivate good relations with the West. But this judgment did not take into account the possibility that the way Stalin sought to guarantee peace and his regime's security would greatly increase international conflict. Thus it is not so surprising that the post-World War I system was consciously designed to bring about peace and stability and yet produced war within a generation, whereas the system after World War II was not designed at all yet endured much longer.[21]

Outcomes do not correspond to intentions because effects are often indirect, in two senses of the word. First, outcomes are often produced through a chain of actions and reactions. Second, the result of trying to move directly toward a goal may be movement in the opposite direction. Perhaps best known are examples of diplomatic and military surprise. A state believes that the obstacles to a certain action are so great that the adversary could not undertake it; the state therefore makes no additional efforts to block that action; the adversary therefore works especially hard to see if it can take it. More generally, actors often pursue "he thinks that I think that he thinks" reasoning in an effort to do what the adversary does not expect.

Some indirect effects work through fairly short-run calculations. For example, permitting members of a group to write a minority report could actually increase the chance of eliciting a unified document. The knowledge that a minority report is possible may induce a general spirit of compromise in order to avoid such an open split. The authorities in West Berlin made good use of this kind of dynamic at the beginning of the Berlin blockade. Knowing that much of the water for the city came from the East, West Berliners started to fill their tubs as insurance, thus dangerously depleting the water supply. Rather than urging people to conserve, the authorities assured them that water supplies were ample and they could use all they wanted. Demand quickly dropped to manageable levels.[22]

Nonlinear Relationships

More of a good thing is not necessarily a better thing. All physical and social scientists and most of us in our everyday lives know of cases in which the relationship between two variables is curvilinear. Nevertheless, our first impulse is to assume that a linear relationship obtains. Thus leaders commonly infer that if the adversary is difficult when it is weak, it will be more difficult when it is stronger. Of course, this prediction often is correct. But in other cases the adversary is intransigent because it knows it cannot defend itself and fears that any concessions will encourage others to push it further. Thus China's leaders apparently believed that others would see the country as weak when it was experiencing domestic unrest and therefore felt it especially important to be unyielding during those periods.[23] As such a nation grows stronger, it may become more reasonable. Eventually, however, its greater power will allow it to impose its desires and it will stiffen its bargaining position. Similarly, we might expect a direct and monotonic relationship between the resources an actor controls and his or her ability to influence others. But often the dynamics of the system defeat this logic: others react adversely to the actor's increase in power and his ability to harm their interests by mobilizing their resources and forming coalitions to contain him or her.[24]

When a policy instrument yields insufficient effects, proponents often call for increased effort. Since a little power, military force, economic aid, antidiscrimination program, or government intervention has made some but insufficient progress against an ill, common sense indicates that more will produce a greater effect. But the use of the instrument may have changed the environment so that continued or increased use will produce perverse effects. In the early 1960s, for example, when the U.S. provision of helicopters to the South Vietnamese army failed to produce continued advantage, attention should have focused on how the Viet Cong had countered the new tactic. Instead, the American military "requested *more* helicopters to conduct similar operations at a higher level of intensity. The new emphasis on air mobile operations also affected the [South Vietnamese army], which became dependent upon helicopters and fire power as a crutch in lieu of sustained patrolling."[25]

Linear thinking also underlies the common assumption that an ability to cope with the most severe threat or contingency automatically enables us to deal with lesser difficulties. Thus in the 1950s many defense analysts believed the forces that could deter the Russians from starting a nuclear war would also deter limited wars as a lesser included evil—"the dog we have to keep the cat will keep the kittens too" was the saying at the time. But when deterrence of all-out war is mutual, the ability to prevent the worst outcome is not automatically sufficient to cope with lesser threats.

Networks, By-Products, and Complexity

Because system elements are interconnected, a change at one point will have wide-ranging effects. Thus when the European settlers in North America made friends or enemies of a tribe of native inhabitants or gave them modern tools and weapons, they altered relations between that tribe and its neighbors, setting in motion a ripple effect. As one historian noted, "a tribe whose enemies had the weapons which it lacked had few alternatives, and all of them were unpleasant. It inevitably made war upon the competitor. So quickly did such hostilities arise after the entry of the European, and so fiercely did they continue, that observers were prone to consider war as the usual intertribal relationship, not knowing how they themselves had transformed these relations. . . . So swift was [the transformation], in fact, that it is doubtful whether first-hand [European] observers ever saw intertribal relations exactly as they had been before."[26] Intertribal relations were themselves interrelated through normal alliance dynamics, and so the initial stimulus provided by settlers' good or bad relations with a particular tribe in their immediate vicinity could affect the extent and shape of hostilities hundreds of miles away.[27]

Ripple effects move through channels established by actors' interests and strategies. Because the strategies are intricate, usually the ramifications are also, and so the results can surprise the actor who initiated the change. Maladroit German diplomacy in the late nineteenth and early twentieth centuries supplies several examples. Dropping the Reinsurance Treaty with Russia in 1890 simplified German diplomacy, as the kaiser and his advisers had desired. More important, though, was the indirect and delayed consequence—Russia turned to France and signed the Franco-Russian alliance of 1894. This increased Germany's need for Austrian support, thereby making Germany hostage to its weaker and less stable partner. In 1902, the Germans hoped that the Anglo-Japanese alliance, motivated by Britain's attempt to reduce its isolation and vulnerability to German pressure, would actually have the opposite effect by worsening relations between Britain and Russia (which was Japan's rival in the Far East) and between Britain and France (which wanted to pressure Britain into making colonial concessions), thereby increasing British dependence on Germany.[28] There were indeed ramifications, but more to Britain's liking than to Germany's. The British public became less fearful of foreign ties, easing the way for ententes first with France and then with Russia. Furthermore, Japan, assured of Britain's benevolent neutrality, was able to challenge and then fight Russia. This war initially increased Anglo-Russian tensions and then, because Britain thought Germany was egging Russia on when the latter's fleet mistakenly fired on British fishing boats, produced a war scare between Germany and England. The Russian defeat at Japanese hands, coupled with the strengthening of the Anglo-Japanese treaty, effectively ended Russian pressure on Britain in India, making it much easier for these two rivals to cooperate, much against Germany's interests and expectations.

In other cases, the existing network of alliances and interests was strong enough to guide ripple effects in ways that actors should have been able to predict but failed to. Because "the enemy of my enemy is my friend" and "the friend of my enemy is my enemy," it is not surprising that the American opening to China in 1971 not only distressed the Soviet Union (as it was meant to) but made other adversaries of China, such as India, more hostile to the United States and encouraged them to seek closer ties with the Soviet Union. Even South Korea responded by exchanging secret visits with North Korea.[29] We do not know whether Chinese officials were surprised by these effects, but American ones were: Kissinger has reported that the signing of the agreement between India and the USSR came as a "bombshell."[30]

The actors' behavior will be guided by the connections and ramifications they can foresee. Thus American policy in the Indo-Pakistani war of 1971 was based not on the direct issue but on the expected impact on China. Frequently, a state decides not to intervene in an issue because doing so will offend a third country whose favors it requires. When Austria argued that the city of Scutari should go to the new Albanian state in 1913, Britain's foreign secretary acknowledged that while this claim had validity in the abstract, Russia would object. "To my mind it is a matter, selfishly speaking, of perfect indifference to us as to who should be the possessor of Scutari, but it is of great importance that we should adopt no line which would in any way weaken or impair our understanding with Russia."[31] In other cases, a state's policies in a local area may be driven by the need to avoid the adversary's trap. Thus in 1915 Secretary of State Robert Lansing wrote in his diary:

> Looking at the general situation I have come to the following conclusion: Germany desires to keep up the turmoil in Mexico until the United States is forced to intervene; therefore we must not intervene. Germany does not wish to have any one faction dominant in Mexico; therefore we must recognize one faction as dominant in Mexico.

> When we recognize a faction as the government, Germany will undoubtedly seek to cause a quarrel between that government and ours; therefore we must avoid a quarrel regardless of criticism and complaint in Congress and the Press. It comes down to this: our possible relations with Germany must be our first consideration; and all our intercourse with Mexico must be regulated accordingly.[32]

But regardless of the form of the dynamics that are at work, contemporary and later observers will misunderstand the state's policy if they examine it only in local terms. British behavior on India's border issues in the late nineteenth century was largely regulated by policy toward Russia, which was in turn conditioned by general calculations of European politics. So when Russia asked Britain to join in putting pressure on Japan to moderate its peace terms in the wake of the Japanese victory over China in 1885, British diplomats were placed in a difficult position. They did not wish to offend Japan, but neither did they wish to sacrifice Russian support. In the end, they compensated for rejecting Russia's request by conciliating it on Indian issues—a connection that escaped contemporary observers and later historians who examined the border question through the perspective of the seemingly most relevant documents in the India office. As Gordon Martel, to whom I owe this discussion, points out: "Foreign secretaries were not in the habit of explaining their Moroccan policy to the Viceroy of India, nor were they in the habit of showing their Ambassador at Paris how events in the North of India influenced negotiations in Nigeria."[33]

The propensity to concentrate on bilateral relations is so strong that it can lead us to miss even the relatively manageable complexity that is produced when three states interact. Thus one scholar has nicely argued that American, British, and Soviet diplomacy in the 1940s has often been misunderstood because we have not appreciated the extent to which one country's policy toward another often had—and sometimes was designed to have—consequences that ramified throughout the triangle.[34]

The effects of one actor's behavior toward another are conditioned by the possible arrangements the other can make with the third party. Winston Churchill understood that such interactions would nullify some of his possible initiatives during the year of Britain's maximum isolation after France fell and before Germany attacked Russia. He saw that one consequence of Britain's successful efforts in the summer of 1940 was not to weaken Germany but to increase the latter's need for French support in what now looked to be a longer struggle. "Owing to our unexpected resistance," Churchill trenchantly remarked, "the Vichy authorities have been able to market their treachery at a slightly higher rate than would otherwise have been possible."[35] Similarly, although he wanted to improve relations with Russia, he rejected Foreign Secretary Anthony Eden's suggestion that he fly to Moscow: "A mere visit would do no good. They might simply trade it to Germany."[36] Britain's efforts could then allow others to strike better bargains with Germany, but Britain could do little to actually gain their support.

Coalition formation with as few as three parties may have no determinant solution. Indeed, the problem is not only one of choice and volition: many physical systems with three elements can be modeled only probabilistically. "A system as simple as the sun, the earth, and an asteroid . . . can become chaotic. Although all three bodies act according to Newton's laws of motion, the complex influences of the two larger bodies can make the movement of the asteroid so irregular that its future positions can only be described in terms of probabilities."[37] As the number of actors increases, the paths of interaction in the system multiply and become extremely intricate. For example, differences in the patterns of eating, aggression, and behavior toward the young in two closely related species of monkeys have been traced to whether the female or the male took the initiative in mating. Through a complex chain of causation, this one difference had far-reaching effects on many other aspects of the species' social structures.[38] Changes over time also display complex ramifications. It took a close observer seven years to figure out that the sudden shift from a territorial to a nonterritorial mating system among pronghorn antelope in a Montana national park was caused by a change in the age structure of the males stemming from a harsh winter three years before the study began. Furthermore, when the age structure returned to normal, the territorial system was not reestablished because it could not develop incrementally. Even a large male can defend his territory and harem only if many of the other males are tied down to their areas and females. As long as a great many males are free to be intruders, no territory can be defended.[39]

Implications for Testing and Method

When we are dealing with systems, static comparisons are not likely to be appropriate. This central implication of economics is sometimes neglected. Thus analysts often conclude that because the United States relies heavily on imports for vital raw materials, it is at the mercy of foreign suppliers. Neglected is the fact that cutting off the primary sources would prompt many other changes as the system adapted to the shock. Generally speaking, the price would increase sharply, leading to conservation, the search for substitutes, and the development of new sources of supply that previously were too expensive to be worth pursuing. Of course these processes do not solve all problems. But one cannot make sense of what will happen without understanding the interconnections that exist or will be called into being.

Even those who stress the importance of systems dynamics may make this error. Thus economists have been among those who have carried out the misleading studies of American vulnerability; and Kenneth Waltz, the leading analyst of international systems, has argued that the difference between American and European policies toward the Middle East can be explained by the fact that the Europeans are much more dependent on oil from the Persian Gulf.[40] But the market for oil is an integrated one; in the event of shortages the Europeans would seek oil from countries that now supply the United States and, if the market was not subject to political controls, even from American oil fields. Similarly, during World War I thinking in static terms led the British navy to conclude that convoys would not defeat the German submarine menace. Such tactics were seen as merely defensive, promising temporary relief at best. Only tracking down the German U-boats could put an end to the threat. In fact, convoying merchant ships forced the U-boats either to abandon their attacks or to come to a place where they could be destroyed by the naval escorts.[41]

When elements are interconnected, success or failure cannot be readily attributed to them individually. It seems obvious that one could try several tactics in different areas and then adopt the one that works best on a wider scale. But the tactic's success could be attributable to the entire ensemble that had been employed; the ones that had apparently failed might have contributed to the successes. The critics argued that in Vietnam resources should be shifted from the large search-and-destroy operations, which appeared to yield few results, to the pacification program, which had cleared the enemy from the areas to which it had been applied. But the army's reply may have been valid: pacification worked only because the large conventional offensives engaged and contained the enemy's most effective forces, which would have destroyed the pacification efforts if American policy had changed.

Even in a system of just two actors, processes such as these can escape the notice of those who are not sensitive to them. Thus in the fall of 1940, Winston Churchill believed that the threat of invasion of the British Isles had declined to a low level, but he resisted the suggestion that England should therefore send more troops to other fronts. It was the very presence of these troops that had reduced the threat of invasion, he insisted.[42] Leaders less sophisticated than Churchill may build their policies on the assumption that nothing else will change. Thus it is often asserted that an increase in arms will make the state more secure (ignoring adversaries' likely responses), or that if a state increases its contribution to a common venture, the result will be a greater combined effort (overlooking the possibility that the partners will respond by slacking off).

When actors take steps to influence others, they often forget that the change in their behavior will itself be noted, perhaps with unintended consequences. A husband may believe that he can please his wife by listening more patiently to her complaints and being more solicitous. But she may find this new behavior suspicious, if not alarming, and react accordingly. One of my graduate school roommates thought he was securing extra protection for his possessions by putting a lock on his bedroom door. In fact I am sure he was increasing his risk: any burglar would assume that the one room with a lock contained what was of most value.[43] On the international scene, when one state moves to commit itself to standing firm in a dispute with another, the latter may *lower* its estimate of the probability that the state will stand firm, rather than increase the estimate as standard bargaining theory argues.[44] The adversary may reason that if the state really had sufficient incentives to pay a high price in order to prevail, it would not have needed to resort to the tactic of commitment. Similarly, if a state increases its defense spending, the adversary may infer that the state feels militarily unprepared—and so probably will not fight. It is true that, all things being equal, increasing defense spending or becoming committed to standing firm will increase the chance that the other side will back down. But it can never be the case that "all things are equal," because a very important element is the other side's beliefs, which will be modified by the state's actions.

Our standard techniques for testing the validity of propositions assume independences that are not present in a system. We can see this by looking at commitment from a different perspective. Deterrence theory indicates that in situations resembling the game of chicken (i.e., those in which each side wants to stand firm, but the worst outcome for each arises if both do so and collide), an actor can increase his chance of prevailing by staking his reputation on maintaining his position before the other has actively challenged it (thus the problem of the other side's inferences discussed in the previous paragraph does not arise as strongly).[45] This proposition might be tested by comparing the outcomes of two sets of crises, one in which an actor had committed himself to stand firm and another in which he had not, and seeing whether the actor prevailed in a higher percentage of the former cases. But this method would in fact be inappropriate. Given a commitment, a challenge will not be issued unless the challenger either does not understand the situation or is extremely strongly motivated to prevail. In either case, the challenger will be difficult to dissuade. Thus commitment might decrease the number of challenges but not increase the committed actor's chance of prevailing when there is a challenge. This is so because any challenges will be a special subset of the crises that would have occurred even in the absence of commitments.[46] In other words, the characteristics that lead to a crisis are not independent of the actor's use of the tactic of commitment.

Even if actors are not in conflict, their interactions can cause changes over time that defeat the methodological assumption that the comparison involves looking at two cases which are the same on all dimensions except one. Many colleges use yield rate as a measure of their quality: if only 40 percent of the people we accepted actually enroll in our program this year, we must be doing worse than we were five years ago, when 60 percent enrolled. This inference seems especially compelling if the yield rate in competitors' programs did not drop. But perhaps the college's reputation has improved so that better applicants now apply: because many of these attractive candidates also are admitted to other institutions, the yield may fall. This explanation could hold even if the total number of applicants did not increase, since weaker ones might no longer apply.

More drastic changes can undermine the utility of yardsticks of success that were initially valid. This is especially likely to be the case when two sides seek advantage over each other. As each alters its behavior in response to the other's action, many of the standard indicators of success will be drained of meaning. For example, in the early 1960s the United States and South Vietnam established the strategic hamlet program in order to provide security for the rural population. They then used the percentage of the hamlets that were overrun by the Viet Cong as a measure of the program's success. But because many of the initial hamlets were able to withstand direct assault, the Viet Cong were forced to change their tactics and rely more on infiltration, inducements, and intimidation. As a result, while the percentage of hamlets conquered or even attacked decreased, this measure no longer was a good indicator of South Vietnamese strength.[47] Similarly, Israel's use of air power in the middle of the War of Attrition with Egypt in 1969 produced success as measured by a reduction in Egyptian artillery fire, but this impression is misleading because the Egyptians reacted by shifting to small-arms fire.[48]

Simpler dynamics of this type are also possible: if an actor lets it be known that he or she is drawing inferences from certain aspects of the other's behavior, those inferences may not be valid in the future. For example, when the Soviets asserted that nuclear superiority was possible, many American defense analysts argued that such statements showed that the USSR was aggressive. Soon afterward, such statements all but disappeared. The Soviets' outlook may have changed; alternately, once they saw the effect of their statements, they may have manipulated this source of information to create a more desired image.[49]

Games Against Nature Are Not "Games Against Nature"

Many of the errors we have discussed can be summarized in the claim that people often think that they are playing games against nature when in fact they are dealing with actors who will respond to them. But although nature does not scheme to defeat human efforts, it does react—or, more precisely, the elements in nature compose a system. While William McNeill may go too far when he talks of "the tendency towards the conservation of catastrophe," he is certainly correct to point out that many attempts to "tame" natural forces have unleashed more or different kinds of disasters.[50]

> In my lifetime the Army Corps of Engineers began to control Mississippi floods by building an elaborate system of levees along the river's lower course. This had the undesired effect of concentrating sediment on the river bottom between the levees. As a result, the water level now rises each year, and the levees have to be raised higher from time to time. Under this regimen, sooner or later the mighty Mississippi will break its banks and inflict far greater damage on the surrounding landscape than if there were no levees and the river were free to overflow each spring and deposit sediment across the breadth of its natural floodplain, as it did in my childhood.[51]

Attempts to control beach erosion provide several examples of perverse effects. To preserve the sand on her beach, a property owner sometimes erects groins that trap sand moving laterally along the beach. But stopping the flow of sand creates severe erosion on the other side of the groin, forcing the neighbor to build his own groin if his area is not to be completely stripped. And so it goes all the way down the beach. Realizing the dangers of this individualistic approach, other communities have tried dealing with the problem frontally—i.e., by constructing barriers to weaken the power of the waves and stabilize the beach. These rarely work: the beach is indeed prevented from migrating inland as it would have done without intervention, but slow erosion is replaced by periods of temporary stability broken by catastrophic failures when the waves, no longer able to dissipate their energy on a beach shaped by natural forces, break through the barriers.[52]

Most people's ideas of evolution assume one-way causation. That is, species compete with one another within the environment, thus driving evolution by natural selection. In fact, however, there is coevolution: plants and animals not only adapt to the environment, they change it. As a result, it becomes more hospitable to some life forms and less hospitable to others.[53] Indeed, the very atmosphere that supports current life was produced by earlier forms of life, some which could not survive in the new environment. On a smaller scale as well, most living things alter their environments, rendering them more suitable for some, less suitable for others, and open to colonization by new species. For example, elephants thrive on acacia trees. But the latter can develop only in the absence of the former. After a while, the elephants destroy the trees, drastically altering the mix of other animals that can live in the area, and even affecting the physical shape of the land.[54] In the process, they render the area uncongenial to themselves, and they either move on or die. The land is adapting to the elephants just as they are to it. The dynamics of a complex system cannot be captured by arbitrarily labeling one set of elements "causes" and others "effects."

Acting in a System

It is not possible to control a system by behaving as though straightforward, one-way, linear processes dominate. But can knowledge of systems dynamics be used to produce desired outcomes?[55] This may be possible when others can be outguessed or are heavily constrained. In some cases, one may be able to reach a desired goal by taking a path that leads directly in the opposite direction. For years, the United States tried to convince its allies to increase their defense spending by increasing its own. It is possible that more favorable results would have been secured had the United States done the opposite and decreased its spending, but such an outcome was not guaranteed, especially if the allies believed they were being manipulated. It is also possible that Britain might increase the chances of brokering a stable and benign relationship between the PRC and Hong Kong if it granted British citizenship to the island's residents. To gain a viable Hong Kong, China would have to come to terms with its people, who would have the option of departing. But the residents of Hong Kong might demand too much, either because they miscalculated or because emigration to Britain looked better than any offer China was willing to make. In many of the cases we have noted, decisionmakers were aware of systems dynamics, tried to manipulate them, yet still ended up with perverse effects due to their limited understanding of the situation or their miscalculations about what others could do.

One interesting possibility is that a state might be better able to protect another by *not* committing to its defense. Although commitment can produce a deterrence, three other effects should not be overlooked. First, such a commitment can increase the client's freedom of action, leading it to behave in ways the protector does not want. Second, commitment may reduce the incentives of third parties to promise assistance to the client. Third, commitment may provoke the adversary either by threatening it or by inflating what it will gain if it prevails (because victory would now damage the patron state's reputation). There might have been greater regional opposition to the Soviet invasion of Afghanistan if the United States had not quickly supplied Pakistan with support and arms. Marc Trachtenberg argues that reducing the American commitment to West Germany during the Berlin crisis of 1958–62 might have ameliorated the conflict by moderating Adenauer's behavior and decreasing the Soviet fears that German interests were dictating American policy.[56] Similarly, Liddell Hart argues that refraining from guaranteeing Poland's borders in 1939 would have been the best way to prevent World War II, or at least to improve Britain's ability to fight it:

> If we had not given that delusory guarantee, Poland would have been forced to accept Russia's help, as the only chance of withstanding German pressure. And Russia would have been forced to give Poland such support, because of her then existing value as a buffer state, and as an auxiliary army. Under these circumstances, it would have been much less likely that Germany would have attacked Poland.[57]

This may be too clever by half, however. Stalin may have signed the Nazi-Soviet pact primarily because he feared the Western powers were maneuvering him into fighting Germany alone, a fear that Britain had reason to believe could have been assuaged only by an unequivocal commitment to Poland.

Being aware of systems dynamics is likely to reduce the incidence of perverse effects somewhat; trying to judge how others will seek to increase their security in reaction to the state's effort to do so will often benefit both sides. In some cases the successful use of systems effects by one actor must mean disadvantage to another. In other instances, however, by improving their ability to deal with the web of forces within which they must act, people can gain mutual or even general advantage.

Notes

1. Studies from cognitive psychology have shown that people much more readily detect additive, linear patterns than interactive ones. See Jerome Bruner, Jacqueline Goodnow, and George Austin, *A Study of Thinking* (New York: Wiley, 1956).

2. The classic treatment is Kenneth Waltz, *Theory of International Politics* (Reading, MA: Addison-Wesley, 1979), to which this essay is broadly indebted.

3. One obvious question, to which I return later, is what happens when actors are aware of the prevalence of perverse effects. Under what circumstances can they act to avoid them and produce the result they wanted in the first place? Indeed, the whole notion of what is a straightforward effect and what is a perverse one depends on the actors' expectations and knowledge.

4. Sam Peltzman, "The Effects of Automobile Safety Regulation," *Journal of Political Economy*, vol. 83, Aug. 1975, pp. 677–725; Gerald S.J. Wilde "The Theory of Risk Homeostasis: Implications for Safety and Health," *Risk Analysis*, vol. 2, Dec. 1982, pp. 209–225; Charles Perrow, *Normal Accidents* (New York: Basic Books, 1984), pp. 179–180. For more critical reviews of the data, see Robert Crandall, *Regulating the Automobile* (Washington, D.C.: Brookings Institute, 1986), pp. 57–84 and the literature cited there.

5. It is extremely difficult to determine when one element is affecting others and when all of them are responding to the same kind of stimulus. Did Berkeley's free speech movement lead to student unrest around the country, or were students reacting to similar conditions in different locations?

6. Albert Hirschman, *The Rhetoric of Reaction* (Cambridge: Harvard University Press, 1991), pp. 11–42.

7. John Herz, "Idealist Internationalism and the Security Dilemma," *World Politics*, vol. 2, January 1950, pp. 157–180; Herbert Butterfield, *History and Human Relations* (London: Collins, 1951), pp. 19–20; Arnold Wolfers, *Discord and Collaboration* (Baltimore: Johns Hopkins University Press, 1962),

pp. 84–85; Robert Jervis, *Perception and Misperception in International Politics* (Princeton: Princeton University Press, 1976), chap. 3.

8. The classic discussion is Schelling, *Strategy of Conflict* (Cambridge: Harvard University Press, 1960).

9. *Ibid.*, pp. 16–19.

10. Andrew Krepinevich, Jr., *The Army and Vietnam* (Baltimore: Johns Hopkins University Press, 1986), pp. 140–41; but also see p. 159.

11. See, for example, *ibid.*, pp. 19–26.

12. Quoted in R.W. Apple, Jr., "Margaret Thatcher: A Choice, Not an Echo," *New York Times Magazine*, April 29, 1979, p. 36.

13. Charles Kindleberger, *The World in Depression* (Berkeley: University of California Press, 1973), p. 305; also see Kindleberger, "Hierarchy versus Inertial Cooperation," *International Organization*, vol. 40, Autumn 1986, pp. 841–47.

14. For an argument that this was the case for the operation of the gold standard in the nineteenth century, see Giulio Gallarotti, *The Anatomy of Spontaneous Order* (New York, Columbia University Press, forthcoming).

15. Donald Reinken, "Computer Explorations of the `Balance of Power,'" in Morton Kaplan, ed., *New Approaches to International Relations* (New York: St. Martin's Press, 1968), p. 469; also see Morton Kaplan "A Poor Boy's Journey," in Joseph Kruzel and James Rosenau, eds., *Journeys Through World Politics* (Lexington, Mass: Lexington Books, 1989), pp. 45–47.

16. Stanley Hoffmann, *The State of War* (New York: Praeger, 1965), pp. 88–122; Raymond Aaron, *Peace and War* (Garden City, N.Y.: Doubleday, 1966), pp. 99–104, 147–49, 373–403.

17. See the fascinating and careful argument by Paul Schroeder, for example in his "The Nineteenth-Century International System: Changes in the Structure," *World Politics*, vol. 39, October 1986, pp. 1–26, and "The Nineteenth Century System: Balance of Power or Political Equilibrium?" *Review of International Studies*, vol. 15, April 1989, pp. 135–54.

18. The clearest statement is Waltz, *Theory of International Politics*. Also see Inis Claude, *Power and International Relations* (New York: Random House, 1962), pp. 11–39, and Robert Jervis, "Security Regimes," *International Organization*, vol. 36, April 1982, pp. 357–78.

19. This is stressed in Waltz, Theory of International Politics.

20. E. J. Dionne, Jr., "Coming Up: The Debate America Wanted" *New York Times*, November 13, 1988.

21. John Lewis Gaddis, *The Long Peace* (New York: Oxford University Press, 1987), pp. 215–16.

22. Frank Howley, *Berlin Command* (New York: Putnam's, 1950), pp. 202–203.

23. Allen Whiting, *The Chinese Calculus of Deterrence* (Ann Arbor: University of Michigan Press, 1975); Melvin Gurtov and Byong-Moo Hwang, *China under Threat* (Baltimore: Johns Hopkins University Press, 1980).

24. Zeev Maoz, "Power, Capabilities, and Paradoxical Conflict Outcomes," *World Politics*, vol. 41, January 1989, pp. 239–266.

25. Krepinevich, *The Army and Vietnam*, p. 76; also see pp. 84, 90. In this case, as in others, motivational and other cognitive dynamics explain why this inference was drawn, but the propensity to expect linear relationships is still important.

26. George Hunt, *The Wars of the Iroquois* (Madison: University of Wisconsin Press, 1940), p. 19.

27. For a discussion of European alliance configurations in these terms, see Robert Jervis, "Systems Theories and Diplomatic History," in Paul Lauren, ed., *Diplomacy* (New York: Free Press, 1979), pp. 226–39.

28. P.J.V. Rolo, *Entente Cordiale* (New York: St. Martin's Press, 1969), p. 121.

29. Raymond Garthoff, *Détente and Confrontation* (Washington: Brookings Institution, 1985), p. 245.

30. Henry Kissinger, *White House Years* (Boston: Little, Brown, 1979), p. 866.

31. Quoted in R.J. Crampton, The Hollow Détente: Anglo-German Relations in the Balkans, 1911–1914 (London: George Prior, 1980), pp. 83–4.

32. Quoted in Friedrich Katz, The Secret War in Mexico: Europe, the United States and the Mexican Revolution (Chicago: Chicago University Press, 1981), p. 302.

33. Gordon Martel, "Documenting the Great Game: 'World Policy' and the ' Turbulent Frontier' in the 1980's," *International History Review*, vol. 2, April 1980, p. 291.

34. Fraser Harbutt, The Iron Curtain: Churchill, America, and the Origins of the Cold War (New York: Oxford University Press, 1986).

35. Quoted in John Colville, *The Fringes of Power: 10 Downing Street Diaries, 1939–1955* (New York: Norton, 1985), p. 283.

36. Quoted in Harbutt, *The Iron Curtain*, p. 33.

37. Robert Pool, "Chaos Theory: How Big an Advance?" *Science*, vol. 245, July 9, 1989, p. 26.

38. Charles Janson, "Capuchin Counterpoint," *Natural History*, February 1986, pp. 45–52.

39. John Byers, "Pronghorns in—and out of—a Rut," *Natural History*, April 1989, pp. 39–48.

40. Waltz, Theory of International Politics, pp. 152–58.

41. This was not the most egregious of the navy's miscalculations, most of which were rooted in the desire to preserve its traditional ways of doing things.

42. Colville, The Fringes of Power, p. 283.

43. We never had a robbery, and my friend went on to become a distinguished political scientist.

44. Schelling, Strategy of Conflict.

45. *Ibid.*

46. To use Morgan's terms, commitment may then positively correlate with the success of general deterrence and negatively correlate with the success of immediate deterrence. See Patrick Morgan, *Deterrence: A Conceptual Analysis* (Beverly Hills, Calif.: Sage, 1977), pp. 25–45.

47. See, for example, Krepinevich, *The Army and Vietnam*, pp. 87–88.

48. Jonathan Shimshoni, *Israel and Conventional Deterrence: Border Warfare from 1953 to 1970* (Ithaca: Cornell University Press, 1988), pp. 154–55.

49. For further discussion of the manipulation of signals and indices, although in a different framework, see Robert Jervis, *The Logic of Images in International Relations*, second edition (New York: Columbia University Press, 1989).

50. William McNeill, "Control and Catastrophe in Human Affairs," *Daedalus*, Winter 1989, pp. 1–12.

51. *Ibid.*, pp. 1–2.

52. See Wallace Kaufman and Orrin Pilkey, Jr., *The Beaches Are Moving* (Durham: Duke University Press, 1983), and Robert Dolan, "Barrier Dune System along the Outer Banks of North Carolina," *Science*, vol. 176, April 21, 1972, pp. 286–8.

53. Insightful if sometimes polemical is Richard Levins and Richard Lewontin, *The Dialectical Biologist* (Cambridge: Harvard University Press, 1985).

54. Roger Lewin, "In Ecology, Change Brings Stability," *Science*, vol. 234, November 28, 1986, pp. 1071–73.

55. See Waltz, *Theory of International Politics*, p.197–99; also see the ingenious discussion in Paul Watzlwick, John Weakland, and Richard Fisch, *Change* (New York: Norton, 1974). A great deal of recent game theory has explored nonmyopic equilibria, but the restrictive conditions may limit the applicability of the conclusions.

56. Marc Trachtenberg, "The Berlin Crisis," in Trachtenberg, *History and Strategy* (Princeton: Princeton University Press, 1991).

57. Basil Liddle Hart, *Why Don't We Learn from History?* (London: Allen & Unwin, 1954), p. 39.

3

The Transformation
of Political Thinking, 1787–1848

Paul W. Schroeder

Monsieur Jourdain, the protagonist of Molière's *Le Bourgeois Gentilhomme*, was surprised and pleased to learn that he had been speaking prose all his life. Robert Jervis's introductory essay on linear-additive versus indirect-systemic thinking in international politics has given me a similar gratifying discovery.

For years I have been researching the history of the European international system from 1787 to 1848, the period of the French Revolution, Napoleon, the Vienna Congress, and the post-Vienna era.[1] The central argument of my forthcoming book concerns the transformation of international politics occurring in this period, a transformation that made the politics of the post-1815 era not merely more peaceful and stable for a time but decisively different in nature from the politics of the preceding and following eras. I have tried elsewhere to indicate the structural or institutional changes involved in this transformation[2] and to analyze the different language of 19th-century politics and the changed outlook that different language represented.[3] A critical difficulty, however, remained. The difficulty lay not in detecting and demonstrating the widespread difference between the prevailing 18th- and 19th-century approaches to international politics—the changes in assumptions, attitudes, and goals held by leaders in practicing politics—but rather it lay in defining and analyzing these changes and thus in more satisfactorily accounting for what amounted to a shift in collective mentality. A change in generations or elites could not account for the transformation, for by and large the same elites were in power before and after 1815. In important instances one could see the same leaders (Prince Metternich of Austria, Prince Talleyrand in France, Tsar Alexander in Russia,

Viscount Castlereagh in Great Britain, Prince Hardenberg of Prussia)
thinking and operating differently in the two eras. For purposes of
analysis, it did not seem to me enough simply to describe how this
change developed over time as a product of or reaction to the wars,
revolutions, and disasters of the era. Though this descriptive task
still remains primary for the historian, understanding and explaining
this transformation of thought and practice in theoretical terms, as an
instance of a general phenomenon, is also important.

The Jervis essay suggested to me a way to do so. The collective
change I had detected and tried to describe in historical terms
represented in theoretical terms a transition from linear-additive to
indirect-systemic thinking. I therefore address in this essay the
general theme of this book, linear versus systemic thinking in
international politics, by analyzing a specific historical illustration
of how they differ, showing how linear thinking gave way to systemic
thinking in the European international politics of the mid-1780's to
1815. I will try to indicate how in this period linear thinking at first
was exclusively dominant, shook off an initial challenge and
maintained its hold for most of the period, and then yielded to
systemic thinking at the very end. For obvious reasons of space, the
historical narrative and analysis will be extremely compressed,
schematized, and oversimplified, and the evidence available from a
massive documentary and secondary literature will be only alluded to.
International historians may therefore object to this analysis,
especially those who believe in the essential uniqueness of historical
events, the vital importance of details, and the impossibility of
devising any systemic ordering of choices, possibilities, and outcomes
in international politics without distorting the process and
diminishing the decisive role of contingency.[4] The essay may also
disappoint the social scientist by giving him/her no help in forming or
operationalizing a working hypothesis. It may, however, go beyond
merely providing an important historical example of the difference
between linear and systemic thinking (perhaps worth something in
itself) in suggesting an answer as to why linear thinking seems so
pervasive and persistent in international politics. I.e., it may
illustrate how such thinking is not simply or mainly the result of the
dispositions, habits, learning, and perception of individual actors but
a collective phenomenon solidly rooted in the constitutive
understandings and practices of international politics in a particular
era. Linear thinking thus constitutes part of a network of ideas and
assumptions, highly functional at least up to a certain point, resilient
and adaptable, resistant to major change and difficult to break. Linear
thinking, in other words, is an integral aspect of a particular kind of

system and structure in international relations. The real difficulty may not lie in persuading or teaching individual actors in international politics to think systemically but in bringing about overall conditions under which systemic thinking and action can become a rational choice, effective in practical terms.

18th-Century Linear Thinking

Eighteenth-century international politics was based necessarily on linear-additive thinking. The core concept of the balance-of-power and its operation required it. Balance-of-power doctrine, as then conceived and practiced by state leaders, was simple and direct: a proper distribution of power was supposed to maintain the independence and relative security of all actors in the system (or most actors, or the essential actors, or simply one's own state). Exactly what constituted a proper distribution or balance of power was naturally a matter of constant dispute and a frequent source of conflict; just how a putatively correct equilibrium would achieve the desired ends of checking aggression and/or preventing bids for hegemony and empire—whether the needed counteraction or blocking coalition would arise automatically from the balance or would require a conscious collective decision or the action of a holder of the balance—was highly debatable and obscure, as is almost everything about balance-of-power theory to this day.[5] Whether the balance of power had to work by exploiting the naturally opposed interests of rival powers or could lead to an associative balance of power which harmonized the interests of all participants in a general equilibrium was at least a theoretical question—or so it has been claimed.[6] Yet whatever the theory may have been (and it is doubtful that it made much concrete difference), the actual practice of balance-of-power politics was clear and consistent enough, its prevailing rules were strictly competitive and conflictual, and the thinking behind them was linear-additive. Each state, to preserve the balance, was supposed to keep up with and, if possible, surpass its rivals, who might be any or all of the other powers, depending on shifting circumstances. To preserve this balance, and above all to prevent itself from falling in rank and status, each state had to insist on receiving compensations at least equal to those of a rival in any transaction and seek indemnities for any loss or exertion involved in war. Compensations and indemnities were calculated on the basis of more or less measurable factors of state power (territory, defensible frontiers, state revenue, population, readily mobilized resources). But an imponderable, the prestige and honor (in French, *"consideration"*) of the monarch and his government, was an equally vital element in the balance of power and aim to pursue in the general competition.[7]

The linear-additive character of balance-of-power practices engendered many unintended and often undesired systemic results. It added the problem of achieving supposedly balanced compensations and indemnities to almost every international transaction, burdened every alliance with side payments, and complicated every attempt at cooperation with the problem of who would gain the most from it and thereby rise or fall in the balance. Still worse, it drove the powers into conflict over their inherently incompatible and mutually contradictory concepts of what the balance of power should be. Throughout the 18th century, particularly toward its close, there was not only no overall consensus on what constituted a desirable balance of power but also no agreement between any of the great powers' particular concepts of the balance. The British idea of the balance called for France to be restrained and confined to the continent so that Britain could have a free hand in Europe and rule the seas; the French called for security for France in Europe so that French sea power could balance Britain's on the seas. Prussia's concept of the German balance called for Prussian equality with Austria and a stalemate in the German Empire; Austria's, for Austrian superiority over Prussia and Austrian control over the Reich. The same held for Austrian and Russian ideas of the balance in eastern and southeastern Europe, Prussian and Russian ideas of a balance in the North, and English, French, Russian, and Ottoman notions of a balance in the Mediterranean.

Obviously, linear balance-of-power thinking was far from the only source of the endemic international conflict and instability of 18th-century politics. Another major factor was the nature and constitution of the monarchial state, based as it was upon dynastic succession; every succession dispute represented simultaneously a potential opportunity for expansion to the various states concerned and a threat to their integrity and survival.[8] The whole process of state formation and modernization, the military revolution of the 16th and 17th centuries, the struggle between monarchs and their bureaucratic ministers and old elites for power, the expansion of Europe into the non-European worlds, and various other political and socioeconomic developments all played their roles.[9] But the powerful contribution to international instability made by linear balance-of-power thinking cannot be ignored.

Nor can one doubt what kind of international system resulted. The once-common notion of a late 18th century system which gradually settled down to limited warfare and controlled competition only to have the emerging equilibrium wrecked by the ideological and military forces unleashed by the French Revolution is untenable. Well before the revolution began in 1789, the international system was out of control and headed toward general conflict. It was first of all riddled with natural and necessary enmities and rivalries which were constitutive of international politics rather than accidental—Anglo-French, Austro-Prussian, Austro-Bavarian, Catholic-Protestant in Germany, Russo-Ottoman, and others. The supposed checks on these rivalries, so-called natural alliances between certain powers and the general desire of all to preserve a balance against hegemony or empire, simply did not work either to restrain conflict or to satisfy the mutual interests of the allies or to promote an overall balance. For decades, Britain, inherently the most invulnerable great power, courted Russia, the next most invulnerable, as its natural ally against France, thereby unintentionally aiding Tsarina Catherine II in her expansionist policies. The French-Austrian alliance served to restrain France and Austria themselves but did nothing to reduce their particular vulnerabilities. Russia used its alliances with Prussia and Austria in turn to control and partly partition Poland, defeat the Ottoman Empire and seize vital territory from it, dominate the Baltic, annex the Crimea, and increase its influence in Germany, all the while keeping its alliance partners paralyzed in rivalry.

The result was that by the mid-1780's, if not earlier, Europe was in the midst of a profound general security crisis which threatened first and foremost various smaller and weaker states and political units in Europe, often referred to at the time as "intermediary bodies." The importance of these intermediary bodies in separating the great powers, serving as buffers and barriers against expansion, and thereby promoting peace was widely acknowledged.[10] Yet they became the prime target for takeover in the escalating systemic breakdown and conflict. The most obvious target was Poland, victim of a first partition at the hands of Russia, Prussia, and Austria in 1772 and doomed to disappear in further partitions in 1793 and 1795—all done quite genuinely in the name of general peace and the balance of power. In addition, the Ottoman Empire; the German Empire and some of its component states and principalities, especially Bavaria; the United Provinces (Holland); Sweden and Denmark; and even Switzerland and the various states of Italy (especially the Venetian Republic) were seriously threatened and undermined in various degrees by the prevailing unrestrained competition. Smaller states, however, were not alone in recognizing an imminent systemic collapse. Well in advance of the French Revolution, Prussian, Austrian, and French leaders saw that the security crisis threatened to destroy their countries' independence and status as great powers. Conversely, Britain and Russia, especially the latter, perceived opportunities in the current competition to win the game decisively, exploiting the paralysis and weakness of the others to gain a free hand and control of the system in their respective spheres.

The Crisis of 1792: The Triumph of Linear over Systemic Thinking

The general security crisis in Europe came to a head in 1787 when a war broke out between Russia and the Ottoman Empire in the East, soon joined by Austria as Russia's ally, and the Prussians and British intervened in Holland to overthrow a Dutch revolt and thereby destroy the influence of France. The Eastern War lasted four years, involved additional powers (Sweden, Denmark, and Poland), and repeatedly threatened to become general. When the wars of the French Revolution began in 1792 with war between France and Austria and Prussia, this only added a new and at the time fairly minor dimension to an ongoing international crisis. A narrative of events is impossible; a mere indication of what the crisis meant for the various great powers will have to do.

For France, swept up since 1789 in an increasingly radical revolution, domestic politics had clear primacy. The main reason that France from mid-1791 on took the belligerent stance toward Austria and the German Empire which finally led to war was that both the court (Louis XVI) and the dominant republican revolutionary faction, the Girondins, believed that they could best achieve their respective goals, Louis that of stopping and the Girondins that of accelerating the revolution, through a foreign war. Yet this does not mean that the foreign dangers France faced were imaginary or unreal. By early 1792 it had lost all its allies and prestige in Europe, was involved in serious quarrels with its neighbors in Germany and Italy, was being harassed by émigré counterrevolutionary activity, and faced war with Austria and Prussia, all while its government struggled with rampant inflation, political confusion in Paris, latent civil war in the provinces, and the undermining of its army and navy, especially their noble officer corps, by revolution and emigration. When the revolutionary leaders declared the fatherland in danger in midsummer 1792 after war had begun, they were only recognizing very tardily a desperate international situation which any government in France, revolutionary or conservative, would sooner or later have had to confront.

Prussia in 1792 also faced grave dangers. Some of its leaders, especially King Frederick II, the so-called Frederick the Great (1740-86), had long been aware that Prussia was intrinsically the weakest and most threatened of the great powers. Prussia was dependent on Russia yet could not count on its alliance; it was locked in an irreconcilable and unwinnable rivalry with Austria in Germany; and in 1792 Prussia found itself tied by a risky and burdensome alliance to Poland, which was bent on liberating itself by a revolution from Russian domination and reforming itself into a viable constitutional monarchy. While the Polish question thus threatened to involve Prussia in conflict with Russia, the revolution in France menaced Prussia's territories on the Rhine and threatened to involve Prussia in a war against France. Yet Prussians in 1792 saw opportunities as well as dangers in their situation. The Prussian army was large and supposedly efficient (its actual deficiencies would only become apparent later in the revolutionary and Napoleonic Wars); it had Britain and Holland as allies; it had the advantages as well as dangers of a central geographic position; and above all, the crisis seemed to threaten its main rival, Austria, still more, thereby opening up chances for Prussia to make gains in Germany or Poland and to become a genuine rather than a would-be great power. The main goal of Prussia's king, Frederick William II (1786–97) and some, though not all, of his advisers was to exploit these opportunities through diplomacy and/or war.

Russia in 1792 had just victoriously survived a series of dangers and challenges in the previous four years from the Turks, the Swedes, the Prussians, and the British. Now Catherine's goal was to destroy the Polish reform movement and reinstate Russian control over Poland. There was some danger that Austria and Prussia might stop Russia by uniting in defense of Poland. But Prussia's ambitions and fears, the Austro-Prussian rivalry over Germany, and the French Revolution with its threat to the German Empire and to Austria as leader of the Empire gave the Tsarina powerful weapons for preventing that from happening.

For Britain 1792 brought no crisis or danger at all, only increased security and opportunity. France was collapsing into anarchy; Spain was effectively deprived of its traditional ally, France; and Austria and Prussia were in a position where at least one of them had to check revolutionary France and guard the Low Countries on Britain's behalf for nothing. This freed the British from all danger, leaving them free to concentrate on their domestic problems, such as Ireland, and their world interests, such as India and trade—or so they thought.

For four of the great powers, then, the general security crisis of 1792 meant either a mixed bag of threat and opportunity, or, for two of them, almost pure gain. For the Habsburg Monarchy under Emperor Leopold II (1790–92), however, 1792 offered no opportunities at all, only a bewildering array of complex challenges and dangers. Leopold, one of the most shrewd and reasonable rulers ever to wear a crown, had by early 1792 largely fended off the most acute of the many external and internal threats he had inherited on the death of his brother Emperor Joseph II (1780–90). He had extricated Austria from its joint war with Russia against the Ottoman Empire, avoided a threatened war with Prussia, regained control of the rebellious Austrian Netherlands (Belgium), and managed to quiet actual or incipient revolts in Hungary, Bohemia, the Tyrol, and other Austrian provinces. Yet these defensive victories did nothing to solve Austria's basic security dilemma, the heart of which lay in eastern Europe. For decades Austria had felt itself slipping into dependence and vulnerability vis-à-vis an increasingly invulnerable and expansionist Russia.[11] Now this long decline seemed about to reach its climax in and to be sealed by Russia's resumption of exclusive control over Poland. This would surely be followed by renewed Russian penetration of the Ottoman Empire and expansion into the Balkans toward Constantinople and the Straits.

No amount of armaments, if Austria could have afforded them, or alliances, even had they been available, would have enabled Austria to meet this threat. For its basic insecurity with Russia arose not from inequality of power, i.e., the respective size, resources, and development of the two empires; on these scores Austria still measured up against Russia quite well. Instead, Austria was intrinsically vulnerable and Russia was not, due to conditions rooted equally in geography and in the nature of 18th-century politics. Austria could not use its armed power directly to confront Russia, even when, as regularly happened in Russia's wars against the Turks, Russia's flank was dangerously exposed to an Austrian attack. This was because any Austro-Russian confrontation automatically exposed Austria to a standing threat from Prussia in Germany and a latent one from France in the Low Countries. (The latter threat was now acute because the revolution had spread from France to Belgium and because various parties in France were reviving and exploiting the traditional Bourbon-Habsburg rivalry for domestic political purposes.) A defensive alliance for Austria against Russia (even if one were available and reliable, which was not the case) would have required Austria to pay its ally with compensations and indemnities at the expense of Austria's already weakened and exposed positions in Germany and northern Italy. Finally, Austria's actual alliance with Russia since 1781, which it had concluded in order to gain security against Prussia and a measure of control over Russian policy, had not served these purposes at all but had only enabled Russia to exploit Austria's exposed position and drag it into even greater dangers and an unwanted Turkish war. Austria's dilemma, as clearly diagnosed by Emperor Leopold and the veteran Austrian foreign minister and chancellor Prince Kaunitz, was that no direct means were available to combat its progressive loss of great-power position and independence; indeed, every direct move would make its situation worse.

Each great power developed a strategy in 1792. Britain's was the simplest: do nothing. Let France degenerate into revolutionary chaos, or exhaust itself fighting the German powers, while Britain attended to its domestic and commercial interests.[12]

France's strategy was also simple, though more active and dangerous: to take arms against a sea of external and internal troubles and by opposing end them. As already noted, the dominant motive for the French declaration of war on Austria on April 20 lay in revolutionary domestic politics, the Girondin faction's aim of thereby exposing the king's treasonous links with foreign powers and thus paving the way to a republic. The French also had other motives for war, both traditional and revolutionary. But France's actual strategy in international politics was wholly traditional and power-political: France proposed to wage war against the hereditary enemy, Austria, for traditional expansionist gains in its historical theaters of war, Belgium, Germany, and Italy, hoping as in the past either to gain Prussia and some of the German states as allies or to keep them neutral.

Prussia's strategy was much more complicated and uncertain. All parties agreed on the goal: enhance Prussia's security and independence, primarily by gaining strategic territories. But there were at least three main ways to go about this: (1) Bury the hatchet more or less durably with Austria, Prussia's new partner in a defensive alliance signed in February 1792, and make this alliance the foundation for a successful war against France, from whom no serious resistance was expected. A joint victory in France and a joint stand with Austria against Russia in Poland would bring Prussia greater security and territorial gains in both East and West. (2) Fulfill Prussia's alliance obligations to Austria against France, but only to the letter, with an eye to involving Austria more deeply in the war in the West and gaining Austria's consent to the maximum gains possible for Prussia, especially in the East at the expense of Poland. (3) Begin the war against France in alliance with Austria and then, when Austria was tied down, pull out and make profitable deals with France and Russia at Austria's expense. In other words, Prussia could solve its security problem by genuine partnership with Austria, manipulation of Austria, or betrayal of Austria. What Prussia actually did was follow the first strategy in negotiating the alliance, the second in launching the war, and the third while fighting it.

Catherine never wavered in her basic policy: try to push both German powers into war with France and then intervene to destroy the reform movement and regain unilateral control in Poland. She and her advisers had not decided the exact form that control would take, direct annexation or indirect domination. But in any case, Russia would continue to exploit the German powers' rivalry in Central Europe and their preoccupation with France to gain Russia a free hand with both Poland and the Ottoman Empire.

All these policies represented linear thinking. They all proposed direct responses to threats and opportunities and expected certain desired results to arise directly from them. The governments, moreover, were not so much ignoring the systemic implications of their policies as they were recognizing but refusing to worry about them. Nothing, after all, could be done to change the possibility of negative consequences, and each supposed the worst results would fall on someone else. All, in game theory parlance, were defecting in the hope that others would pay the penalties of cooperation, and all were determined to avoid the "sucker's payoff" themselves. No state believed it within its power or purview to do anything about Europe as a whole, or the European balance, or the threatened intermediary states. The British knew that France, an essential actor, might collapse in revolutionary chaos or be crushed and mutilated territorially by war; this was not their problem. Russia and Prussia knew that Poland would certainly be paralyzed and perhaps destroyed by another intervention. No matter; a reformed, independent Poland represented a threat, at least to Russia, and such threats were usually handled under the system, as Russia had done with Poland before, by direct action. No one was conscious of behaving in a lawless or particularly reckless way; all believed that what they were doing was normal and legitimate, in conformity with prevailing rules and standards of statecraft.

One great power's program was different, not linear but systemic— that of Austria under Leopold. (He was the only advocate at first for systemic thinking and had difficulty winning even Kaunitz over to it.) Leopold's change in strategy derived, as noted, from his recognition of the impossibility of any direct, frontal answer to Austria's security problem. That problem arose from a combination of Austria's internal problems; its central geographic position; its open and concealed rivalries with Russia, Prussia, and France; and the vulnerable, weakened condition and positions of the vital intermediary bodies of Europe. All of these intermediary bodies—Poland, the Ottoman Empire, the German Empire, the Low Countries, Italy—were neighbors of Austria, and Austrian security depended on their existence. Any direct balance-of-power response to a particular one of these various threats through Austrian armaments, alliances, military actions, or other measures of deterrence or compellance would both fail to solve that particular threat and indirectly exacerbate the others.

This meant that Austria's security problem was not contingent and specific (like, for example, the contingent threat to Russia of an independent reformed Poland supported by Austria and Prussia) but systemic in nature, bound up inextricably with the whole system of international politics then being pursued and clearly resulting from that system. By the same token, Austria's security crisis was also part and parcel of the general European security crisis, almost indistinguishable from it and wholly inseparable from it. Austria would become safe and secure only when Europe as a whole became safe and secure, and not before. But since all the other great powers, and even most of the threatened smaller ones, saw things differently and did not identify their individual security with that of Europe as a whole in any practical sense, Austria had to try to solve its security problem by leading them, through persuasion and diplomatic maneuver, into likewise identifying their own security problems with that of Europe as a whole so that they would abandon or subordinate their individual programs in the interest of meeting the larger problem. I.e., Leopold needed to convert them from linear to systemic thinking. Leopold's foreign policy is usually explained as the common tactic of using one threat to nullify another. For example, he exploited Prussian fears of the French Revolution to deter the Prussians from attacking Austria in the East or joining with Russia to subvert and partition Poland and cited the danger of French and Prussian expansion to try to persuade Russia to follow a conservative policy of preserving Poland as a buffer state, and so on. This explanation is obviously true as far as it goes; Leopold followed precisely the same tactics in playing off discontented peoples and factions within the monarchy against each other to solve or manage Austria's internal problems. But any skillful politician will try to do this; the explanation misses what is distinctive about Leopold's strategy, a genuine and skillful, if doomed, effort to create a European consensus on a general system of peace.

To explain his complicated strategy, inevitably oversimplifying it: he first defined the threat of the French Revolution as one arising not so much from revolutionary doctrines and propaganda as from the French aggression and the international war likely to result from

France's internal anarchy and its political and ideological quarrels with its neighbors. He used this danger of a revolution-bred war, a danger to the French throne and all others, to urge a broad European concert to restrain France from external aggression without overtly intervening in its internal affairs. The so-called circular of Padua and the joint declaration of Pillnitz with Prussia in the summer of 1791, both calling for a European concert toward the revolution, were issued by Leopold partly to deal with the revolution itself. His aim was in a nonprovocative way to warn the revolutionaries off aggression and subversion and perhaps to moderate the course of the revolution internally in order to save the French royal family. He wanted at the same time to curb the French émigrés and calm the frightened German princes in the Rhineland. Another aim was to get states like Russia, Sweden, and Spain, who were constantly calling on Austria to rescue the French royal family and stop the spread of anarchy, to join in or keep quiet. But Leopold's action was not mainly focussed on France; it was focussed where his worst fears of war and revolution lay, in eastern Europe, especially Poland. The primary purpose of his proposed concert was to involve Russia and Prussia in a joint Eastern policy and tie them down there, to save the Polish rather than the French monarchy. He constantly warned St. Petersburg and Berlin that the only way to save the European social order, threatened by revolution and war in Paris and Warsaw, was for the great powers to unite for their own safety in a general European program of peace and moderate reform under their joint supervision, starting with Poland. If any of them took advantage of the current anarchy for individual gains, French revolutionary ambitions would be enflamed, other revolutionary programs in Poland and elsewhere would be ignited, and Europe, including themselves, would be engulfed in flames. Within a general European concert to deter and reassure France and so help Louis XVI stabilize his regime under a moderate constitution, the three eastern powers had to unite in a special concert to preserve Poland under its new monarchial constitution, jointly guaranteeing it as an independent, neutral buffer state useful to them and to Europe. The alternative would be a revolutionized Poland which would endanger all its neighbors, Russia with its massive servile peasant population worst of all. If Austria, Russia, and Prussia decided to eliminate this danger by dividing Poland, they would only gain more direct frontiers with each other over which they would constantly quarrel, and more rebellious subjects to govern. A Poland preserved and reformed under joint eastern power protection and guarantee would pacify the Poles, unite the three powers in a common conservative task to their mutual benefit, and promote general peace in Europe.[13]

It is not hard to see what this program represented. It was a shrewd response (indeed, the only realistic one) to Austria's insoluble security dilemma—an attempt to make Austria safe by indirect systemic methods that would incorporate Austrian security into a scheme for a secure, pacified Europe as a whole. It also represented, a generation before 1815, the essence of the Vienna system—a great-power alliance for peace, a Concert of Europe, a conservative union of the three eastern powers, and guarantees to preserve the independence of smaller states and intermediary bodies. The program was, moreover, the Vienna system unmarred by the repressive antiliberalism and anticonstitutionalism that would later be brought to bear by others, notably Austria's chancellor Prince Metternich and Russia's tsars Alexander I and Nicholas I, to exploit it. Not only did Leopold specifically want to preserve an autonomous Poland with a moderate monarchial constitution and the 1791 constitution in France, but on general principles he favored constitutions for other European states, including Austria. The British prime minister William Pitt is often credited, especially by British authors, with having proposed in 1804 the main features of the 1815 settlement. Closely examined, this claim has little basis in fact. The real spiritual progenitor of the Vienna system was Emperor Leopold II.

It is also easy to see what happened to this program, and why. It was beginning to fail even before Leopold's untimely death in March 1792 and collapsed completely thereafter. Moreover, it never had a chance to succeed; its defeat was massively overdetermined, given the dominance of linear thinking everywhere. The British simply ignored all pleas to cooperate in regard to France, even in a purely diplomatic way, until late in 1792 when France's revolutionary victories began to threaten British interests in the Low Countries. Then, typically, London began calling for the concert it had hitherto ignored in the hope of getting more and better military efforts against France from Austria, Prussia, and other states. In April Catherine II, sweeping aside Austria's pleas, intervened militarily in Poland to overthrow the constitution, declaring that her contribution to the struggle against revolution was to destroy the Jacobins at Warsaw. The French, as noted, relied on revolutionary élan to solve their problems. Prussia hesitated a short while and then abandoned the war against France and the alliance with Austria to seek compensations and gains in Poland. Worst of all, Austria itself under Leopold's son and successor Francis II relapsed into the worst kind of linear thinking. Austria found itself caught in a major war with France, which it was losing, and was dependent on Prussian aid and unable to save Poland, control Prussia, or stop Russia. Because of this it decided to go on fighting France and to give a reluctant consent to Prussian and Russian actions in Poland so that it might secure the compensations and gains it especially wanted, i.e., the exchange of its remote and threatened Belgian territories for nearby Bavaria, plus any additional indemnities and compensations it might get from a successful war against France. In other words, since Austria was already losing badly in the ongoing balance-of-power game of compensations and indemnities, the solution was to try harder and gamble more. The snares and disasters into which this fool's strategy led Austria over the next decade, the repeated desperate and costly efforts to make war pay off in real security, cannot even be touched on here.[14]

Thus Leopold's effort to construct a peace system for Europe based on systemic rather than linear thinking passed quickly into an oblivion from which, to my knowledge, no historian has yet rescued it. But this is not the whole story; it is hardly the beginning. The failure of Leopold's program, Europe's rejection of systemic thinking in 1792, opened the door to twenty-three more years of almost continuous war, two solid decades of futile, disastrous efforts by rival allied and French-led coalitions to solve Europe's general security crisis through direct action. The allied side tried persistently to defeat the French enemy, reduce its power, and establish a new balance of power against France through alliances, armaments, and instruments of deterrence such as barrier systems. The French side attempted to win security through military victory, revolutionary expansionism, and finally, under Napoleon, through boundless imperialism. It was not simply or mainly Napoleon's power and ambition, or allied disunity and weakness, that kept a solid peace from being achieved until 1814–15. Each one of the many proposed allied peace settlements from 1792 to 1812, if achieved, would soon have collapsed on account of their failure to define and construct a peaceful Europe and their essential reliance on direct power-political methods for achieving peace.[15] As for Napoleon, he simply took the linear thinking prevalent in Europe to its ultimate and unbearable conclusion. He never defined peace at all, and he always sought his version of peace, i.e., that nothing and nobody should be able to stand in his way or defy his will by the direct means of war and conquest.

The Emergence of Systemic Thinking in 1813–1815

The real story of 1792–1815 in international politics is therefore not one of battles and campaigns in which the allies, after repeated failures, finally gained military victory. Nor is it the surface diplomatic one of repeated negotiations and short-lived peace treaties. These stories, though parts of the whole, are not even the main elements in the construction of peace. Still less is the story one of a transformation of Europe under the impact of the French Revolution and Napoleon, which modernized Europe and aroused a new spirit of liberalism and nationalism so that in the end peoples as well as governments rallied against Napoleonic imperialism, turning the principles of the revolution against France in the War of Liberation. So far as international politics is concerned, that interpretation is almost entirely false. Neither French-style modernization nor liberal reforms and modern nationalism had much to do either with final victory or with the construction of peace. Instead, the main story in international politics is one of how the countries and leaders of Europe learned through repeated, disastrous failure; of how, having exhausted all possibilities for constructing peace through direct action, they slowly, fitfully, unevenly came to adopt systemic thinking and systemic solutions as the only way out. The process of learning cannot be described here, nor can the new system be analyzed. All that is possible is to point to a few salient features in support of the claim that the peace settlement at Vienna, clearly the most successful the modern world has ever seen, resulted from the emergence of systemic thinking.

First, the concept of security, both for individual states and for Europe as a whole, was redefined in systemic terms. Linear thinking, as has been seen, defines security in terms of balance of power, the capacity and will of each individual state, or at least each great power, to protect itself against all plausible threats, either individually or by temporary, ad hoc alliances. Systemic thinking accepts the impossibility of producing a stable, harmonious system of general security in this linear way and recognizes that attempts to do so are ultimately counterproductive because of the well-known security dilemma: one power's efforts to gain security by capability aggregation only stimulates others to do the same, thus increasing its own and the general insecurity and establishing a vicious downward spiral. Systemic thinking instead calls for each state, great or small, to possess only the power necessary to support its independence and enable it to play its particular, appropriate role in an organized, planned system of general, mutual security. It assumes that security must be shared throughout the system, that all units, large and small, must be reasonably secure for any unit genuinely to be so; and it adapts the distribution of power to this goal.

This is the kind of thinking which pervades the Vienna settlement. It took a long time, in a very uneven learning process, for the diplomats of the era to learn it and to accept its necessity; some never did. Most Austrians had learned it, or most of it, by 1801; almost all Prussians by 1807; most Russians before 1812, and almost all thereafter; and (fortunately) a few Britons in key places, above all Lord Castlereagh, just in time, in 1813–14.[16] The danger of relapse into old ways of thinking and acting was always present and was frequently acute. But the breakthrough occurred at last in enough minds to make things work. One cannot read the documents of this era without finally recognizing that the incessant references by state leaders to the unity of Europe; to the vital need to protect the independence and security of all its member states, including the current enemy France; and to the indispensable necessity of harmonizing and guaranteeing all legitimate rights really meant something new and different. These leaders insisted on a proper distribution of power that would enable each state to enjoy its legitimate independence and play its rightful role in the European family of states. This idealistic language was not a fig-leaf for continuing the balance-of-power competition of the 18th century. It marked the transition in regard to state security from linear to systemic thinking.

The same holds for the allied approach to coalition-building for the sake of victory and peace. The old linear approach had been to form a coalition by first identifying the common enemy (often demonized) and stressing the universal and overriding character of the threat that enemy posed (often exaggerated, always viewed in isolation from other threats or general systemic problems). Having defined the enemy and the threat it posed as the root source of evil and having stipulated its destruction as the central, almost unique object of the war, the coalition's initiators, usually Britain and Russia, would then try to persuade or coerce other governments into fighting the war under their leadership. The primary goal of military victory over the common enemy would then also largely shape the peace settlement, which would be directed above all to ensure that the enemy would not threaten the peace again. This approach to coalition-building, with inessential variations, dominated allied policy from 1792 to 1812 and failed time and again to achieve a satisfactory outcome.

The systemic, indirect approach to coalition-building pursued in 1813–14 reversed this procedure. It began not by defining the enemy and the threat but by trying to define "peace," i.e., by trying to develop a concrete conception of what would constitute a satisfactory, peaceful Europe. It sought to develop this conception, moreover, not through edicts drawn up by the self-appointed leaders of the coalition but by asking the responsible leaders of states being recruited for the coalition for their definition of peace. What did they need in order to be reasonably secure and satisfied? How could their needs for security and independence be fitted into a general workable and durable system of peace in Europe? Once a mutually acceptable definition of peace was reached by this kind of negotiation, the coalition partners would then decide how far existing conditions would have to be changed to realize it; how much military force and effort would be required to reduce the power of the enemy so that these new conditions could be realized, and how the enemy could be brought to accept them (i.e., how much military "victory" was really necessary); whether enough military force was available to the coalition or whether more partners were needed, and how to bring them in on what terms (i.e., how much "military victory" would cost politically); and above all, how to enlist all the necessary actors, including if possible the enemy itself, in the task of building and sustaining the agreed-upon common conception of peace during the war and after it.

This is basically how the final coalition of 1813–15 was formed and maintained up to the final victory and peace settlement and following it. Obviously the story was much messier and more complicated than this; but the details should not obscure the fundamental process and how it differed decisively from the preceding coalitions and their principles. The coalition of 1813 did not begin by identifying an enemy, vowing to destroy it, calling on everyone to join in the crusade for military victory, and pursuing that goal to the end. It began, with Russia and Prussia in February–March 1813, by defining the minimal terms of peace. It continued by fighting to achieve these, at first unsuccessfully, but also by recruiting new adherents to this defined and limited conception of a peaceful Europe—first Sweden, already allied with Russia; then Britain in June; then Austria in August, after Austria's own intensive efforts at mediating a compromise peace had failed; then a host of Napoleonic satellites and conquered territories in October to January 1813–1814. At every step the appeal to coalition members was not "Join us to destroy the common enemy." Neither was it "Join us or we will destroy or punish you." (That kind of message was sent by some German patriots, including the famous Prussian reformer Baron vom Stein, who headed the Central Administration Department set up to administer liberated territories, and it backfired badly.) Rather, the message was, "Join us to create a peaceful Europe. Tell us what you need in order to take your part in it, and we will do everything possible to guarantee that you get it."

The appeal was made not just to potential allies and defectors from the Napoleonic camp but above all to the enemy itself. From June 1813 to mid-March 1814, two weeks before the end of the war, members of the allied coalition were in almost constant negotiation with Napoleonic France, attempting to persuade the emperor through his ministers (most of whom were desperately eager for peace) that France could end the war, retain some of its conquests, and keep Napoleon on his throne if he would join in building a peaceful Europe. There is final proof that military victory, far from being the goal or indispensable foundation of peace, was almost a by-product of the search for systemic peace and security: the last battle of the 1814 spring campaign, before the walls of Paris on March 30, was fierce but indecisive. What led to the French surrender was negotiations in which the allies convinced Napoleon's marshals that they were offering France an honorable peace and that only Napoleon was standing in its path.

One cannot, I think, understand the peace offer—even seriously discuss it—without an awareness that a fundamental shift in thinking had occurred: from the belief that the way to construct peace is to beat an enemy into submission, compelling it to bow to your will, to the belief that the way to construct peace is to draw everyone, if possible also the enemy, into a shared conception of peace and joint activity in building it.

One more signal of the transition from linear to systemic thinking must be mentioned: the abandonment of *Realpolitik*. Eighteenth-century international politics conformed fully to the realist paradigm of a structural anarchy which compels everyone to resort to self-help and issues in a recurrent pattern of shifting balances of power. Whatever theorists may say, most state leaders of 1813–15 abandoned this model of international politics, and the practical politics of the period reflect it. They had learned from bitter experience that international anarchy was intolerable, that self-help was impossible and self-destructive, and that equilibrium had to be sought not in a balance of power but in, or political equilibrium ("equilibre politique" was the actual term they constantly used, of which "balance of power" is an English mistranslation). "Balance of power" means independence and security via a balanced opposition of power and interests, backed where necessary by the use of armed force. "Political equilibrium" meant for the state leaders of 1813–15 essentially a balance of rights, satisfactions, responsibilities, and duties, elaborated and guaranteed under a system of sanctions based on consensus and backed by law. The leaders (and, for that matter, the great mass of citizens and subjects) of Europe in 1815 had no doubts as to where their preference lay. They chose political equilibrium.

Two quick examples to back up this naked assertion (and, incidentally, to explain certain puzzles inexplicable to anyone who relies on a balance-of-power explanation of the politics of this era).

(1) Why did the continental allies, after they had virtually destroyed Napoleon's army at Leipzig in mid-October 1813, thereby driving him from Germany, threatening his hold on Italy, and opening France itself to invasion, continue for months thereafter to offer Napoleon a peace based upon the natural frontiers, which would have left him in possession of much valuable German territory west of the Rhine and in control of the most powerful state on the Continent? In ordinary balance-of-power terms, this offer makes no sense. It could be compared with the Allies in late 1944 offering Hitler's Germany a peace based on Germany's retaining Austria, Bohemia, and part of Poland. The answer (not necessarily a justification of the policy) lies in the conviction, constantly voiced and shared at least by most leaders in Austria, Prussia, and Russia, that the most vital requirement for European peace was not the reduction of French power to harmless dimensions, or the expansion of their own power to overmatch any threat that France might conceivably produce. The indispensable requirements for peace were instead the restoration of their individual independence as great powers, the liberation of Germany, and the maintenance of unity among themselves. The first two goals were achieved once Napoleon was pushed back across the Rhine; now the essential task above all was to maintain their wartime cooperation into the postwar world. Too much military victory over France and reduction of French power might work against a durable allied unity by reducing too far their joint need of each other and by raising quarrels over the spoils of victory. (As everyone knows, this happened at the Congress of Vienna over Poland and Saxony.) Some had argued for years (e.g., Friedrich von Gentz, Metternich's secretary and a famous political philosopher and publicist, as early as 1806)[17] that if Germany east of the Rhine was liberated from French control and if Austria, Prussia, and Russia were reconciled in a permanent defensive alliance, even Napoleonic France could not hurt them and probably would not try. However, if Prussia and Austria continued to be rivals and if Russia continued to exploit their divisions, even the complete liberation of Germany, total defeat of Napoleon, and a sweeping reduction of French power would not make them secure. In other words, the key to enduring peace lay less in reducing French power than in managing their own relations with each other. The eastern powers, having tried the direct linear route to security against France time and again since 1792 with disastrous results, now were ready to try another indirect, systemic route.

(2) Why was Austria willing, even eager, to grant its enemy, Napoleon's ally Bavaria, remarkably favorable terms in the Treaty of Ried in October 1813 to persuade it to defect to the allies under

Austria's protection? In that treaty, not only was the sovereignty and independence Bavaria had gained under Napoleonic protection guaranteed regardless of any future reorganization of Germany, but Bavaria was also carefully protected against territorial loss even though for years it had aggrandized itself hugely by wars fought as Napoleon's ally against Austria and Prussia. It would be fully compensated for any territory it had to give up in the final peace, including old Austrian territory, and could continue to occupy these Austrian territories until the peace as a guarantee. Austria and Bavaria had been traditional enemies for almost a century, with Bavaria in recent decades the major target of Austrian territorial ambitions. At the time the treaty was signed in 1813 Bavaria had been abandoned militarily by Napoleon and was helpless. Some Austrians as well as Prussians and Russians urged Austria to recoup its losses in southern Germany at the expense of Napoleon's client states, especially Bavaria. One can see why Bavarians might want to seize on this treaty as salvation from disaster (though in fact they had to be lured and pressured into it). But what made Austria urge it on them?[18]

As always, particular circumstances and contingent calculations (in this case, fear of Russian influence and of Baron vom Stein and the so-called Prussian Jacobins) entered into Austrian reasoning. But again they were not the main considerations and should not be allowed to obscure a basic change in thinking that had taken place, especially in Austria. The old linear method for securing Austria's leading position in Germany had meant lining up clients behind Austria's leadership within the Reich and holding them in line, by force if necessary, against pressures and lures from Prussia, Russia, France, and their own ambitions. One school of thought in Austria in 1813 called essentially for renewing that policy: regaining and fortifying Austria's territorial hold in southwest Germany, reducing the southern German states to manageable levels of weakness and dependence, and thereby ensuring Austria's control over a bloc of states in Germany, along with effective power-political leadership of whatever German empire or confederation would be established. Metternich, Emperor Francis, and other Austrians knew better, understood that if Austrian leadership was to be restored in Germany, it had to be on a different, more indirect basis. The vital systemic requirement for Austria's security and its leadership in Germany alike was that the states of Germany, which together constituted a critical intermediary body between Austria and Western Europe (France, the Low Countries, and Britain), be themselves tranquil and nonrevolutionary. If they were not reasonably safe and satisfied, Austria could not be. Austria could no longer rule or dominate Germany; Germany had grown beyond it, and Austria's own need for repose and its other burdens dictated that while it could and must lead Germany, it could not control or govern it. Besides, Austria's security required a friendly Prussia as well. A Germany of confederated but essentially independent states, led and managed by Austria in partnership with Prussia, was compatible with Austro-Prussian friendship; a united Austrian-dominated Germany was not. Preserving a satisfied, reconciled, independent Bavaria would help Austria manage Prussia, curb Prussian ambitions, and promote its own influence. An alienated Bavaria would sooner or later throw itself into Prussia's arms, or Russia's, or even France's. Once again all this shows the change from linear to systemic thinking.

Conclusions

European politics in 1787–1815 thus offers a great lesson in the possibility of systemic thinking and reveals its superiority over linear thinking for purposes of durable peace. The operation of the Vienna system from 1815 to 1848 and beyond is a further lesson in systemic thinking, though that story cannot be pursued here.[19] Both periods prove that systemic thinking in international politics can emerge and work durably—a point important for history, political theory, and practical politics alike.

Other conclusions, however, must be more pessimistic. Just as impressive as the ultimate emergence of systemic thinking as a constitutive and regulative element of international politics in 1813–15 is the great amount of time and the complicated, cumulative learning process required for this to happen. The conversion and/or education of individual leaders, or even of whole elite groups in certain countries, clearly did no good so long as the new way of thinking had not triumphed in all the main centers of power and decision, or at least in a critical mass of them. There seemed frequently in 1787–1812 to be a kind of Gresham's law at work in international politics: bad linear thinking repeatedly drove good systemic thinking out of circulation. It is not hard to see why. Linear thinking had the weight of tradition, routine, and entrenched habit behind it. It often promised short-run gains which systemic thinking required one to forgo. Most of all, unless systemic thinking and solutions were adopted and their requirements observed by everyone, or at least all essential actors, the system would fail to work and the power or powers that did adopt it would find themselves being cheated and exploited by others (in game theory, the Stag Hunt). In short, systemic thinking and practice requires a level of mutual trust and cooperation hard to achieve and harder still to maintain over the long run and inevitably leads to powerful temptations to cheat.

Furthermore, the process of learning in this period was not merely uneven, spiral, and tortuous, filled with relapses; it was driven by powerful coercive factors, and needed to be. Europe's leaders, by and large, did not actively look for new and better ways of thinking about international politics and practicing it; nor did they willingly accept them. They were forced into systemic thinking by repeated failures, the exhaustion of alternatives, their inability to make any form of the old politics or any combination of the old and the new politics work— and finally, by the ruthless imperialism of one of the most insatiable conquerors Europe has ever seen. It is doubtful that systemic learning will come more easily to today's elites and masses.

Worst of all, one of the most powerful and beneficial aspects of the developments which have transformed Western and, to a great extent, world society since 1815, i.e., the rise and spread of liberal representative democracy, the politization of the masses, and the increasing need for governments to legitimate themselves through constitutional processes of election, may work in an important way against a learning process promoting systemic thinking in international politics. For even in mature liberal representative democracies, the short-term political rewards of appealing to a mass electorate on the basis of linear thinking with its readily grasped catchwords and slogans are so great (witness the short-term political rewards of "successful" wars in the Persian Gulf and Panama for the American president) as to overwhelm efforts to teach the broad public, or even responsible leaders, to see events and developments in complex, indirect, systemic terms.

This means that even a determined skin-of-our-teeth Thornton Wilder type of optimist about the human race such as myself may find it hard to see how systemic thinking about international politics can ever come to the fore, especially in the United States, which does not have Europe's long experience of failure and disaster.

Notes

1. It is forthcoming as a volume in the *Oxford History of Modern Europe* series under the title *The Transformation of European Politics, 1763–1848* (Oxford: Clarendon Press).

2. "The 19th-Century International System: Changes in the Structure," *World Politics* 39 (1986), pp. 1–26.

3. "The nineteenth century system: balance of power or political equilibrium?", *Review of International Studies* 15, 2 (April 1989), pp. 135–53.

4. For an argument along these lines, see Jeremy Black, "On the 'Old System" and the "Diplomatic Revolution" of the Eighteenth Century," *International History Review* 12, 2 (May 1990), pp. 301–23, and Black's *The Rise of the European Powers 1679–1793* (London: Edward Arnold, 1990), chaps. IV–V, especially pp. 184–85 and 206–07. In my view, Black's arguments represent an important but penultimate truth. History, including international history, is certainly disorderly and chaotic; but it remains intelligible chaos. System and order are concealed in it because it is human history, and human beings act in distinctively human ways, constantly seeking order in history and putting system into it. In any case, explanation can only proceed by simplification, generalization, the conception of ideal types. Not everything can happen; the range of possibilities is indefinite, but limited, and capable of being conceived and ordered.

5. There is a massive literature on this theme; for recent discussions, see the articles by Inis L. Claude, Jr., Richard Little, Michael Sheehan, and Moorhead Wright in the *Review of International Studies* 15, 2 (April 1989).

6. Richard Little, "Deconstructing the Balance of Power: Two Traditions of Thought," *ibid.*, 87–100.

7. The best descriptions of the actual working of the 18th century balance of power system, breaking with the British biases dominating the English-language literature, are Harm Klueting, *Die Lehre von der Macht der Staaten* (Berlin: Duncker and Humblot, 1986), and Heinz Duchhardt, *Gleichgewicht der Kräfte, Convenance, Europäisches Konzert* (Darmstadt: Wissenschaftliche Buchgesellschaft, 1976). Two good surveys of 18th century international politics are Derek McKay and H. M. Scott, *The Rise of the Great Powers, 1648–1815* (London: Longman's, 1983) and Jeremy Black, *Rise of the European Powers* (n. 4). A valuable analysis of the evolution of European international politics, stressing changes from one era to another, is David Kaiser, *Politics and War: European Conflict from Philip II to Hitler* (Cambridge, MA: Harvard University Press, 1990).

8. See especially Johannes Kunisch, *Staatsverfassung und Mächtepolitik* (Berlin: Duncker and Humblot, 1979).

9. See, for example, Charles Tilly, ed., *The Formation of National States in Western Europe* (Princeton: Princeton University Press, 1975); Johannes Kunisch and Barbara Stillinger, eds., *Staatsverfassung und Heeresverfassung in der europäischen Geschichte der frühen Neuzeit* (Berlin: Duncker and Humblot, 1986); William H. McNeill, *The Pursuit of Power* (Chicago: University of Chicago Press, 1982); Geoffrey Parker, *The Military Revolution: Military Innovation and the Rise of the West 1500–1800* (Cambridge: Cambridge University Press, 1988);and Andre Corvisier, *Armies and Societies in Europe 1494–1789* (Bloomington, IN: Indiana University Press, 1979).

10. For more on intermediary bodies and their importance under the 1815 Vienna system, see Schroeder, "19th Century International System" (fn. 2 above), pp. 17–25.

11. Karl A. Roider Jr., *Austria's Eastern Question 1700–1790* (Princeton: Princeton University Press, 1982).

12. John Ehrman, *The Younger Pitt*: Vol. 1, *The Years of Acclaim* (New York: Dutton, 1969); Jeremy Black, "Anglo-French Relations in the Age of the French Revolution 1787–1793," *Francia* 15 (1987), pp. 407–33.

13. This narrative of developments and analysis of Leopold's policy is all summarized from my forthcoming book (fn. 1). The sources are listed there; the documents I used were partly unpublished ones in the *Haus-Hof-und Staatsarchiv* in Vienna, but mainly those published in various collections, in particular Alfred von Vivenot and Heinrich Zeissberg, eds., *Quellen zur Geschichte der deutschen Kaiserpolitik Osterreichs während der franzîsischen Revolutionskriege, 1790–1801* (5 vols., Vienna: W. Braumüller, 1873–90). An excellent biography of Leopold is Adam Wandruszka, *Leopold II* (2 vols., Vienna: Herold, 1963–65).

14. It is this fact that keeps me from entirely subscribing to Tom Christensen's interesting argument in this volume ("Conclusion: Systemic Stability and the Security of the Most Vulnerable Actor," p.) that leaders of vulnerable states can be the best systems thinkers. They can indeed, as Leopold illustrates; but so can others, like Lord Castlereagh of Great Britain. And while it is always vital to pay attention to the needs and fears of vulnerable essential actors, these needs and fears may also drive them into some of the worst forms of linear thinking, Much of Austria's history in this period and others (say, 1859 or 1914) illustrates this; so might much recent history in the Middle East.

15. I argue this case, and apply it especially to the Second Coalition, in my "The Collapse of the Second Coalition," *Journal of Modern History* 59, 2 (June 1987), 244–90.

16. The standard work on Castlereagh, still indispensable for any study of the era, is Charles K. Webster, *The Foreign Policy of Castlereagh, 1812–1815* (London: G. Bell, 1931). For more discussion on how Castlereagh became a European statesmen, see my "The Unnatural 'Natural Alliance': Castlereagh, Metternich, and Aberdeen in 1813," *International History Review* 10, 4 (November 1988), 522–40.

17. "MÇmoire sur les moyens de mettre un terme aux malheurs et aux dangers de l'Europe et sur les principes d'une pacification générale," in Gentz, *Aus dem Nachlasse Friedrichs von Gentz* (2 vols., Vienna: C. Gerold, 1867), II, 1–99.

18. On Metternich's German policy, see Enno Kraehe, *Metternich's German Policy* (2 vols., Princeton: Princeton University Press, 1963–1983); on the Treaty of Ried, Hans W. Schwarz, *Die Vorgeschichte des Vertrages von Ried* (Munich: Beck, 1933).

19. See William Daugherty's essay in this book, "Systems Management and the Endurance of the Concert of Europe."

4

System Management
and the Endurance of the
Concert of Europe

William H. Daugherty

Robert Jervis's essay on system effects emphasizes that the dynamics of the international system are often perverse. Because of the anarchic nature of the international environment, conflict can arise even among states satisfied with the status quo. Conversely, aggressive states are normally restrained by the self-interested reactions of their would-be victims, not by policies consciously directed toward equilibrium. The system is difficult to manage, and efforts to do so may backfire. In light of these tendencies, the pattern of cooperation among the five European great powers in the years after the Napoleonic wars is puzzling. Austria, Britain, France, Prussia, and Russia overcame pressures for conflict, avoided war, and cooperated in resolving several international problems. How and why were these states able to manage the international system between 1815 and 1848?

In this essay I argue that the Concert of Europe was a social institution that constrained competition among the great powers while enhancing their opportunities and techniques for cooperation. This institution identified special rights and responsibilities for the great powers. The Concert prescribed rules, norms, and principles whereby the powers expected each other to reaffirm their common interests in maintaining peace, to forswear unilateral pursuit of advantage, and to commit themselves to acting together in response to threats. Norms of joint action and self-denial reinforced expectations that others would cooperate, sustaining the feedback process responsible for the endurance of the Concert.

I begin this study with a brief discussion of the problem of cooperation under anarchy and the role that expectations can play in overcoming obstacles to cooperation. I then outline an approach to studying the impact of social institutions on international cooperation. Starting with the Congress of Vienna, I illustrate how the pattern of cooperation in the Concert of Europe may be understood in terms of the dynamics of a social system. I focus on the endurance of cooperation and restraint among the great powers in their management of several international problems which threatened to shatter the peace of Europe. This pattern is particularly evident in the powers' approach to the independence of Greece, the independence of Belgium, and the Near Eastern Crisis of 1839–1841.

The great powers continued to jockey for position and influence during the Concert period. By manipulating rules, norms, and principles, they sought to restrain each other while they pursued their own individual interests. Yet even those states that manipulated Concert norms for selfish purposes were constrained by the need to demonstrate consistency and to preserve the effectiveness of those norms. As a result, while great-power competition was not eliminated, it was moderated so that these states could maintain order and avoid war.

This essay demonstrates the inadequacy of alternative explanations of the period of cooperation that followed the Napoleonic Wars. One argument is that the Concert was an alliance formed to prevent renewed French aggression, and that it deteriorated as soon as the French threat faded. Another is that the Concert was a conspiracy of conservative leaders determined to preserve the status quo. Related to these two is an argument that the period of cooperation is really not so difficult to understand since, by collaborating to prevent war, the great powers were simply pursuing their self-interests. These arguments fail to recognize the Concert's enduring capacity for mitigating the pernicious effects of anarchy.

My analysis illustrates that the Concert became a system of management that endured long after the conditions responsible for its formation had passed. The reintegration of France was an important step in this transformation. It is also clear that the great powers were willing to permit changes in the status quo as long as the changes enhanced stability, and that the Concert institution facilitated an orderly process of change. This study demonstrates that by shaping the great powers' expectations and encouraging them to incorporate long-term interests into their short-term calculations, Concert norms helped them to cooperate in spite of divergent interests and pressures for conflict.

In the conclusion I discuss the implications of this research for systems theory. A systems approach is useful in studying the Concert because the pattern of cooperation reflects complex interactions, feedback effects, and unintended consequences. In addition, Concert participants referred to it as a "system" of European equilibrium. Analyzing the Concert in this way demonstrates that a social system depends on actors' conceptions of it and of their roles within it. Activity can transform the system, often in ways unintended by the actors. The rules of the system are subject to manipulation, but they impose constraints on action at the same time that they facilitate orderly behavior. Finally, I suggest several lessons drawn from the Concert for efforts to manage the emerging international system.

The International System
and the Problem of Cooperation

The Realist perspective stresses the anarchic nature of the international system. Because there is no central authority to make or enforce binding agreements, states cannot rely on each other to maintain peaceful intentions. Each must provide for its own security because there is nothing to ensure that today's allies will not become tomorrow's enemies. In such a self-help environment states find it difficult to cooperate for mutual benefits. The environment creates pressures to seek advantage over one another.[1]

Moreover, the anarchic environment makes it difficult for actors to cooperate even when each prefers cooperation to any other outcome. Despite their realization that in the long run, they are better off cooperating than trying to exploit each other, actors may still face formidable obstacles. The actors might want to cooperate, but because they cannot rely on others to do so, they can find themselves forced to defect in order to protect themselves from exploitation.[2] If we expect that others might defect, then it is sensible for us to defect in order to avoid the costs of being exploited, especially when those costs are severe. Even if we believe that others want to cooperate, we may think that others expect us to defect. Since these expectations would lead them to defect, we should defect. Such anticipations of others' expectations can lead to mutual defection even though everyone would prefer to cooperate. The solution to this problem is to create widespread expectations that the game will last and that all actors will cooperate. The actors would benefit from the ability to credibly reassure one another of their intentions to cooperate. If they could commit themselves to mutual cooperation, they could enjoy a pattern of enduring cooperation.

The game-theory literature provides insights into the conditions that increase the prospects for cooperation under anarchy. These studies suggest that international cooperation may depend on the extent to which states incorporate long-term interests into their short-term calculations, share an awareness of the durability of their interaction, and maintain confidence in each other's willingness and ability to cooperate.[3] Yet the processes through which states achieve and maintain the expectations that promote cooperation have not been fully explored. Robert Jervis concludes that the game-theory approach does not provide a full explanation, observing that "without the power of at least some shared values, without some identification with the other, without norms that carry moral force, cooperation may be difficult to sustain."[4]

A Sociological Approach

By illuminating the impact of rules, norms, roles, and institutions, a sociological approach to the study of the international system reveals ways that actors can control the dynamics of international politics and maintain a pattern of cooperation.[5] The game-theory perspective is consistent with the *homo economicus* view of human beings as rational egoists who carefully calculate and weigh their options in order to select the most rewarding course of action. In contrast, the *homo sociologicus* approach treats humans as social creatures who are motivated and constrained by social norms.[6] Human beings form bonds in response to the demands of their environment. These bonds alter the environment by providing new and different resources for and constraints on action. A network of social bonds affects individuals' conceptions of their interests. Observers of a social system may find it difficult to separate individual actors from the environment of social interactions that they compose.[7] Hedley Bull asserts that a sociological approach is appropriate for the study of international relations. In an "international society," he argues, states "conceive themselves to be bound by a common set of rules in their relations with one another, and share in the working of common institutions."[8]

Although the international system lacks central authority, states can manage the pressures of anarchy through institutions that limit conflict and facilitate cooperation. According to Robert Keohane, institutions specify "rules that constrain activity, shape expectations, and prescribe roles."[9] States can intentionally form institutions in order to establish a regular pattern of interaction. Powerful states could design arrangements that supported their interests and sustained their positions of strength,[10] yet international institutions exert reciprocal—

and possibly unintended—influence on states. "Institutions do not merely reflect the preferences and power of the units constituting them," says Keohane. "The institutions themselves *shape those preferences and that power.*"[11] Institutions become part of the environment in which states interact. They alter the conditions of international relations, often in ways that escape the awareness of actors. Thus institutions take on lives of their own, evolving and expanding, not necessarily because actors consciously modify them but because, as Keohane explains, "prior institutions create incentives and constraints that affect the emergence or evolution of later ones."[12] Moreover, institutions become increasingly resistant to manipulation or change by individual actors as time passes.[13]

International institutions enable states to manage their relations. States may initiate patterns of cooperation in recognition of their mutual interests. Institutions facilitate the maintenance of cooperation by providing "rules of thumb" that guide patterned behavior so that states do not have to recalculate their interests continually. In fact, institutions themselves become part of the interests that states pursue. Institutions can "lead nations to consider others' interests in addition to their own," observes Arthur Stein. "Those who previously agreed to bind themselves out of self-interest may come to accept joint interests as imperative."[14] International order requires more than states recognizing that they have common interests. It depends on rules and norms that specify what kind of behavior is orderly.[15]

Rules and norms are mechanisms that can sustain a pattern of cooperation. The above discussion of the problem of cooperation under anarchy illustrated the pivotal role of expectations. Cooperation is most likely when actors share expectations of cooperation. But where do these expectations come from, and how are they maintained? Norms specify and clarify the types of behavior that are expected. As guides for action and guides to the behavior that can be expected from others, norms shape expectations of future interactions.

Actors base their expectations of others on past behavior. But when conditions change, as in a crisis, for example, actors may not know whether their expectations are still valid. Actors may be tempted to violate a pattern of cooperation if opportunities for short-term gain appear. Even if we intend to continue cooperating, we may worry about others' intentions, or others' expectations of our intentions, and so on. Challenges to the uniformity of expectations that everyone will cooperate intensify incentives to defect. Conversely, cooperation is more likely when expectations of cooperation are high. Thus all can benefit from widespread cooperative reputations. Actors may strengthen their reputations as cooperators simply by cooperating. But rules, norms, and institutions provide additional mechanisms through which actors can signal their intentions and reaffirm their commitments to cooperation. When actors acknowledge norms of cooperation, they place themselves within the expectations of those norms and solidify their reputations as cooperators, thereby enhancing the prospects for cooperation.[16]

Rules, norms, and institutions are both resources and constraints. They restrict behavior by proscribing certain actions, such as challenging each other's interests, and by prescribing joint responses to common threats. They enable cooperative behavior by providing the means for actors to communicate their intentions and commitments. They tell actors what others expect of them and what to expect of others. By shaping actors' expectations and interests, institutions constrain the range of likely interactions and limit the scope of conflict.

Activity in a social system involves complex interactions, feedback mechanisms, and unintended consequences.[17] Behavior that is guided by social institutions reproduces and alters the conditions that enable that behavior in the first place. An analogy to language is helpful: the rules of language restrict our forms of communication at the same time that they enable us to communicate. When we use a language, we unintentionally reproduce and alter the rules of grammar and vocabulary that permit use in the first place.[18] In a social system, according to Anthony Giddens, "the flow of action continually produces consequences which are unintended by actors, and these unintended consequences also may form unacknowledged conditions of action in a feedback fashion."[19]

A skeptic, pointing out that social norms can be manipulated, might claim that norms are nothing more than reflections or tools of self-interest. Yet the fact that rules and norms are subject to manipulation by actors that can exploit them in pursuit of self-interest does not diminish the impact of institutional arrangements. If norms had no impact on behavior, there would be no point in trying to exploit them. Even those states or individuals capable of manipulating the norms of the international system will be constrained. A state that gains influence by invoking rules or principles will find that its freedom of action is limited by relying on these institutional elements. In his study of social norms, Jon Elster recognizes that while norms may be used to rationalize self-interested behavior, they have real and autonomous effects on human activity. Norms are more than tools of manipulation, even when they are used as tools of manipulation. The manipulator is constrained by a limited universe of norms with which to exert influence, by the need to demonstrate consistency, and by the desire to preserve the effectiveness of those norms being manipulated.[20]

The international system is more stable when states feel compelled to justify their actions in terms of common norms and principles. Addressing the possibility that states merely pay "lip-service" to international institutions, Hedley Bull argues that "the state which at least alleges a just cause, even where belief in the existence of a just cause has played no part in its decision, offers less of a threat to the international order than one which does not." Such a state "is at least acknowledging that it owes other states an explanation of its conduct, in terms of rules that they accept." When states disrupt a pattern of cooperation without justifying their actions in terms of accepted rules and institutions, they jeopardize "all the settled expectations that states have about one another's behavior."[21] Conversely, when states repeatedly justify their actions in terms of commonly accepted rules and institutions, they reinforce those expectations that are central to the maintenance and reproduction of a pattern of cooperation. Recognizing the long-term benefits of cooperation, states are less likely to diverge from cooperative behavior when they expect others to continue to cooperate.

Having outlined the elements of a sociological approach to studying the international system, I next demonstrate the ability of this approach to illuminate the Concert of Europe. I focus on the institutional mechanisms through which cooperation was established and maintained.

The Concert Is Established

The Concert of Europe was an informal institution that enabled the five European great powers—Austria, France, Great Britain, Prussia, and Russia—to manage the international system. The institution dampened and moderated the perverse effects of anarchy that can turn small disturbances into general war. The great powers created a new "system" of diplomacy embodying rules, principles, and procedures of self-restraint and joint action. Cooperation took three forms in the Concert. First, the powers refrained from attacking or threatening each other directly. Second, they exercised restraint in the pursuit of gains that were at the expense of each other's interests. Third, they collaborated in resolving potential threats to a stable order.[22] Great-power competition was not eliminated but was regulated because the powers expected one another to forgo unilateral gains in order to maintain stability. Even when they sought to manipulate the Concert's institutional arrangements for selfish purposes, the powers found themselves constrained by the need to explain their actions in terms of Concert principles.

Cooperation was initially based on great-power interests in avoiding war. Instead of seeking to maximize relative gains, these states sought to minimize the mutual losses that all would suffer if competition led to war. As part of the institutional arrangements of the Concert, the great powers consciously assumed *roles*: along with the *right* to impose their collective will on themselves and other European states, they took on the *responsibility* for preserving international order. While these roles reflected the five states' strength relative to the rest of Europe, the roles represented more than awareness of the distribution of capabilities. By assuming rights and responsibilities, the great powers placed themselves within a set of expectations regarding the kinds of behavior they were authorized and obligated to perform. As a result, these states' conceptions of themselves shaped the nature of great-power behavior and the outcomes of their interactions.

Cooperation endured because the Concert's norms continued to reinforce great-power expectations. The rules and norms of the Concert called for the great powers to consult in times of crisis or potential conflict, to reassure each other of their intentions to cooperate in the future, to explicitly acknowledge their commitments to maintaining peace and stability, to forswear unilateral advantage, and to act together in resolving disturbances.[23] These norms served the interests of the powers by providing the means for managing each other. Each sought to manage and control the others; they did not think in terms of being managed themselves, yet the result was that all were constrained.[24] At the same time that it helped the powers to coordinate their actions, the Concert regulated their behavior in ways that exceeded their individual intentions. Both a resource and a constraint, the institution provided the means for cooperation and imposed limits on competition.

The norms of the Concert facilitated cooperation by strengthening the powers' confidence in the durability of their interaction. By prescribing joint action and self-denial, the norms encouraged deferment of short-term selfish gains in favor of long-term common interests. In spite of opportunities and pressures for unilateral action that could have generated conflict, the institutional arrangements reminded leaders of their long-term interests and gave them the forum within which to reaffirm their commitments so that long-term interests weighed heavily in short-term calculations. The causal path of this process ran through the actors' expectations. The norms simultaneously depended upon and reinforced expectations of future collaboration. By continuing to engage in collaborative behavior, the powers regenerated those crucial expectations.

In keeping with the tendency of social institutions to take on lives of their own, the Concert evolved and expanded from an alliance designed to contain France into an institution with a much broader goal and capability: the management of great-power competition. This transformation was not planned in the initial arrangements but was effected through the institution's operation. The Concert endured long after the conditions responsible for its establishment had passed. It continued to operate until external shocks jolted the central mechanism of self-reinforcing norms and expectations.

The Congress of Vienna, 1814–15

As Paul Schroeder explains in his contribution to this volume, by 1814 the great powers had realized that their actions could have undesired consequences. They began to think in terms of the European system as a complex and interconnected environment rather than an arena in which all-out pursuit of interests would bring individual rewards. They recognized the need to restrain competition in order to avoid war. Instead of seeking relative gains, the powers shared the goal of avoiding mutual loss. F.H. Hinsley observes that the powers

> were prepared, as they had never previously been prepared, to waive their individual interests in the pursuit of an international system. This fact is not rendered any less impressive by the recognition that they were prepared to waive their individual interests because it was in their individual interests to do so. They had recognized for the first time that it was in their interests to do so.[25]

The powers agreed in 1814 to meet in Vienna to establish the post-Napoleonic War settlement and to design a new system of European diplomacy.[26] Austria, Britain, Prussia, and Russia initially took positions of dominance at Vienna, reflecting power capabilities and their roles in the coalition against Napoleon.[27] The Congress included France because the first Treaty of Paris of March 1814 called for the participation of "all the Powers engaged on either side" of the war against Napoleon. Thus, as René Albrecht-Carrié observes, France was "implicitly acknowledged as a legitimate member of the community of Europe."[28]

Castlereagh's goal at Vienna was to establish a "just equilibrium" in Europe.[29] This meant that all the great powers should be satisfied and secure from threat of attack. While this goal required the reallocation of population and territory, the leaders were seeking something more stable and durable than an equal distribution of power capabilities. Their concept of equilibrium required institutional arrangements that would bind them to ongoing maintenance of that equilibrium. The agreements made at Vienna shaped the powers' goals and behavior throughout the Concert period. Paul Schroeder emphasizes that "political equilibrium meant a balance of satisfactions, a balance of rights and obligations and a balance of performance and payoffs." This understanding of political equilibrium was powerful as "an ideal to which almost everyone had to pay lip service no matter how much it was distorted for individual purposes."[30] These observations support the view that the Concert, as a social institution, exerted an independent influence on the great powers. The operation of the Concert reshaped the interests of the great powers so that continued participation became a value in itself. Indeed, according to Schroeder, the criteria for "a good European equilibrium" became recognition of honor and dignity, satisfaction of national rights, maintenance of treaties, unity of the great powers, and equal representation of all the great powers in the Concert, rather than the equal distribution of power.[31]

Despite their desire to establish equilibrium, the powers first had to overcome several disputes at the Congress of Vienna.[32] For example, serious tensions over the control of Poland and Saxony led all the great powers to begin preparing for war in November 1814. "I witness every day," said Castlereagh, "the astonishing tenacity with which all the Powers cling to the smallest point of separate interest."[33] When Prussia threatened war on December 29, 1814, Britain, Austria, and France countered five days later with a secret treaty, and war was averted. As a result of this stalemate, France gained entrance to the directing committee of the Congress. The diplomats resolved the Poland-Saxony dispute and were now able to work more harmoniously toward a general settlement.[34]

The leaders contemplated the value of a public commitment and joint guarantee of the Vienna treaty.[35] Castlereagh argued that in order to form "the best alliance that could be formed," the powers should make a "public declaration" to Europe of "their determination to uphold and support the arrangements agreed upon" at the Congress.[36] Such a declaration could deter potential challengers from disturbing the established equilibrium. It would also support the powers' efforts to bind each other to a system of management. Such joint and public commitments signal intentions and expectations of future cooperation. They provide opportunities to reinforce such expectations. These commitments constrain states by imposing high reputational costs on violators, who will be scrutinized by all parties and observers of the agreement. As I demonstrate below, joint and public commitments played an important part in binding the great powers to Concert principles.

The German Confederation and the Swiss Constitution were outcomes of the Vienna negotiations.[37] The German Confederation gave joint management of German affairs to Austria and Prussia; their long-standing rivalry, evident in the Poland-Saxony standoff, prevented them from agreeing on a system for uniting Germany. In the case of Switzerland, the great powers agreed to guarantee Swiss neutrality and the inviolability of its territory. Charles Webster considers this new principle to have been

> one of the most important results of the period, for the great powers had definitely recognized that their own interests, as well as those of all Europe, were best served by the exclusion of a small state from participation in future conflicts.[38]

Schroeder points out the unintended impact of these developments on the long-term stability of Europe. Both Switzerland and the German confederation served as "intermediary bodies" that "separated the great powers, making it more difficult for them to fight, [and] linked them by giving them something in common to manage."[39] The stabilizing effect of these intermediary bodies reflects characteristics of a social institution. The powers made joint commitments that in turn shaped their interests so that the pattern of cooperation was reinforced.

The Congress was disrupted by Napoleon's escape from Elba on February 25, 1815, the subsequent Hundred Days, and the final defeat of Napoleon at Waterloo. A debate ensued over the terms of the new treaty. Several diplomats urged that France be severely punished. But Castlereagh stood by his goal of European equilibrium. He warned that the allies should seek "security, and not revenge."[40] Wellington advised that if the powers sought "peace and tranquillity . . . they must make an arrangement which will suit the interests of *all the parties* to it."[41]

On November 20, 1815, the powers signed the second Treaty of Paris, restricting France roughly to its 1790 borders, providing for its military occupation, and imposing an indemnity. On the same day Austria, Britain, Prussia, and Russia signed a treaty renewing the Quadruple Alliance. In Article VI of the treaty, the four agreed that in order to "consolidate the connections which at the present moment so closely unite" them "for the happiness of the world," they would "renew their Meetings at fixed periods" so that they could consult "upon their common interests." Their stated goals were to secure "the repose and prosperity of Nations" and to maintain "the Peace of Europe."[42] This article explicitly established the principles of the Concert as an ongoing system of management in which the great powers had joint responsibility for Europe. The agreement produced an expectation of consultation and provided the framework in which the powers could continually reaffirm their common interests in peace. This arrangement was an informal institution in that it articulated norms, shaped expectations, and prescribed roles. The norms embodied in this article supported a self-reinforcing process of enduring cooperation.

Shortly after the Quadruple Alliance was renewed, tension arose between Austria and Russia due to Metternich's suspicion that Tsar Alexander was meddling in Naples, the Ionian Islands, and Spain in order to facilitate an invasion of Turkey. Castlereagh recognized that these tensions threatened the Quadruple Alliance and the peace and stability of Europe. His response in December 1815 and January 1816 illustrates the application of Concert principles. Instead of responding to Alexander's intrigues with those of his own, and instead of forming an opposing coalition, Castlereagh sought to restrain the tsar by appealing to the commitment he had made at Paris. Castlereagh did not want to alienate Alexander; to do so would be a "hazard to the great machine of European safety, which if it does not consist of the four powers is shaken to its foundations."[43] Castlereagh instructed all British foreign representatives to

> inspire the states of Europe . . . with a sense of the dangers which they have surmounted by their union, of the hazards they will incur by a relaxation of vigilance, . . . and that their true wisdom is to keep down the petty contentions of ordinary times, and to stand together in support of the established principles of social order.[44]

He hoped to reinforce the powers' commitments to cooperation by reminding them of their long-term common interests. Castlereagh's policy in dealing with threats to the integrity of the Ottoman Empire was to cooperate with the powers in preserving the Empire, but most importantly, to ensure that the powers did not appear hostile to Russia. If Russia were to feel isolated from the Concert, a Russian attack on Turkey might become inevitable. A war in the region could not possibly be contained, Castlereagh thought, so the overriding concern was to maintain peace.[45] In other words, self-restraint and unity were essential parts of restraining Russia and limiting conflict.

The Conference of Aix-la-Chapelle, 1818

Aix-la-Chapelle was an important step in the Concert's institutional transformation. Originally a response to fears of resurgent French aggression, the Concert reintegrated France and gained strength as a system of managing European order. Having convened at Aix-la-Chapelle to consider ending the occupation of France, the powers discussed admitting France into the Quadruple Alliance. The success of the Quadruple Alliance bred confidence that joint action would be valuable in the future. In a memorandum submitted at Aix-la-Chapelle, the British plenipotentiaries noted that the Alliance had promoted remarkable peace during the last four years. The memo observed that the influence of the Quadruple Alliance had surpassed the powers' expectations. Although the Alliance had been "formed upon principles altogether limited," the "unparalleled unity" of the allies had enabled them to cooperate in ways that exceeded their "immediate and primitive obligations." As a result, they were successful in maintaining order and "watching over the peace of Europe." Britain acknowledged the "beneficial effects . . . produced by the four Allied Powers consulting together . . . for the preservation of peace and order," and argued that "the introduction of France into such a system" would "add immensely to the moral weight and influence" of the Concert.[46]

The powers agreed to admit France as a member of the Concert. In their note to France, the other four powers invited France "to take part in their present and future deliberations, consecrated to the maintenance of the peace" and to "the rights and mutual relations" of the great powers.[47] France accepted the invitation and affirmed its commitment to the Concert's principles. In a note to the other powers, France acknowledged its duty to strengthen "the benefits which the complete re-establishment of general Peace promises to all Nations." Because "the intimate union of governments is the surest pledge" of lasting peace, France "could not remain a stranger to a system" of Concert principles and great-power cooperation.[48]

The five powers then signed a joint protocol in which they asserted that "assuring to France the place that belongs to her in the European system will bind her more closely to the pacific and benevolent views in which all the Sovereigns participate, and will thus consolidate the general tranquillity." As part of this protocol, France pledged "henceforth to concur in the maintenance and consolidation of a System which has given Peace to Europe, and which can alone insure its duration."[49]

The final act of the five powers at Aix-la-Chapelle was to issue a declaration to all the states of Europe publicizing their understandings of the Concert, its purpose, and its obligations. They offered "the most sacred pledge" of Europe's "future tranquillity." The powers had established an "intimate Union" with "no other object than the maintenance of Peace, and the guarantee of those transactions on which the Peace was founded and consolidated." They resolved "never to depart, either among themselves, or in their Relations with other States, from the strictest observation of the principles of the Right of Nations," which would "guarantee the Independence of each Government." The powers reaffirmed their intentions to hold meetings "for purpose of discussing in common their own interests, . . . and the repose of the world will be constantly their motive and their end."[50]

The transition from the great-power settlement at Vienna in 1815 to their agreement at Aix-la-Chapelle in 1818 reflects the dynamics of a social system. The reintegration of France illustrates that institutional arrangements formed in the Quadruple Alliance for the security of Europe took on a life of their own. Action in accord with Concert norms reinforced expectations that the Concert was a useful means of managing European international relations. As these expectations gained strength, they facilitated further reliance on the Concert institution. In the documents issued at Aix-la-Chapelle the powers emphasized their commitments to joint action in maintaining peace. Such reaffirmation was consistent with Concert norms and served to reproduce those norms. By enhancing expectations that all the powers would participate, these statements fostered ongoing cooperation.

Congresses of Troppau, Laibach, and Verona, 1820–22

Frictions in the Concert appeared in connection with the Congresses of Troppau, Laibach, and Verona. The powers met to consider intervening to suppress rebellions in Italy, Spain, and Greece. A dispute between Britain and the continental powers arose over the interpretation and application of Concert principles. Britain did not participate in the Congress of Verona and refused to sanction its decisions.[51] Despite open disagreement and unilateral pursuit of interests in this period, the Concert institution was influential. The powers continued to explain and justify their actions in terms of jointly accepted principles. Although states sought to manipulate norms to serve their own interests, these efforts ultimately were constrained by Concert norms.

Because he appreciated the utility of jointly accepted principles, Metternich proposed the preliminary Protocol of Troppau endorsing great-power intervention in revolutionary states.[52] After Austria, Prussia, and Russia resolved at Troppau to sanction Austrian intervention in Naples, these powers sought to clarify their intentions, reassure other states, and portray their actions as consistent with generally accepted principles. They denied that they were driven by a "spirit of conquest," by a desire to infringe "on the Independence of other governments in their Internal Administration," or by an effort to prevent "wise alterations, freely undertaken, and consistent with the true interests of the peoples." Their "only wish," they declared, was "to maintain Peace."[53]

Castlereagh explained the objection of the British government to the principle of intervention resolved at Troppau. While Britain could not support such interventions, it would not stand in the way as long as the powers engaging in intervention "were ready to give every reasonable assurance that their views were not directed to purposes of aggrandisement subversive of the Territorial System of Europe." Britain did not want its toleration of Austrian intervention to signal acceptance of a general principle. Castlereagh made it clear that for Britain the right of intervention was "only to be justified by the strongest necessity." At the same time he tried to preserve the pattern of great-power cooperation. Castlereagh instructed the British foreign representatives to acknowledge the other powers' "purity of intention" so that their "difference of sentiment" would not cause any "alteration whatever in the cordiality and harmony of the Alliance on any other subject." He wanted to ensure that the great powers did not "abate their common zeal" in maintaining the Concert.[54]

The fact that Concert principles were the subject of so much attention, clarification, and interpretation indicates their impact on the thinking of the powers. Both sides in this dispute were clearly interested in maintaining common understandings and a common set of expectations. Neither side wanted disagreement to disrupt the system of joint management. The powers pursued divergent interests, but within the framework of Concert principles. They tried to manipulate these principles to support their own positions yet were confined by the obligation to justify their actions in terms of a European order.

Metternich's strategy was to manipulate principles and use them to commit other powers to policies of self-restraint. At Troppau Metternich exploited Tsar Alexander's desire for great-power solidarity in order to gain support for Austrian intervention in Naples and to bind Russia to a policy of self-denial.[55] Later, horrified by Turkish cruelties toward Greek-Orthodox rebels, the tsar wanted to intervene in support of the Greek rebellion. Britain and Austria shared an interest in preventing unilateral Russian action against the

Ottoman Empire. Now Metternich appealed to the principle of great-power unity to develop a policy of nonintervention that kept Alexander out of Turkey. Castlereagh also adjusted his interpretation of the danger of European revolutions, urging Russian restraint pursuant to Alexander's commitment to the "consecrated structure" of Europe.[56] Citing "the danger of my intervention for my allies," Alexander decided not to support the Greek rebellion.[57]

Metternich's strategy of restraining others in a "web" of Concert principles ultimately imposed constraints on him. He wrote:

> I feel as if I were in the middle of a web, like my friends the spiders whom I love because I have so often admired them. . . . I have brought to bear my moral means in all directions . . . but this state of things forces the poor spider to remain in the center of its fine web.[58]

Having relied so heavily on unity to restrain Russia, Metternich got caught in his own web. Metternich's ties with Tsar Alexander motivated Canning, the new British foreign secretary after Castlereagh's suicide, to try to split the Holy Alliance. Because he could no longer rely on Britain to support Austria's position, Metternich now could not afford to risk his relationship with the tsar. Thus allied unity became a necessity for Metternich, not a tool for gaining influence. Metternich was a victim of his own success in using principles to bind Tsar Alexander.[59]

In assessing great-power relations from 1820 to 1822 we find friction and disagreement. But we should not overlook the fact that although the powers tried to manipulate principles in competitive ways, their competition was nevertheless regulated within the Concert. The powers sought to maintain unity and peace, and they were constrained by their appeals to Concert principles. Disputes over the content and applicability of those principles never went so far as to reject or overturn them. In fact, these disputes served the important function of refining the powers' understandings of what kinds of behavior were expected of them and of the appropriate role for the Concert institution in managing international affairs.[60]

Yet the evidence of manipulative and self-interested behavior in this period leads many observers to mark this as the failure or end of the Concert of Europe.[61] One line of reasoning is that the Concert had been held together by fear of France. This logic implies that alliance ties deteriorated as memories of the Napoleonic Wars and the French threat faded.[62] The reintegration of France at Aix-la-Chapelle contributed to the Concert's demise, it is argued, because the powers now had more interests in conflict than in common.[63] But, as I show in the next section, the Concert did not fall apart. The institution endured and enabled the great powers to manage several threats to the international order. Moreover, the reintegration of France transformed and strengthened the Concert by reinforcing the powers' expectations that they could maintain peace.

Another argument is that the powers had been bound together by their fear not so much of France but of revolutions in general. In 1823 the French envoy to Naples predicted that the French overthrow of the Spanish revolution would undermine the Concert:

> The fear of revolutions is the common sentiment which, for the past eight years, has held the great powers united and Europe in peace. A peril, once past, is quickly forgotten, and this fear will be greatly enfeebled once the Peninsula will have been restored and pacified. Then the politics of the interests, of the ambitions of one power versus the other, the old politics, if you wish, will resume all its rights.[64]

In addition, this argument implies that the Concert could not have been sustained in light of Britain's divergence from the Continental powers, especially the three eastern powers, on the dangers of revolution and the legitimacy of interventions.[65]

But, again, the Concert was sustained. While the powers may have differed on the legitimacy of intervention, they agreed on the need to maintain peace. They recognized that revolutions could cause war, and they were determined, above all, to prevent disturbances in Europe from drawing them into general war. They also understood that changes in the status quo could be stabilizing as long as the process of change was carefully managed. The Concert institution enabled joint management of the process through which Greece and Belgium gained independence. The norms of the Concert facilitated great-power cooperation by encouraging consultation and reassurance. Concert norms also reinforced the pattern of restraint. Although the powers jockeyed for position and influence, competition was constrained because they remained aware of their basic obligations to maintain order, and because they expected each other to abide by these obligations.

The Concert Endures

In this section I explain how the Concert of Europe endured well after the frictions of 1820–22. A pattern of restraint is evident in the powers' management of Greek independence, Belgian independence, and the Near Eastern crisis. These were serious matters in which divergent interests could have sparked war. The great powers competed for influence but were able to prevent their competition from getting out of control because they continued to acknowledge their common interests in maintaining peace, to forswear the unilateral pursuit of advantage, and to commit themselves to joint action. Concert norms and actions consistent with them continually reinforced expectations that others would cooperate. The endurance of the Concert reflects its nature as a social institution.

The Independence of Greece, 1821–32

Pressures for conflict arose from the strong interests of four of the great powers with respect to the Ottoman Empire. Russia sought control of the Straits of the Bosphorus and the Dardanelles, or at least open access to them. Russia also wanted to protect and support Christian subjects of the Ottoman sultan. Austria sought to prevent the rise of Balkan nationalism which threatened to break apart the Austrian Empire. France wanted to maintain commercial relations and religious ties in the eastern Mediterranean and had developed strong ties to Egypt. Britain had naval outposts at Malta and in the Ionian Islands and wanted to prevent any other powers from controlling this region, so it opposed French dominance in Egypt and Russian control of the Straits. Unstable internal affairs put the Ottoman Empire in danger of collapse. Balkan nationalities resisted Turkish rule and would have welcomed outside assistance. The resulting opportunities for individual powers to gain influence could have led to conflict. The powers could not agree on any system of dividing the Ottoman Empire, and they knew that their conflicting interests could cause war, so it was essential that they maintain stability in the region.[66]

Revolutions in Greece against Ottoman rule began in 1821. Britain tried to restrain Russia from intervening and strengthening its influence at the expense of the Ottoman Empire. As a result of these efforts, the two powers signed a joint protocol in 1826 in which they proposed joint mediation between the Greek rebels and the sultan.[67] The two powers promised not to seek "any increase of Territory, nor any exclusive influence, nor advantage in commerce for their Subjects, which shall not be equally attainable by all other Nations." They communicated their plans to the other three powers so that all five could jointly support stability in the region.[68]

Rejecting the proposal of mediation, the sultan sought assistance from Mohamed Ali of Egypt to suppress the Greek rebellion. The entrance of Egypt into the affair intensified the conflict of interests between France, Britain, and Russia.[69] But in 1827 the three powers signed a treaty in which they reaffirmed their "interests for the tranquillity of Europe," forswore any individual advantage, and agreed to joint enforcement of an armistice between the Ottoman sultan and the Greeks. The Sultan was given one month to establish an armistice, or else the powers would impose it.[70]

The powers were forced to execute their threat of force. A combination of British and French naval forces destroyed the Turco-Egyptian fleet at Navarino on October 20, 1827. Representatives of Britain, France, and Russia explained to the Turkish foreign minister that "the three Allied Powers make common cause" with respect to the Greek question.[71] The purpose of the three-power alliance and its military action was joint management—to restrain the pursuit of unilateral advantage and to ensure European stability.[72]

When war broke out between Russia and Turkey in April 1828, France sent troops to support Greece. The French explained that they preferred multilateral action, that they "would act in the name of the three Courts, and for the common interest," and that they would withdraw their forces as soon as the sultan was defeated and stability was established. The three powers continued meetings in London to discuss arrangements for Greece. The sultan accepted defeat in September 1829.[73]

Britain, France, and Russia granted Greek independence in the joint protocol of February 3, 1830. They stated that their goal was to introduce into the alliance "whatever improvements might be best adapted to assure new pledges of stability." They agreed that the new Greek monarch would not have any ties to the royal families of Britain, France, or Russia. They planned to guarantee the independence of Greece. Furthermore, "no troops belonging to one of the Contracting Powers shall be allowed to enter the territory of the new Greek State, without the consent of the other two Courts who signed the Treaty." Finally, the powers expressed confidence that "the maintenance of their union . . . will not cease to contribute to the confirmation of the peace."[74] The convention of May 7, 1832, established Otho of Bavaria as the Greek monarch and finalized Greek independence.[75]

In a note to the sultan the powers explained the principles that had guided them in their response to the Greek problem. Their motives were "to safeguard Europe from a conflagration," to establish a stable order in the region, and "to consolidate the very existence of the Ottoman Empire."[76] In spite of opportunities and temptations to pursue individual interests, the powers had successfully managed the establishment of an independent Greece. They used joint consultations and declarations to reaffirm Concert principles of multilateral action and self-denial. The Concert constrained conflict and provided the great powers with the institutional resources for maintaining order.

The Independence of Belgium, 1830–39

Disturbances began in Brussels in August 1830 in protest against Dutch rule. After the Belgians proclaimed their independence from Holland, King William of the Netherlands appealed for international assistance to suppress the revolt. The issue was especially significant for the great powers because the union of Belgium and Holland had been part of the Vienna settlement and was designed to promote stability. Opinion in France supported Belgian independence. Louis Philippe, the French king, indicated that he would not intervene in Belgium as long as the other powers would exercise similar restraint. Britain was willing to accept Belgian independence from Holland as long as Belgium did not then fall under French control. Recognizing the threat to European peace, the powers decided to meet in London to discuss their response to the revolution.[77]

The great powers differed in their views of Belgian independence, but they agreed on the importance of avoiding war. In a protocol of December 20, 1830, the five powers stated that the purpose of the union of Belgium and Holland in the treaties of 1814 and 1815 had been "to found a just balance in Europe, and to secure the maintenance of general peace." They acknowledged that maintaining peace would now require the separation of Belgium and Holland. They asserted their intention to establish the situation that would best combine Belgian independence "with the interests and security of other Powers, and with the preservation of the balance of Europe."[78] By obliging the powers to consult one another and to focus on preserving peace, the principles of the Concert helped the powers to defer pursuit of unilateral gains and thus to maintain order.

In January 1831 the powers reiterated "the principles which actuate their common policy." They were determined not to seek "any augmentation of territory, any exclusive influence, [or] any isolated advantages" in their management of the Belgian problem. Instead, they were committed to providing "the best guarantees of repose and security" to Belgium and all its neighbors. The five powers guaranteed the "perpetual neutrality" of Belgium, "as well as the integrity and inviolability of its territory."[79] They recognized that they were establishing the same obligation that they had created with regard to Greek independence. Accordingly, they agreed that the new Belgian monarch could not be a prince of a reigning family of any of the great powers.[80]

In February 1831 there was still concern that France might seek to gain some advantage in Belgium. Holland and Belgium were not able to agree on borders or to abide by the terms of their armistice. The great powers clarified their motives in a joint declaration. They unanimously acknowledged their obligation to "the cause of general peace." They repeated that Belgium and Holland had originally been united in order to maintain peace and equilibrium. Now that the union was broken, the powers "had the right, and events rendered it their duty, to prevent the Belgian provinces, [having] become independent, from disturbing the general security and the balance of power in Europe." Joint actions by the powers resulted from the "identity of their opinions upon the force and upon the principles of the solemn transactions which bind them together." As an independent state, they argued, Belgium was bound by obligations not to overturn the "general system." If it were to infringe on the treaties and principles which "governed" Europe, Belgium would bring on "confusion and war. The Powers alone could prevent this evil, and as they could do so, it was their duty." The powers acknowledged that the nature of Europe as a collective social order produced international obligations: "Each nation has its particular rights; but Europe has also her rights; it is social order that has given them to her."[81]

In August 1831 hostilities flared between Belgium and Holland. The Dutch army routed the Belgians and was marching to Brussels when the French army intervened. This unilateral action by France raised fears that France was seeking some advantage and heightened the danger of European war.[82] The five powers discussed the French intervention, its motives, and the extent to which it could be justified. They reached an understanding recorded in the protocol of August 6, 1831. The French army would return from Belgium as soon as the armistice was restored. The powers felt that the French action was acceptable because it was consistent with jointly accepted principles and goals—maintaining the armistice. They acknowledged that the intervention was not aimed at "any object personal to France," and that France "had not had time to comply with the obligation which she wished to fulfil, of concerting measures with her allies." Recognizing the danger that military actions could "give rise to serious complications," the powers agreed to restrict the movements of the French troops so that the war would not get too close to Prussian and German borders.[83] Belgian independence was granted in a treaty with the five great powers, signed on November 15, 1831, but King William did not accept the development until 1838, when he realized that he must relieve his Dutch subjects of the tax burden needed to keep his army ready for war against Belgium. At this point Belgium stubbornly appealed to the great powers in an effort to gain territory in Luxemburg and Limburg. But the great powers were determined to maintain the unity they had reached in the London Conference.

Belgium relented and finally received its independence on April 19, 1839.[84]

Despite heightened tensions that could have produced a spiral of hostility, the great powers had successfully managed the process of Belgian independence. The Concert's institutional arrangements continued to limit conflict and facilitate cooperation. Concert principles required self-denial and joint efforts to preserve peace. By continually reaffirming these principles and seeking common understandings, the powers reinforced expectations of cooperation. Aware of long-term common interests, each power was willing to exercise restraint because it expected the others to be restrained.

The Near Eastern Crisis, 1839–41

Mohamed Ali of Egypt had acquired Syria by defeating Turkish forces in 1832. In June 1839 the Ottoman sultan, trying to reestablish the Ottoman Empire's position, attacked Syria and was again defeated. This development threatened the integrity of the Ottoman Empire and precipitated a division of the great powers. All of the powers wanted to maintain the independence of the Ottoman Empire and restrict Mohamed. But France and Egypt had strong ties, so France did not want to see Mohamed humiliated. France preferred to concentrate on limiting Russian domination in the region. Britain was intent on eliminating Mohamed as a threat to the Ottoman Empire. After considerable maneuvering and debate over the appropriate form of joint action, Russia, Prussia, and Austria joined Britain in opposing Mohamed Ali.[85]

The four powers signed a convention with the sultan on July 15, 1840, in which the powers agreed to secure the Straits and Constantinople against Mohamed's aggression. Their forces would withdraw simultaneously as soon as the sultan decided that they were no longer necessary. The sultan agreed to close the Straits to all foreign warships in times of peace. Annexed to the convention were terms that required Mohamed to withdraw from Ottoman territory and return the Ottoman fleet,[86] but he stood firm in the expectation that France would support him. Britain sent a naval force to drive Mohamed back. The four powers once again formally declared that in their actions against Mohamed they would "seek no augmentation of Territory, no exclusive Influence, no Commercial advantage for their subjects, which those of every other nation may not equally obtain."[87] This forswearing of unilateral advantage had become an effective way for the powers to reinforce expectations of cooperation.

The isolation of France generated resentment in the French public and government, led by Adolphe Thiers, against the other powers. The French called for aggressive action. Their hostility was directed against Prussia and Austria, the most vulnerable of the great powers, and led to a war scare on the Rhine in October 1840. Thiers hoped that French bellicosity would intimidate the other powers into compromising. Louis Philippe, the French king, supported military preparations but remained committed to peace.[88] In a note to the four powers he assured them that France "wishes to maintain the European equilibrium, the care of which is the responsibility of all the Great Powers. Its preservation must be their glory and their main ambition."[89] The king forced Thiers to resign and replaced him with Guizot, who informed the French ambassador to Britain that France had "no intention of remaining outside the general affairs of Europe." France was convinced that its participation was beneficial to itself and to others. Guizot believed "in the necessity of the concert" and in "higher interests" which required that Europe "operate in concert and in unity."[90]

According to Schroeder, the French response to the four-power alliance illustrates that in the minds of the leaders, European equilibrium was a matter of "rights, status, and prestige, rather than power." France was alarmed not by a threat to its security or an attack on its interests, but by the others' willingness to exclude it.[91] The isolation of France was a way for the other powers to draw France back into conformity with Concert principles of joint management and self-denial.[92]

In November 1840 Mohamed Ali was driven back to Egypt, where he was reinstated by the sultan as the hereditary leader. The powers then sought to reintegrate France into the Concert; there was no effort to punish or humiliate France in the process. The four powers and Turkey issued a protocol which emphasized the principle prohibiting foreign warships from entering the Straits. In addition, they invited France to join them in pledging support for this principle.[93] France insisted that it would sign the convention only after the other powers had promised that the convention of July 15, 1840, which had isolated France, was now finished.[94] On July 13, 1841, the five powers signed a convention with Turkey in which the powers professed "their sincere desire to see consolidated the repose" of the sultan's empire and recorded "their unanimous determination to conform" to the prohibition of foreign warships in the Straits while the Porte was at peace. Once again, the powers expressed confidence "that their union and their agreement offer to Europe the most certain pledge for the preservation of the general peace."[95]

The management of the Near Eastern crisis illustrates that while great-power competition was not eliminated, it was moderated by Concert principles. The prompt decision to reintegrate France indicates the value that the great powers placed in the Concert as a system of management. The powers continued to recognize their interests in peace, the importance of joint action, and the need for self-restraint. The pattern of cooperation endured in the twenty-five years after the Congress of Vienna because Concert principles and norms created expectations that others would cooperate and provided opportunities to reinforce those expectations.

The Concert in Decay?
The Revolutions of 1848 and the Crimean War

My goal in this essay has been to demonstrate how and why the Concert endured as long as it did. A full discussion of the Concert's decay is beyond the scope of this work, but a few observations show that my explanation of the Concert's endurance can also help us to understand its demise.

The bedrock of the Concert was the powers' confidence in their joint ability to manage European affairs. Having recognized the desirability of cooperation, each cooperated because it expected others to cooperate as well. These expectations were shaped by the Concert's norms and reinforced every time states acknowledged or followed those norms. But if that confidence was undermined, states would worry more about the penalties they would suffer if they cooperated while others did not. Actors are less likely to obey norms of cooperation when they do not expect others to obey them. In the same way that cooperation can be self-reinforcing through the causal channel of expectations, a pattern of cooperation can quickly unravel if confidence in others' intentions or ability to cooperate is shaken. When expectations about the durability of a cooperative relationship are challenged, the shadow of the future shrinks, actors focus on short-term interests, and cooperation is less likely.

These dynamics were responsible for the Concert's decay. In 1844 Russia was not confident that the powers could continue to preserve the Ottoman Empire. Count Nesselrode, the Russian foreign minister, sent a memorandum to Britain acknowledging the two powers' common interest in maintaining the integrity of the Ottoman Empire. Close cooperation offered the greatest hope of success, but Nesselrode was worried that cooperation might fail. He wrote that the great powers "must not conceal from themselves how many elements of dissolution that Empire contains within itself. Unforeseen circumstances may hasten its fall, without it being in the power of the friendly Cabinets to prevent it."[96] Britain did not agree that the Ottoman Empire would inevitably collapse. This divergence contributed to the unraveling of the powers' confidence in the Concert system.

The revolutions of 1848 shocked leaders and undermined their expectations of continued joint action. Even if a leader intended to maintain his commitment to the Concert, the effect of the revolutions was to diminish his confidence in the willingness and ability of other leaders to participate. Other states were uncertain about the significance of France's emergence from the revolutions as a republic. As a result they were less confident that France would perform its Concert duties.[97]

Intensified popular national sentiments frightened the eastern powers, especially Austria. Nationalism widened the ideological gap between the liberal and conservative powers and threatened to divide Austria and Prussia. As diplomats became more sensitive to the danger that their states could be overthrown, they were less able to focus on the long term. Rising democratic pressures ended the isolation of leaders from the public. Domestic public opinion exerted a greater influence on leaders.[98] In her essay in this volume, Susan Peterson shows that although the powers tried to exercise restraint in the crisis leading up to the Crimean War, the British public would not permit a conciliatory policy. These developments support Paul Schroeder's observation that democracy can be an obstacle to long-term, complex systems thinking because democratic leaders must appeal to the short-term, simplistic demands of the public.[99]

The revolutions undermined the Concert because the powers were now more vulnerable to the costs of a single exploitation and because they could not be confident that all leaders shared expectations of cooperation. However, the Concert was a social institution, and social institutions do not always die quickly. Despite the new obstacles to Concert diplomacy, it apparently continued to operate to some extent. The Crimean War was limited in its scope; it did not develop into a general European war. During the conflict the powers met at Vienna seeking a jointly acceptable resolution that would maintain peace. At the postwar Congress of Paris in February 1856, the powers sought to expand the influence of the Concert by admitting Turkey.[100]

A degree of commitment to joint management of European stability thus survived revolutions and the Crimean War. The great powers occasionally appealed to the Concert to solve diplomatic problems during the rest of the nineteenth century, but these efforts were usually unsuccessful. The Concert's effectiveness was degraded because the great powers were less confident in each other's commitments to principles of joint action and self-denial.

Conclusion

The Concert of Europe was an institution that enabled the great powers to manage the European international system, maintain stability, and avoid war. The institution gave the powers special rights and responsibilities. Its principles called for the powers to reaffirm their common interests in peace, to forswear unilateral pursuit of advantage, and to act together to resolve potential threats to stability. These norms were central to the regulation of great-power competition. By shaping the powers' expectations of joint action and self-denial, Concert norms helped the powers to overcome the obstacles to cooperation under anarchy. A pattern of cooperation endured because the powers expected a durable and rewarding relationship. By providing institutional means for reassurances and commitments, the Concert tended to reinforce itself.

Some observers might criticize the Concert for being effective only at the margins: the great powers were relatively satisfied with the status quo after the Napoleonic Wars, and there were no severe challenges to their interests or stability. This position fails to recognize that the Concert itself enabled the powers to maintain satisfactions and prevent severe challenges. The great powers managed potential disturbances, seeking to ensure that none of their members became too threatening or too vulnerable. The Concert was an institution that did more than reflect its members' interests. It reshaped their conceptions of their interests so that they remained committed to the benefits of enduring cooperation. They came to think in terms of the Concert itself and of their roles within it instead of focusing solely on the interests that led them to create the institution in the first place.

Moreover, one of the main findings of systems approaches is that the margins can have central importance. Through feedback effects and unintended dynamics, small perturbations can have disastrous consequences in international politics. War can result from spirals of hostility. States may be satisfied with the status quo but unable to maintain peace due to the anarchic nature of their environment. There were pressures for conflict and several dangerous incidents between 1815 and 1848, but no great-power war occurred. The Concert constrained competition and facilitated collaboration. The pattern of cooperation endured long after the conditions initially responsible for its establishment had passed.

These conclusions have several implications for how we think about the international system. The most significant is that in light of the Concert, it appears possible to manage the dynamics of the international system. Rather than being prisoners of their environment, the great powers in some ways were architects of their environment. They could not escape the anarchic nature of the system and the competitive pressures it creates, but they were able to form an institution to regulate those pressures. They established conditions that increased the stability of their interactions. Most interesting, although great-power leaders designed the Concert in its initial stages, the institution took on a life of its own. So the Concert did hold the states captive, but this was a system in which states benefited from being constrained. The Concert institution illustrates that such a system is not simply a fixed constraint on behavior but also a resource that permits action. The Concert limited conflict by imposing obligations of consultation, reassurance, joint action, and self-denial. It also enabled the powers to enjoy the benefits of a stable order by making it easier for them to reinforce the expectations that foster a pattern of cooperation.

The nature of the international system can depend on the ways that actors think about it. The system changed after the Napoleonic Wars because great-power leaders began to think in terms of managing the system to maintain order. The Concert could not have operated unless the leaders believed that it operated. Indeed, the Concert functioned precisely because leaders expected it to function. Recognition of the social nature of the international system allows us to understand that actors may create and alter system rules. Some rules exist only to the extent that actors believe them to exist. Furthermore, some systems are systems only because actors conceive them to be. For example, there is no such thing as a working monetary system or collective security system independent of the awareness and expectations of the human beings within those systems.[101]

Yet the system and its rules exert an independent impact on actors within it. Social systems exhibit complex interactions, feedback processes, and unintended consequences. Social actors form institutions, then reproduce and alter those institutions, both consciously and unconsciously, by acting within them. Thus action in a system tends to transform it. Actors can manipulate rules and norms, but even the manipulators will be constrained by the institutions they seek to exploit. In the international system, these dynamics can promote order even in the absence of central authority.

The enduring impact of the Concert suggests that institutions can support contemporary efforts to manage the international system. The end of the Cold War may be the beginning of an era of multipolarity, uncertainty, and instability,[102] but it also provides an opportunity to build institutions to cope with these problems. Leaders should recognize that institutions tend to take on lives of their own. What appears today to be an imperfect or incomplete solution may gain influence and effectiveness as it is used. Institutions can constrain conflict and foster cooperation in ways that are not immediately apparent.

The Concert demonstrates that a small group of "great powers" can work together to maintain order. Yet it is essential that such states understand that leadership roles carry responsibilities as well as privileges. Accordingly, new institutions should clarify and emphasize the obligations of great power status. These states should make joint and public commitments, justify their actions in terms of generally accepted principles, and reassure each other and other states of their intentions. When they respond to crises, the leading states should consult one another and forswear unilateral efforts to gain advantage. These norms of joint action and self-denial can constrain conflict and reinforce the expectations that facilitate cooperation.

Since a doctrine of self-restraint is easier to follow when a state knows that it can defend itself if attacked, institutions should not seek to eliminate the threat of military action. Rather, they should establish standards for nonprovocative force postures so that states can demonstrate peaceful intentions. Institutions should also acknowledge that maintaining a stable international order occasionally requires changes in the status quo. The Concert of Europe enhanced stability by granting independence to Greece and Belgium. Designers of new institutions must establish principles for recognizing new states and reorganizing troubled regions. This will be difficult because borders today are more sacred than in the nineteenth century.

Recognition that actors try to manipulate rules, norms and principles should not cause leaders to shy away from international institutions. Even an actor who manipulates principles will be constrained. As long as actors find it necessary or profitable to act within institutions, their activity tends to reinforce international order. For example, when President Bush appealed to the U.N. in order to sanction military action against Iraq, it is possible that he was paying "lip service" to norms of the international community in order to justify actions in the interests of the U.S. However, President Bush set an important precedent. The next time that U.S. interests call for military intervention, the U.S. president will be constrained by domestic and international expectations. It is difficult to imagine that the U.S. Senate would have endorsed the war against Iraq if the U.N. Security Council had not passed a resolution authorizing the use of force. The Senate, the U.S. public, and prospective military coalition partners are likely to hold a future U.S. president to the same standard of U.N. consultation. So by acting within the framework of the U.N., President Bush may have reinforced the institution and the obligations it imposes on international behavior. Principles of consultation, joint action, and self-denial are subject to manipulation, but they tend to constrain even the manipulators and to promote international order in the process.

Notes

1. See, for example, Kenneth N. Waltz, *Man, the State, and War* (New York: Columbia University Press, 1959); Kenneth N. Waltz, *Theory of International Politics* (Reading, Mass.: Addison Wesley, 1979); and Joseph M. Grieco, *Cooperation Among Nations: Europe, America, and Non-Tariff Barriers to Trade* (Ithaca: Cornell University Press, 1990). For a critique of the argument that pursuit of relative gains obstructs international cooperation, see Duncan Snidal, "Relative Gains and the Pattern of International Cooperation," *American Political Science Review*, Vol. 85, No. 3 (September 1991), pp. 701–726.

2. The iterated Prisoners' Dilemma can be analyzed as a Stag Hunt, in which each player's first choice is mutual cooperation, while each player's last choice is to cooperate while others defect. See Robert Jervis, "Cooperation Under the Security Dilemma," *World Politics*, Vol. 30, No. 2 (January 1978), p. 171.

3. See Jervis, "Cooperation Under the Security Dilemma"; Robert Axelrod, *The Evolution of Cooperation* (New York: Basic Books, 1984); Kenneth A. Oye, ed., *Cooperation under Anarchy* (Princeton: Princeton University Press, 1986); and Robert Jervis, "Realism, Game Theory, and Cooperation," *World Politics*, Vol. 40, No. 3 (April 1988), pp. 317–349.

4. Jervis, "Realism, Game Theory, and Cooperation," p. 348. See also Robert Axelrod and Robert O. Keohane, "Achieving Cooperation under Anarchy: Strategies and Institutions," in Oye, ed., *Cooperation under Anarchy*, pp. 226–254.

5. On an international society see Hedley Bull, *The Anarchical Society* (New York: Columbia University Press, 1977); Herbert Butterfield and Martin Wight, eds., *Diplomatic Investigations* (Cambridge, Mass.: Harvard University Press, 1966); Hedley Bull and Adam Watson, eds., *The Expansion of International Society* (New York: Oxford University Press, 1984); Hedley Bull, Benedict Kingsbury, and Adam Roberts, eds., *Hugo Grotius and International Relations* (Oxford: Clarendon Press, 1990); Stanley Hoffman, "Hedley Bull and His Contribution to International Relations," *International Affairs*, Vol. 62 (Spring 1986), pp. 179–195; Hayward R. Alker, Jr., "The Presumption of Anarchy in World Politics," unpublished manuscript; J.W. Burton, *Systems, States, Diplomacy and Rules* (Cambridge: Cambridge University Press, 1968); and Evan Luard, *Types of International Society* (New York: The Free Press, 1976). Works emphasizing institutions include Friedrich Kratochwil and John Gerard Ruggie, "International Organization: A State of the Art on an Art of the State," *International Organization*, Vol. 40, No. 4 (Autumn 1986), pp. 753–775;

Friedrich V. Kratochwil, *Rules, Norms, and Decisions* (Cambridge: Cambridge University Press, 1989); Robert O. Keohane, "International Institutions: Two Approaches," *International Studies Quarterly*, Vol. 32, No. 4 (December 1988), pp. 379–396; Stephen D. Krasner, ed., *International Regimes* (Ithaca: Cornell University Press, 1983); Stephan Haggard and Beth A. Simmons, "Theories of International Regimes," *International Organization*, Vol. 41, No. 3 (Summer 1987), pp. 491–517; Oran R. Young, "International Regimes: Toward a New Theory of Institutions," *World Politics*, Vol. 39, No. 1 (October 1986), pp. 104–122; David Strang, "Anomaly and Commonplace in European Political Expansion: Realist and Institutional Accounts," *International Organization*, Vol. 45, No. 2 (Spring 1991), pp. 143–162; Joseph S. Nye, Jr., "Neorealism and Neoliberalism," *World Politics*, Vol. 40, No. 2 (January 1988), pp. 235–251; and Oran R. Young, *International Cooperation: Building Regimes for Natural Resources and the Environment* (Ithaca: Cornell University Press, 1989).

6. See Jon Elster, "Social Norms and Economic Theory," *Journal of Economic Perspectives*, Vol. 3, No. 4 (Fall 1989), pp. 99–117; Elster, *The Cement of Society* (Cambridge: Cambridge University Press, 1989), Chapter 3; Elster, *Nuts and Bolts for the Social Sciences* (Cambridge: Cambridge University Press, 1989), Chapter 12; and Diego Gambetta, *Were They Pushed or Did They Jump?* (Cambridge: Cambridge University Press, 1987), pp. 7–22.

7. Alexander Wendt argues that "the capacities and even existence of human agents are in some way *necessarily* related to a social structural context—that they are *inseparable* from human sociality." Alexander Wendt, "The Agent-Structure Problem in International Relations Theory," *International Organization*, Vol. 41, No. 3 (Summer 1987), p. 355.

8. Bull, The Anarchical Society, p. 13.

9. Keohane, "International Institutions," p. 384. See also Young, "International Regimes," p. 107.

10. On the processes through which international institutions may be formed see Oran R. Young, "Regime Dynamics: The Rise and Fall of International Regimes," in Krasner, ed., *International Regimes*, pp. 93–113; and Young, "International Regimes," pp. 108–111.

11. Keohane, "International Institutions," p. 382, emphasis added.

12. Keohane, "International Institutions," p. 390. See also Kratochwil and Ruggie, "A State of the Art"; Andrew Schotter, *The Economic Theory of Social Institutions* (Cambridge: Cambridge University Press, 1981); and Michael Hechter, "The Emergence of Cooperative Social Institutions," in Michael Hechter, Karl-Dieter Opp, and Richard Wippler, eds., *Social Institutions: Their Emergence, Maintenance and Effects* (New York: Aldine de Gruyter, 1990), pp. 13–33.

13. For example, see Anthony Giddens, *The Constitution of Society* (Berkeley: University of California Press, 1984), p. 171.

14. Arthur A. Stein, "Coordination and Collaboration: Regimes in an Anarchic World," in Krasner, ed., *International Regimes*, p. 139. See also Robert O. Keohane, *After Hegemony: Cooperation and Discord in the World Political Economy* (Princeton: Princeton University Press, 1984), pp. 110–132.

15. Bull, The Anarchical Society, pp. 53–76.

16. Charles A. Kupchan and Clifford A. Kupchan observe that reputations for resolve are less important in a system of collective security: "Collective security, by reducing the uncertainties associated with balancing under anarchy, dampens the need to bolster resolve to make deterrence more credible." Charles A. Kupchan and Clifford A. Kupchan, "Concerts, Collective Security, and the Future of Europe," *International Security*, Vol. 16, No. 1 (Summer 1991), p. 135. It is also important to reduce uncertainties regarding others' cooperative intentions. Widespread expectations that all actors intend to cooperate make them more willing to do so. So reputations for cooperation are useful, and efforts to bolster these reputations would support a pattern of cooperation.

17. See Robert K. Merton, "The Unanticipated Consequences of Purposive Social Action," *American Sociological Review*, Vol. 1 (December 1936), p. 903.

18. See David Dessler, "What's at Stake in the Agent-Structure Debate?" *International Organization*, Vol. 43, No. 3 (Summer 1989), pp. 441–473; Giddens, *The Constitution of Society*, p. 171 and passim; and Roy Bhaskar, *The Possibility of Naturalism* (Atlantic Highlands, N.J.: Humanities Press, 1979), pp. 42–43.

19. Giddens, The Constitution of Society, p. 27.

20. Elster, *The Cement of Society*, pp. 97–151; and Elster, "Social Norms and Economic Theory," pp. 103–104.

21. Bull, The Anarchical Society, p. 45.

22. For general analysis of the Concert of Europe see René Albrecht-Carrié, *The Concert of Europe* (New York: Walker and Company, 1968); Paul Schroeder, "The 19th-Century International System: Changes in the Structure," *World Politics*, Vol. 39, No. 1 (October 1986), pp. 1–26; Paul Schroeder, "The Nineteenth Century System: Balance of Power or Political Equilibrium?" *Review of International Studies*, Vol. 15, No. 2 (April 1989), pp. 135–153; Robert Jervis, "From Balance to Concert: A Study of International Security Cooperation," in Oye, ed., *Cooperation under Anarchy*, pp. 58–79; Robert Jervis, "Security Regimes," in Krasner, ed., *International Regimes*, pp. 173–194; Richard Elrod, "The Concert of Europe: A Fresh Look at an International System," *World Politics*, Vol. 28, No. 2 (January 1976), pp. 159–174; and Paul Gordon Lauren, "Crisis Prevention in Nineteenth-Century Diplomacy, in Alexander George, ed., *Managing U.S.-Soviet Rivalry: Problems of Crisis Prevention* (Boulder: Westview Press, 1983), pp. 31–64.

23. See Jervis, "From Balance to Concert," pp. 71–73; and F.H. Hinsley, *Power and the Pursuit of Peace: Theory and Practice in the History of Relations Between States* (Cambridge: Cambridge University Press, 1963), p. 225.

24. See Paul Schroeder, "Alliances, 1815–1945: Weapons of Power and Tools of Management," in Klaus Knorr, ed., *Historical Dimensions of National Security Problems* (Lawrence: University Press of Kansas, 1976), pp. 227–262.

25. Hinsley, Power and the Pursuit of Peace, p. 197.

26. On the Congress of Vienna see Charles K. Webster, *The Congress of*

Vienna, 1814–1814 (London: H.M Stationery Office, 1919; reprint, London: G. Bell & Sons, 1945) (page references are to reprint edition); Charles K. Webster, *The Foreign Policy of Castlereagh, 1815–1822: Britain and the European Alliance* (London: G. Bell & Sons, 1925); Harold Nicolson, *The Congress of Vienna: A Study in Allied Unity, 1812–1822* (New York: Harcourt, Brace and Company, 1946); Walter Alison Phillips, *The Confederation of Europe: A Study of the European Alliance, 1813–1823 as an Experiment in the International Organization of Peace* 2d ed. (New York: Howard Fertig, 1966); Enno E. Kraehe, *Metternich's German Policy*, Vol. 2, *The Congress of Vienna, 1814–1815* (Princeton: Princeton University Press, 1983; Henry A. Kissinger, *A World Restored: Metternich, Castlereagh and the Problems of Peace, 1812–1822* (Boston: Houghton Mifflin, 1957; reprint, New York: Grosset and Dunlap, 1964) (page references are to reprint edition); and Edward Vose Gulick, *Europe's Classical Balance of Power: A Case History of the Theory and Practice of the One of the Great Concepts of European Statecraft* (Ithaca: Cornell University Press, 1955; reprint, New York: W.W. Norton & Company, 1967), pp. 132–291 (page references are to reprint edition).

27. See Webster, *The Congress of Vienna*, pp. 54–77.

28. Albrecht-Carrié, *The Concert of Europe*, p. 30.

29. Quoted in Webster, *The Congress of Vienna*, p. 99.

30. Schroeder, "The Nineteenth Century System: Balance of Power or Political Equilibrium," p. 143.

31. Schroeder, "The Nineteenth Century System: Balance of Power or Political Equilibrium," p. 144.

32. See Webster, *The Congress of Vienna*, pp. 98–122.

33. Quoted in Webster, *The Congress of Vienna*, p. 109.

34. See Webster, *The Congress of Vienna*, pp. 74–75, 113–115; Gulick, *Europe's Balance of Power*, pp. 237–243; and Nicolson, *The Congress of Vienna*, pp. 176–179.

35. See Webster, *The Congress of Vienna*, pp. 79–83.

36. Quoted in Webster, *The Congress of Vienna*, p. 83.

37. See Webster, *The Congress of Vienna*, pp. 128–134; and Paul Schroeder, *The Transformation of European Politics, 1787–1848* (forthcoming), Chapter 12.

38. Webster, The Congress of Vienna, p. 134.

39. Schroeder, "The 19th-Century International System," p. 17.

40. Quoted in Webster, *The Congress of Vienna*, p. 139.

41. Quoted in Gulick, Europe's Classical Balance of Power, p. 274.

42. Treaty of Alliance and Friendship between Great Britain, Austria, Prussia, and Russia. Signed at Paris, November 20, 1815. Edward Hertslet, *The Map of Europe by Treaty* (London: Butterworths, 1875), Vol. I, p. 375.

43. Quoted in W. Alison Phillips, "Great Britain and the Continental Alliance, 1816–1822," in A.W. Ward and G.P. Gooch, eds., *The Cambridge History of British Foreign Policy, 1783–1919* (Cambridge: University Press, 1923), Vol. II, p. 7.

44. Quoted in Phillips, "Great Britain and the Continental Alliance," p. 8.

45. Phillips, "Great Britain and the Continental Alliance," p. 11.

46. Memorandum on the Treaties of 1814 and 1815 Submitted by the British Plenipotentiaries at the Conference of Aix-la-Chapelle, October 1818. Webster, *The Congress of Vienna*, pp. 170–171.

47. Note addressed by the Plenipotentiaries of Great Britain, Austria, Prussia, and Russia to the Duke of Richelieu. Aix-la-Chapelle, November 4, 1818. Hertslet, *The Map of Europe by Treaty*, Vol. I, p. 566.

48. Note addressed by the Duke of Richelieu to the Plenipotentiaries of Austria, Great Britain, Prussia, and Russia, in reply to their Note of the 4th November, 1818. Aix-la-Chapelle, November 12, 1818. Hertslet, *The Map of Europe by Treaty*, Vol. I, pp. 567–568.

49. Protocol of Conference, between the Plenipotentiaries of Austria, France, Great Britain, Prussia, and Russia. Signed at Aix-la-Chapelle, November 15, 1818. Hertslet, *The Map of Europe by Treaty*, Vol. I, pp. 571–572.

50. Declaration of the Five Cabinets (Great Britain, Austria, France, Prussia, and Russia). Signed at Aix-la-Chapelle, November 15, 1818. Hertslet, *The Map of Europe by Treaty*, Vol. I, pp. 573–574.

51. See Paul W. Schroeder, *Metternich's Diplomacy at its Zenith, 1820–1823* (Austin: University of Texas Press, 1962); Phillips, "Great Britain and the Continental Alliance"; H.W.V. Temperley, "The Foreign Policy of Canning, 1820–1827," in Ward and Gooch, eds., *The Cambridge History of British Foreign Policy*, Vol. II, pp. 51–118; Kissinger, *A World Restored*; Webster, *The Foreign Policy of Castlereagh*; and Albrecht-Carrié, *The Concert of Europe*, pp. 47–59.

52. The Protocol is quoted in Phillips, "Great Britain and the Continental Alliance," pp. 37–38.

53. Circular of the Austrian, Prussian, and Russian Sovereigns to their respective Missions at Foreign Courts, respecting the Affairs of Spain, Portugal, and Naples. Troppau, December 8, 1820. Hertslet, *The Map of Europe by Treaty*, Vol. I, pp. 660–661.

54. Circular Despatch to British Missions at Foreign Courts. London, January 19, 1821. Hertslet, *The Map of Europe by Treaty*, Vol. I, pp. 665–666.

55. Kissinger, *A World Restored*, pp. 260–269.

56. Quoted in Kissinger, *A World Restored*, p. 295. See also Phillips, "Great Britain and the Continental Alliance," pp. 42–44; and Schroeder, "Alliances, 1815–1945," p. 232.

57. Quoted in Kissinger, *A World Restored*, p. 308. See also Schroeder, *The Transformation of European Politics*, Chapter 13.

58. Quoted in Kissinger, *A World Restored*, p. 286.

59. See Kissinger, *A World Restored*, p. 313.

60. See Hinsley, Power and the Pursuit of Peace, pp. 212–213.

61. See, for example, Kissinger, *A World Restored*, p. 310; Jervis, "Security Regimes," p. 184; Gulick, *Europe's Classical Balance of Power*, p. 295; and Nicolson, *The Congress of Vienna*, pp. 257–274.

62. See Jervis, "From Balance to Concert," p. 61.

63. In Nicolson's view, the Aix-la-Chapelle conference "disclosed the

ideological rift between the democratic and the autocratic Powers and marked, to all acute observers, the beginning of the end." Nicolson, *The Congress of Vienna*, p. 261.

64. Quoted in Schroeder, Metternich's Diplomacy at its Zenith, p. 236

65. On Canning's program to break up the Congress system at Verona, split the Holy Alliance, and maintain British influence on the Continent, see Temperley, "The Foreign Policy of Canning," pp. 113–118.

66. Temperley, "The Foreign Policy of Canning," pp. 83–90; Schroeder, *The Transformation of European Politics*, Chapter 14; and Albrecht-Carrié, *The Concert of Europe*, pp. 99–102.

67. See Temperley, "The Foreign Policy of Canning," pp. 90–94; and Schroeder, *The Transformation of European Politics*, Chapter 14.

68. Protocol of Conference between the British and Russian Plenipotentiaries, relative to the Mediation of Great Britain between the Ottoman Porte and the Greeks. Signed at St. Petersburg, April 4, 1826. Hertslet, *The Map of Europe by Treaty*, Vol. I, p. 743.

69. See Albrecht-Carrié, *The Concert of Europe*, pp. 106–107.

70. Treaty between Great Britain, France, and Russia, for the Pacification of Greece. Signed at London, July 6, 1827. Hertslet, *The Map of Europe by Treaty*, Vol. I, pp. 769–774. Article V of the treaty committed the powers again to self-denial: "The Contracting Powers will not seek, in these arrangements, any augmentation of territory, any exclusive influence, or any commercial advantage for their subjects, which those of every other Nation may not equally obtain" (pp. 771–772).

71. Quoted in Albrecht-Carrié, *The Concert of Europe*, p. 112.

72. See Schroeder, "Alliances, 1815–1945," p. 233.

73. Temperley, "The Foreign Policy of Canning," pp. 99–101; and Albrecht-Carrié, *The Concert of Europe*, pp. 113–114.

74. Protocol (No. 1) of the Conference held at the Foreign Office. London, February 3, 1830. Albrecht-Carrié, *The Concert of Europe*, pp. 115–119.

75. Convention between Great Britain, France, and Russia, on the one part, and Bavaria on the other, relative to the Sovereignty of Greece. Signed at London, May 7, 1832. Hertslet, *The Map of Europe by Treaty*, Vol. II, pp. 893–899.

76. Quoted in Albrecht-Carrié, *The Concert of Europe*, p. 122.

77. G.W.T. Omond, "Belgium, 1830–1839," in Ward and Gooch, eds., *The Cambridge History of British Foreign Policy*, Vol II, pp. 119–127; Schroeder, *The Transformation of European Politics*, Chapter 15; and Albrecht-Carrié, *The Concert of Europe*, pp. 62–63.

78. Protocol (No. 7) of a Conference held at the Foreign Office. London, December 20, 1830. Albrecht-Carrié, *The Concert of Europe*, pp. 65–67.

79. Protocol (No. 11) of a Conference held at the Foreign Office. London, January 20, 1831. Albrecht-Carrié, *The Concert of Europe*, pp. 67–70.

80. Protocol (No. 14) of a Conference held at the Foreign Office. London, February 1, 1831. Albrecht-Carrié, *The Concert of Europe*, pp. 80–81; Omond, "Belgium," pp. 132–138.

81. Protocol (No. 19) of a Conference held at the Foreign Office. London, February 19, 1831. Albrecht-Carrié, *The Concert of Europe*, pp. 71–76.

82. Omond, "Belgium," pp. 143–145.

83. Protocol (No. 31) of a Conference held at the Foreign Office. London, August 6, 1831. Albrecht-Carrié, *The Concert of Europe*, pp. 77–79.

84. Omond, "Belgium," pp. 148–159. The three treaties of April 19, 1839 appear in Hertslet, *The Map of Europe by Treaty*, Vol. II, pp. 979–998.

85. Schroeder, *The Transformation of European Politics*, Chapter 16; R.B. Mowat, "The Near East and France, 1829–1847," in Ward and Gooch, eds., *The Cambridge History of British Foreign Policy*, Vol. II, pp. 161–176; and Sir Charles Webster, *The Foreign Policy of Palmerston, 1830–1841: Britain, the Liberal Movement, and the Eastern Question* (London: G. Bell & Sons, 1951), Vol. II, pp. 621–664.

86. Convention between Great Britain, Austria, Prussia, and Russia, and Turkey, for the Pacification of the Levant. Signed at London, July 15, 1840. Hertslet, *The Map of Europe by Treaty*, Vol. II, pp. 1008–1015.

87. Protocol (3) of Conference between Great Britain, Austria, Prussia, Russia, and Turkey, respecting Pacification of the Levant. London, September 17, 1840. Hertslet, *The Map of Europe by Treaty*, Vol. II, p. 1023.

88. Webster, *The Foreign Policy of Palmerston*, Vol. II, pp. 672–708.

89. Quoted in Albrecht-Carrié, *The Concert of Europe*, p. 142.

90. Quoted in Albrecht-Carrié, *The Concert of Europe*, p. 143.

91. Schroeder, "The Nineteenth Century System," p. 145.

92. See Schroeder, "Alliances, 1815–1945," p. 235.

93. Protocol of a Conference held at the Foreign Office, July 10, 1841. Albrecht-Carrié, *The Concert of Europe*, pp. 148–149.

94. Webster, The Foreign Policy of Palmerston, Vol. II, p. 769.

95. Convention between Great Britain, Austria, France, Prussia, Russia, and Turkey, respecting the Straits of the Dardanelles and of the Bosphorus. Signed at London, July 13, 1841. Hertslet, *The Map of Europe by Treaty*, Vol. II, p. 1024.

96. Memorandum by Count Nesselrode, delivered to Her Majesty's Government, and founded on communications received from the Emperor of Russia subsequent to His Imperial Majesty's visit to England in June 1844. Albrecht-Carrié, *The Concert of Europe*, p. 156.

97. Albrecht-Carrié, *The Concert of Europe*, pp. 152–153.

98. See Kupchan and Kupchan, "Concerts," p. 142n.

99. See the final comments in Schroeder's contribution to this volume.

100. See Hinsley, *Power and the Pursuit of Peace*, pp. 226–231; Schroeder, "The 19th-Century International System," pp. 5–6; and Albrecht-Carrié, *The Concert of Europe*, pp. 159–191.

101. See the essays in this volume by Kathleen McNamara, Jeffry Frieden, and Richard Betts.

102. See John J. Mearsheimer, "Back to the Future: Instability in Europe After the Cold War," *International Security*, Vol. 15, No. 1 (Summer 1990), pp. 5–56.

5

The Domestic Politics of Crisis Bargaining and the Origins of the Crimean War

Susan Peterson

The Crimean War has been called "the only perfectly useless modern war that has been waged" and "the outcome of a series of misjudgments, misunderstandings and blunders, of stupidity, pride and obstinacy rather than of ill will."[1] Russian and British decisionmakers may well have been stupid, proud, and obstinate in the early 1850s, but Jervis's introductory essay provides a much simpler and more systematic explanation of the escalation of a minor conflict over religious rights to a war involving all the major European powers. In addition to explaining the origins of the Crimean War, systems theory also provides insights for policymakers concerned with avoiding conflict escalation.

The period from 1852 to 1854 witnessed the death rattle of the Concert of Europe and the final retreat into the linear thinking that had characterized European diplomacy before 1815. From 1848 to 1854, the European powers unlearned many of the lessons painstakingly acquired in the late eighteenth and early nineteenth centuries and reverted to direct, nonsystemic approaches to security. This chapter chronicles a blatant example of this linear thinking—Russian and British diplomacy on the eve of the Crimean War.

In an interconnected system, actions often have indirect and complicated effects, outcomes may not correspond with the intentions of any of the actors, and linear thinking may lead to incorrect predictions about the consequences of one's actions. The conventional wisdom on crisis bargaining—that states should respond immediately and forcefully—is often inadequate for explaining the evolution of international crises and misleading as a guide for policymakers in part because it fails to account for such indirect effects. Specifically, the international environment interacts with existing domestic conditions to shape outcomes of international crises. External bargaining moves influence the domestic distribution of power in the opposing state and thereby determine what policy response becomes dominant.

Russian bargaining strategy on the eve of the Crimean War closely followed the policy prescriptions of deterrence theory and attempted to resolve the conflict through a demonstration of firmness. Such a strategy was a throwback to the linear thinking of 1792 described by Paul Schroeder in his contribution to this volume. Had either Russia or Britain initially tried to define the minimal terms of peace, as Schroeder argues they did in 1813, the crisis might have been peacefully resolved. Instead of securing the direct response Russia sought, that country's coercive tactics interacted with the domestic British subsystem to produce war.

Russian strategy inadvertently led to escalation by arousing suspicions of Russian intentions and weakening a friendly British government which advocated moderation. The initially coercive strategy had the unintended consequence of strengthening hard-line elements within the British government, precisely those parties which had a stake in provoking and prolonging the conflict. By the time Russia offered significant concessions, public opinion was so inflamed and the position of the main hard-liner in the British government, Lord Palmerston, was so advanced that the Aberdeen government could no longer take yes for an answer.

Deterrence theory predicts that an initially coercive strategy followed by limited concessions will always lead an opponent to form perceptions of a resolved adversary. Such linear thinking neglects the domestic determinants of foreign policy during a crisis and the interaction between the international and domestic environments. The main rival approach, cooperation (or spiral) theory, is also characterized by linear thinking, however, when it suggests that an initially conciliatory strategy followed only if necessary by coercion will lead to benign perceptions of the adversary and a peaceful resolution of the conflict. Both approaches ignore the unintended consequences of employing their policy prescriptions. As the Crimean case suggests, the nexus between the international and domestic arenas means that the success or failure of a particular bargaining strategy depends upon the configuration of influence in the adversary state. The linear nature of deterrence and cooperation theory prescriptions can have dangerous, even catastrophic, results. The recognition of indirect effects and of the importance of the domestic political context can improve the fit between theory and practice by determining the conditions under which the strategy prescribed by each model of international conflict is appropriate and effective.

This chapter is divided into two sections. The first discusses the literature on crisis bargaining and domestic politics. The second section presents the chronological evolution of the Crimean War crisis—the Russian bargaining strategy of initial coercion followed by concessions and its impact on the perceptions and domestic political situations of the four key British decisionmakers.[2]

Deterrence, Cooperation, and the Domestic Politics of Crisis Bargaining

The standard wisdom on bargaining in international crises, which is derived from deterrence theory, holds that states should start out tough and shift to concessions only in the later phase of the conflict after cooperation is forthcoming from the adversary. Recently, cooperation theorists have criticized deterrence theory for ignoring the unintended consequences of threats and have prescribed the use of an initially conciliatory bargaining strategy. However, these theorists also have frequently neglected the dangers of conciliation. And because both deterrence and cooperation theorists ignore the interaction between the domestic and international environments during a crisis, they argue that their policy prescriptions for the appropriate sequencing of coercive and conciliatory bargaining tactics are universally valid.

The conventional wisdom on crisis bargaining has its origins in deterrence theory's emphasis on coercion and the importance of effectively communicating the willingness to stand firm.[3] Such analyses stress the dangers of allowing one's opponent to believe that one is weak in capability or resolve. The proper response when faced with an international crisis, according to this school of thought, is to employ a bargaining strategy which is first firm and then conciliatory in order to clarify the comparative resolve of both parties to the conflict. If accommodative tactics are attempted too soon, the result will be war or diplomatic defeat since the recipient of the accommodative offers will expect further concessions.

The prescription that a state should start high—that any cooperative attempt must be preceded by coercive moves to be effective—rests on the assumptions that decisionmakers learn from initial concessions that the other state lacks resolve and that they incorporate this inference into their own decisions about what policy to adopt. This argument is supported by social psychological literature concerning "levels of aspiration." These goals that an individual seeks to achieve are revised during the bargaining process, upward following success and downward following failure.[4]

Deterrence theory has been criticized for failing to consider the indirect effects of its policy prescriptions. Recent literature which focuses on the difficulties of achieving "cooperation under anarchy" argues that threats intended to deter and convey resolve often produce unintended escalation.[5] According to this school, states exist in a security dilemma in which the actions of one state to gain security have the effect of making other states less secure.[6] This approach emphasizes the use of conciliation, the dangers of escalation, and the need to consider the security requirements of other states. Cooperation theorists advocate a bargaining strategy which starts out "nice" by offering concessions and then reciprocates coercion as well as accommodation. A state facing a crisis should respond initially with an accommodative signal to indicate its willingness to cooperate to resolve the conflict and only shift to coercive tactics later if the opponent fails to compromise. If coercive tactics are attempted too soon, the result will be escalation of the crisis and possibly war.

The prescriptions of both cooperation theory and deterrence theory rest on the assumption that information processing mediates between bargaining behavior and decision-making. Unlike deterrence theory, however, cooperation theory assumes that policymakers infer from initial coercion that the other is overly hostile. The first approach predicts that concessions will raise the level of aspiration of the other party, whereas the second school predicts that concessions will promote trust and reciprocity. Since the state undertaking early concessions risks exploitation, it credibly demonstrates that it can be trusted in the future. A bargaining strategy which is first conciliatory and then firm conveys an image of a reasonable but strong opponent who, if s/he resorts to coercive tactics, does so only grudgingly and as a last resort.[7]

Deterrence theory emphasizes the unintended consequences of conciliation, and cooperation theory focuses on the dangers of employing coercive tactics. Both approaches claim universal applicability for their policy prescriptions and predict policy failure if the other's prescriptions are implemented. Both are based on models of information processing. Both assume that policymakers learn from the opponent's bargaining strategy during a conflict and incorporate these lessons into their own decisions about what policy to adopt. Because they assume that states learn and behave as individuals do, both deterrence and cooperation theory ignore the interaction between the international environment and the existing domestic situation in each state.

Recent work on bargaining and conflict resolution emphasizes the interaction of international and domestic factors. The international environment often influences the domestic political structure of and coalition building within states.[8] Recent analyses of "two-level games" and "nested games"[9] also suggest that the domestic political context, in turn, influences actors' payoffs, which influence their choice of policy response. Richard Ned Lebow similarly argues that weakness in a state's political system or leadership limits the ability of decisionmakers to accurately perceive and interpret the influence attempts of other states.[10]

Students of bureaucratic politics recognize the reciprocal effects of domestic and international politics when they prescribe bargaining strategies which "strengthen the soft-liners" and "avoid strengthening the hard-liners" in the adversary's government.[11] Jack Snyder's examination of the impact of international leverage on domestic change in the Soviet Union suggests a way of implementing this policy prescription. Snyder finds that a highly threatening international environment will turn a weak liberal state toward militarism and imperialism, whereas a more favorable international environment characterized by inducements will help institutionalize the liberal regime. Similarly, threats will discredit a weak imperialist opponent, while the use of inducements will allow such a regime to survive.[12]

Students of international conflict generally agree that exclusively coercive or conciliatory strategies are ineffective in resolving disputes. This has been recognized by both deterrence and cooperation theorists who argue that the two forms of influence tactics should be combined in different sequences. Together with Snyder's findings, this suggests that the different sequences of coercive and accommodative tactics advocated by the two schools are appropriate under different conditions, depending upon the configuration of influence in the recipient state.

This argument is supported by a recent analysis of U.S.-Soviet disarmament negotiations in the 1950s. Matthew Evangelista has found that these negotiations did not fail because of misperception of the other side's intentions, as cooperation theory suggests. The United States recognized Soviet concessions and refused to compromise for domestic political reasons.[13]

Building on these works, I argue that domestic political factors interact with the international environment to produce the crisis outcome. A state's external bargaining strategy affects the balance of power within the opponent's political system. It does so by supporting or undermining the arguments of hard- or soft-line factions and by shaping the incentive structures of domestic actors, thereby determining which policy response becomes dominant. Specifically, initially coercive strategies undermine the faction in power whose policy is being pursued and support the opposition, whereas an initially conciliatory strategy strengthens the influence of the ruling coalition, whether hard- or soft-line. External bargaining strategies affect the domestic distribution of power and the policy response by shaping actors' incentive structures. Whether the crisis is resolved through compromise, war, defeat, or victory depends upon the interaction of the two sides' bargaining strategies, but the process by which each strategy influences the other state is domestic and political, not perceptual.

In the case of the Crimean conflict, a focus on the domestic balance of power within the adversary states leads to several hypotheses that contradict those offered by deterrence and cooperation theory. Deterrence theory predicts that the initially coercive Russian strategy should have led the British to lower their expectations and to welcome Russian concessions, leading to a peaceful resolution of the conflict. Cooperation theory suggests that the Russian strategy should have led British decisionmakers to form hostile perceptions of an aggressive opponent and to resist subsequent concessions, leading to escalation. While it also predicts escalation, the domestic politics approach presented here leads to several opposing hypotheses about the process by which the crisis escalated to war. First, this approach predicts that the Russian strategy of initial coercion should have undermined the moderate British government and strengthened its hard-line opposition. Subsequent Russian concessions should have failed, but not because they were misperceived, as suggested by cooperation theory. Rather, a domestic politics approach predicts that Russian strategy would have shifted the domestic distribution of power in London against conciliation, resulting in a coercive British policy and escalation of the conflict.

In fact, this is precisely what happened in the Crimean case. The process by which the coercive Russian strategy contributed to the escalation of the crisis was more political than perceptual. The strategy largely reinforced the preexisting beliefs of British decisionmakers but significantly altered the balance of power among them. Public opinion strengthened the hand of the hard-liners in London, leading to a more coercive policy response and, ultimately, to war. In short, the abandonment of the systemic thinking described in the Schroeder and Daugherty chapters in this volume caused Russian decisionmakers to ignore the consequences on British domestic politics of a strategy intended to coerce the Turks into submission. Ultimately, the domestic situation in Britain also precluded the systemic thinking necessary to prevent escalation of the conflict.

The Crimean War Crisis

Diplomatic bargaining on the eve of the Crimean War exhibited a remarkable degree of feedback between the international and domestic bargaining environments. It is unfair to berate policymakers in London and St. Petersburg for stupidity and inaccurate to say that the primary cause of the war was misperception; rather, these decisionmakers engaged in linear thinking. Tsar Nicholas, in particular, failed to adequately gauge the effects of his policy on the already volatile domestic atmosphere in London.

Russian diplomacy during the diplomatic crisis preceding the outbreak of the Crimean War can be divided into two phases. The sequence of coercive and accommodative bargaining moves closely followed that prescribed by deterrence theory. In the initial stage of the conflict, Nicholas engaged in coercive diplomacy, mostly in the guise of a menacing mission to Constantinople headed by the former minister of the navy Count Menshikov, in an attempt to intimidate the Turks and impress the Europeans with Russian resolve on the issue of the Holy Places. Near the end of the Menshikov mission, the Russians shifted to concessions, and following the occupation by Russia of two Turkish principalities, Nicholas shifted to a highly conciliatory strategy, cooperating with European diplomatic efforts to resolve the crisis.

The British response to this strategy was that predicted by the literature on domestic politics. Early Russian coercive bargaining behavior shifted the balance of power within the British government against the soft-liners, Aberdeen and Clarendon, and reinforced the arguments of the hard-liners, Palmerston and Russell. British decisionmakers recognized Russian attempts to compromise in the second phase of the conflict, but the soft-liners within the government were so discredited at home that they could no longer afford to compromise.

Origins of the Conflict

The conflict over the Holy Places was an ongoing struggle between a small population of Catholic subjects of the Ottoman Empire, whose rights were guarded by France, and 13 million Greek Orthodox subjects. The rights of the Greek population, which comprised one-third of the population of the Ottoman Empire, had been protected historically by

Russia, whose tsar was the nominal head of the Church. Catholic rights in the Holy Places were codified in a Franco-Turkish treaty in 1740, and Greek Orthodox rights were contained in a 1774 treaty with Russia. Throughout the next 75 years there were periodic conflicts over religious rights in the Ottoman Empire, particularly over access to the churches of Jerusalem, Nazareth, and Bethlehem.

Although the issue of the Holy Places was a source of tension in Anglo-Russian relations, the atmosphere improved following the tsar's 1844 visit to London. In a series of notes known as the Nesselrode Memorandum, which were exchanged during this visit, Russia and Britain agreed to maintain the *status quo* in Turkey as long as possible and to open discussions if the fall of the Ottoman Empire appeared imminent.[14]

Beginning in May 1850 Napoleon made a series of demands on behalf of the Latin Church based upon the 1740 treaty. Following French strong-arm tactics, including the passage of a French warship through the Dardanelles in violation of the 1841 Straits Convention, the sultan relented. By December 1852, the Turks conceded everything Napoleon had demanded on behalf of the Catholic Church, including keys to the doors of the Church of Bethlehem.

Russian Strategy

The initial Russian response to the 1850 French challenge and subsequent Turkish concessions was coercive. As this section demonstrates, St. Petersburg undertook limited mobilization and dispatched a menacing diplomatic mission to Constantinople. The tsar simultaneously engaged in conversations with the British ambassador to St. Petersburg about the future of the Ottoman Empire. Nicholas's bleak outlook meant that these conversations took on a threatening tone. Only near the end of this first phase of the conflict did Russia begin to make limited concessions. This was followed, however, by the withdrawal of the Menshikov mission, the severing of diplomatic relations with the Turks, and the occupation of two Turkish principalities.

Nicholas "felt the necessity of speaking to these wretched Turks with firmness" and speed.[15] The immediate Russian response was the mobilization on December 30, 1852, of two army corps on the Turkish border and the preparation of forts and flotillas on the Black Sea. This act was accompanied by conversations with the British on the future of the Ottoman Empire. Against the advice of his foreign minister, Count Nesselrode, in January 1853 Nicholas engaged the British ambassador, George Seymour, in the first of a series of conversations. The tsar expressed his concern about the increasingly unstable situation in Turkey, saying "[W]e have on our hands a sick man—a very sick man; it will be I tell you frankly, a great misfortune if, one of these days, he should slip away from us, especially before all necessary arrangements were made."[16] Nicholas went on to say that although he had no intention of establishing himself at Constantinople, circumstances might force him into a temporary occupation. Although Nesselrode later toned down the comments, in the final talk on February 21 Nicholas told Seymour, "The Turkish Empire is a thing to be tolerated, not to be reconstructed; in such a cause I protest to you I will not allow a pistol to be fired."[17]

The most visible aspect of Russian policy in the early stage of the conflict was the tsar's decision to send Prince Alexander Menshikov on a diplomatic mission to Constantinople. Menshikov's instructions were designed to meet two major Russian goals: to obtain satisfactory arrangements on the Holy Places and to secure guarantees for the future.[18]

From the outset there was no mistaking the intent of the mission. On the day after Menshikov's arrival on a war vessel, another war ship arrived carrying Vice Admiral Kornilov, commander of the Black Sea fleet, as well as several other military officers. On March 2 Menshikov paid a visit to the Turkish grand vizier. Contrary to diplomatic custom, he was dressed in a frock coat and hat, not his uniform, and walked by the open door of the waiting foreign minister, who immediately resigned over the insult contained in this breach of diplomatic protocol.

Menshikov did not formally present Russia's demands until March 16. This note stated that any agreement could "no longer be confined to barren and unsatisfactory promises which may be broken at a future period."[19] On March 22 Menshikov delivered a second note to the new Turkish foreign minister, Rifaat Pasha, calling for action on the Holy Places. He demanded immediate negotiations and presented a Russian draft convention.

By late April Russia had reached an agreement with Turkey on the immediate issue of the Holy Places and a *firman*, or royal decree, was issued by the Turkish government on May 3. Menshikov replied that the Turkish proclamation met Russian demands regarding the Holy Places, thereby settling that issue, but that it provided no guarantee for the future. Russia still wanted a formal treaty guaranteeing that the Greeks would share any future rights secured by other Christians, and Menshikov presented a draft and an ultimatum requesting a reply within five days.[20]

On May 10 the Turks rejected the Russian ultimatum, claiming it violated their sovereignty. Menshikov did not sever relations, however, as he had originally been instructed. Instead, he made the first of several concessions. He wrote to Reschid Pasha, a sometimes member of the Turkish government who held no office at the time, asking him to act as an intermediary with the sultan. Menshikov repeated his demands, but this time he avoided the words "sened", "treaty", or "convention" and called only for "an act emanating from the sovereign will of the Sultan, a free but solemn engagement."[21] This was a substantial concession since the Turks in 1852 had broken such a commitment. The Turkish Council of Ministers voted to reject the offer, and on May 15 Reschid Pasha appealed to Menshikov for an extension of the ultimatum until May 17. Again, Menshikov conceded and extended the deadline, but the Grand Council again voted to reject the offer, as well as two subsequent ones. The Russian diplomat then broke off relations and left Constantinople on May 21.

Following Menshikov's departure, the tsar issued preliminary orders for the occupation of the semiautonomous Turkish principalities of Moldavia and Wallachia, threatening to occupy these territories until he received satisfaction. On May 31, Russia issued a final ultimatum to the Turks and, when the Turks rejected it, Russian troops crossed the border into Wallachia and Moldavia.

In the first phase of the crisis, St. Petersburg followed the sequence of coercive and accommodative bargaining tactics prescribed by deterrence theory. It responded to the initial French and Turkish challenge with mobilization and the dispatch of a coercive mission to Constantinople. The later stages of the Menshikov mission were characterized by Russian moderation and offers of limited concessions, although still backed by the threat to sever diplomatic relations. When the Turks refused to cooperate, this threat was carried out and the Russians invaded the Turkish principalities.

British Response

Deterrence theory argues that the initially coercive Russian strategy should have convinced British decisionmakers that St. Petersburg was resolved to stand firm on the Holy Places. Cooperation theory, in contrast, suggests that this strategy should have led British policymakers to view Russia as hostile and aggressive. Although cooperation theory is correct in its emphasis on the difficulties and dangers of resolving the conflict through the use of coercive tactics, the evolution of the first stage of the crisis is best explained by the domestic politics approach. The Russian coercive strategy gradually undermined the arguments of the soft-liners in London and began to shift the balance of power within the cabinet toward a more coercive response. The prime minister, Lord Aberdeen, retained his conciliatory outlook throughout this stage of the conflict, while Lord Palmerston, the home secretary, remained bellicose. John Russell, leader of the House of Commons and foreign secretary at the outset of the crisis, initially blamed France for the conflict, but he was quick to join Palmerston in advocating resistance. Lord Clarendon, foreign secretary throughout the rest of the conflict, initially agreed with Aberdeen but shifted his view in response to the Menshikov mission. This change clearly was more a response to domestic pressure than to Russian policy, however. Increasing domestic outcry undermined the arguments of soft-liners in the Aberdeen government and caused Clarendon to begin changing his policy stance in the later phase of the Menshikov mission. In this section a discussion of the domestic situation in London in 1853 precedes a chronicle of the views of the four major British decisionmakers in the first stage of the crisis.

The Aberdeen cabinet was a coalition government formed in December 1852 after the sudden fall of the Derby government. Aberdeen was a Peelite, a free trade conservative, or Tory, but Palmerston, Russell, and Clarendon were Whigs, or aristocratic Liberals. In addition to suffering differences within the core of the Liberal-Conservative cabinet, the government enjoyed little parliamentary support. Although the Peelites numbered only 30 of the 662 members in the House of Commons, they held a disproportionate number of cabinet offices.[22]

Aberdeen's own position in the cabinet was weak. In addition to the problems he faced as the leader of a coalition government, he was not a popular politician, was a poor public speaker, and could not effectively use a threat of resignation since Russell was waiting in the wings to fill his office. When Aberdeen formed his ministry in 1852, it was generally understood that Russell would succeed him as prime minister after a brief period.[23]

Not one of the major decisionmakers in Britain was alarmed by the outbreak of the crisis or by early Russian responses to it. On January 7, 1853, when Seymour, the British ambassador to St. Petersburg, communicated to London reports of the Russian mobilization, he explicitly connected it to a French threat to send an expedition to Syria and attributed no hostile intentions to the Russians. The British ambassador in Paris also shared the belief that the outbreak of the crisis "was the fault of France."[24] Lord Russell argued that Britain was not interested in the merits of the dispute over the Holy Places but that since France had been in the wrong in initiating the conflict, it should make the first concessions.[25] Clarendon blamed "the restless ambition and energy of France,"[26] while Aberdeen did not hesitate to blame the Turks. Early in 1853 he told Ernest Brunnow, the Russian ambassador in London, "I hate the Turks for I regard their government as the most repressive in the world. One of the most difficult duties of my political life has been to lend my support to the maintenance of the Ottoman Empire."[27] Even the hard-line Palmerston, who harbored a long-term suspicion of Russia, did not immediately question Russian intentions or British restraint. "The Emperor of Russia is ambitious and grasping," he stated on April 11 during the initial phase of the Menshikov mission, "but he is a gentleman and I should be slow to disbelieve his positive denial of such things as those in question."[28] Both hard- and soft-line British policymakers recognized legitimate Russian interests in the region and French and Turkish encroachments against them.

The early Seymour conversations also did not alarm the British despite Nicholas's repeated suggestions for the partition of the Ottoman Empire. Not only did the conversations not distress the cabinet members but Harold Temperley goes as far as to suggest that they produced good feelings between Britain and Russia.[29] Seymour's own reactions to the tsar's comments nicely summarize the early British sentiments. On January 12 he reported that

> although the Emperor walks about in a helmet, sleeps on a camp-bed, and occasionally talks gunpowder, he is not more keen on war than his neighbours. He occasionally takes a precipitate step; but as reflection arrives, reason and Count Nesselrode make themselves heard. He is not sorry to be able to recede if he can do so without a loss of dignity. He cannot, however, give up his pretensions as to the Holy Places; his case is too clear, and the question is one which is very interesting to the feelings of the Church of which he is in some measure the head.[30]

There was little response in London to the Seymour conversations, and what there was seemed positive or indifferent. On February 9 Russell acknowledged "the moderation, frankness, and the friendly disposition of His Imperial Majesty," Tsar Nicholas.[31]

The arrival of the Menshikov mission in Constantinople on February 28, 1853, had little effect except on Russell, who questioned Russian intentions and situated himself squarely in the hard-line camp. Clarendon remained unperturbed by Menshikov's arrival and the resignation of Fuad Effendi, the Turkish foreign minister, since "on more than one occasion [the British Government has] received the personal assurances of the Emperor of Russia that he planned to uphold the Turkish Empire."[32] Aberdeen was again quick to condemn the Turks.

These barbarians hate us all, and would be delighted to take their chance of some advantage, by embroiling us with the other powers of Christendom. It may be necessary to give them moral support, and to endeavor to prolong their existence; but we ought to regard as the greatest misfortune any engagement which compelled us to take up arms for the Turks.[33]

The prime minister's policy preference was clear: "Whether right or wrong, we advise the Turks to yield."[34]

Following Menshikov's presentation of his demands on March 16, Turkey appealed to Britain and France for assistance. The French responded on March 19 by sending a fleet to Salimas in Greece, but the British refused to join this action. At the meeting at which this decision was made, Russell, Palmerston, and, to a lesser degree, Sir James Graham, secretary of the admiralty, favored immediate action, but the moderate Aberdeen and Clarendon coalition was able to convince them not to order naval action.[35]

Russell's stance at this meeting represented at least a partial shift in response to Russian coercive diplomacy. By March 20, in a letter to Clarendon, Russell stated, "The Emperor of Russia is clearly bent on accomplishing the destruction of Turkey, *and he must be resisted....* "The vast preparations at Sevastopol show a foregone purpose, and that purpose is, I fear, to extinguish the Turkish Empire."[36] To the extent that these statements marked a slight shift from his early condemnation of France for the outbreak of the crisis, Russell's stance supports the predictions of cooperation theory. Lord Russell inferred from early Russian coercion that the adversary was hostile and must be resisted.

Menshikov's coercive tactics following the May 5 settlement of the immediate conflict of interests increased British suspicions of Russian intentions. While reinforcing Palmerston and Russell's beliefs, Russian behavior in the later stage of the Menshikov mission also resulted in a shift in Clarendon's policy preference. However, this change appears to have been more a response to domestic public opinion, which was increasingly aroused by Russian policy, than a significant shift in the foreign secretary's expectations of Russian behavior.

In late May, following reports of Russian mobilization, the British cabinet authorized the British ambassador in Constantinople to call up the fleet at Malta to any place he considered it necessary to protect Turkey. This authorization was accompanied by a warning to encourage the Turks to undertake a conciliatory policy. Clarendon stated that rather than being a response to Russian action, this move was undertaken as "the least measure that will satisfy public opinion and save the government from shame hereafter."[37] Public opinion was increasingly turning against the soft-liners in the Aberdeen cabinet. In fact, by early June the Tory newspapers were demanding the impeachment of both Aberdeen and Clarendon for aiding Menshikov in his mission.[38]

In the first week of June the cabinet met and decided to send the fleet to Besika Bay, outside the Dardanelles in the Aegean Sea.[40] During the meeting Russell, Clarendon, Lansdowne (a minister without office), and Palmerston agreed on the need for prompt action. Only Aberdeen and, possibly to a lesser extent, Sir James Graham of the admiralty opposed the action. Clarendon had clearly been influenced by public opinion and was on Palmerston's side by this point in arguing the need for a dramatic move.[40] The British fleet arrived in Besika Bay on June 13 and was joined by the French fleet on the following day.

The failure of the Menshikov mission and the subsequent Russian decision in late May to sever relations with Turkey increased hard-liners' suspicions and pressured the more moderate members of the cabinet to resist Russian aggression. Aberdeen appeared wounded by Menshikov's final demands, saying that they were "unreasonable and ought to be resisted. But I cannot yet believe that it will be necessary to do so by war if the Emperor should hitherto have been acting in good faith; if his whole conduct should have been a cheat the case is altered."[41]

Palmerston and Russell remained bellicose and attributed aggressive intentions to the Russians. In response to Menshikov's departure from Constantinople, Russell complained that if *"[e]very privilege* of the Greek Orthodox (not of all Christians) is to be made a matter of engagement with Russia, it is intolerable. It is the way of the bear before he kills his victim!" Palmerston's belief in the need to resist Russian expansionism also was reinforced by Menshikov's coercive tactics. On May 22 he wrote to Clarendon:

> The policy and practice of the Russian Government has always been to push forward its encroachments as fast and as far as the apathy or want of firmness of other Governments would allow it to go, but always to stop and retire when it was met with decided resistance, and then to wait for the next favourable opportunity to make another spring on its unintended victim.[42]

He was a strong advocate of sending the fleet to Besika Bay, saying, "I feel strongly that if we allow a long delay to intervene, circumstances may arise which make us the laughing stock of Europe."[43]

Clarendon's views continued to be mixed. While showing a marked shift from those he held at the outset of the crisis, as the above evidence suggests, his statements appeared to be made in direct response to domestic pressures more than to a dramatic change in his perceptions of the Russians. Menshikov's actions in the final phase of his mission further convinced Clarendon of the need to resist Nicholas's efforts to achieve a protectorate over the Ottoman Greeks.

> Our trusty and well-beloved Nicholas has not been quite honest or disinterested, for while adhering to the religious questions that were to be the sole object of Prince M[enshikov]'s mission, he has sought to divide the Turkish Empire with the Sultan by making himself the protector of the Greeks.[44]

Now, Clarendon too advocated firm action, tipping the balance against restraint. He instructed Seymour to inform the tsar that Britain supported the sultan and ought not to have advised him to accept Menshikov's demands. He also supported sending the fleet and authorizing the ambassador, Stratford Canning, to summon the fleet if necessary, saying he wished they had done it earlier.[45]

The Russian occupation of the principalities only exacerbated British views of Russian aggressiveness. Palmerston considered the occupation an act of war and "an unjust aggression," and he advocated a firm response, suggesting that "the excessive forbearance with which England and France ha[d] acted" had led to Russian aggression.

> [T]he result might have been foreseen. It is in the nature of men whose influence over events and whose power over others are founded on intimidation, and kept up by arrogant assumptions and pretensions, to mistake forbearance for irresolution, and to look upon inaction and hesitation as symptoms of fear, and forerunners of submission. . . . [T]he Russian Government has been led on step by step by the apparent timidity of the Government of England.[46]

Although increasingly frustrated and disappointed that the situation was "drifting fast toward war," Aberdeen remained concerned that Britain not engage in coercive and provocative behavior. As late as July he still felt that they were on the verge of resolving the crisis and opposed Palmerston's suggestion to send the fleet into the Bosphorus Straits or the Black Sea.[47]

Clarendon remained squarely in the Palmerston-Russell camp in advocating resistance, but his views of Russian intentions were little changed. Following the Russian occupation, Clarendon continued to recognize the difficult position of the Russian emperor and the need "to spare his dignity as much as possible."[48]

In short, by the time Menshikov left Constantinople on May 21, his coercive tactics had reinforced existing suspicions and aroused new ones within the British cabinet. The subsequent Russian threats and occupation of Moldavia and Wallachia only increased the mistrust. Of the inner cabinet, Palmerston and, to a lesser degree, Russell distrusted Nicholas from the outset, and initial Russian coercion only reinforced their beliefs about the nature of Russian intentions and the appropriate British response. Aberdeen seemed equally set in his trust of the tsar, although even this was shaken by the summer. Only Clarendon showed a significant shift in his statements during the second phase of the Menshikov mission. He still recognized the need to placate the tsar, however, and it was only when Russian tactics inflamed domestic opinion that Clarendon shifted the balance of power in favor of resistance and coercion.

Deterrence theory's hypotheses are completely falsified by the evolution of the crisis. The initially coercive Russian strategy conveyed aggressive intentions, not resolve. Although the outcome is consistent with cooperation theory, the process by which the crisis escalated is that predicted by the domestic politics approach. Although at least one British policymaker changed his view of Russia based on its choice of bargaining strategy, initial Russian coercion shifted the British balance of power, resulting in a coercive response. The swing voter, Clarendon, consciously changed his policy preference for domestic political reasons.

Russian Strategy

Following the occupation of the principalities, Russian strategy shifted dramatically as diplomatic efforts to resolve the crisis intensified. Between June and December 1853 the European nations pursued eleven different diplomatic solutions to the crisis. As this section demonstrates, Russia generally cooperated with these efforts and made significant concessions. This shift is consistent with the sequence of coercive and accommodative tactics prescribed by deterrence theory. After the Turks declared war, Nicholas maintained a primarily defensive stance, and it was ultimately up to Britain to declare war.

In late July the four neutral European powers—Austria, France, Britain, and Prussia—adopted the Vienna Note as the basis for negotiations. This document bound the sultan to observe forever the rights of the Greek Orthodox Church in the Ottoman Empire and not to change the *status quo* concerning the Holy Places without the prior consent of the French and the Russians.[49] The tsar immediately accepted the note on the condition that the Turks accept it without modification. A month later the Turks rejected the European effort and suggested several amendments to the note. The *Porte* demanded the deletion of the stipulation that Ottoman Greeks share in all rights granted to other Christian subjects, the paragraph suggesting that the "active solicitude" of the tsars was responsible for Greek rights had only been granted "spontaneously" by the sultans, and any mention of previous treaties.[50]

The Russians responded with restraint to the Turkish demands for modification of the Vienna Note. On September 7 Nesselrode sent a moderate but firm response to Vienna, saying that Russia would allow no modifications to the proposed settlement and that it was the responsibility of the four powers to obtain Turkish compliance.

Meanwhile, on September 7, Nesselrode sent a dispatch to all his ambassadors in the field analyzing the proposed modifications to the Vienna Note and explaining why Russia could not accept them. This document also interpreted the original note as favorable to Russian interests. News of this dispatch, which subsequently became known as the "violent interpretation," reached London on September 16.[51]

When word of the violent interpretation appeared to spoil the chances of the Vienna Note, Nicholas undertook his greatest concession yet. He again assured his European colleagues that Russia desired no new rights in Constantinople and was willing "to meet every legitimate wish" of the European powers, implicitly refuting the violent interpretation. At Nicholas's request, the Austrian foreign minister drew up a new proposal, known as the Buol Project or the Olmütz Proposal, which built upon the failed Vienna Note. In it, the tsar offered to withdraw from the principalities as soon as the original Vienna Note was signed.[52]

Events in Constantinople were beginning to overtake European diplomatic efforts, however. On October 4 the Turkish Grand Council officially declared war on Russia. Not only was the Russian response to maintain a defensive posture but the tsar continued to pursue a negotiated settlement, saying that Russia would accept an agreement based upon the Buol Project and a direct Russo-Turkish understanding but that Turkey had to make the first move.[53] Britain and France refused.

Even after the failure of the Olmütz Proposal and the Turkish declaration of war, the tsar continued to act with restraint toward both the Turks and the British and to make sporadic efforts to resolve the crisis short of war. It was too late, however, since Britain refused to restrict Turkish ships to port as requested by the Russians, and on February 4 and 5, 1854, the Russian ambassadors left London and Paris.

Although they severed diplomatic relations with the British and French, the Russians still did not declare war. This action was left to the French and British, who declared war on March 27 and 28, 1854, respectively.

In sum, Russian strategy closely followed the sequence of coercive and accommodative bargaining tactics prescribed by deterrence theory. In the initial stage of the conflict, Nicholas sent a menacing diplomatic mission to Constantinople to coerce the Turks and impress the Europeans. When this failed, Russia shifted to concessions and cooperated with repeated European diplomatic efforts to resolve the crisis.

British Response

In the second phase of the Crimean crisis, from June 1853 to the outbreak of war in March 1854, British decisionmakers recognized Russian willingness to make concessions and forge a compromise. The conflict had progressed too far, however. Public outrage in Britain and Turkish opposition, both of which had been hardened by Russian coercive tactics early in the crisis, placed severe limits on the Aberdeen ministry. Following the disclosure of the violent interpretation, although not necessarily in response to it, the British gave their unqualified support to the Ottoman Empire against the Russians. Russia's continued concessions were recognized in London, but British policymakers simply decided not to reciprocate for domestic political reasons. Although diplomatic efforts continued throughout the fall of 1853, it is difficult to think what more the tsar could have done at that point, short of accepting total defeat, to resolve the crisis. Aberdeen and other soft-liners were so discredited at home that the British government could no longer compromise.

Among the four members of the inner cabinet, there was a general consensus that the Vienna Note should be the basis for negotiation, that Nicholas had compromised by accepting the note immediately, and that he should not be asked to accept the Turkish changes. Clarendon found nothing in the note which might offend the "dignity or the independence of the Sultan," suggested that the Turks had proposed the modifications "under the conviction that they could not be complied with," and asserted that the tsar was "perfectly free to reject" them.[54] Like Clarendon, Aberdeen felt that the changes were petty and suspicious and concluded that "we have no right to ask [Nicholas] to agree to further alterations, after what he has already done."[55]

Even Russell thought the Turks were being treacherous, although his views changed somewhat throughout the course of negotiations over the proposed modifications. Initially, he argued that the Turks should be forced to yield, although a week later, while still thinking the Turks "immense fools," he expressed his hope that Nicholas would concede and accept the changes. He clearly recognized Russia's "last compliance" but fretted that "this Eastern question has got us into as entangled a position as can well be." By early September, before the violent interpretation which is so often blamed for negative British images of the Russians, Russell suggested that Britain stand by the Turkish decision. "If the Emperor of Russia rejects both the [proposed] amended note of the conference and the Turkish note of July 23, we must conclude that he is bent on war, and prepare our measures accordingly."[56]

Much of the specific explanation for Russell's stance, given his recognition of Russian concessions and the general explanation of the failure of efforts to resolve the conflict, can be found in domestic public opinion in Britain, which had been exacerbated by earlier Russian actions. In addition to the general furor which had been growing throughout the crisis, by August there was an increasing sense that war was inevitable. This not only pressured decisionmakers directly but by the time of the proposed Turkish modifications, it was also wreaking havoc in British financial markets.[57] Throughout the summer, parliamentary debate on foreign policy became increasingly heated and hard-line. By the last night of the session on August 16, when a severely anti-Russian speech was delivered, only one member of Parliament defended the policy of the Aberdeen government.[58]

On September 17, the day after news of the violent interpretation reached London, Britain and France abandoned the Vienna Note. It is difficult to say, however, that the British action was in response to the violent interpretation, since attitudes in London had already begun to shift. A more accurate analysis would be that the violent interpretation was used as a rationalization for an action the British had already decided was necessary for domestic political reasons— unqualified support of the Ottoman Empire against the Russians.

Before the violent interpretation had become known in London, the British and French ambassadors in Constantinople called up four steamships, but Stratford, the British ambassador in Constantinople, resisted efforts to call up the whole fleet. The Turkish attacks against Christians which had followed the Russian occupation of the principalities had escalated to a near state of revolution in Constantinople with the Turkish war party using riots to warn the sultan against conceding to Russia. Soon after news of Nesselrode's dispatch reached London and Paris, the French suggested a joint naval action, and the British agreed. On September 23 the British and French authorized their fleets to pass through the Dardanelles to Constantinople, in violation of the 1841 treaty. This move by Clarendon and Aberdeen was apparently taken to protect British subjects, not in response to the violent interpretation.[59]

Stratford certainly took the dispatch as evidence of Nicholas's aggressive intentions, but the ambassador continued to be little trusted in London, especially by Aberdeen and Clarendon. The foreign minister concluded by early November that Stratford "is bent on war." Queen Victoria, too, concluded that Stratford's dispatches "exhibit clearly on his part a *desire* for war, and to drag us into it."[60]

The public response was swift and severe, however, and the moderate government lost considerable ground. The *Daily News* denounced the Vienna Note, saying it had been offered to help the Russians, and it was suggested in the London press that the Aberdeen government was in Russian pay. Even the *Times*, which had been sympathetic to the Aberdeen cabinet, suggested that Turkey had been justified in rejecting the original Vienna Note. Greville noted in his memoirs on September 20, 1853: "Day after day the Radical and Tory papers, animated by very different sentiments and motives, pour forth the most virulent abuse of the Emperor of Russia, of Austria, and of this Government, especially of Aberdeen."[61]

Palmerston continued to view Russian intentions as hostile and to advocate firm resistance, commenting on November 1 that "Russia must, by fair means or foul, be brought to give up her pretensions and withdraw her aggression."[62] Russell's distrust of Russia and desire to support the Turks only intensified, and on September 17 he threatened to resign rather than force the unmodified Vienna Note on the Turks.[63]

Clarendon continued to walk a middle line between the extreme positions represented by Palmerston and Aberdeen, leaning more toward the former as the crisis progressed. Although he argued that the construction put on the Vienna Note by Nesselrode was grounds for suspicion, at the end of September Clarendon expressed his belief that the tsar could not be expected to submit to any more humiliation at the hands of the Turks.[64] While he recognized the limited intentions of the Russians, he also was aware of the growing public furor. Although he knew the tsar would like a way to back down with honor, Clarendon argued, "We cannot press the Turks too hard about the Note because public opinion would be against it, and secondly, because they would fight it out single-handed." He advocated sending the British fleet, saying, "With reference to public feeling in England, we could not well do less, and if any Russian attack were made upon Turkey that our fleet might have prevented, we never should have heard the end of it."[65] Statements like these have prompted Paul Schroeder to conclude that Clarendon had decided to reject the Vienna Note before the violent interpretation surfaced but that he used Nesselrode's dispatch as a rationalization. "Had no violent interpretation come along from Russia, they would have invented one and were in fact in the process of inventing or provoking one in order to justify the move they intended to make anyway."[66] The official British response to the violent interpretation was to abandon the Vienna Note as the basis for negotiations and to suggest that the four powers adopt the Turkish modifications as their interpretation of the original note.[67]

Russia continued to offer concessions and to act with restraint toward Constantinople despite the October 4 declaration of war by the Turks. Like the earlier concessions, the Olmütz offer was recognized in London, but British policymakers decided not to reciprocate. Of the major decisionmakers, only Aberdeen positively perceived Russian intentions and wanted to respond favorably to Nicholas's efforts at accommodation. On October 3 the prime minister wrote to the queen, "Last night despatches were received from Olmütz, which gave an account of a very strong declaration on the part of the Emperor of Russia, of his desire to obtain nothing in Turkey beyond the actual *status quo* in religious matters." The next day he said he would resign rather than be a party to war with Russia "on such grounds as the present."[68] The prime minister was alone in his views, however, and he was in an increasingly tenuous position at home. Aberdeen's support within his own cabinet and in Parliament was weak, and Russell's recent threat to resign had revived the issue of his succession to the office of prime minister.

The rest of the cabinet opposed the Olmütz proposal, but in Clarendon's case, this was not because he questioned Nicholas's intentions. Rather, he appears to have correctly perceived the nature of the tsar's offers at Olmütz when he recognized that Nicholas "did eat dirt and went far to neutralize the dispatch of objections to the modifications. . . . Nicholas seems now prepared to eat a great deal of dirt and to swallow modifications and other things he would not look at four months ago but I suppose there must be a limit." Seymour also agreed that the Olmütz Proposal was "a notable specimen of what can be done in the way of backing" down.[69]

The foreign secretary opposed the Olmütz Proposal for domestic political reasons, not because he misperceived Russian intentions. Clarendon ultimately provided the swing vote, with Palmerston and Russell, against accepting the Olmütz Proposal, however. The reason for this rejection was not simply suspicion of Russian intentions but fear

of Turkish refusal and the "false and embarrassing" position in which
that would put the British cabinet, particularly in the face of public
opinion. On October 5 Clarendon wrote, "The public seems to think
that there is nothing to do but to declare war against Russia, just when
she is yielding the point in dispute."[70] In addition to rejecting the
Olmütz concessions by Russia as failing to repudiate the violent
interpretation, on October 8 the British cabinet ordered the fleets to
proceed to Constantinople immediately. A week later the government
authorized the fleets to pass through the Bosphorus and enter the
Black Sea if Russia attacked the Turks. This represented a more
coercive British stance.

On November 30 the Russian pattern of fighting defensively in its
ongoing war with the Turks was dramatically altered. In the Battle of
Sinope the Russian navy went on the offensive, destroying the Turkish
fleet and the city of Sinope and killing thousands of Turks. The news of
the "massacre" did not reach London until December 12. When it did,
as Graham noted, the reaction of the public and press was swift and
vicious.

> The attack on Sinope has produced an immense effect on the public
> mind both in France and in England. It is difficult to put any restraint on
> the national desire to avenge what is regarded as a contempt and
> defiance of our flags.
> I have been one of the most strenuous advocates of peace with
> Russia until the last moment; but the Sinope attack and recent events
> have changed entirely the aspect of affairs. I am afraid a rupture with
> Russia is inevitable.[71]

Within a few days of hearing the news of Sinope, Palmerston
resigned from the government, ostensibly in opposition to a franchise
reform bill. It was widely assumed, however, that the real reason for
his departure was the Aberdeen government's failure to take a firm
stand against Russia, and the public furor intensified. The *Morning
Post* even reported that the home secretary had resigned for foreign
policy reasons.[72] The news of both Sinope and Palmerston's
resignations led to public attacks on Prince Albert, who reportedly
brought about the secretary's departure through his unconstitutional
interference in foreign policy. These attacks reached a high point in
January 1854, and at one point it was even rumored that the prince had
been impeached for high treason.[73] Both Lansdowne and Russell also
reportedly threatened resignation around this time.[74]

In response to the public outcry generated by the Sinope massacre,
the British cabinet decided on December 22, in Palmerston's absence, to

send the fleet to join the French in the Black Sea and to inform the Russians that any Russian ship caught out of harbor would be seized or sunk. Public opinion was now largely determining the British response. Although Russian concessions and willingness to continue negotiations were recognized in London, the diplomatic process had been overtaken by the events of the Russo-Turkish war, especially the battle at Sinope.

Throughout the second phase of the Crimean conflict, British decisionmakers recognized Russian attempts to compromise. However, the early Russian strategy of coercion had aroused public opinion in Britain and undermined the position of soft-liners within the Aberdeen cabinet. The prime minister and Clarendon, the other major soft-liner in the government, were so discredited at home by Russian bargaining behavior that they could no longer afford to compromise. Clarendon provided the decisive vote in shifting the balance of power within the British cabinet toward a policy of coercion. Russian strategy had so inflamed public opinion that the foreign secretary felt he and his government could not survive compromise.

Conclusions

In the diplomatic crisis preceding the outbreak of the Crimean War, the international environment interacted with the domestic arena in Britain to shape the outcome of the conflict in a manner unintended by Russia or Britain. Russia followed the sequence of coercive and accommodative bargaining tactics prescribed by deterrence theory—it started out tough and shifted to conciliation in the later phase of the conflict—but the crisis still escalated to war. This illustrates deterrence theory's failure to consider the unintended domestic consequences of its policy prescriptions. Russian bargaining moves influenced the domestic distribution of power in London and thereby determined that a coercive policy response would become dominant. The interaction of this coercive British stance with Russian policy resulted in the Crimean War.

Deterrence theory's prescriptions failed miserably in this case, but its major rival, cooperation theory, also failed to capture the indirect effects of external bargaining on the domestic political situation. The initially coercive Russian strategy led to escalation of the conflict, as predicted by cooperation theory. The process by which it did so, however, was political, not perceptual. Russian strategy did not fail because it changed the perceptions of British policymakers but because it aroused public opinion and undermined the arguments of the soft-line government.

In systemic terms, Russian actions had indirect and complicated effects; the outcome did not correspond with the intentions of any of the actors. Despite the fact that Russia employed the policy prescriptions of deterrence theory, the standard wisdom on crisis bargaining, the Crimean conflict escalated to war. The information-processing models used by deterrence and cooperation theory to explain the consequences of bargaining and negotiation fail to accurately predict the results of a state's actions because they fail to account for the indirect domestic effects of external bargaining moves.

The final disintegration of the Concert of Europe reflected in the Crimean War was, to a large extent, a result of the failure of the key actors to remember the lessons they had learned so well in 1813–15. Russia attempted a frontal assault in response to a threat to its security only to discover too late that its actions had backfired. As both Daugherty and Schroeder conclude in their contributions to this volume, democracy itself may have been an obstacle to the learning process which produces systemic thinking. Although Russian policymakers ignored the unintended consequences of their policy, public opinion in Britain ultimately prevented the Aberdeen government from compromising.

The Crimean case suggests that the key task in advising decisionmakers on foreign policy is to avoid the linear thinking of most prior analysts and practitioners of crisis bargaining. No single strategy or sequence of tactics will be successful against every opponent. Although avoiding linear thinking is certain to be a difficult task, policymakers need to be aware of the domestic balance of power in an adversary state and to carefully design a bargaining strategy which takes it into account.

Notes

For their helpful comments and suggestions, I would like to thank Miriam Avins, Teresa Johnson, Jonathan Mercer, Jack Snyder, and the other participants in the November 1991 conference on systems effects held at Columbia University.

1. Sir Robert Morier as quoted in J. A. R. Marriot, *The Eastern Question* (Oxford University Press, 1940), p. 249; and M.S. Anderson, *The Eastern Question 1774–1923: A Study in International Relations* (London: Macmillan, 1966), p. 132.

2. Because of space limitations, this chapter examines only the effect of Russian strategy on the British policy response and the escalation of the conflict, although the same sort of analysis could be applied to British policy and Russian response.

3. The best known of these works is Glenn H. Snyder and Paul Diesing, *Conflict Among Nations* (Princeton: Princeton University Press, 1977). Also see Alexander L. George, David K. Hall, and William E. Simons, *The Limits of Coercive Diplomacy: Laos, Cuba, Vietnam* (Boston: Little, Brown, 1971); Russell J. Leng and Stephen G. Walker, "Comparing Two Strategies of Crisis Bargaining: Confrontation, Coercion, and Reciprocity," *Journal of Conflict Resolution* 26 (December 1982): 571–91; Charles Lockhart, *Bargaining in International Conflicts* (New York: Columbia University Press, 1979); and Oran R. Young, *The Politics of Force: Bargaining During International Crises* (Princeton: Princeton University Press, 1968).

4. Sidney Siegel and Lawrence E. Fouraker, *Bargaining and Group Decision Making: Experiments in Bilateral Monopoly* (New York: McGraw-Hill, 1960). For laboratory experiments which support the argument, see Jeffrey Z. Rubin and Maryanne R. DeMatteo, "Factors Affecting the Magnitude of Subjective Utility Parameters in a Tacit Bargaining Game," *Journal of Experimental Social Psychology* 8 (1972): 412–26; and Gary A. Yukl, "Effects of Situational Variables and Opponent Concessions on a Bargainer's Perception, Aspirations and Concessions," *Journal of Personality and Social Psychology* 29 (1974): 227–36.

5. The best known works within this school are: Robert Axelrod, *The Evolution of Cooperation* (New York: Basic Books, 1984); Robert Jervis, *Perception and Misperception in International Politics* (Princeton: Princeton University Press, 1976), ch. 3; and Charles E. Osgood, *An Alternative to War or Surrender* (Urbana: University of Illinois Press, 1962).

6. Robert Jervis, "Cooperation Under the Security Dilemma," *World Politics* 30:2 January 1978): 167–214.

7. S. S. Komorita and James K. Esser, "Frequency of Reciprocated Concessions in Bargaining," *Journal of Personality and Social Psychology* 32 (1975): 699–705; Ronald L. Michelini, "Effects of prior interaction, contact, strategy, and expectation of meeting on game behavior and sentiment," *Journal of Conflict Resolution* 15:1 (March 1971): 97–103; Dean G. Pruitt and Jeffrey Z. Rubin, *Social Conflict: Escalation, Stalemate, and Settlement* (New York: Random House, 1986); and Robert L. Swinth, "The establishment of the trust relationship," *Journal of Conflict Resolution* 11:3 (September 1967): 335–44.

8. Alexander Gerschenkron, *Economic Backwardness in Historical Perspective* (Cambridge: Harvard University Press, 1962); Peter Gourevitch, *Politics in Hard Times* (Ithaca, NY: Cornell University Press, 1986); Peter Gourevitch, "The Second Image Reversed:The International Sources of Domestic Politics," *International Organization* 32 (Autumn 1978): 881–911; Jack Snyder, *Myths of Empire: Domestic Politics and Strategic Ideology* (Ithaca: Cornell University Press, 1991).

9. Robert Putnam, "Diplomacy and Domestic Politics," *International Organization* 42:3 (Summer 1988): 427–60; George Tsebelis, *Nested Games: Rational Choice in Comparative Politics* (Berkeley: University of California Press, 1990).

10. See especially Richard Ned Lebow, *Between Peace and War: The Nature of International Crisis* (Baltimore: Johns Hopkins University Press, 1981), pp. 169–92; and Richard Ned Lebow, "The Deterrence Deadlock," in *Psychology and Deterrence* ed. Robert Jervis, Richard Ned Lebow, and Janice Gross Stein (Baltimore: Johns Hopkins University Press, 1985), pp. 180–81.

11. Snyder and Diesing, *Conflict Among Nations*, pp. 510–22.

12. Jack Snyder, "International Leverage on Soviet Domestic Change," *World Politics* 42:1 (October 1989): 1–30.

13. Matthew Evangelista, "Cooperation Theory and Disarmament Negotiations in the 1950s," *World Politics* 42:4 (July 1990): 502–28.

14. For the text of the treaties, see Great Britain, *Parliamentary Papers, Accounts and Papers, Eastern Papers*, 31 January – 12 August 1854, vol. 71, Part I, pp. 27–8. (hereinafter *Eastern Papers*) For the text of the notes, known as the Nesselrode Memorandum, see *Eastern Papers*, vol. 71, Pt. VI, pp. 2–4.

15. Cited in Harold Temperley, *England and the Near East: The Crimea* (Archon Books, 1964), p. 304.

16. *Eastern Papers*, vol. 71, Pt. V, pp. 2, 4.

17. Ibid., pp. 4, 8, 11. On Nesselrode's statements, see G. H. Bolsover, "Nicholas I and the Partition of Turkey," *Slavonic and East European Review* 27 (1948), p. 141; and Charles Emerson Walker, *The Role of Karl Nesselrode in the Formulation and Implementation of Russian Foreign Policy, 1850–1856* PhD Dissertation (West Virginia University, 1973), p. 115.

18. Nicholas selected Menshikov because he felt his brusque manner would allow him to be more aggressive with the Turks. H. E. Howard, "Brunnow's Reports on Aberdeen, 1853," *Cambridge Historical Journal* 4 (1932–34), p. 317; and Walker, *Role of Karl Nesselrode*, p. 123. For the content of Menshikov's instructions, see: John Sheldon Curtiss, *Russia's Crimean War* (Durham, NC: Duke University Press, 1979), pp. 85–88; Temperley, *England and the Near East*, pp. 306–7; and Walker, *Role of Karl Nesselrode*, pp. 123–35.

19. *Eastern Papers*, vol. 71, Pt. 1, p. 149.

20. See *Eastern Papers*, vol. 71, Pt. I, pp. 185–86.

21. Ann Pottinger Saab, *The Origins of the Crimean Alliance* (Charlottesville, VA: University Press of Virginia, 1977), p. 39.

22. Conacher, *Aberdeen Coalition*, p. 35; Malmesbury, *Memoirs of an Ex-Minister*, pp. 286–87.

23. Chamberlain, *Lord Aberdeen*, p. 478. This was in direct conflict with the power of Russell and, especially, the more popular Palmerston to threaten resignation. As Chamberlain sums up Aberdeen's position within the cabinet, "At best Aberdeen could only negotiate with his own cabinet. He could not command it." Also, see Maxwell, *Life and Letters of Clarendon*, vol. II, pp. 21–23.

24. On Seymour's views see: Vernon John Puryear, *England, Russia, and the Straits Question 1844–1856* (Hamden, CT: Archon Books, 1965, originally published in 1931), pp. 206–7; *Eastern Papers*, vol. 71, Pt. I, p. 56. For Cowley's comment, see A. J. P. Taylor, *The Struggle for Mastery in Europe 1848–1918*

(London: Oxford University Press, 1954), p. 53. Also see the February 9, 1853 letter from Cowley to Russell in *The Later Correspondence of Lord John Russell, 1840–1878*, ed. G. P. Gooch (London: Longmans, Green, 1925), vol. II, p. 147.

25. Puryear, England, Russia, and the Straits Question, pp. 220–21.

26. Taylor, Struggle for Mastery in Europe, p. 53.

27. Quoted in Walker, *Role of Karl Nesselrode*, p. 141. Also see the January 1853 letter from Aberdeen to Russell quoted in Muriel E. Chamberlain, *Lord Aberdeen: A political biography* (London: Longman, 1983), p. 479.

28. Temperley, England and the Near East, p. 270.

29. Temperley, *England and the Near East*, pp. 272–78, 312–15. Also see Gavin Burns Henderson, *Crimean War Diplomacy and Other Historical Essays* (Glasgow: Jackson, Sons & Company, 1974), p. 6; Puryear, *England, Russia, and the Straits Question* pp. 214–15; and Norman Rich, *Why the Crimean War?*, pp. 29–33. Temperley also argues, however, that the first British suspicions were those voiced by Russell on April 29, an assertion which is disputed below but one which is also cited in Wetzel, *Crimean War*, p. 48.

30. *Later Correspondence of Lord John Russell*, vol. II, p. 145.

31. *Eastern Papers*, vol. 71, Pt. 5, p. 8; *British Foreign Policy*, vol. II, p. 340. Temperley claims that Russell was disturbed by the Seymour conversations (*England and the Near East*, pp. 272–75), but this shift in perceptions seems to have occurred later in response to Menshikov's actions.

32. Cited in Curtiss, *Russian's Crimean War*, p. 96. Also see F. A. Wellesley, *The Paris Embassy during the Second Empire* (London: Thornton Butterworth, 1928), p. 24.

33. Quoted in Walpole, *Life of Lord John Russell*, p. 178.

34. Puryear, England, Russia, and the Straits Question, p. 232; and Rich, Why the Crimean War?, p. 32.

35. Herbert Maxwell, The Life and Letters of George William Frederick, Fourth Earl of Clarendon (London: Edward Arnold, 1913), vol. II, p. 3.

36. Walpole, *Life of Lord John Russell*, vol. II, p. 181; Chamberlain, *Lord Aberdeen*, p. 481.

37. Quoted in Conacher, *Aberdeen Coalition*, p. 151.

38. Conacher, *Aberdeen Coalition*, p. 155.

39. Conacher, *Aberdeen Coalition*, p. 153. This move also apparently was not a response to the Russian occupation, since news of the occupation plans only reached London on June 5.

40. Chamberlain, *Lord Aberdeen*, p. 482. Also see Rich, *Why the Crimean War?*, pp. 62–63.

41. Quoted in Conacher, *Aberdeen Coalition*, p. 151.

42. Evelyn Ashley, *The Life and Correspondence of Henry John Temple, Viscount Palmerston* (London: Richard Bentley & Son, 1879), vol. II, p. 273.

43. Quoted in Conacher, *Aberdeen Coalition*, p. 152.

44. Wellesley, *Paris Embassy*, p. 25. Also see *Eastern Papers*, vol. 71, Pt. I, pp. 163, 183, 203.

45. *Eastern Papers*, vol. 71, Pt. I, p. 204; Chamberlain, *Lord Aberdeen*, pp. 481–82.

46. *Later Correspondence of Lord John Russell*, vol. II, pp. 150–51; Ashley, *Life and Correspondence of Palmerston*, pp. 227–28. For similar statements by Palmerston during this period, see Walpole, *Life of Lord John Russell*, p. 183.

47. Maxwell, *Life and Letters of Clarendon*, vol. II, p. 15; Conacher, *Aberdeen Coalition*, p. 160; and Sir Arthur Gordon, *The Earl of Aberdeen* (London: Sampson, Low, Marston, 1893), pp. 225–26.

48. Temperley, England and the Near East, pp. 343–44; Eastern Papers, vol. 71, Pt. I, p. 265; Later Correspondence of Lord John Russell, vol. II, p. 147.

49. *Eastern Papers*, vol. 71, Pt. II, pp. 26–7, 81.

50. *Eastern Papers*, vol. 71, Pt. II, pp. 69–70, 78–79, 81.

51. There is conflicting evidence on whether the violent interpretation was inadvertently leaked or deliberately given to the press. For the two views, see: Paul W. Schroeder, *Austria, Great Britain, and the Crimean War: The Destruction of the European Concert* (Ithaca: Cornell University Press, 1972), p. 69; and A. J. P. Taylor, *The Struggle for Mastery in Europe 1848–1918* (London: Oxford University Press, 1954), pp. 55–6 n. 1. Walker says that Brunnow mistakenly gave the dispatches to Clarendon who "was not particularly upset with them." *Role of Karl Nesselrode*, p. 237.

52. Curtiss, *Russia's Crimean War*, p. 197; Rich, *Why the Crimean War?* p. 84. On the Buol Project see *Eastern Papers*, vol. 71, Pt. II, pp. 128–9.

53. In response Count Buol, the Austrian Foreign Minister, convened another conference of ambassadors and drafted another proposal, according to which Constantinople was to send a representative to negotiate with Russia in a neutral place. *Eastern Papers*, vol. 71, Pt. II, pp. 187–88.

54. *Later Correspondence of Lord John Russell*, vol. II, p. 152; Eastern Papers, vol. 71, Pt. II, pp. 95, 86.

55. Maxwell, *Life and Letters of Clarendon*, vol. II, p. 17.

56. Walpole, *Life of Lord John Russell*, pp. 184, 186, 187. Also see Conacher, *Aberdeen Coalition*, pp. 177–80.

57. *Greville Memoirs*, vol. VI, p. 437.

58. Conacher, *Aberdeen Coalition*, pp. 166–74.

59. Conacher, *Aberdeen Coalition*, p. 188.

60. For Stratford's views, see Lane-Poole, *Life of the Right Honourable Stratford Canning*, vol. II, p. 303. For Clarendon's and Victoria's statements, see: Maxwell, *Life and Letters of Clarendon*, vol. II, p. 29; *The Letters of Queen Victoria*, ed. Arthur Christopher Benson and Viscount Esher (London: John Murray, 1908), vol. II, p. 460.

61. Martin, Triumph of Lord Palmerston, pp. 129–35; Greville Memoirs, vol. VI, p. 450.

62. Ashley, Life and Correspondence, p. 285.

63. Walpole, *Life of Lord John Russell*, p. 190; Maxwell, *Life and Letters*, vol. II, pp. 22–23; Bell, *Lord Palmerston*, vol. II, pp. 87–88.

64. *Eastern Papers*, vol. 71, Pt. II, pp. 110–11; Schroeder, Austria, Great Britain, and the Crimean War, p. 87.

65. Maxwell, *Life and Letters of Clarendon*, vol. II, p. 26. On the public outcry see Martin, *Triumph of Lord Palmerston*, pp. 128–37.

66. Schroeder, *Austria, Great Britain, and the Crimean War*, p. 65.

67. Conacher, *Aberdeen Coalition*, pp. 182–83; *Eastern Papers*, vol. 71, Pt. II, p. 217.

68. Quoted in Conacher, *Aberdeen Coalition*, p. 192; quoted in Chamberlain, *Lord Aberdeen*, p. 486. For other statements by Aberdeen throughout October and November see: *The Correspondence of Lord Aberdeen and Princess Lieven, 1832–1854* Third Series, E. Jones Parry, ed. (London: Royal Historical Society, 1938–9), vol. 62, p. 653; Gordon, *Earl of Aberdeen*, p. 238.

69. Schroeder, *Austria, Great Britain, and the Crimean War*, pp. 79, 102.

70. Martin, *Triumph of Lord Palmerston*, p. 140. Such sentiments were frequently expressed in the later part of the crisis. The British ambassador to Paris, Cowley, stated, "I must say that I never expected to get as much out of the Czar." "The real difficulty for us appears to me to avoid getting again into *the fix* out of which we have just escaped—that is finding ourselves advocating Russia against Turkey." Schroeder, *Austria, Great Britain, and the Crimean War*, p. 79.

71. Charles Stuart Parker, *Life and Letters of Sir James Graham* (London: John Murray, 1907), vol. II, p. 226. On the reaction of the British press to the Battle of Sinope, see Breeze, *British Opinion of Russian Foreign Policy*, pp. 156–57.

Contrary to Graham's statement, however, this public outcry apparently was not echoed in Paris where the business and political elite were enraged by the massacre, but the mass public had very little reaction. Lynn M. Case, *French Opinion on War and Diplomacy during the Second Empire* (Philadelphia: University of Pennsylvania Press, 1954), pp. 16–18. This reaction was apparently reflected in the French ambassador's reaction to the incident. Castelbajac reportedly welcomed news of the Sinope victory as meaning a quick end to the war. Vitzhum von Eckstaedt, *St. Petersburg and London*, vol. I, p. 9.

72. Martin, *Triumph of Lord Palmerston*, p. 148.

73. *Letters of Queen Victoria*, vol. III, p. 3; Walpole, Life of Lord John Russell, pp. 202–3.

74. Taylor, *Struggle for Mastery in Europe*, p. 58; Walpole, *Life of Lord John Russell*, p. 200.

6

The Dynamics of
International Monetary Systems:
International and Domestic Factors
in the Rise, Reign, and Demise
of the Classical Gold Standard

Jeffry A. Frieden

An international monetary system of fixed nominal rates is at one and the same time very simple and very complex. Such a system is rudimentary in that all participants simply agree to a set of stable values of their currencies. The prime example of a fixed-rate system is the classical gold standard, which was a pillar of the world economy from about 1870 until 1914. That such a system is complex in many ways is indicated by the abject failure of continued attempts to reestablish the gold standard during the interwar years, and by the involved and extended negotiations over a limited fixed-rate system among the members of the European Community since 1973.

The purpose of this essay is to examine the dynamics of international monetary systems, specifically systems of fixed nominal exchange rates. The broad question is how such systems can arise and become stable over time. More specifically, I focus on explaining how and why the classical gold standard arose, and how and why it was as stable as it was before World War One. This explanation provides the tools to understand why subsequent attempts at establishing fixed-rate systems have met with less stability and success. I end by exploring some of the implications of the analysis of the gold standard for prospects of success in the ongoing process of European monetary integration and ultimate movement toward a single currency.

A Fixed-Rate International Monetary System:
Description, Definitions, and Analysis

An international monetary system can be compared to a domestic monetary standard on the three traditional roles of money: unit of account, medium of exchange, and store of value. The international monetary regime establishes a way to equate currency values for the purposes of measuring or accounting for relative prices, either by way of a fixed rate among currencies or against a commodity such as gold, or by way of market-based floating rates. For international payments, monetary systems use as a medium of exchange either national currencies—usually a limited number of key currencies—or such a common tender as precious metals. And some mix of national currencies and common tender are held for investment (store of value) purposes.

All of these purposes *can* theoretically be served by atomistically derived and maintained markets in which national currencies are traded freely. However, historically most international monetary systems have included some function for explicit government policy regarding the exchange rate. One such set of policies is that which constitutes a fixed-rate international monetary system. In a fixed-rate system, currencies are tied to each other at established parities, and governments commit themselves not to alter these parities. The most famous such system was the classical gold standard of the late nineteenth and early twentieth century, in which the currencies of the world's leading economies were fixed to gold by their national governments at some legal rate. Typically (with some exaggeration) each national monetary authority on the gold standard stood ready to exchange gold for its currency, or its currency for gold, at the established rate and on demand.

Traditional discussions of the international monetary system focus on the efficiency effects of a particular system, that is, its effects on global welfare (trade, payments, economic growth). In less grandiose discussions the implications of exchange-rate arrangements on national welfare or on specific groups within nations are considered. These discussions are primarily normative and policy-oriented. From an analytical perspective, we can ask two parallel sets of questions along these lines, one at the global and the other at the national level.

The first set of analytical questions is concerned with how at the international level an exchange-rate regime is adopted and sustained. In posing such questions, we abstract from global welfare considerations to ask how it is that nation states are able to cooperate in establishing and maintaining a global standard. In this regard, international monetary coordination is an exercise in collective action, with the normal free rider and informational problems and criteria for overcoming them.

Indeed, there is some reason to regard an international monetary regime as a public good. From a global standpoint, as with domestic money, any standard is almost certainly better than none at all. Some generally agreed rules of the game—even if only to allow free trading in national currencies—are needed to provide the stability necessary for international trade and payments. In the context of a fixed-rate regime, and inasmuch as international exchange-rate stability is something of a public good, there is an incentive (especially for small countries) to defect. A country can, for example, reap specific benefits by devaluing its currency. This makes its exports more competitive but does not challenge the stability of the system. Of course, if enough countries act similarly, the regime will collapse.

The experience of international monetary relations suggests one set of dynamics, at the international level, that can help create and reinforce a regime such as the gold standard. The more countries participate in such a system, the greater the incentives to any one country to affiliate with it. This is because participation in the system gives greater access to trade and investment with other members. All else equal, firms and individuals are more likely to trade with, invest in, and borrow from countries whose currency values are more predictable. So such a system can exhibit a synergistic feedback mechanism or virtuous circle: the more countries are members of the system, the more attractive is membership. Of course, the circle can be vicious as well: once the size of the regime begins to decline, the system can collapse rapidly as countries defect.

In this context, the crucial question is how the synergistic process gets started and reinforced. Experiences from other such processes suggest the importance of a focal point around which actors can converge—in the international monetary realm, perhaps a major trading and investing nation that can lead others toward a mutually beneficial agreement on international monetary norms.[1]

Although interstate considerations are important, in the final analysis exchange-rate regimes are the result of a series of national choices. Analysts thus need to examine a second set of questions, those that concern the determinants of national policies toward the international monetary system. How, in other words, do countries come to make and sustain a commitment to an international currency standard? Determinants of such a choice include both "national interest" calculations of the optimal national policy and more political considerations based on the role of interest groups within national societies.

The national welfare implications of different monetary regimes have especially to do with the degree to which they allow national policymakers to sustain or restore internal and external macroeconomic balance.[2] Perhaps the best way to examine this is by way of the contrast between fixed and floating rates. Fixed rates provide for stability and predictability, while floating rates allow national policymakers more independence to respond to country-specific economic conditions. This is especially true in a world in which capital can move freely from country to country.

Where capital is not mobile across borders, there is no contradiction between fixed rates and national monetary autonomy, as the monetary authorities can affect domestic macroeconomic conditions by altering the interest rate. However, where capital is mobile, interest rates are by definition set on world markets; the exchange rate is the only tool the monetary authorities have for affecting macroeconomic conditions. This sets up a trade-off between the benefits of exchange-rate stability and the benefits of national policy autonomy. This trade-off can be (and typically is) evaluated on a national-interest basis in terms of such characteristics of the country as how open to trade the economy is, how vulnerable it is to unique shocks, and so on. For example, consideration of such aggregate national-level characteristics leads to the conclusion that small open economies dependent on the export of a few commodities whose prices tend to fluctuate widely are almost certainly better off with floating than fixed rates. In this context, the choice of regime is affected by structural characteristics of the national economy.

This suggests a second set of dynamics in the evolution of international monetary regimes. As a stable regime grows in importance and extent, and more countries associate with it, the level of foreign trade and payments for each member grows as well. In other words, not only does the existence of the system attract more members but the existence of a stable system leads these members to trade, invest, and borrow more. As this happens the countries become more open on current and capital accounts, and their economies become more integrated and less vulnerable to unique shocks. These trends in turn give the countries stronger national-welfare reasons to maintain their commitment to the regime. So another feedback mechanism or virtuous circle can operate: the growth of a stable international monetary regime increases its members' international trade and investment and, therefore, their interest in ensuring regime stability.

National welfare considerations are important, but domestic distributional considerations are also central to the choice of exchange-rate regimes. In explaining any national policy, we must carefully delineate the ways in which national welfare considerations translate into pressures on policymakers and therefore into influences on outcomes. We know all too well that the fact that a policy is welfare-improving from the standpoint of society as a whole does not guarantee its adoption. The process is mediated through the interests of domestic groups and the effects of domestic political institutions.

In fact, different exchange-rate policies have different effects on domestic socioeconomic interest groups. For those heavily engaged in international trade and payments, the stability and predictability of a fixed rate is eminently desirable. However, in a financially integrated world (as today and before 1914), a fixed rate eliminates the possibility for independent national monetary policy (as discussed above). This may matter little to those whose economic horizons are global (international banks, multinational corporations, major exporters), but it is a real sacrifice for those tied to the domestic market. For this reason, we expect internationally oriented economic actors to favor fixed rates, and domestically oriented economic actors to favor floating or adjustable rates. By the same token, those that favor a devaluation (essentially producers of import or export-competing tradable goods) tend to oppose a fixed-rate system that prohibits devaluations.

National choices on whether and how to associate with an international monetary regime are the consequence of domestic bargaining among interested groups in national society and within national political institutions. The stronger those who favor a fixed rate, the more likely it will be adopted. Here again, a virtuous-circle feedback mechanism can be at work. The more encompassing the international monetary regime, the greater the interest of internationally oriented firms in national societies in encouraging their governments to associate with the regime. Once a government becomes a member of the regime, the proportion of the economy that is oriented to foreign trade and payments is likely to grow, and with it the influence of that sector's policy preferences—especially to remain committed to the system. Of course, here as elsewhere the mechanism can operate in reverse: as an international monetary system collapses it pulls the political rug out from under its supporters in national political economies by reducing the economic influence of internationally oriented groups and lessening their commitment to the system.

In summary, two important analytical questions dominate the discussion of any international monetary regime. First, what are the "national interests" in play and what are their domestic political determinants? Second, how do independent nation states interact in their policies toward the international monetary arena? In answering both questions I have identified important dynamic effects. At the subnational level, the more extensive and stable the international monetary regime, the greater the incentives for internationally oriented groups within any individual country to pressure their government to affiliate. At the national level, the larger the international monetary regime, the higher the level of national trade and payments of each member country and the more linked the markets among countries, and thus the stronger the national welfare argument for each country to affiliate with the regime. At the interstate level, the greater the number of countries that are members of the regime, the greater the incentive for additional countries to affiliate.

This is really one set of dynamics—a feedback mechanism that includes both strategic interaction among states and politics within them—but it can usefully be divided between its international and domestic components. Internationally, we should observe convergence of ever greater numbers of states around an international monetary focal point as such a focal point becomes more and more attractive and credible. Domestically, we should observe more domestic support for affiliation with this focal point (regime) as it grows in extent and credibility.[3] In the next section I trace these interrelated processes through the history of the classical gold standard.

The Rise of the Gold Standard: International Dynamics

It is unclear when the classical gold standard began, for the world's major countries went on gold at different times. For example, from the 1820s onward the United Kingdom, France, and the United States were all on a specie standard quite similar to the subsequent monometallic gold standard.[4] By 1880, however, every major trading and financial nation on earth had tied its currency legally to gold at a fixed rate. This situation was to prevail—indeed, more and more countries were to join the regime—until 1914, when World War One brought the system down. During these decades, the advanced industrial countries of the world, and many developing countries as well, grew at unprecedented rates. International trade and payments increased continually until the world economy was probably more integrated than it has ever been before or since. In purely economic terms, the gold standard era was something of a truly golden age.

The near automaticity assumed to inhere to the gold standard was expressed eloquently, and not without some nostalgia, by John Maynard Keynes in 1920:

The inhabitant of London could order by telephone, sipping his morning tea in bed, the various products of the whole earth, in such quantity as he might see fit, and reasonably expect their early delivery upon his doorstep; he could at the same moment and by the same means adventure his wealth in the natural resources and new enterprises of any quarter of the world, and share, without exertion or even trouble, in their prospective fruits and advantages; or he could decide to couple the security of his fortunes with the good faith of the townspeople of any substantial municipality in any continent that fancy or information might recommend. He could secure forthwith, if he wished it, cheap and comfortable means of transit to any country or climate without passport or other formality, could despatch his servant to the neighboring office of a bank for such supply of the precious metals as might seem convenient, and could then proceed abroad to foreign quarters, without knowledge of their religion, language, or customs, bearing coined wealth upon his person, and would consider himself greatly aggrieved and much surprised at the least interference. But, most important of all, he regarded this state of affairs as normal, certain, and permanent.[5]

The classical gold standard was a remarkably uncomplicated mechanism. To be "on gold," a country simply fixed a legal value in national currency at which the monetary authorities (typically the mint or the central bank) would buy or sell gold. This effectively established a fixed legal rate of exchange between gold and the currency, and thus between all other gold-standard currencies and the national currency. A number of subsidiary "rules of the game," not formal but widely understood, were designed to ensure that the government would be able to guarantee free convertibility of the currency into gold.[6]

The economic implications of the gold standard were also quite simple and were understood in late medieval times. If a country ran a persistent trade deficit, gold would flow out and the money supply would contract.[7] This would drive domestic prices down relative to world prices, thus increasing exports and reducing imports—and bringing trade back into balance. The process ran in reverse for countries with persistent surpluses.

To repeat the points made more generally above, a credible commitment to gold provided economic agents with a marvelously predictable exchange rate, but it also greatly restricted the ability of national governments to affect national monetary conditions. This trade-off was also widely recognized, especially in the common practice of all governments of going off gold during major crises, such as wars, in which policy autonomy was unarguably more important than exchange-rate stability.

The classical gold standard's prehistory began in 1717, when Britain's master of the mint, Sir Isaac Newton, set the price of an ounce of gold at £3 17s 10 1/2d.[8] Silver remained coin, and the country was legally bimetallic, but at this rate gold was overvalued at the mint, so silver gradually disappeared from circulation.[9] Silver was demonetized in 1774 in recognition of the fact that only gold circulated in the United Kingdom.

In 1797, in the midst of the Napoleonic Wars, the British government suspended gold convertibility. The country remained off gold until 1821, and this "paper pound" period led to one of the most famous debates in the history of economics, the Bullionist Controversy. Inconvertibility had been accompanied by inflation in Britain, and discussion of the causes of inflation raged throughout the suspension. Of the position that prevailed in the parliamentary Bullion Committee report of 1810, David Laidler has written, "No other discussion of economic policy issues prepared by working politicians has had so sound an intellectual basis and has stood the test of time so well."[10] The report presaged much of modern monetary theory, pointing out that inconvertibility allowed the monetary authorities to increase the money supply at will and thus created the potential for inflation.[11] It similarly argued for a commitment to gold as a safeguard against such a danger. In other words, it recognized the trade-off between the ability of the government to affect monetary conditions and commitment to a fixed exchange rate.

At much the same time as Britain was going back to gold, France was settling into a stable bimetallic standard. The gold-silver rate was, in other words, set so that neither metal was overvalued relative to the other. In these conditions, bimetallism was consonant with the gold standard. The United States, after shifting the rates a bit in the search for balance, settled in the 1830s on a rate that essentially drove silver out of circulation and put the country on gold. Almost all other countries were on a monometallic silver standard.

Conditions were disturbed somewhat by California and Australia gold discoveries, which increased annual world gold production from about $36 million in the 1840s to about $119 million in the 1850s.[12] Countries solely on silver or gold were safe, but those on a bimetallic standard found gold increasingly overvalued at the previous mint price—the market price was dropping while the legal price remained the same. Most bimetallic countries, which tended to favor silver over gold, readjusted the gold-silver rate to avoid a *de facto* shift to gold; some demonetized gold.

In some ways, this experience can be taken as the starting point of our dynamic international story. By the 1850s, two things were clear.

First, the United Kingdom was irrevocably on the gold standard. Neither changing gold market conditions nor intermittent panics would shake the Bank of England's commitment to the general principles of the gold standard.[13] Second, the United Kingdom was the world's financial and commercial center. London had come to dominate international finance, shipping, and trade; the country as a whole was far and away the world's most important economy; and the pound sterling was becoming the vehicle currency for most international trade and payments.[14] This process was especially clear in the financial realm: after averaging £5.5 million a year in the 1830s and 1840s, British net foreign investment rose to £20 million a year in the 1850s and £37.2 million a year in the 1860s.[15]

The centrality of the British economy to the global economy, and unshakable British commitment to gold, exerted a gradually increasing pull on the rest of the world. The areas of recent settlement both in and out of the British Empire, which were tightly integrated into British trade and payments in this era, were early adherents to gold. They relied on London for almost all their foreign finance, and foreign finance was quite important to their economies (especially to the construction of a transportation infrastructure). Their all-important commodity exports also found their major market in London.

The rationale was straightforward. British importers and investors were more likely to sign contracts with countries whose currencies had stable values against sterling. The simplest way to signal such predictability was to go onto gold. British traders and financiers could (and often did) specify payment in sterling, but currency instability in the foreign country added an unnecessary risk to business transactions. From the standpoint of the foreign country's economic agents, of course, local currency movements were especially unsettling if contracts were in sterling: an unexpected fluctuation of the local currency could bankrupt a sterling debtor. For both reasons, those drawn into the British commercial and financial orbit had strong reasons to gravitate toward gold as well.

Germany was perhaps the single most important such case. From 1837 on the process of unification went hand in hand with movement toward currency union, largely around silver. However, internationally oriented financial and commercial interests after 1860 pressed continually for conversion to gold. This was facilitated after the country's victory over France in 1871, which led to a substantial French indemnity payment in gold. The resulting increase in the government's gold reserves allowed it to go onto gold with little difficulty between 1871 and 1873.

The French resisted longer. In 1865 France, Belgium, Switzerland,

and Italy created the Latin Monetary Union, which attempted to establish a stable bimetallic standard with realistic gold-silver rates. An international monetary conference convened at French initiative in 1867 attempted to arrive at internationally coordinated bimetallism, with no success. Indeed, only the French were enthusiastic about bimetallism per se; the other members of the union preferred going onto gold.

In the Latin Monetary Union as in other countries wavering between gold and bimetallism, the issue was forced after 1873, as silver dropped in price after major discoveries in the United States. Bimetallic countries were faced with either having to buy silver at an overvalued rate, thus driving gold out of monetary use, or engaging in another round of recalibrations of the gold-silver rate. The latter course seemed unstable, as silver continued to flood onto the market. The former course meant forgoing the use of gold as money at a time in which gold

was more and more important to international trade and payments. Virtually all countries chose gold over silver, commitment to the international regime over domestic policy independence.

By 1878 the members of the Latin Monetary Union had declared for gold. Meanwhile another international monetary conference, called at US initiative to try to salvage bimetallism, was a fiasco. Britain, Germany, Belgium, and Switzerland refused to go along, and while a few countries were sympathetic to the American position they did not represent a critical mass.[16] For Italy the issue was a bit contrived. In the face of chronic fiscal imbalances, the country went to inconvertibility in 1866 and did not go back to gold until 1884, only to go off again in 1894.

Italy was the exception. As Germany went to gold between 1871 and 1873, Sweden, Norway, and Denmark followed suit. With Britain and Germany accounting for the vast majority of their trade and payments, their way was clear. The three Scandinavian countries also formed a Scandinavian Monetary Union, which largely consisted of provisions to allow each country's currency to circulate freely in all three nations. By 1875 the Netherlands was *de facto* on gold, and in that year the United States (which had suspended convertibility during the Civil War) announced that it was going back to gold by 1879. In 1877 Finland, politically dependent upon Russia but economically similar to the Scandinavian countries, linked to gold.

Austria-Hungary and Russia had been on depreciated paper currencies since 1848 and 1839 respectively. As silver prices dropped, the paper currencies actually rose *above* their legal silver prices in the 1870s. In 1879 Austria-Hungary announced its intent to go to gold, which it achieved in 1892. In 1885 Russia went to bimetallism but was forced off silver and onto gold alone between 1893 and 1895. Even Japan went from bimetallism to gold in 1871, only to be forced off during a financial crisis in 1878. Fifteen years later the government declared its intention to go back to gold, and the process was assisted by a military victory over China in 1895 and the subsequent payment of a £39 million gold indemnity.

As this account indicates, the process exhibited much of the synergistic feedback expected. The incentives to go to a monometallic gold standard increased especially after international financial flows out of London became very large in the 1850s and 1860s. The issue was forced by the drop in the market price of silver over the course of the 1870s. German accession to the gold standard in 1871–1873 pulled Scandinavia, the Netherlands, and Finland along by 1877. Japan went to gold in 1871 and the U.S. in 1875, while Belgium, France, and Switzerland were officially monometallic by 1878. By this point, a precipitate seven-year rush toward gold had placed virtually every major trading and financial nation on earth on the gold standard. This would appear to be clear evidence of the upward spiral or feedback effect at the international level, in which each additional member (especially larger members) served in a dynamic way to attract further members of the regime until the gold standard was essentially universal among major nations.

The Rise and Reign of Gold:
Domestic-International Dynamics

The international dynamic described above relied upon a more nuanced domestic dynamic. Countries' choices to go on or off gold were made in the context of often bitter debates among groups in society that had vested interests for or against the fixed-rate standard. The contours of these distributional divisions were outlined above; in this section I discuss how international trends and national policies interacted to speed the rise and strengthen the reign of the classical gold standard.

Even in Britain, the gold standard was controversial at a crucial turning point. The debate over resumption after the end of the Napoleonic Wars was not just about economic theory; it involved economic interests. Those tied to international trade and investment, such as Dutch-Portuguese Jewish merchant and financier David Ricardo, were favorable to early resumption of specie convertibility at the preexisting rate. Those producing tradable manufactures, especially in and around Birmingham, were opposed. They wanted a depreciated currency, not the appreciated one resumption implied, even if this required staying on paper money.[17] City of London (financial and commercial) interests prevailed, an outcome that accords with recent arguments about the political power of the city against manufacturing.[18]

In Germany, the politics of gold was more complex. The powerful rye farming interests, the Junkers, were strong supporters of silver, which implied a relatively depreciated currency. A weak currency would raise the amount of German currency received per pound of rye exported, and the domestic price of imported grain. The Junkers were dismayed after 1871, when the German government sold off its monetary silver in order to go to a monometallic gold standard. Silver sales drew money out of circulation and tended to appreciate the gold mark, thus making German rye less competitive on world markets. Debates over silver raged in tandem with debates over trade protection.

Both issues were decided when, in 1879, Bismarck shifted toward protectionism. The Junkers had previously been indifferent to agricultural protection (as exporters) and hostile to industrial protection. Bismarck essentially cut a deal with Junker soft-money supporters. In return for their support for high levels of industrial *and* agricultural tariffs, Bismarck halted the selling of monetary silver, thus arresting the real appreciation of the mark. This sop to the silver interests was sufficient to win them to the side of protection, and it was mild enough not to threaten the German commitment to gold.[19] The Scandinavian countries were dominated by economic actors closely tied to the import-export trade and foreign finance; they strongly supported gold and were quickly triumphant.[20]

In some cases the domestic-international dynamic was most clearly operative when the gold standard came under domestic political challenge. In these circumstances, political conflict over gold tended to divide those strongly tied to international commercial and financial activities, who had an interest in affiliation with the system, from those who either were domestically oriented or wanted a depreciated exchange rate, who had an interest either in paper currency or in devaluation (usually both). In the parlance of the day, these two positions were commonly known as "hard money" and "soft money," respectively.[21]

By far the most important and striking example of the domestic-international dynamic was the United States. Although international trade and payments affected only small portions of the American economy in the late nineteenth century, groups tied to the foreign sector were powerful. American financial markets were in fact closely linked with those abroad, especially in London.[22]

Support for hard money came from Northeastern traders, bankers, and investors, and from most export-oriented manufacturers. Soft money, devaluation, and going off gold was preferred by farmers and manufacturers from the interior, whose markets were domestic and who worried primarily about the low domestic prices of their products. The division persisted throughout decades of conflict, which was exacerbated when international conditions made the preferences of either of the groups more intense—such as when the growth of British trade and finance increased the incentives for the internationalist groups to tie themselves to London, or when falling farm prices increased the desire of agricultural groups for a devaluation.

During the Civil War the United States went off gold as prices more than doubled under a paper currency ("greenback") standard. After the Civil War, the Treasury shrank the money supply to appreciate the dollar and move toward resumption of gold convertibility at the prewar rate. This real appreciation put severe pressure on tradables producers, especially manufacturers. The Greenback movement first developed as a response among the iron and steel manufacturers of Pennsylvania. They were the country's leading protectionists and recognized that devaluation cum reflation would reverse the relative price decline. This could only be accomplished if the country stayed off gold. The railroadmen concurred, as did investment bankers and others tied to these industries. Soft-money advocates worried little about the international credibility gold might bring, for they bought and sold next to nothing abroad. For them the world economy was a threat from which to be protected. As a Chicago merchant put it, "these gentlemen on the seaboard base all their calculations on gold, to bring them to par with foreign countries, leaving us in the West to take care of ourselves."[23]

Around 1873 two important groups were drawn into the soft-money camp. Farmers were originally indifferent, for farm prices held up quite well in the first years after the Civil War. However, the Panic of 1873 initiated a secular decline in farm prices. Like manufacturers, farmers recognized that devaluation would raise the domestic price of imported farm products and would raise farm prices relative to the prices of such nontradables as transportation and financial services.

The second important group brought into play after 1873 was silver miners. In 1873 silver was removed from circulation ("de-monetized"). As the price of silver declined relative to gold, miners and Greenbackers devised a common program to meet both their needs. If silver was "remonetized" at the old 16:1 rate against gold, the government would be forced to buy silver at well above the market rate. This would act as a subsidy to the miners; it would inject money into the economy as the government bought up silver; and it would force the country off gold and onto a de facto (and depreciated) silver standard. A powerful alliance of Midwestern manufacturers, farmers, associated nontradables producers, and miners opposed the return to gold under the banners of greenback issue and free silver.[24]

Supporters of gold were concentrated in the Northeast among the financial and commercial communities with strong ties to European trade and payments. As the New York Chamber of Commerce put it in complaining about the risk attached to a floating exchange rate: "Prudent men will not willingly embark their money or their merchandise in ventures to distant markets . . . with the possibility of a fall [in gold] ere their return can be brought to market."[25]

This fundamental disagreement caused bitter political battles. In April 1874 Congress passed an inflation bill by a wide margin. The vote on the bill, which mandated expansion of the supply of paper money, illustrated the overlap of economic and regional differences. Over 95% of northeastern congressmen opposed the bill, while over three quarters of congressmen from the agrarian South and the agrarian and industrial West (including Pennsylvania) supported it. Northeastern hard-money interests immediately mounted a furious campaign to overturn the bill. President Ulysses Grant came through with a veto, but this cost the Republicans the congressional elections of 1874.

After the Republican electoral debacle, Grant and Republican Party leaders attempted a display of party unity to salvage their chances for the 1876 presidential elections. In January 1875 they convinced lame duck Republicans to vote for the Resumption Act, mandating a return to gold on January 1, 1879.

In 1876 Republican Rutherford B. Hayes, a supporter of hard money, was elected. The new Congress remained dominated by soft-money interests, and one of its first acts in February 1877 was to pass the moderately silverite Bland-Allison Act; President Hayes's veto was easily overridden. However, in late 1877 an attempt to repeal the Resumption Act was barely defeated: it passed the House and failed by one vote in the Senate. Hayes's Treasury secretary, John Sherman, had in fact worked with Republicans and Democrats alike to find a compromise and had determined that Bland-Allison was the price of defeating repeal of the Resumption Act. Even so, Hayes was forced to wield the blunt instrument of patronage in order to gather enough votes to save the gold standard.[26]

In the meantime, some soft-money supporters became disgusted with the two major parties. They founded the Greenback Party, which stood strongly for devaluation and a flexible exchange rate. The party ran Peter Cooper for president in 1876, with little success, but did better in the 1878 congressional elections. However, by then Hayes and Sherman had traded for or bought enough votes in Congress to save resumption, and the country went back to gold at the beginning of 1879.

American commitment to its fixed rate against gold was relatively unquestioned during the 1880s. However, silver sentiment erupted amid the agricultural depression that began in 1888. Farm prices dropped precipitously, and—unlike in manufacturing—productivity advances were not sufficient to counteract this trend. Reflation and devaluation under the silverite banner would have mitigated the farm crisis, and farmers were well aware of this. The silver miners, for obvious reasons, continued to support silver monetization.

The most striking reflection of agrarian interests was the rise of Populism. In 1890 the Farmers' Alliance movement scored major electoral successes in the western states. In 1892 the People's (Populist) Party was formed by the southern and western alliances, along with labor groups; in that year the Populists got over a million votes for president and sent hundreds of legislators to state houses and Congress.

Devaluation cum inflation ranked at the top of the Populists' demands. They called for a paper money-silver standard, with the dollar fluctuating against gold. The Treasury would have been directed to regulate the money supply to avoid deflation. Gold clauses, tying contracts to the value of gold as a hedge against devaluation, would have been made illegal.[27]

In the opposing corner, northeastern commercial and financial interests remained at the core of the hard-money camp. The bankers' position had if anything hardened. World trade and payments were at their high point, and huge amounts of European money were flowing into the United States through New York. Indeed, many on Wall Street had come to hope that New York would soon be an international financial center, for which commitment to gold was a prerequisite.

Manufacturers were more receptive to hard-money arguments than they had been in the 1870s for three reasons. First, declining prices of manufactured products were more than compensated for by rapid productivity increases, so few manufacturers felt substantially disadvantaged by the real appreciation. Second, by the 1890s larger portions of American industry were internationally oriented: manufactured exports had expanded and foreign direct investment was increasing.[28] Third, the manufacturers' interest in the money question had become secondary to their concern to defend tariff protection, which was under attack from agricultural interests.

Republican Benjamin Harrison beat eastern Democrat and gold supporter Grover Cleveland in the 1888 election by promising support for silver. Harrison made good on his promise with the 1890 Sherman Silver Purchase Act. This doubled the amount of silver purchased by the Treasury under the Bland-Allison Act. The bill was too mild to satisfy antigold interests, and it was coupled with the prohibitive McKinley Tariff of 1890, which generated agrarian opposition. The result was that the Republicans lost the House in the 1890 midterm elections, then lost both chambers and the presidency to Cleveland in 1892.

The Democrats had run on a silverite platform, but Cleveland was known as a gold supporter—a "Gold Democrat" in contemporary parlance. In 1893 the country was hit by a severe panic, which the financial community blamed on uncertainty about commitment to the gold standard. Despite his party's platform, President Cleveland pushed Congress to repeal the Sherman Act. Cleveland allied with gold Republicans against the majority of his own party and, as Grant and Hayes before him, used patronage to bludgeon key Democrats into submission. This repudiation of soft money was responsible for the Democrats losing the 1894 midterm elections. In turn, the gold conservatives lost the battle for control of the Democratic Party to free silver supporters.

The 1896 election was fought largely over the gold standard. Democrats and Populists jointly fielded William Jennings Bryan, who ran against the "cross of gold" upon which, Bryan thundered, the country was being crucified. The Republicans, in response, cobbled together a hard money-high tariff coalition with presidential candidate William McKinley as the link. He had impeccable protectionist credentials, having designed the tariff of 1890; despite his long-standing support for silver, he switched to gold in 1896. This made the McKinley candidacy a peculiar coalition of hard-money eastern trading and financial interests and high-tariff Midwestern manufacturers. McKinley's striking reversal on gold lost him the western states' silver Republicans. However, once the election became a referendum on money, the Republicans became the conduit for millions of dollars in eastern business contributions to ensure the victory of gold.[29]

The narrow defeat of Bryan effectively sealed the fate of silver, and in any event antigold sentiment dampened over the next few years as economic conditions improved. In 1900 Congress passed the Gold Standard Act, Bryan was defeated a second time, and the country's commitment to the gold standard was firm.

The stories told until now might be read to indicate that the domestic order simply, albeit often slowly and painfully, validated national-welfare arguments for a decision to link to gold. This would be a mistake, as the decision was not always and everywhere taken. One fascinating example is that of Argentina.[30] The pampean country was economically and politically dominated by wheat farmers and cattle ranchers. In the 1870s a secular decline in farm prices began. In this context, farm producers clamored for a currency depreciation to increase their peso returns from declining sterling prices for wheat and beef. The dominant tradables producers, in other words, wanted a paper currency that could depreciate and compensate them (in peso terms) for the decline in the world prices of their goods. This they achieved in 1880, when Argentina went off gold and onto inconvertible paper money.

However, Argentina went back to gold in 1900 and stayed on until World War One. The reason for this is not hard to discover. In 1897 world prices of beef and wheat began to rise. This meant an increased inflow of foreign currency into Argentina, and a decline in its price relative to paper pesos—in other words, an appreciation of the paper peso. In these circumstances, farmers were receiving *fewer* pesos for every pound of beef or wheat exported. In response, they demanded that the exchange rate be fixed against gold at a depreciated rate—to avoid the real appreciation that would make their export earnings less valuable in peso terms. This they achieved in 1900. In other words, Argentine policy toward gold was purely and entirely a function of the interests of the beef and wheat producers: whatever exchange-rate policy would maximize their earnings was adopted—floating rates and depreciation as farm prices fell, a low fixed rate as farm prices rose.

The American episodes, along with the parallel Argentine experience, illustrate the dynamic interaction of international economic trends and the domestic politics of gold. As farm and silver prices dropped, farmers and silver producers pushed for the government to go off gold and onto a depreciated silver standard; in Argentina the demand was for a depreciated paper currency. However, internationally oriented trading and financial groups pressed for maintenance of the gold commitment in order to ensure their fullest possible participation in world trade and payments. For reasons that are far beyond the scope of this paper, in the United States gold won, while in Argentina gold lost until the interests of export-based farmers and ranchers shifted in the late 1890s.

The historical record, then, shows how the growth of the solidity and scope of the classical gold standard reinforced the gold sentiments of internationally oriented economic actors within national policy debates. However, increased international competition (especially the secular decline in farm prices) drove many others, primarily export-competing farmers, to desire a devaluation against gold. This sort of feedback mechanism is an important intermediate step in the growth of the gold standard. Indeed, the mechanism by which this feedback operated often ran through groups in domestic societies who saw their interests closely linked to national commitments to gold.

The Demise of Gold:
The Circle Becomes Vicious

The dynamic described here operated in reverse as the gold standard unraveled. This is analytically reassuring, for an explanation of how the presence of certain international and domestic factors can lead to the adoption and stability of an international fixed-rate regime should also predict that their absence would make such an outcome less likely. This is in fact what we observe in the interwar period; both the lack of an international focal point and the tenuous nature of domestic political support for international monetary cooperation made a return to the classical gold standard untenable.[31]

The failure to reconstitute the gold standard was not for lack of trying. Many international monetary conferences were held in the 1920s, but they were unable to arrive at the sort of commitment to gold—or anything else—that had evolved in the 1870s.[32] It is indeed ironic that the conferences of this era, which tended to take place and end with a show of unity of purpose, were accompanied by a weakening of international monetary cooperation and that the conferences of the 1860s and 1870s, which were failures, were accompanied by a continual increase in international monetary stability.

The causes of the interwar difficulties were, as expected, twofold. First was the lack of an international focal point: there was no stable commercial and financial core around which expectations could converge. No one country played the same crucial role in world trade and payments that Great Britain had in the 1860s and 1870s. The United States was arguably as important to the world economy in the 1920s as the UK had been in a previous epoch, but the US consistently refused to participate fully in international monetary affairs, which made it a most unsuitable leader.[33] Leadership might have been provided by an Anglo-French-German consortium, but the three countries were at loggerheads on a whole range of international economic and noneconomic issues, and such a consortium was most unlikely.

In the absence of a suitable focal point at the global level, the interwar gold standard was highly unstable. Most countries took years after the end of World War One to go back to gold; many cheated on the implicit "rules of the game"; and almost all went off gold when the Depression hit.

The international dynamic was reinforced by the second factor identified: the lack of domestic political support for a fixed-rate system. The domestic political environment had been altered by several circumstances. Many of those previously strongly committed to gold had lost influence with the collapse of the prewar system; and the Depression of the 1930s further reduced the sociopolitical clout of these groups. Even where, as in Great Britain, the financial and commercial sectors remained powerful, the weakness of the interwar gold standard tempered their commitment to it.[34] Elsewhere, the war and associated political developments had strengthened such groups as labor, which had far more interest in domestic economic growth than in links to the world economy.[35]

Domestic ambivalence about going back to gold made government commitments less than fully credible, even where gold convertibility was resumed rapidly.[36] And as the Depression hit, everyone from labor to import-competing manufacturers and farmers clamored for governments to go off gold. This clamor typically led to an abandonment of the gold standard in short order.

The result, on both counts, was a very weak interwar gold standard. The U.S. resumed convertibility in 1919, but it was not until 1928 that the major European countries were all on gold; Japan did not resume until December 1930. Almost as soon as the gold link was relatively widely established, the Depression brought it down: Great Britain, Germany, Scandinavia, most of Central and Eastern Europe, Canada, and Japan went off gold in 1931, while the United States waited until 1933.[37]

The tentative nature of the interwar monetary system, and its precipitous collapse under the strain of the Depression, illustrate the importance of the two dynamics discussed in relationship to the happier experience of the pre-World War One gold standard. The lack of a strong and visible international focal point around which national policies could converge weakened the interwar gold standard. Similarly, the tenuous nature of domestic political support for the economic policies necessary to a commitment to gold further weakened the system. Attempts to build, or rebuild, an international fixed-rate system need to take these two factors to heart.

Contemporary Implications:
The European Monetary System and Beyond

The most striking contemporary analogue to the classical gold standard is the ongoing process of European monetary integration.[38] From the late 1960s through 1979, the members of the European Community (EC) attempted to stabilize their currencies against each other. This attempt foundered for reasons similar to those discussed above. First, there was no clear focal point for the system—especially given continual jockeying for position between France and Germany. Second, domestic political forces were quite unfavorable to the loss of policy independence represented by fixed exchange rates within Europe. Most important, powerful groups in France and Italy opposed the austerity measures that would have been necessary to bring their inflation rates in line with those of Germany.

In 1979, the EC announced the formation of a European Monetary System (EMS) with an exchange-rate mechanism that would link member currencies together on a narrow band. Most commentators at the time expected the EMS to go the way of previous unsuccessful attempts at European monetary union. Indeed, in the early 1980s the system seemed shaky at best, experiencing frequent realignments. However, by 1985 the EMS was quite firmly in place, and despite subsequent disturbances it appears to have been the prelude to gradual movement toward a single EC currency.

This development recalls the movement toward gold in the 1870s. Indeed, the international and domestic dynamics present there also came to the fore in the EC of the 1980s. First, German predominance in European money and finance meant that the Deutschemark served as an anchor for the EMS. This led to some grumbling, especially from the French, but Germany's growing economic predominance within Europe made the mark a powerful focal point for other EC members. Second, domestic political conditions had changed since the 1970s. More and more economic agents had become heavily committed to EC trade and payments as the EC liberalized commercial and financial relations. Indeed, the commitment to a single market by the end of 1992 quickened the pace of monetary union by suggesting that firms from countries not linked to the EMS would be at a disadvantage—and might not even be able to participate fully in the reinvigorated European market. This strengthened the backbone of internationally oriented (especially European-wide) businesses and tended to erode the opposition of more domestically based groups in business and labor. The evolution of the system has indeed shown that German leadership and solid domestic support within member counties are crucial to the possibility of an ever-stronger EMS leading to a single European currency.

Although movement toward stable exchange rates is somewhat more advanced in Europe than elsewhere, there have been suggestions that EC experience might presage similar developments elsewhere. Members of the Group of Seven have discussed attempts to reduce exchange-rate volatility among their currencies for years, with little success. Bilateral talks over the dollar-yen relationship have also been very limited in their results. And discussions about the possibility of a currency union among Mexico, Canada, and the United States to accompany the North American Free Trade Area are only in the most embryonic of stages.

Early as it may be to look toward broader extensions of current European trends, there are reasons to expect the topic to continue to be important. Inasmuch as the discussion here is relevant, it implies that positive results depend on favorable international and domestic conditions. Internationally, there needs to be some nucleus around which coordination can be organized, whether this is one currency or a cooperative effort. Domestically, there needs to be support for the national economic policies to sustain a commitment to such a system, especially from groups strongly oriented toward the international economy. It is not hard to imagine scenarios in which these two factors are present, and so we cannot rule out some form of reconstituted fixed-rate international monetary system as the 1990s progress.

Conclusions

An international monetary system requires implicit or explicit agreement among member states about the characteristics and requirements of membership. This agreement in turn appears, both analytically and historically, to be more likely to ensue if two sets of dynamics are operative. First, at the international level, governments cohere best when there is a clear focal point around which their policies can converge. This process of cohesion is interactive inasmuch as the greater the number of countries that converge around the focal point, the stronger the focal point. Second, at the domestic level, governments are able to commit to convergence more successfully when they can muster domestic political support to sustain national policies required by the system in question.

Under the classical gold standard, both such dynamics were present. The United Kingdom so dominated world trade and investment that the incentives for other countries to gravitate toward Britain and its gold-backed currency were great, and they grew ever greater as more countries so gravitated. The extraordinary growth of world trade and payments in the nineteenth century greatly increased the size, wealth, and political power of those groups within national societies that stood to gain from being part of the gold standard. The greater the influence of these groups, the more likely their governments were to link to gold; the more governments linked to gold, the more rapid the growth of world trade and investment; the more the world economy grew, the stronger the incentives for groups in yet other countries became to press for *their* governments to go onto the gold standard; and so on.

A linked international and domestic dynamic drew more and more of the world onto the classical gold standard; the absence of this dynamic doomed the interwar gold standard to failure. An analogous process appears to account for the success so far of European monetary integration and may be relevant to broader attempts at building a new international monetary system.

Notes

The author acknowledges support form the Social Science Research Council's Program in Foreign Policy Studies and from the German Marshall Fund and comments from Barry Eichengreen, Giulio Gallarotti, Lisa Martin, Allan Rousso, and Tami Stukey.

1. For a related discussion of such considerations in general, see the articles in Stephen Krasner, Ed. *International Regimes* (Ithaca: Cornell University Press, 1983).

2. For more on this topic see my "Invested interests: The politics of national economic policies in a world of global finance," *International Organization* 45, No. 4 (Autumn 1991), pp. 425–451.

3. The two dimensions discussed here are similar to those that serve to orient Barry Eichengreen, *Golden Fetters* (New York: Oxford University Press, 1992). Eichengreen focuses on the twin pillars of cooperation and credibility. Cooperation, the collaborative efforts of national monetary authorities, is comparable to the inter-state component of my discussion. Credibility, the reliability of national commitments to cooperative ventures, is related to the domestic aspects of my discussion.

4. The principal divergence from "classical" gold rules was that both the United States and France were legally bimetallic. As will be discussed further on, this was not a problem until the gold-silver rate began to shift, especially in the 1870s. In other words, inasmuch as the gold-silver rate was stable, being on a bimetallic standard (as many countries were or came to be over the course of the early nineteenth century) was tantamount to being on gold. In this sense we can push the origins of the international gold standard back to the 1820s.

5. John M. Keynes, *The Economic Consequences of the Peace* (New York: Harcourt, Brace and Howe, 1920), pp. 11–12.

6. The best collection on the mechanism is *The Gold Standard in Theory and History* Ed. Barry Eichengreen (London: Methuen, 1985).

7. This ignores all of the fascinating complexities of the mechanism, such as slippage between gold reserves and currency issue and the role of capital movements. These are not important for our purposes. That at some level the rules operated as constraints is all that matters here. For the debates see Eichengreen, *The Gold Standard*; and *A Retrospective on the Classical Gold Standard, 1821–1931* Ed. Michael Bordo and Anna Schwartz (Chicago: University of Chicago Press, 1984).

8. This history is drawn especially from Marcello de Cecco, *Money and Empire: The International Gold Standard, 1890–1914* (Oxford: Basil Blackwell, 1974); R. G. Hawtrey, *The Gold Standard in Theory and Practice* (London: Longmans, Green, and Company, 1927); and Jacques Merten, *La naissance et le développement de l'étalon-or 1696–1922* (Louvain: Editions Warny, 1944). Other sources include the essays in Eichengreen, *The Gold Standard* and in Bordo and Schwartz, *A Retrospective*; Arthur Bloomfield, *Monetary Policy Under the International Gold Standard* (New York: Federal Reserve Bank of New York, 1959); and Charles Kindleberger, *A Financial History of Western Europe* (London: George Allen and Unwin, 1984), pp. 55–70. The facts are relatively uncontroversial, and specific citations will only be provided for specific quotations or somewhat more controversial data. For a perspective on the events that focuses especially on gold as a commitment mechanism, see Michael Bordo and Finn Kydland, "The Gold Standard as a Rule" (mimeo, 1991).

9. To clarify the process for those unfamiliar with it, where the mint price of a precious metal (the price the government offered) was below the market price, private agents would not bring the metal to the mint for coining but would instead sell it at the higher market price. Where the mint price was above the market price (as Newton's rate accomplished), gold would be brought in for coining. On a bimetallic standard, if the mint price of one metal is overvalued relative to the other, the undervalued metal will disappear from circulation. Both metals can be maintained in circulation if their mint prices are kept in line with market prices, which requires adjustments in the event of major discoveries of one or the other metal. This relationship was important in the latter part of the nineteenth century, discussed further on.

10. In *The New Palgrave*, under "Bullionist Controversy." The classic study of the process and its aftermath is Frank W. Fetter, *Development of British Monetary Orthodoxy 1797–1875* (Cambrdige: Harvard University Press, 1965).

11. On the actual experience, see Ian Duffy, "The Discount Policy of the Bank of England During the Suspension of Cash Payments, 1797–1821," *Economic History Review* 35 (February 1982), pp. 67–82.

12. Calculated from David Martin, "The Impact of Mid-Nineteenth Century Gold Depreciation Upon Western Monetary Standards," *Journal of European Economic History* 6 (Winter 1977), p. 643.

13. Ironically, this perception was probably reinforced by the Bank's issue of uncovered banknotes during the Panic of 1847, as this indicated that temporary quasi-suspension in times of dire crisis would not threaten long-term adherence to the rules of the game. Bordo and Kydland, "The Gold Standard as a Rule," discuss this use of a contingent rule. On this see also Rudiger Dornbusch and Jacob Frankel, "The Gold Standard and the Bank of the England in the Crisis of 1847," in Bordo and Schwartz, Eds., *A Retrospective*, pp. 233–264.

14. On the theory of which see Paul Krugman, "Vehicle Currencies and the Structure of International Exchange," *Journal of Money, Credit, and Banking* 12, No. 3 (August 1980), pp. 513–526. The rise of a vehicle currency is closely related to the development of an international monetary regime, of course.

15. Michael Edelstein, *Overseas Investment in the Age of High Imperialism* (New York: Columbia University Press, 1982), p. 21.

16. On these international episodes see Charles Kindleberger, "International Monetary Reform in the Nineteenth Century," in Richard Cooper, Peter Kenen, Jorge Braga de Macedo, and Jacques van Ypersele, Eds. *The International Monetary System Under Flexible Exchange Rates* (Cambridge: Ballinger, 1982), pp. 203–216.

17. Charles Kindleberger, "British Financial Reconstruction, 1815–22 and 1918–25," in Charles Kindleberger and Guido di Tella Eds., *Economics in the Long View* (London: Macmillan, 1982), pp. 105–120. See also Fetter, pp. 64–95.

18. See especially P.J. Cain and A.G. Hopkins, "The Political Economy of British Expansion Overseas, 1750–1915," *Economic History Review* 33, No. 4 (November 1980), pp. 463–490.

19. On the German case see Mertens, pp. 142–147; and Paul McGouldrick, "Operations of the German Central Bank and the Rules of the Game, 1879–1913," in Bordo and Schwartz, Eds., *A Retrospective*, pp. 311–349.

20. On which see Lars Jonung, "Swedish Experience under the Classical Gold Standard, 1873–1914," in Bordo and Schwartz, *A Retrospective*, pp. 361–399.

21. It should be noted that the dichotomous division masks nuances. It is possible to support a fixed but depreciated rate, for example. However, inasmuch as devaluation implied going off gold, preferences over the level of the exchange rate tended to coalesce with preferences over its flexibility. Soft-money advocates typically wanted both a flexible rate against gold (paper or silver currency) and a low (depreciated) rate; hard-money advocates typically wanted both a fixed rate and a high (appreciated) rate. For more on this see my "Invested Interests."

22. For a couple of representative studies, see Larry Neal, "Integration of International Capital Markets: Quantitative Evidence from the Eighteenth to Twentieth Centuries," *Journal of Economic History* 45, No. 2 (June 1985), pp. 219–226; and Lawrence Officer, "The Efficiency of the Dollar-Sterling Gold Standard, 1890–1908," *Journal of Political Economy* 94, No. 3 (1986), pp. 1038–1073.

23. Cited in Irwin Unger, *The Greenback Era: A Social and Political History*

of American Finance, 1865–1879 (Princeton: Princeton University Press, 1964), p. 157. See also James Kindahl, "Economic Factors in Specie Resumption in the United States, 1865–1879," *Journal of Political Economy* 69 (February 1961), pp. 30–48.

24. It is interesting in this context to note that Junker silver interests in Germany at the time wanted the government to stop selling off its monetary silver, while American silver interests wanted the government to buy up silver for monetary purposes. The results of course would have been parallel.

25. Cited in Unger, *The Greenback Era*, p. 151.

26. Unger, *The Greenback Era*, p. 371. Against the argument that resumption of gold payments at the pre-Civil war parity was economically or morally inevitable, we can cite a source above suspicion for its monetary responsibility: "Our own judgement in retrospect is that, given that a gold standard was to be reestablished, it would have been preferable to have resumed at a parity that gave a dollar-pound exchange rate somewhere between the pre-Civil War rate and the rate at the end of the war" (Milton Friedman and Anna Schwartz, *A Monetary History of the United States, 1867–1960* (Princeton: Princeton University Press, 1963, p. 82n). This would put Friedman and Schwartz somewhere between the moderate greenbackers and the strong silverites.

27. The classic study is John Hicks, *The Populist Revolt* (Minneapolis: University of Minnesota Press, 1931).

28. See David A. Lake, *Power, Protection, and Free Trade* (Ithaca: Cornell University Press, 1988), pp. 91–118, for a survey of American trade policy in this period.

29. How many millions is not clear; the formal audit showed $3.5 million, with $3 million from New York; the actual figure could have been twice or three times this. Herbert D. Croly, *Marcus Alonzo Hanna* (New York: Macmillan, 1912), p. 220. For details of these two episodes—Republican commitment to gold and reliance on corporate contributions—see pp. 192–204 and pp. 209–227.

30. The classic study of this is the masterful A.G. Ford, *The Gold Standard 1880–1914: Britain and Argentina* (Oxford: Clarendon Press, 1962), especially pp. 81–169.

31. This section draws heavily on Eichengreen, *Golden Fetters*, with which it shares a common analytical orientation as well.

32. See, for example, Stephen V.O. Clarke, *Central Bank Cooperation 1924–1931* (New York: Federal Reserve Bank of New York, 1967).

33. On American ambivalence in this period see my "Sectoral conflict and U.S. foreign economic policy, 1914–1940," *International Organization* 42, No. 1 (Winter 1988), pp. 59–90.

34. See, for example, Philip Williamson, "Financiers, The Gold Standard, and British Politics, 1925–1931," in *Businessmen and Politics* Ed. John Turner (London: Heinemann, 1984). Detailed studies of the British case are D. E. Moggridge, *British Monetary Policy 1924–1931: The Norman Conquest of $4.86* (Cambridge: Cambridge University Press, 1972); and Diane Kunz,

The Battle for Britain's Gold Standard in 1931 (London: Croom Helm, 1987).

35. A broad-gauged interpretation of changes at this level and their implications for post-World War Two economic agreements is John G. Ruggie, "International Regimes, Transactions, and Change: Embedded Liberalism in the Postwar Economic Order," *International Organization* 36 (Spring 1982), pp. 379–415.

36. This is one of the principal points of Eichengreen, *Golden Fetters*.

37. A good survey is Ben Bernanke and Harold James, "The Gold Standard, Deflation, and Financial Crisis in the Great Depression: An International Comparison," NBER Working Paper No. 3488, October 1990.

38. The literature on this topic is now so enormous that it even a brief survey would be inadequate. Two good places to start are, on the earlier experiences, Peter Ludlow, *The Making of the European Monetary System* (London: Butterworth, 1982); and, on the more recent record, Francesco Giavazzi and Alberto Giovannini, *Limiting exchange rate flexibility: The European Monetary System* (Cambridge: MIT Press, 1989).

7

Independence or Interdependence: Testing Resolve Reputation

Jonathan Mercer

Robert Jervis stresses in his chapter that failure to appreciate systemic effects often leads policy astray. An integral part of a system is interconnectedness. Jervis warns that decisionmakers often fail to recognize that events are connected or interdependent; this leads to simplistic and counterproductive policies. But the opposite is also true: policies may founder when decisionmakers assume an interdependence which does not exist.

For example, policymakers and deterrence theorists have long believed that states develop reputations for resolve. Using systems logic, they reason that how they behave in one area will be used by others to predict how they will behave elsewhere. This results in behaving resolute over trivial stakes to acquire a general reputation for being resolute. As Herman Kahn bluntly put it: U.S. security depends upon "a willingness to incur casualties in limited wars just to improve our bargaining position moderately."[1] Some soldiers must be sacrificed to create a reputation that can be exploited in later crises.

In this essay I argue that this reasoning is theoretically flawed and empirically unsubstantiated. Reputations do not form as easily as deterrence theory expects. Actors generally do not explain outcomes as a result of another state's or policymaker's character. When decisionmakers do infer a character trait of resolve or irresolve, this trait is not always used to explain or predict subsequent behavior. There also appears to be a difference between the way we explain our adversaries' and the way we explain our allies' behavior. By wrongly believing that reputations form easily, actors may find themselves trapped by a number of unintended and usually undesirable consequences. In viewing commitments as interdependent, and thus believing that our past behavior will be used to predict our future behavior, deterrence theorists illustrate the danger of bad systems theory.

I critique deterrence theorists' assumptions of reputation by examining how decisionmakers explained one another's behavior in the 1905–1906 Moroccan crisis and the 1908-1909 Bosnian crisis. These were part of the complex of crises that led to the maelstrom of 1914. Fluid alliance patterns, multipolarity, and the powerful force of hypernationalism characterized international politics at the beginning of the twentieth century. The close of this century may share many of these characteristics. By better understanding the connections between commitments that policymakers did and did not make, we may gain insight into how reputations form and design our policies accordingly.

Before beginning the case study, I present deterrence theory's assumptions about the interdependence of commitments and define a reputation for resolve. I then note some problems with deterrence theory's hypotheses on resolve and review the positions of several critics who also doubt the interdependence assumption in deterrence theory. I conclude with some speculative reasons for the fact that resolve reputations may not form as easily as expected by deterrence theory. I do not offer a full-blown theory or set of hypotheses to explain actors' explanations of each other's behavior in my case study. Instead, I aim to raise a flag of caution. While this book naturally focuses on the interconnections of complex systems, we must be careful not to see interdependence where *independence* may reign.

The Centrality of Resolve Reputation
to Deterrence Theory

The objective of deterrence is to convince a potential challenger that the costs and risks of a challenge outweigh its benefits. The defender needs to convince would-be challengers that it may defend its interests. In some areas this is easy. It is assumed that a state will defend its own territory, but it is less clear that it will defend someone else's. It is in the area of extended deterrence that deterrent threats may not be believed.

The Russians may not believe an American president when he warns that "an attack upon Munich is the same as an attack upon Chicago."[2] Credibility—defined as resolve plus capability—is inversely related to its cost: the more costly it is to implement a threat, the less likely it is to be implemented and therefore the less likely to be believed.[3] Successful deterrence depends on credibility, but credibility is difficult to establish. One of the most important ways to make incredible threats credible is by manipulating reputation.[4] However, before reputation can be manipulated, it must be perceived by others to exist, and it cannot exist unless commitments are interdependent. In other words, reputation must first exist as a fact before it can be used as a tool.

Deterrence theorists contend—and decisionmakers believe—that threats and promises are interdependent whether we like it or not. "The main reason why we are committed in many of these places," wrote Schelling, "is that our threats are interdependent. Essentially we tell the Soviets that we have to react here because, if we did not, they would not believe us when we say we will react there."[5] This will sometimes result in bloody fights not for the immediate stake but for saving and building a reputation. As a result, most disputes are not about the issue at hand but about expectations of future behavior: if we are weak now, they think we will be weak in the future, so we must be tough.[6] Because interdependence is generally considered a fact, decisionmakers are obligated to play by the logic of interdependence. This reasoning is similar to that found in the game of Chicken.

In the game of Chicken, the only thing more dangerous than acquiring a reputation as a chicken is attempting to fix that reputation. Although I swerved off the road last time, how can I convince my adversary that this time I really am serious? Such an image, wrote Jervis, "can be a handicap almost impossible to overcome."[7] An effort to get rid of a chicken image may result in a head-on collision, killing both parties. In international politics, as in the game of Chicken, it is not only desirable to have a reputation for resolve, it is essential to one's security. Dean Rusk captures this view:

> The integrity of the U.S. commitment is the principal pillar of peace throughout the world. If that commitment becomes unreliable, the communist world would draw conclusions that would lead to our ruin and almost certainly to a catastrophic war.[8]

Precisely because reputation is so important it can, like any other vital security interest, be manipulated to further diplomatic objectives. Reputation is thus believed to be not only a fact but also a tool.

The essential problem of deterrence is making one's threats and promises credible: "A potent means of commitment, and sometimes the only means, is the pledge of one's reputation."[9] A common way to show resolve in bargaining is to stake one's reputation on the outcome.[10] Another way to increase one's commitment is by establishing a reputation at lower levels of conflict for keeping one's commitments. In this case, a state will want to show resolve by either provoking a crisis or fighting a costly war over a minor issue in the "expectation of getting a 'free ride' on its resulting reputation."[11]

Deterrence means preventing certain events from happening; it is about the future. If commitments are interdependent, they strengthen deterrence by allowing one to suggest future behavior by present behavior. At the same time, they allow one to justify present behavior because one is creating expectations of future behavior. Without the fact of interdependence, the tool of reputation is unavailable and with it an important means of imparting credibility to threats which otherwise seem incredible.

Defining Resolve Reputation

A reputation is an assessment of character. What we think of our own character is a self-perception; what we think of another's character is a reputation. States may be given reputations, but they do not own them: a reputation is not the same as a self-image. As one observer remarked, "A man's reputation is not a quality that he possesses, but rather the opinions which other people have about him."[12] Another way to examine this point uses David Baldwin's distinction between "property" and "relational" concepts. A property concept can be defined and measured without reference to another state. A relational concept refers to "an actual or potential relationship between two or more actors." Here are some pairs of property and relational concepts: foreign policy and international politics, lever and leverage, policy and power, intentions and capabilities.[13]

For example, credibility is a relational concept. It implies the existence of other actors. Whether a threat or promise is credible depends entirely on the perceptions of others. It makes no more sense to speak of inherent credibility than it does to speak of inherent leverage, inherent power, or inherent capability. Nonetheless, it is commonplace to refer to inherent credibility.[14]

Reputation is also a relational concept. One would not say, "Chuck possesses his reputation for being a bully"; rather, one would say, "People have given Chuck this reputation," or "Chuck believes he has a reputation for being a bully." Nonetheless, reputation is usually thought of as a property concept.

For example, Schelling contends that "Soviet expectations about the behavior of the United States are one of the most valuable assets we possess in world affairs." William Kaufmann, referring to recent U.S. behavior, notes: "This then is the record—the credit, as it were—

that we have at our disposal in making credible any policy of deterrence." Glenn Snyder and Paul Diesing make the same mistake: "As 'resolve credit' with adversaries can be earned and 'banked' by repeated instances of firmness, so 'loyalty credit' with present or potential allies can be generated and drawn upon in the future by repeated demonstrations of support."[15]

This is no mere semantic quibble. Treating reputation as a property concept leads scholars and decisionmakers to think of it as a tool which can be readily controlled and manipulated. It fosters the misconception that others view our reputation as we do. If we understand that reputation is a relational concept, then it becomes obvious why we must study others' perceptions to understand our reputation. To the extent that state B may think about A's reputation, such thinking is done from B's perspective, and B may have very different concerns and interests than does A.

Explaining others' behavior as a consequence of their character is necessary but may not be sufficient for a reputation to form. A decisionmaker must first use another's character to explain behavior and then infer that the actor will behave similarly in the future. Perceptions must be interdependent. For example, in the Bosnian crisis the Russians would have had a reputation for lacking resolve only if the Germans believed St. Petersburg yielded in 1909 because it was irresolute *and* if Berlin later used this explanation to explain or predict Russian behavior.

A resolve reputation consists of character judgments that are later used to explain or predict behavior. Without a character judgment, there can be no interdependence, and a resolve reputation may not form.

Problems with Deterrence Theory's
Interdependence Assumption

There are three problems with the interdependence assumption in deterrence theory. The first problem is methodological. Deterrence theory's assumption that commitments are interdependent results in indeterminate predictions. How should decisionmakers explain a state that is first resolute then irresolute, or first irresolute then resolute? Which behavior reflects its "true" character? One proposed solution adds "effort" into the calculation.[16] A state that tries but fails gets credit for effort and may be viewed as resolute. But what happens when a state does not try in one crisis but tries in the next? Should it be viewed as resolute or irresolute? Regardless, the addition of effort makes deterrence hypotheses on resolve unfalsifiable: a state that tries is one that does not get a reputation for irresolve. It might be possible to determine effort independent of other states' perceptions, though it would be difficult and would still be indeterminate. In this essay I make deterrence's resolve hypothesis falsifiable by simplifying it: a state that yields should be viewed as irresolute, and a state that stands firm should be viewed as resolute.

The second problem with the interdependence assumption on resolve is theoretical. There are no theoretical reasons for policymakers basing their estimation of another's resolve on past behavior.[17] The game of Chicken illustrates some of the logic behind the resolve hypotheses[18] but does not explain the relationship between the independent and dependent variables: past behavior and perception.

Deterrence theorists generally assume that to back down in one crisis means the vanquished acquires a reputation for lacking resolve and the victor a reputation for resolve. For example, Glenn Snyder stresses the consequences of repeated plays of Chicken: "to yield on one occasion . . . creates an expectation that one will yield again on future occasions, which will encourage 'toughness' in the adversary and put oneself at a disadvantage in future plays."[19] He qualifies this assumption by noting that the defeated state may become resolved to resist any future challenges because of its earlier retreat. Russia and Austria in 1914 are typically used to illustrate the "never again" phenomenon: the Russians vowed to stand firm in part because of their past retreats, but the Austrians assumed the Russians would yield as they had before.

While this is a sensible interpretation of potential consequences from repeated plays of Chicken, it is equally plausible that the victor in the first Chicken game will fear that the defeated state will vow "never again"; as a result, the victor may expect the loser to be resolute in the next crisis. Although this game is usually invoked to show the dangers of capitulation, it could just as easily be invoked to show the dangers of winning: beware a state that is defeated, for it will seek revenge. The victor could assume that the vanquished will be more, not less, resolute in the future and will seek to avenge its earlier defeat.

When deterrence theorists recognize the possibility of the "never again" reaction, they nevertheless contend that the victorious state blithely assumes its defeated adversary will not seek revenge. By doing so, deterrence theorists tap only part of the logic of Chicken. The game of Chicken has no dominant strategy and no determinate outcome. Since defeat may result in a reputation for either resolution or irresolution, it provides a shaky foundation on which to build assumptions about resolve.

Only a reckless or extremely motivated actor would assume that because a state was irresolute once, it would be similarly irresolute in the future. Given deterrence's counterintuitive interdependence assumptions about resolve, it is all the more important that these assumptions have sound theoretical support.[20]

The third problem is empirical. Despite its importance to deterrence, there is little empirical evidence on the interdependence of commitments and thus on reputation. For example, Glenn Snyder and Paul Diesing found only one instance where a decisionmaker believed another state had a particular kind of reputation; they therefore concluded that "statesmen are apparently overly concerned about resolve reputation."[21] They speculate that resolve reputation may be acquired or lost in specific geographic regions or on a group of related issues. But a 1984 study by Paul Huth and Bruce Russett found that past behavior had no impact on the outcome of crises. Their more recent studies suggest that Snyder and Diesing were on the right track: Huth and Russett found that the defender's past behavior and reputation are important only when the two combatants have a continuing rivalry with prior confrontations.[22] These later works suggest that A's past behavior toward B, C, and D is irrelevant to E, who infers A's future behavior only from A's past behavior toward E.

In a more recent empirical study, Huth found that if A retreats from B's challenge in one crisis, this often results in another challenge by B in a subsequent crisis.[23] However, Huth also found that if A defeats B's challenge in one crisis, this often results in another challenge by B in the next crisis. The only way to prevent another challenge by B is to end the crisis in stalemate. If a history of either prevailing *or* backing down will prompt a challenge, then a state's reputation cannot be the cause of these outcomes.

Ted Hopf's work also casts doubt on deterrence theory's interdependence assumption. In an exhaustive study of Soviet perceptions from 1965 to 1989, Hopf found that Soviet decisionmakers continued to view the United States as a highly credible adversary even after U.S. defeats in the Third World. The Soviets reasoned that the United States would continue to respond vigorously to roll back Soviet gains.[24]

In the next section, I provide background to the Moroccan and Bosnian crises. I then use the cases to illustrate three central points about reputation. First, I demonstrate that decisionmakers often differ significantly in how they explain one another's behavior. This shows that states may acquire different reputations with different states for the same behavior. Second, I examine the tendency to confuse self-perceptions with reputation. This reinforces the argument that reputation is a relational, not a property, concept. Third, I show that past demonstrations of resolve (or irresolve) may not translate into expectations of future resolve (or irresolve). This undermines further the interdependence assumption in deterrence theory.

Background to the 1905–1906 Moroccan and 1908–1909 Bosnian Crises

"If Russia keeps her hands free in Europe and if I conclude my agreements with England, Italy and Spain, you will see Morocco fall into our garden like ripe fruit."[25] The French foreign minister, Théophile Delcassé, was right; Morocco did wind up in the French garden, but only partially and only after a bruising diplomatic campaign. The French planned to strengthen their position on the continent and obtain a chunk of North Africa through a series of colonial agreements with Italy, Spain, and England. But the Germans were not willing to allow France to control Morocco as England controlled Egypt. Out of concern for Germany's reputation and to strengthen its international position, Chancellor Bernard Bülow sent Kaiser Wilhelm in 1905 to Tangier to demonstrate German interest in Morocco. "Under the circumstances," said Bülow, "Your Majesty may await the outcome of the Moroccan question with a quiet mind."[26]

Both sides confidently executed their plans; the issues at hand were minor. But what at first appeared to be a trivial colonial dispute quickly spiraled into a major confrontation which had little to do with Morocco, and much to do with the future. The architect of Germany's Moroccan policy, Baron Friedrich von Holstein, was mainly concerned with Germany's reputation:

> Not only for material reasons, but even more to preserve her prestige, Germany must oppose the intended annexation of Morocco by France. . . . But if we now allow our feet to be stepped on in Morocco without a protest we simply encourage others to do the same somewhere else.[27]

Although the apparent stakes in the Moroccan crisis concerned German political and economic rights in Morocco, the real stakes, as the parties perceived them, concerned future deterrence (or reputation) and the future configuration of international alliances.

The crisis has two stages: the German victory in ousting Delcassé and the subsequent French victory over the Germans at the Algeciras Conference. The French cabinet feared that Delcassé's policy would lead to a disastrous war. In secret negotiations with Berlin, the French prime minister, Maurice Rouvier, offered Delcassé's removal from office for a peaceful resolution to the crisis.[28] By forcing the resignation of the French foreign minister, the Germans won a diplomatic battle and the French were humiliated.

The Germans were not satisfied. In the second stage of the crisis, Berlin demanded a conference to settle the dispute, which was eventually held at Algeciras. This was the first showdown between the Triple Alliance of Austria, Germany, and Italy, and what was shortly to become the Triple Entente of France, England, and Russia. Despite the superior capability of the Austro-German bloc, they yielded before the Triple Entente. Over German protests, the French secured most of their objectives in Morocco.

Two years later Europe was again in crisis, this time over the Austrian effort at formal annexation of Bosnia and Herzegovina, which they had occupied since 1878. In 1908, the Austrian foreign minister, Alois Aehrenthal, decided to annex these two provinces. In a limited gambit to ensure Austrian security, Vienna intended to annex Bosnia and Herzegovina and support the independence of Bulgaria. This would be a blow to the Serb dream of a Greater Serbia, which was a threat to the territorial integrity of the Austrian monarchy.[29]

The Russian foreign minister, Alexander Izvolsky, sought to profit by the Austrians' intent to annex Bosnia. In exchange for his promise to support the annexation, Izvolsky obtained an Austrian promise to support Russian ambitions in the Straits.

The announcement of the Austrian annexation of Bosnia and the simultaneous announcement of Bulgarian independence created a sensation in Europe. Izvolsky repudiated his agreement and denied complicity. The Russians, supported by the French and British, challenged the Austrians, who were supported by the Germans. Whereas the British and French offered St. Petersburg only diplomatic support, the Germans gave Vienna a blank check.

The Austrians, backed by Germany, pressed the Russians to force Serbia to abandon its hope of territorial aggrandizement and to accept the annexation of Bosnia and Herzegovina without compensation. The Russians delayed. At the end of March 1909, the Germans delivered a note to the Russians—some say an ultimatum—demanding that the Russians accept the Austrian proposals or risk war. Izvolsky yielded to the demand and the crisis ended.

The Russians were humiliated, the Austrians and Germans triumphant. While the British gave only diplomatic support and the French barely that, the Austrians obtained a blank check from their German ally. Following the Triple Entente's victory in the Moroccan crisis, the Triple Alliance now tied the score.

People Explain Behavior Differently

Deterrence theory is wrong to assume that resolute behavior will always be interpreted as showing resolve, or that apparent irresolute behavior will be viewed as revealing irresolution. People often explain the same behavior differently. Simply put, we may have as many reputations as there are observers. In both the Moroccan and Bosnian crises, the British and Germans differed fundamentally in how they explained their allies' and adversaries' behavior.

Contrasting British and German Views of the French in Morocco. In the Moroccan crisis, the British and Germans viewed French behavior differently. Most key British decisionmakers believed French irresolution explained Delcassé's resignation. Lansdowne, the British foreign minister, thought the resignation "disgusting."[30] To his ambassador in Paris he wrote:

> Delcassé's resignation has, as you may well suppose, produced a very painful impression here. What people say is that if one of our Ministers had a dead set made at him by a foreign Power the country and the Government would not only have stood by him but probably have supported him more vigorously than ever, whereas France has apparently thrown Delcassé overboard in a mere fit of panic. Of course the result is that the "entente" is quoted at a much lower price than it was a fortnight ago.[31]

Lansdowne later complained: "Recent events have, I am afraid, undoubtedly shaken people's confidence in the steadfastness of the French nation."[32] Like Lansdowne, British prime minister Arthur Balfour thought the French "could no longer be trusted not to yield to threats at the critical moment of a negotiation."[33] The ouster of Delcassé led Lansdowne and Balfour to think the French were irresolute.

After the French/British victory at Algeciras, the British were pleased that the French stood firm against the Germans. Indeed, the new British foreign minister, Edward Grey, recalled Delcassé's resignation differently than his predecessor: "After their attempt to be civil to Germany last year by discarding Delcassé they cannot be expected to make advances again till it is clear that German policy has changed."[34] And much later, in his memoirs, Grey wrote:

> It was in the preceding months in 1905 that France had consented, under German pressure, to the humiliation of dismissing M. Delcassé. She had felt compelled to consent because the German armaments were so much more ready for war than her own. The German pressure left her no option but to bring her own forces and equipment up to date.[35]

It is not that the French lacked resolve in dismissing Delcassé; they were merely being "civil" to the demanding Germans.

The Germans explained Delcassé's resignation differently than did the British. We might expect the Germans to view Prime Minister Rouvier and his colleagues as wholly lacking in resolve: the French had given in to German threats and Rouvier had negotiated Delcassé's dismissal. Contrary to the expectations of deterrence theory, Berlin did not view Rouvier as irresolute; they thought the whole affair was Delcassé's fault. Had he not followed his foolish, anti-German, "stormy and brutal" policy, relations between France and Germany would be wonderful.[36] Now that the unreasonable Delcassé was gone, good relations with Rouvier and France were possible. The day after Delcassé's resignation, Holstein wrote to a colleague that the problem between the two countries was "now a matter of form; for we don't want to upset France's future." Both Holstein and Chancellor Bülow held Delcassé responsible for the lamentable state of French-German relations.[37]

Rouvier now sought bilateral talks to end the crisis, but Bülow felt that a conference had to be held.[38] The Germans continued to demand a conference to settle Moroccan affairs. Rouvier—like Delcassé— refused. Rouvier was puzzled that the Germans refused to settle now that Delcass was gone, and the Germans were puzzled that Rouvier should adopt the Delcassé program. German explanations of Rouvier's behavior began to change when he assumed an increasingly uncompromising position—but they did not change in the direction that deterrence theory would expect.

As Rouvier continued to refuse any concessions to the Germans, they began to speak of him in disparaging terms. Rouvier thought that Holstein had to be a weak man because he submitted to Delcassé's policy, which subverted France's and Rouvier's position:

> It is definitely a great weakness of Rouvier's and shows a lack of logical reflection that he has not realized how, by adopting the Delcassé program, he is helping Delcassé back to his feet, the man who is now probably his worst enemy. . . . I still have the hope that Rouvier will come to his senses before it is too late and adopt a reasonable policy again instead of wrapping himself in the prophet's cloak of Delcassé.[39]

And later, Holstein wrote that Rouvier "is really a weak man and allows himself to be terrorized by the Delcassé group."[40] "However, who knows?" wrote Holstein, "Perhaps a few sensible people may yet be found in France."[41]

The German and British views of French resolve were inversely related. The Germans viewed Delcassé's policy as reckless and foolish, placing both Rouvier and Germany in a difficult situation. Rouvier did France a great service by removing him. This was statesmanship. In contrast, the British thought Delcasse's course best and Rouvier and his colleagues unreliable and irresolute. The German view changed with Rouvier's refusal to meet the "legitimate" German demands. They began to view Rouvier as a weak and duplicitous man. Indeed, when Rouvier showed the greatest resolve, he was reviled by the German leadership and held in contempt as a weak man. In contrast, the British praised French policy for holding firm against the German assault.

The View of Russia's Defeat in the Bosnian Crisis from Berlin, Vienna, and London. There is a similar split in explanations for the Russian defeat in the Bosnian crisis. While the Germans and Austrians viewed the Russian capitulation as sensible given the situation, the British thought it reflected Russian irresolution.

The Germans were pleased with their solution to the Bosnian crisis. Acting Secretary of State Alfred Kiderlen, Chief of the General Staff Hellmuth Moltke, and Chancellor Bülow all used transient and context-specific reasons to explain the Russian capitulation.

Kiderlen took great pride in the démarche he drafted and sent to St. Petersburg that resulted in their retreat: "I knew that the Russians were not ready for war, that they could not go to war in any case, and I wanted to make what capital I could out of this knowledge."[42] Kiderlen reported to the Austrians that he intended with the démarche "to press Izvolsky to the wall and expedite a clear and precise answer."[43] Kiderlen's views accord with those of Moltke. Moltke reported to Franz Conrad von Hötzendorff, his Austrian counterpart:

> Your Excellency, let us look into the future with confidence. As long as Austria and Germany stand shoulder to shoulder . . . we shall be strong enough to blast any ring [around us]. Many will break their teeth [trying to crack] this Central European bloc.[44]

Their adversaries were not irresolute. They would try again to break Austro-German power. But the chance for war had been missed; the entente was growing stronger by the day. The Bosnian crisis, continued Moltke, had offered an opportunity for war "which will not come so soon again under such propitious circumstances." The Triple entente lacked capability, not resolve. The favorable situation of 1909 might not again appear.

Bülow appears to have viewed the event similarly. In his farewell address to the kaiser, Bülow claims to have offered the following advice:

> "Don't repeat the Bosnian business." His Majesty (mistrustfully): "That was a triumph for you." Myself: "Situations in foreign policy seldom repeat themselves. Last winter we had a set of circumstance which will probably never be so favorable to us again."[45]

Bülow's memory may have been "helped" by later events. Nonetheless, it does fit with the contemporary view of his chief of staff. Bülow probably believed that his Bosnian victory was a vindication of his tactics and the military buildup he oversaw. Elsewhere in his memoirs and in spite of 1914, he thought that "by means of our strength as a Continental Power, we tore the web which encompassed us."[46] Again, he used German capability, rather than Russian irresolve, to explain the Austro-German victory.

Like their German ally, the Austrians explained their victory as a product of a unique situation. According to G.P. Gooch, Austrian foreign minister Aehrenthal offered situational explanations for the Austrian victory in a dispatch to Leopold Berchtold:

> The failure of Russian policy, first in the Far East, then in the Near East, was due to a misreading of the real situation by her rulers. Perhaps a more realistic course might now be adopted, virtually involving a return to the policy of the Three Emperors' League.[47]

The Russians were not irresolute, they simply misread the situation. The Russian defeat should awaken the Russians to pursue the "more realistic" course which Aehrenthal had advocated for years: a return to the conservative triumvirate of the Dreikaiserbund.

The Austrian chief of staff, Conrad, believed a great opportunity had been missed. Sooner or later, war would erupt in the Balkans. He reasoned better war now, when Russia was weak, than "before she regained her strength."[48] Austro-German capability had been responsible for the victory, not Russian irresolve.

Unlike their German and Austrian adversaries, British decisionmakers condemned unanimously Izvolsky's capitulation. The permanent under secretary of state, Charles Hardinge, thought "Izvolsky's capitulation . . . is really too deplorable!" To prevent another such rebuff, Hardinge thought it "absolutely necessary to find a new Minister for Foreign Affairs, who shall be endowed with such character and qualities as Monsieur Stolypin possesses. This is, however, not an easy thing to find in Russia."[49] Apparently, not only was Izvolsky irresolute and "not a statesman"[50] but so were most of the decisionmakers in Russia. Like Hardinge, the British ambassador to St. Petersburg, Arthur Nicolson, was "astonished that the Russian Gov[ernmen]t had capitulated with such promptitude and so completely" and regretted Stolypin's absence. "I wish," Nicolson continued, "that Izvolsky and his colleagues had stiffened their backs."[51] He thought they had exaggerated the danger.

As Germany and Britain had different views of French behavior in the Moroccan crisis, Berlin and London had different assessments of Russian behavior in the Bosnian crisis. Whereas the Germans (and Austrians) felt the Russians had no choice but to yield, the British believed the Russians had a choice: their failure to stand firm reflected Russian irresolution.

Confusing Self-Perception with Reputation

The deterrence theory assumption that people explain the same behavior similarly leads directly to the error of confusing our self-perception with our reputation. Our reputation is what others think of us, not what we think of ourselves. Nonetheless, British and German decisionmakers repeatedly make this mistake.

German Self-Perceptions and the British View of Germany. Holstein believed the kaiser's irresolution was responsible for Germany's Algeciras defeat: "I ought to have realized that it would be difficult to make Bülow, and impossible to make his Majesty, resolve on the last resort."[52] Holstein feared that in time, "it will be noticed abroad that His Majesty gives in to strong pressure."[53] Because Holstein believed that German irresolution explained the German defeat, he assumed that others viewed German behavior similarly; he became certain that Germany had acquired a reputation for being irresolute. He believed that all the other countries stood firm "because they hoped . . . that Germany would lose her nerve. Therein lies the danger. This same method will be used again."[54]

British policymakers did not think the Germans were irresolute. In spite of their belief that the balance of capability favored Germany,[55] I did not find any British decisionmakers suggesting that the Germans lacked resolve. If anything, they had the opposite view: the Germans were a threat and would continue to be one. I discuss this further in the section on the indeterminacy of past behavior.

In general, Grey did not understand what the German problem was. There was no reason for Germany to fear Britain; once Germany recognized this, good relations were possible: "All that is necessary is for the Germans to realize that they have got nothing to complain of."[56] Grey continued to view the Germans as a menace and their claims as unjust. This did not, however, translate into a view that the Germans lacked resolve.

Grey's views were common among his Foreign Ministry colleagues. For example, reporting on the aftermath of the Algeciras defeat, the British ambassador to Berlin observed, "it is evident that the idea that Herr von Holstein had been made the scape-goat for the recent failure of German Diplomacy is not without foundation".[57] The Germans might be incompetent in diplomacy, but they were not weak-willed.

British Self-Perceptions After Algeciras. What was salient to British decisionmakers was not the German defeat but the British victory. Just as the German leaders thought Germany irresolute for their Algeciras defeat, so the British thought England had demonstrated resolve at Algeciras, not that the Germans had shown a lack of it. Eyre Crowe, an influential civil servant in the British Foreign Office, illustrates this tendency to assume that one's own state has a particular reputation while in the same breath not giving the defeated state a reputation for lacking resolve.

In his famous memorandum, Crowe argued that the Germans challenged France because of a German perception that England lacked resolve:

> [England's] reluctance for extreme measures, even under severe provocation, had only recently been tested on the occasion of the Dogger Bank incident. It was considered practically certain that she would shrink from lending armed assistance to France.[58]

The Germans challenged because they believed that England was irresolute.

Crowe's belief that the German challenge was inspired by British irresolution was wrong. First, the Germans believed the British would not oppose their challenge, not cravenly surrender to it.[59] Second, there is no evidence that the Dogger Bank episode entered into German calculations of their Moroccan challenge.[60] The Germans did seek to exploit the episode by cashing in on Russian hostility toward Britain and thereby bring the Russians into the German orbit. The policy failed and they blamed Delcassé since he mediated the dispute. British resolve was never an issue with the Germans in the Dogger Bank affair.

Nonetheless, Crowe believed Britain had an image problem. The history of Anglo-German relations was one of "entirely one-sided aggressiveness" met by British "concession after concession."

Somewhat like a "professional blackmailer," the Germans kept exploiting the British because they knew England lacked resolve. After Algeciras, everything was different:

> The events connected with the Algeciras conference appear to have had on the German Government the effect of an unexpected revelation, clearly showing indication of a new spirit in which England proposes to regulate her own conduct towards France on the one hand and to Germany on the other. . . . The time which has since elapsed has, no doubt, been short. But . . . there is an impression that Germany will think twice before she now gives rise to any fresh disagreement.[61]

Because German behavior was thought to be a consequence of a British reputation for lacking resolve, a change in Britain's reputation should have meant a change in German behavior. Like a cold splash of water, the British Moroccan victory would change the German image of England and result in more peaceful relations.

Just as Crowe believed German aggression in Morocco was driven by England's reputation for irresolution, Holstein believed Germany's unblinking support for its Austrian ally in the Bosnian crisis would shake the entente from its alleged belief in German irresolution. After urging Bülow to inform the Austrians (and the world) of total German support for Vienna in the Bosnian crisis, Holstein added: "This cold bucket of water should put a quick end to the most recent concentric bluff probably inspired by King Edward, because no one wants war."[62]

As shown above, Holstein's and Crowe's expectations—and those of deterrence theory—were wrong. Because people often view the same event differently, our reputation may be different than our self-perception. At the Algeciras Conference, Crowe saw British resolve, Holstein saw German irresolve, and neither would have believed the views of the other. Just as the British stance at Algeciras failed to elicit from Holstein an attribution for resolve, so the German retreat at Algeciras failed to elicit from Crowe an attribution for irresolve. Each focused on what was most salient to himself. In this case, Crowe had no reason for his optimism and Holstein no reason for his pessimism. In determining our reputation, what we think of ourselves is irrelevant; only what others think about us counts.

The Indeterminacy of Past Behavior

Past behavior may either not be used as a guide to future behavior, or be used to predict that a state will behave differently in the future than it did in the past. In either case, the assumption that policymakers infer that a state will behave in the future as it did in the past is not sustained in this case.

As noted above, the Germans were confused. They assumed their adversaries shared the view from Berlin that Germany had been irresolute and therefore had a reputation for being irresolute. The danger, they thought, was not only that Germany would now be challenged more often than before but that Germany would no longer be believed when it intended to stand firm. Discussing an issue unrelated to the Moroccan crisis, Holstein warned:

> But to tamper with our land army, that would be the beginning of the end. Yet to stand firm on this question will be more dangerous than on Morocco—*simply because of the fact that people no longer believe we will do so.*[63]

This quote illustrates what is assumed to be the essential problem with bluffing in an iterated game of Chicken.

Far from believing the Germans were irresolute, the British assumed the Germans would challenge again. Even Crowe, who had first thought the British Algeciras victory would force the Germans to recognize British resolution, believed the Germans would continue with their aggressive policies. For example, when the Germans began in September 1908 to resist France's gradual takeover of Morocco, the first Moroccan crisis flashed before Crowe's eyes: "We are face to face with a situation resembling that which preceded the fall of M. Delcassé, and we may expect the beginning of another dose of bullying administered to the French gov[ernmen]t."[64] It seemed likely to Crowe that Bülow would launch "another bullying campaign intended to frighten and cow France into a yielding mood."[65]

Turning Holstein's fears on their head, Crowe reasoned that Germany was more resolved because of its Algeciras defeat:

> We know of the existence of a strong and pent-up feeling of rage in Germany at the want of success she has lately had in the domain of foreign policy. . . . If an "untoward event" were to occur anywhere, it should be remembered that the present is the very time when Germany is most ready for an armed adventure.[66]

The problem was not, as Holstein feared, that the British thought the Germans irresolute but that British decisionmakers believed Germany resolved to avenge its earlier diplomatic defeats. Rather than assuming the Germans would yield again, they assumed the Germans would vow "never again!" and would challenge the entente powers in the same geographical area, over a similar issue, and in the same way.

There is an additional twist on deterrence theory's assumption that decisionmakers use another's past behavior to predict the same behavior in a different crisis. Rather than thinking the British and French were unlikely to bluff in the future because they had demonstrated great resolve, the Germans thought just the opposite: French and British decisionmakers were *more* likely to bluff because they now ostensibly thought that the *Germans* lacked resolve. After the German defeat at Algeciras, Holstein wrote: "More than ever we are being subject to bluff, but no one will push things to extremes."[67] In another memo to Bülow, Holstein warned:

> At Algeciras Germany gave in before collective pressure. If she now allows concessions to be pressured out of her in the Triple Alliance question, then the pressure system will have proved its worth a second time, and will then be used more often and will lead us gradually step by step to a revision of the Peace of Frankfurt. King Edward and Clemenceau are probably already agreed about this final goal, but they want to reach it by peaceful means. . . . *Menacer souvent, frapper rarement* [threaten often, strike seldom] was the advice Marshal Marmont regarded as correct for Russia eighty years ago. Clemenceau and the King are probably planning something similar now. *We must be prepared for all kinds of bluff—they will be tried out one after the other to see how they work.*[68]

Decisionmakers worry more about their own resolve reputation than anyone else's. What was most salient to Holstein was the German defeat, not the French-British victory. He assumed London and Paris viewed the outcome as he did. As a result, and contrary to deterrence expectations, he assumed France and Britain were more rather than less likely to bluff.

Holstein assumed other states inferred future German resolve from their past behavior. Stand firm! implored Holstein during the Bosnian crisis, for then the others will have to yield:

> If we held firm another few weeks three years ago, the Russians would have been compelled—for the sake of their loan—to advise France to give in. Now the opposite will probably occur, because France does not want a war in the east. But first they are trying their luck in Berlin.[69]

Holstein thought the situation would compel the French to urge moderation on its Russian ally in the Balkan conflict. By standing firm, "France will at last be forced to urge Russia to adopt a calm attitude."[70] To the end Holstein remained confident that German adversaries were driven by a perception of German irresolve.

Holstein's fear that Germany needlessly acquired a reputation for irresolution after Algeciras is similar to Grey's view of Russia after its 1909 capitulation to the Triple Alliance. Just as Holstein felt Germany needed to stand firm a bit longer to win, Grey similarly believed Izvolsky, the Russian foreign minister, had needlessly yielded to the Austro-German threat: "The result would not be so bad, if only Izvolsky had withstood German hustling for 48 hours."[71]

In the same dispatch, Grey pondered the consequences of Russia's back-down:

> Germany will not make war upon [Russia] if not provoked, but Russia may have to withstand some provocation and bluff now and then: which however will cease if she makes her internal administration efficient and strong.

Again, this is similar to Holstein's earlier belief that other states were more likely to try to bluff Germany due to Berlin's alleged reputation for lacking resolve. Grey believed that when the St. Petersburg "internal administration" became "efficient and strong," the bluffs would cease. This belief had more to do with organization and leadership than with military capability. In other words, both German and British policymakers believed that victorious states were more, not less, likely to bluff.

In the midst of another German challenge to Morocco in 1908, Crowe recalled Delcassé's ouster but now expected the French to stand firm: "It is at least possible that France will not this time be as conciliatory as was M. Rouvier's government when they dismissed M. Delcassé." And later he noted: "The French are clearly not in a temper to allow themselves to be bullied."[72] Crowe saw no reason why the earlier French "concession" meant the French would yield again. Even if Crowe viewed the Rouvier government as irresolute, a new government in a different situation might behave differently. Neither Crowe nor Grey remembered Delcassé's resignation as revealing an absence of French resolve; this subverts the interdependence assumption of deterrence theory.

To review, this study shows that although actors often interpret the same behavior differently, they nevertheless assume their own view is shared by others. As a result, they turn their self-perceptions into reputations. Additionally, actors use past behavior in ways unanticipated by deterrence theory. Actors may either infer a state will be resolute in the future because it was irresolute in the past, or they may infer that victorious states will be more likely to bluff in the future. More important, actors often prefer transient and context-specific explanations over assessments of character. For example, the British failed to use German irresolution as an explanation for the German defeat at Algeciras. In the Bosnian crisis, the Germans and Austrians used what they perceived to be the transient feature of capability rather than an enduring quality of Russian irresolution to explain St. Petersburg's capitulation.

Conclusions

It is as important to know where interdependence does not exist as where it does exist. Assuming interdependence where it does not operate can be as dangerous as wrongly assuming independence. My case study shows that resolve reputations do not form easily. States which yielded to an adversary's threat were viewed as irresolute by their allies, but not by their adversaries. Even when they were viewed as irresolute by an ally, this did not mean a resolve reputation formed. For example, the British first viewed the French as irresolute for ousting Delcassé but did not assume they would be irresolute in the future. Only by examining later cases would it be possible to determine if the British view that the Russians were irresolute in 1909 carried over to the future. In most cases, decisionmakers used transient features of a particular context to explain an outcome. When they did use character to explain an outcome, this explanation was not used to predict future behavior. Both findings undercut deterrence theory's interdependence assumption.

It should not be surprising that decisionmakers do not use another's past behavior to predict behavior. There are no sound theoretical reasons that counter the commonsense view that past behavior is an unreliable guide to future behavior. As Bülow noted, situations rarely repeat themselves in international politics: governments, leaders, capabilities, issues may all change. The emotional content of crises also varies, though this is often ignored. Deterrence theorists—and realists in general—have never known what to do with emotion, which interferes with assumptions of rationality.[73] But revenge and hate are powerful motives which may reside in the memories of decisionmakers and may affect the outcome of crises even when all other variables are held constant.

Nor is it surprising that deterrence theory rests on the assumption of interdependence. As noted earlier in this essay, reputation—which presumes interdependence—helps policymakers lend credibility to their threats and promises, allows them to create expectations of their future behavior, and may offer a justification for their present behavior. Without the fact of interdependence, the tool of reputation is taken from their diplomatic arsenal.

Though there is no theoretical support for the interdependence assumption, there seemed to be a lot of empirical support. There is an abundance of evidence that policymakers think they acquire reputations. Thomas Schelling offers numerous illustrations of policymakers acting to preserve their reputations. This evidence bears on how decisionmakers perceive themselves, but not on how others perceive them. Similarly, Robert Jervis has demonstrated that decisionmakers "are strongly influenced by where they have been."[74] But this does not mean that decisionmakers are strongly influenced by where *others* have been.

This observation may help explain a puzzling tendency among decisionmakers. While a decisionmaker may not use past behavior to predict another's behavior, he may assume that others make this calculation of his own state's behavior.[75] Worst-case thinking, inspired by the condition of anarchy, may partially explain this tendency.[76] It may be unreasonable to assume we will behave in the future as we behaved in the past, but who says our adversaries are reasonable? Better safe than sorry.

There are two problems with this argument. One, some policymakers (e.g., Holstein and Crowe) are certain that they have reputations for irresolution and believe this is the source of their trouble. Two, decisionmakers sometimes engage in "best case" reasoning. For example, after the British victory at Algeciras, Crowe was confident that Germany now understood British resolve and would remain quiet.

Cognitive and motivated biases may help explain why decisionmakers assume that their own behavior will be used as an index to their future behavior, even while they fail to make the same kind of inference from others' behavior. There can be a reputation only if there is a character judgment. It may be that we are more likely to assess our own behavior as a function not only of the situation but also of our character. We have great confidence in our ability to explain our own behavior and may be quick to see in our policy qualities or characteristics unique to our nation or policymakers. Couple this with a tendency to assume our own view is shared by others and we may have an answer to why actors are quick to give themselves reputations but slow to give reputations to others. If we are likely to make character judgments of our own behavior, and then assume our view is universally held, then we have turned our self-perception into what we believe to be a reputation. While we reject interdependence and prefer common sense in analyzing our adversaries' behavior, we assume the existence and nature of our own reputation and fear or welcome its consequences.

This may explain why we assume a reputation for ourselves and not our adversaries but does not address why we appear to be more likely to worry about our allies' than our adversaries' resolve. Attribution theories may help resolve this puzzle. Social psychologists contend that we often view behavior we find undesirable as caused by internal sources such as character; yet we often take responsibility for, or explain away, another's desirable behavior.[77] Teachers who take credit for the performance of their good students but deny responsibility for their students who perform badly illustrate this tendency.

Along with this motivated bias is a cognitive bias. Decisionmakers adopt policies they think will succeed. When the policy succeeds, they naturally see a covariation between policy and outcome. When policy fails, they often blame whoever interfered with their policy rather than believe their policy was flawed.[78] In this case, the British were disappointed with Izvolsky's capitulation and, consequently, viewed him as lacking resolve. When our allies retreat when we wish them to stand firm, we hold them responsible. Because we generally want our adversaries to yield, we take credit for our successful policy rather than attribute to them a reputation for lacking resolve.[79]

These tentative explanations should not distract from the central point of this essay. We must be careful not to be seduced by the wonderful complexity and often bizarre consequences of systems. Everything is not interdependent, and curvilinear thinking is not always best. Deterrence theory's assumption of interdependence led Thomas Schelling to reason that reputation is one of the few things worth fighting for: "We lost thirty thousand dead in Korea to save face for the United States and the United Nations, not to save South Korea for the South Koreans, and it was undoubtedly worth it."[80] But this reasoning is doubtable. Assuming interdependence can be costly. There is no safe way to play resolve reputation.

Notes

I am indebted to Miriam Avins, Thomas Christensen, Teresa Johnson, Elizabeth Kier, Susan Peterson, Jack Snyder, and the other participants in the Pew Systems Project for their helpful comments. Thanks also are due to the John M. Olin Institute for Strategic Studies at Harvard University for financial and intellectual support.

1. Cited by Fred Kaplan, *The Wizards of Armageddon* (New York: Simon and Schuster, 1983), p. 328.

2. Michael R. Gordon, "Pressure Rises for U.S. Flexibility on 'Star Wars'," *New York Times*, May 25, 1988.

3. For a discussion of the effectiveness vs. threat credibility trade-off, see Steven J. Brams, *Superpower Games: Applying Game Theory to Superpower Conflict* (New Haven: Yale University Press, 1985), pp. 13–19, 44–45.

4. See for example, Schelling, "The Art of Commitment," *Arms and Influence* (New Haven: Yale University Press, 1966), pp. 35–91. Steven Brams uses reputation to solve a fundamental problem in nuclear deterrence: how can one make credible a threat which, if carried out, could cause enormous destruction to one's state? He argues the long term gains in reputation offset short term losses. Brams, *Superpower Games*; and Steven J. Brams and Marek P. Hessel, "Threat Power in Sequential Games," *International Studies Quarterly* Vol. 28, No. 1 (March 1984): 15–36.

5. Schelling, *Arms and Influence*, p. 55.

6. William W. Kaufmann, *The Requirements of Deterrence* (Princeton: Center for International Studies, 1954), p. 7; Schelling, "The Manipulation of Risk," *Arms and Influence*, pp. 92–125.

7. Robert Jervis, *The Logic of Images in International Relations* (Princeton: Princeton University Press, 1970), p. 6. See also Kenneth Oye, "Explaining Cooperation Under Anarchy," Kenneth Oye, ed., *Cooperation Under Anarchy* (Princeton: Princeton University Press, 1986), p. 14.

8. John Lewis Gaddis, *Strategies of Containment* (New York: Oxford University Press, 1982), p. 240.

9. Thomas Schelling, *The Strategy of Conflict* (Cambridge: Harvard University Press, 1960), p. 29. See also Patrick Morgan, "Saving Face for the Sake of Deterrence," Robert Jervis, Richard Ned Lebow, and Janice Stein, eds., *Psychology and Deterrence* (Baltimore: Johns Hopkins University Press, 1985), p. 128; Jervis, *The Logic of Images*.

10. Glenn Snyder and Paul Diesing, *Conflict Among Nations* (Princeton: Princeton University Press, 1977), pp. 203–47; Jervis, *The Meaning of the Nuclear Revolution* (Ithaca: Cornell University Press, 1989), pp. 39–40; Alexander George and Richard Smoke, *Deterrence in American Foreign Policy* (New York: Columbia University Press, 1974), p. 559.

11. Jervis, The Logic of Images, p. 46.

12. F.G. Bailey, "Gifts and Poisons," *Gifts and Poisons: the Politics of Reputation* (Oxford: Basil Blackwell, 1971), p. 4.

13. David Baldwin, *Economic Statecraft* (Princeton: Princeton University Press, 1985), pp. 22–24; see also David Baldwin, "Interdependence and Power," *International Organization* Vol. 34, No.4 (Autumn 1980): 496.

14. Baldwin makes this mistake; see Baldwin's *Economic Statecraft*, p. 107. It is also common among the best deterrence theorists, see Bernard Brodie, "The Anatomy of Deterrence," *World Politics* Vol. 11 (January 1959): 175.

15. Schelling, *Arms and Influence*, pp. 124–25; Kaufmann, *The*

Requirements of Deterrence, p. 10; Snyder and Diesing, *Conflict Among Nations*, p. 432.

16. John McNaughton relied on the measure of effort as a way for the United States to escape from the Vietnam War with minimal damage to its reputation. See *The Pentagon Papers* (New York: Bantam Books, Inc, 1971), p. 438.

17. For a similar view, see Richard Ned Lebow and Janice Stein, "Deterrence: the Elusive Dependent Variable," *World Politics* Vol. 42, No. 3 (April 1990): 355.

18. See Schelling, *Arms and Influence*, pp. 116–125.

19. Glenn Snyder, "'Prisoners Dilemma' and 'Chicken' Models in International Politics," *International Studies Quarterly* Vol. 15 (March 1971): 86.

20. Snyder and Diesing, *Conflict Among Nations*, pp. 186–187, also view this assumption as counter-intuitive.

21. Snyder and Diesing, *Conflict Among Nations*, pp. 187–188.

22. Huth and Russett, "What Makes Deterrence Work?" *World Politics* Vol. 36 (July 1984): 496–526; Huth and Russett, "Deterrence Failure and Crisis Escalation," *International Studies Quarterly* Vol. 32 (March 1988): 29–45; Huth and Russett, "Extended Deterrence and the Outbreak of War," *American Political Science Review* Vol. 82 (June 1988).

23. Paul Huth, *Extended Deterrence and the Prevention of War* (New Haven: Yale University Press, 1988).

24. See Ted Hopf, "Deterrence Theory and Soviet Foreign Policy: Soviet Lessons from their Victories and Defeats in the Third World, 1965–1990," (Ph.D. diss, Columbia University 1989); and Hopf, "Soviet Inferences from Their Victories in the Periphery," Robert Jervis and Jack Snyder, eds, *Dominoes and Bandwagons: Strategic Beliefs and Great Power Competition in the Eurasian Rimland* (New York: Oxford University Press, 1991), pp. 145–189.

25. Delcassé to Paléologue in early 1904, cited by G.P. Gooch, *Before the War: Studies in Diplomacy*, Vol. 1: *The Grouping of the Powers* (New York: Longmans, Green and Co., 1936), p. 153.

26. Cited by Raymond J. Sontag, "German Foreign Policy, 1904–1906," *The American Historical Review* Vol. 33, No. 2 (January 1928): 289.

27. Cited by Norman Rich, *Friedrich von Holstein: Politics and Diplomacy in the Era of Bismarck and Wilhelm II* Vol. 2, (Cambridge: Cambridge University Press, 1965), pp. 683–84. For logic similar to Holstein's, see for example Thomas Schelling, *Arms and Influence*, p. 125.

28. Bertha R. Leaman, "The Influence of Domestic Policy on Foreign Affairs in France, 1889–1905," *The Journal of Modern History* Vol. 15, No. 4 (December 1942): 472; Christopher Andrew, "France and the German Menace," Ernest May, ed., *Knowing One's Enemies: Intelligence Assessment Before the Two World Wars* (Princeton: Princeton University Press, 1984), p. 130; Oron J. Hale, *Germany and Diplomatic Revolution* (Philadelphia: University of Pennsylvania Press, 1931), p. 136.

29. Luigi Albertini, *The Origins of the War of 1914*, Vol. 1, Isabella M. Massey, trans. and ed., *European Relations From the Congress of Berlin to the Eve of the Sarajevo Murder* (New York: Oxford University Press, 1952), pp. 144–145.

30. Lord Newton, *Lord Lansdowne: A Biography* (London: MacMillan and Co., 1929), p. 341.

31. Lansdowne to Bertie (June 12, 1905), C.J. Lowe and M.L. Dockrill, *The Mirage of Power* Vol. 3: *The Documents* (Boston: Routledge & Kegan Paul, 1972), p. 426.

32. Lansdowne to Sir Reginald Lister (July 10, 1905), Lowe and Dockrill, *The Documents*, p. 426.

33. Balfour to the King (8 June, 1905), cited by Sir Sidney Lee, *King Edward VII: A Biography*, Vol. 2: *The Reign: 22nd January to 6th May 1910* (New York: MacMillan, 1927), p. 344.

34. See minute by Grey in Lascelles to Grey (September 24, 1906), *British Documents on the Origins of the War, 1898–1914* (henceforth cited as *BD*) Vol. 3: *The Testing of the Entente, 1904–1906* (London: His Majesty's Stationary Office, 1928), No. 440, p. 390.

35. Lord Grey, *Twenty-Five Years, 1892–1916*, 2 vols. (New York: Frederick A. Stokes Company, 1925), p. 91.

36. Bülow to Radolin (May 22, 1905) cited by Hale, *Germany and Diplomatic Revolution*, p. 127.

37. See for example, Holstein to Radolin (June 7, 1905), *The Holstein Papers: The Memoirs, Diaries and Correspondence of Friedrich von Holstein, 1837–1909* Vol. 4, Norman Rich and M.H. Fisher, eds., *Correspondence* (Cambridge: Cambridge University Press, 1963), No. 890 p. 343.

38. Bülow to the German Embassy in Paris (June 6, 1905), cited by Rich, *Friedrich von Holstein*, pp. 707–708.

39. Holstein to Radolin (June 23, 1905), *Holstein Papers*, pp. 346–347.

40. Holstein to Bülow (July 20, 1905), *Holstein Papers*, p. 354.

41. Holstein to Radolin (February 12, 1906), *Holstein Papers*, p. 396.

42. Kiderlen made this boast to a Romanian politician, Take Jonescu, as reported in Jonescu, *Some Personal Impressions* (New York: 1922), p. 53, cited by Schmitt, *The Annexation of Bosnia*, p. 195. Schmitt observes in a note that one historian doubts that authenticity of the language.

43. Szögyéeny to Aehrenthal (March 21, 1909), cited by Schmitt, *The Annexation of Bosnia*, p. 195.

44. Moltke to Conrad (March 19, 1909), cited by V.R. Berghahn, *Germany and the Approach of War in 1914* (London: MacMillan Press, 1973), p. 80.

45. Cited by Albertini, *The Origins of the War*, p. 287. Bülow offered similar advice to Berchtold, see Geoffrey Dunlop, trans., Vol. 3, *Memoirs of Prince von Bülow* (Boston: Little, Brown, and Company, 1932), p. 15.

46. Cited by Schmitt, *The Annexation of Bosnia*, p. 252.

47. This is Gooch's paraphrase of an Aehrenthal to Berchtold dispatch, cited in Gooch, *Before the War*, p. 416.

48. This is Gooch's paraphrase of July 2, 1909 memo to Aehrenthal, cited in Gooch, *Before the War*, p. 417.

49. Hardinge to Nicolson (March 30, 1909), *BD*, Vol. 5: *The Near East: The Macedonian Problem and Annexation of Bosnia, 1903–1909* (London: His Majesty's Stationary Office, 1928), No. 807, p. 764.

50. Hardinge to Nicolson (May 10, 1909), *BD*, Vol. 5, No. 860, p. 799.

51. Nicolson to Grey (March 24, 1909), *BD*, Vol. 5, No. 764, p. 736.

52. Cited by Taylor, Struggle for the Mastery of Europe, p. 439.

53. Private letter (March 17, 1906), cited by Rich, *Friedrich von Holstein*, p. 741. See also in *Holstein Papers*, Holstein to Brandt (March 28, 1906), No. 959; Memorandum by Holstein (May 17, 1906), No. 983, p. 427.

54. Holstein to Pascal David (May 13, 1906), *Holstein Papers*, No. 980, p. 424.

55. See for example, Memorandum by Grey (February 20, 1906), *BD*, Vol. 3, No. 299, p. 267.

56. See the minute by Grey in Lascelles to Grey (May 28, 1906), *BD*, Vol. 3, No. 416, p. 358.

57. Lascelles to Grey (August 16, 1906), *BD*, Vol. 3, No. 424, p. 366.

58. Memorandum by Crowe (January 1, 1907), *BD*, Vol. 3, Appendix A, p. 400. The Russians attacked British commercial ships in the Baltic thinking they were Japanese torpedo boats. This worsened already bad Anglo-Russian relations. The affair was peacefully settled. For more detailed discussion of the Dogger Bank affair, see Ian H. Nish, *The Anglo-Japanese Alliance: the Diplomacy of Two Island Empires, 1894–1907* (London: The Athlone Press, 1966), pp. 289–292; and Eugene N. Anderson, *The First Moroccan Crisis, 1904–1906* (Chicago: University of Chicago Press, 1930), pp 112–113.

59. Sontag, "German Foreign Policy," p. 289.

60. See note 58.

61. Memorandum by Crowe (January 1, 1907), *BD*, Vol. 3, Appendix A, p. 419, for the other excerpts see pp. 414, 416.

62. Holstein to Bülow (March 12, 1909), *Holstein Papers*, No. 1185, p. 621. Holstein died 8 May 1909.

63. Holstein to Otto Rose (June 18, 1906), *Holstein Papers*, No.986, p. 429.

64. See Crowe's minute in Bertie to Grey (September 2, 1908), *BD*, Vol. 7: *The Agadir Crisis* (London: His Majesty's Stationary Office, 1932), No. 96, p. 84.

65. See Crowe's minute in de Bunsen to Grey (September 7, 1908), *BD*, Vol. 7, No. 101, p. 90.

66. See Crowe's minute in de Bunsen to Grey (September 7, 1908), *BD*, Vol. 7, No. 101, p. 90.

67. Holstein to Bülow (October 25, 1906), *Holstein Papers*, No. 999, p. 442.

68. Holstein to Bülow (October 27, 1906), *Holstein Papers*, No. 1000, pp. 442–443 (my emphasis).

69. Holstein to Bülow (January 27, 1909), *Holstein Papers*, No. 1181, pp. 617–618.

70. Holstein to Bülow (January 27, 1909), *Holstein Papers*, No. 1181, pp. 617–618.

71. Grey to Nicolson (April 2, 1909), Vol. 5, No. 823, p. 772.

72. See Crowe's minutes in de Bunsen to Grey (September 7, 1908), *BD*, Vol. 7, No. 101, p. 90; Bertie to Grey (September 13, 1908), *BD*, Vol. 7, No. 104, p. 93.

73. Snyder and Diesing, *Conflict Among Nations*, p. 187, note that the emotional content of each crisis may differ. Robert Jervis observed that scholars of international relations rarely discuss hatred; see Jervis, "Political Psychology—Some Challenges and Opportunities, *Political Psychology* Vol 10, No. 3 (1989): 488.

74. Robert Jervis, "Realism, Game Theory, and Cooperation," *World Politics* Vol. 40 (April 1988): 321. See also Jervis, "How Decision Makers Learn From History," *Perception and Misperception in International Politics* (Princeton: Princeton University Press, 1976), pp. 217–287; and Yeun Foong Khong, *Analogies at War: Korea, Munich, Dien Bien Phu and the Vietnam Decisions of 1965* (Princeton: Princeton University Press, forthcoming).

75. Snyder and Diesing, *Conflict Among Nations*, p. 457, make the same observation.

76. This argument is also made by Snyder and Diesing, *Conflict Among Nations*, p. 188.

77. For example, see Michael Ross and Garth Fletcher, "Attribution and Social Perception," *Handbook of Social Psychology* Vol. 2, p. 12.

78. For example, see Jervis, *Perception and Misperception*, p. 347.

79. For elaboration on these points, see my dissertation, "Broken Promises and Unfulfilled Threats: Resolve, Reputation, and Deterrence." (Columbia University).

80. Schelling, *Arms and Influence*, pp. 124–125.

8

Weimar Germany and Systemic Transformation in International Economic Relations

William C. McNeil

Over the past century and especially since the First World War, western democratic capitalist states have seen international trade and capital flows become a major, often dominant variable controlling their domestic economic and political health. European states commonly export from 25% to 50% of their national production, and even the United States, which until twenty years ago exported less than 5% of its gross national product (GNP), now exports over 10%.[1] This growing dependence on foreign trade and the emergence of a vast international capital market available to finance both domestic investment and government deficits have combined to tie nations' domestic economies inexorably to the world's economy.

As the world has become integrated economically, the western industrial states have also undergone a profound transformation in the role and responsibilities of their national governments. The emergence of the welfare state and the enormous growth in the size of government spending as a share of national production has given the state a level of responsibility for preserving economic growth and stability that would have been unimaginable prior to the First World War.

These two trends—the evolving dependence on the international market and the expansion of government power—have combined to create an entirely new relationship between domestic and international politics.[2] It has in effect created an entirely new system within which policymakers must operate. States can draw on the world market to finance investment, spending and consumption in ways that would have been unthinkable in the past. But along with these new options have come new complexities and restraints which are all too often misunderstood or misjudged by policymakers.

Politicians can fail to anticipate the consequences of their actions for a vast range of reasons. Too often, they simply misunderstand the system within which they are working. But Jervis's thesis points to a much more interesting source of unanticipated consequences. We find, in the course of history, the occasional historical moment (this can be brief or last for decades) when systems are in the midst of dramatic change. Decisions made in this environment can inaugurate a systemic transformation that changes all the rules of the game. Thus a policymaker may start out in a system with one set of rules and, through his own actions, end up in a world with a radically different set of constraints. Going from peace to war, for example, brings such a systemic transformation. Professor Schroeder notes that sometimes leaders can cooperate to transform the system through a painful learning process that forces them to consider the broader consequences of decisions for peace and war, for stability and disorder.

The emergence of the new linkages between domestic politics and the world economy has been just such a systemic transformation, but one that few policymakers understand or control. States that face domestic pressure to provide full employment and economic stability have won new options with the emergence of world capital markets, but they also face new and very dangerous risks. In the 1920s, for the first time, West European and especially German politicians had to face these new political realities. An economic crisis could cost them elections and even inaugurate civil war. In trying to provide economic security to their electorate they became dependent on a remarkably volatile international monetary system.

The centuries-long transformation of the western world into an integrated, interdependent economic and monetary system moved into a new, dramatic, and painful stage in the aftermath of the First World War. Even today, the process has not settled into the stability that we tend to ascribe to the mythical golden age of the gold standard of the late nineteenth and early twentieth centuries. What is even more remarkable than the slow adjustment of the economic system is the even slower, one might say retarded, response of the western political system.

Germany's Weimar Republic was the first state to face the new, complex relationship between domestic politics and the integrated world economic and monetary system. The failure of its leaders to understand the consequences of their actions would play a central role in destroying the Weimar democracy. The unintended and unanticipated transformation of the systemic relationship between domestic politics and international finance lay at the core of their failure.

In 1924, as Weimar politicians worked to end the inflation and hyperinflation that had racked German society for nearly a decade and would indelibly mark the German conscience for three generations, they faced a society on the edge of both economic and political disintegration. The inflation itself had largely been the product of a political stalemate in which all social groups fought to transfer the costs of war and defeat onto other members of society while paying nothing themselves. The near balance of power between left and right prevented higher taxes while the government tried to buy social peace by spending vast sums which it paid for by printing money. In the end, this exacerbated all the social tensions and also destroyed Germany's financial system. Savings were eroded to the point that by late 1923, Germany's entire wartime debt in marks could have been paid off with one United States nickel.[3] Even after the stabilization of the mark, long-term loans were simply not available at any price, and short-term funds, the vital lubricant of market economies, could be had only at real interest rates of over 50% per year.

In the half decade after the currency stabilization of 1924, the German government played a juggling game as it attempted to balance its economic and political liabilities. On the one hand, it had to promote economic recovery to regain some of the legitimacy lost during the hyperinflation, while on the other, it had to pay the reparations demanded by the allies to repair their own shattered societies. The tie between economic growth and electoral victories, which has become a commonplace in modern capitalist societies, was just emerging in Germany in the 1920s, and Weimar's leaders faced a level of economic catastrophe nearly without precedent in the modern world.[4]

The financial collapse confronting Germany in 1923 forced Germans of nearly all parties to swallow their anger at the Versailles "diktat" and vote for the Dawes Plan with its promise of capital injections from abroad.[5] Germans accepted the Dawes Plan because they were unable to carry on their passive resistance to French reparation demands and because they stood to gain from the import of foreign, and especially American, capital. But they were virtually unanimous in believing that Germany could not pay large-scale reparations and that in the long run, the Dawes Plan was bound to fail. German leaders believed that even with their complete cooperation, Germany would never be able to transfer all the required gold and foreign currency to the allies. When the plan failed, as it inevitably had to, and the costs of the war had to be renegotiated, Germans wanted to have world, and especially American, opinion on the side of reducing reparations. To win this support German leaders formulated a public policy of complete compliance with the Dawes Plan. While abiding by this "fulfillment policy," German officials fully expected that the Dawes Plan would soon collapse from its own weight.[6]

Under the formula set up by the Dawes Committee, Germany was to pay a reduced but progressively rising sum of reparations and in return was to receive a large international loan to stabilize the government's finances and serve as a reserve for the new reichsmark. In addition, it was universally understood that the international tranquility secured by the plan would lead to large-scale foreign loans for Germany.[7] Germany's principal obligation under the plan was to adopt a policy of strict fiscal and monetary restraint. Taxes were to be raised and spending cut in order to create a fiscal surplus large enough to pay for reparations. The domestic implications of this "fulfillment policy" were little understood at that time, but the economic experts who drafted the Dawes Plan correctly believed that if Germany reduced its domestic consumption through higher taxes, Germans would buy fewer goods from abroad and this would produce an export surplus. The gold and currency earned from this export surplus would provide the money to pay reparations.[8]

Germans thus believed that they could try to fulfill the Dawes Plan and it would still fail, while the allied economic experts believed that if Germany adopted the correct policies, it could pay reparations. What neither side considered was the domestic economic and political implications of Germany's acceptance of a fulfillment policy or the destabilizing effects of Germany's emerging dependence on foreign loans. Without anyone intending it, Germany quickly became dependent on imported capital to support the government's policy of economic and political stabilization. A conflict would soon emerge between Germany's commitments under the Dawes Plan and its domestic political needs for greater unemployment relief and social spending. As American loans became the vital tool financing Germany's deficits, the United States and Germany became world leaders in attempting to solve the new foreign policy dilemma of how to achieve both domestic and international stability. New demands, new benefits, new costs and new risks would slowly evolve into a new interconnected system tying international finance to domestic fiscal policies.

As the loans first began to flow into Germany, German policymakers believed that their dependence on foreign loans had both dangers and possible virtues. Initially, most Germans emphasized the risks that the loans might bring with them. The two greatest fears were that lenders would use their financial power to gain control over German industries and city governments and, the more cogent fear, that borrowing abroad would undermine the Dawes Plan and trigger an international financial crisis that would destroy Germany's political independence.[9] One worried Prussian official summed up this anxiety when he warned that if Germany failed to live up to the terms of the Dawes Plan, "We will fall into an enslavement from which there will be no escape and which even the words 'absolute financial control' cannot fully describe."[10] By 1927, as the loans reached serious proportions, a more optimistic view would be expressed by the Foreign Ministry's reparations expert, Hans Simon. He suggested that since Germany could transfer only a fixed amount of money abroad each year, the more it owed in private loans, the less it could be forced to pay in reparations. As he put it, "The greater our private debt, the smaller our reparations burden."[11]

But Germans understood that winning a reduction in reparations required that they demonstrate their good faith by trying to meet the terms of the Dawes Plan. This was most clearly stated in a report sent by the German Embassy in Washington back to Berlin. The embassy included an article from the *New York American* with this note attached. "The article is noteworthy in that it renders German policy in regard to the Dawes Plan essentially correctly in two sentences: 'The ruling circles in Germany are determined not to permit a breakdown of the Dawes Plan to be blamed on German sabotage. Behind this determination, however, lies the hope that the plan itself will demonstrate the impossibility of its continued functioning."[12]

Thus, while German leaders may have hoped they could use the American loans to their own advantage, they also profoundly feared that German political independence could be threatened if their own actions undermined the Dawes Plan and created an international crisis.[13] This specifically meant that Germany had to run a fiscal surplus. As reich chancellor Hans Luther told his cabinet in July 1925, "In terms of foreign policy, it is undoubtedly impossible to present an unbalanced budget."[14]

On balance then, Germans had compelling reasons to pursue a "fulfillment policy" as set out by the Dawes Plan and to try to achieve a positive balance of trade through fiscal restraint. For a brief time in 1924 and 1925, they did in fact raise taxes, cut spending, and generate a large government surplus.[15] But then, in the winter of 1925–26, the German economy fell into a severe depression. Unemployment among union members rose to over 20%. Business profits collapsed and business failures reached frightening numbers.[16]

The government found itself under steady and irresistible pressure to help business by cutting taxes and to help workers by increasing unemployment relief.[17] As the German government responded to the domestic political pressures bred by the collapsing economy, it set in motion a chain of events that not only would produce more severe long-term economic problems but would ultimately undermine its foreign policy as well.

The emergence of a rich international capital market ready to loan to Germany and the emergence of deficit fiscal policies in Germany combined to produce not the enslavement to foreign bondholders feared by German leaders but enslavement to an indifferent capital market. The dependence on imported capital would feed back into German domestic politics and impose new, paralyzing restraints on German policy, not through political pressures but via the free market. The system of linked domestic and international relations that would play such a crucial role in undermining the Weimar Republic in the years after 1929 had hardly existed five years earlier.

When the German economy slipped into the short, but extraordinarily sharp, depression of 1925–26, the German government came under pressure to alleviate the impact of the crisis from two powerful and closely linked domestic spheres of influence. On the one hand, government ministries were intimately tied to interest groups that incessantly lobbied for economic help. In a system in which the Labor Ministry was the passionate defender of worker interests, the Economics Ministry was the equally vocal supporter of business needs, and agriculture used its political connections to win massive government support, government intervention to soften the impact of the business cycle was almost inevitable. As a reluctant finance minister put it in mid–1926, he "was operating on the premise that for both the Economics and Labor Ministries, the advantages of the work creating program outweigh any consideration of financial problems."[18]

On the other hand, in a coalition parliamentary government, these interests also reflected electoral votes for the ruling parties. Failure to pacify labor, or agriculture, or the powerful government bureaucrats' organizations, or the various branches of business could and did lead to losses for parties in the coalition.[19] A disgruntled politician justifiably complained in early 1928 that "recently, there has developed a downright race between the various parliamentary factions to make themselves popular by distributing money."[20]

As the economy staggered through the depression of 1925–1926 and the modest recovery of the next two years, this combination of political pressures pushed the German governments to begin what we now would refer to as a Keynesian economic policy. One official in the Bavarian state government summed up the general feeling when he declared, "It must be the task of state and municipal governments to do everything to create work and lighten the burden of the unemployed."[21] The result was a steady increase in the fiscal deficits of German governments at the reich, state, and local levels.

As in most governments, German policymakers operated in two distinct spheres. Domestic politicians had relatively little interest in foreign policy, while diplomats had no sympathy for the pressures of domestic politics. The decisions to undertake deficit spending in the summer of 1926 were based purely on the fear that if the impact of the depression was not tempered, the German political system would collapse. Foreign policy officials were not consulted about the possible implications of these decisions for Germany's international goals, and they were opposed to deficit spending policies once they were implemented. But the domestic political choices would soon intrude into the foreign policy arena. Government deficits undermined Germany's efforts to prove that even though it fulfilled the demands of the Dawes Plan, it could not pay reparations. In addition, the fiscal deficits brought Germany into a conflict with the allies and with the man given responsibility to see that Germany paid as much as it could, the agent general for reparations, S. Parker Gilbert. While any state might find itself in difficulty as it ran large fiscal and trade deficits, Germany had the unique problem of having to face a tough, single-minded official determined to make Germany achieve a trade surplus.

The fiscal deficits and dependence on foreign loans also reignited the smoldering social struggles that had nearly torn Germany apart between 1918 and 1924. Control of the foreign loans became the center of a domestic war between powerful interest groups within Germany that wanted to use the imported capital for themselves while rejecting as illegitimate the claims of other groups.

As the Germans struggled to control government spending and foreign borrowing, they began to find out just how closely domestic fiscal policy and foreign policy were connected. Historians of international relations have come to expect that domestic interest groups set foreign policy agendas to serve narrow interest group needs, but the Germans would find that domestic politics subverted a shared foreign policy agenda. Everyone in Germany hoped to end or reduce reparation payments. And nearly everyone had agreed that a fulfillment policy was the best way to do that. But German fiscal policy would subvert this shared foreign policy. It is not enough to argue that domestic politics shapes foreign policy. Instead, we need also to consider how domestic actions in one field may cause international pressures to come back, in a circular or interactive fashion, to limit future domestic policy options.

The expectation that the state has the responsibility to stabilize the national economy has transformed the role of the state in modern capitalist nations, and the Weimar Republic was the first to discover the complications of this new burden. The fact that Germany, like many other debtor states since, had to borrow money on the international markets to finance the fiscal deficits brought an entirely new element into the policy process. When domestic fiscal and monetary policies increase dependence on the international capital markets and ultimately produce a monetary crisis, domestic policy becomes a new kind of diplomatic issue. A vital part of foreign policy is now being driven by forces independent of and little understood by the traditional makers of foreign policy. Henry Kissinger would capture the frustration felt by the traditional foreign policy elite when he observed of the American decision to go off the gold standard in August 1971, "The fact was that a decision of major foreign policy importance had been taken about which neither the Secretary of State nor the National Security Advisor had been consulted."[22] Thus the interactive system has emerged as a powerful reality, but even today, it is difficult to restructure the policy-making process to create an effective policy instrument.

For Germany, the crisis began to unfold in late 1928. By that time, German government deficits had reached 3.5 billion RM per year. This represented nearly 5% of German net national product and had become a major stimulant to the German economy. As government spending grew, opposition to the new fiscal deficits also grew both at home and abroad.

Domestically, German business and agriculture leaders were almost unanimous in condemning the government's spending, taxing and social policies even though they were often the recipients of government aid. Conservatives were not prepared to accept the legitimacy of an expanded state role in the economy with its recognition of the rights of other sections of society. They were determined to restore the old order and regain for owners their absolute control over their factories. They saw government as the major challenger to their authority and insisted that government's power in all fields had to be cut.

But the most powerful internal attack on government deficits came from Reichsbank president Hjalmar Schacht. A man of vast ambitions and vanity, Schacht was determined to expand his own power by closing foreign bond markets to German governments, thus making them dependent on Reichsbank credits. The government in turn fought to bring the Reichsbank under control and to get its help in funding the fiscal deficits caused by the government's political weakness. Despite his notorious emotional instability and intense nationalism, Schacht won vital support from Montagu Norman of the Bank of England. Even more important, Schacht also came to exercise a tremendous influence on American money markets. This influence was partially a result of the perception that Schacht represented prudent fiscal policies and partially a product of his alliance with the reparations agent, S. Parker Gilbert. Together Schacht and Gilbert personified the power of international finance as it worked to control German domestic policy.

Parker Gilbert had gone to work for the U.S. Treasury during the First World War as a protégé of Russell Leffingwell, who had become one of the dominant partners in J.P. Morgan and Company, America's most powerful bank. When the Wilson administration was replaced by the Republican regime of Warren G. Harding, Gilbert stayed on at the Treasury and became an intimate of Andrew Mellon, another of the most powerful businessmen and bankers in the United States. Gilbert's ability to work with both parties and his reputation as an apolitical bureaucrat had led to his selection as reparations agent in 1924. Throughout the late twenties, it was widely rumored that Gilbert hoped to make his fortune by joining Morgan when he left his position as reparations agent. The rumors were true, and one can hardly doubt the close ties—both ideologically and personally—between Gilbert and the Morgan partners. Germans assumed that this meant that Gilbert was the representative of American bankers' interests in Europe. The German Embassy in Washington reported that in spite of the fact that most Americans admitted that at some future date, reparations and loan repayment would come into conflict, they were not worried. "At the present time neither those involved in German business nor public opinion are racking their brain. They soothe themselves [in the knowledge] that a confidant of the administration and big finance keeps guard in Berlin as Agent General."[23] The assumption was reasonable, but the reality was far different.

Gilbert was close to Mellon, Morgan and to Benjamin Strong, governor of the Federal Reserve Bank of New York. But this did not mean that he represented the interests of Wall Street bankers. The Morgan partners were absolutely opposed to extensive lending to Germany. Although the firm put together the syndicates that sold the Dawes and Young Plan bonds, it sold no other German bonds, and the partners, especially J.P. Morgan, Jr., remained strongly anti-German and unwilling to establish close ties to German banks or the government. Thus the firms that made the billions of dollars in loans to Germany did so despite the skepticism of Morgan and the growing opposition of Parker Gilbert. This division reflected the splits within the American banking community, not only between inland and New York bankers but within the international banking group as well.

Within the American government, Benjamin Strong had taken a position as the most ardent supporter of European interests. Herbert Hoover would call Strong a "mental annex" of Europe. But this was true only compared to Hoover's suspicions of both the Europeans and the New York bankers who loaned American money to them. Although Strong wanted to help Europe he would not let foreign conditions dictate Federal Reserve policy.[24] And Hoover, who was soon to be elected president, had opposed extensive lending to Europe since 1922 and fought a running battle to reduce the loans and force banks to provide greater security checks on foreign loans.

The result of this conglomeration of conflicts in the United States was a passive acceptance of the German loans for a time. But neither Gilbert nor the new president, Herbert Hoover, felt any commitment to protect the loans by reducing reparations. And certainly, American officials felt no obligation to continue to make loans to Germany in the future.

German policymakers were misled by their assumptions about how policy was made in the United States and who influenced it. Their belief that powerful economic institutions must determine policy rested on the assumption that economic power can be directly translated into political power. It ignored the very real influence of Congress in American politics (a mistake that many Europeans and others continue to make in dealing with the United States). And it assumed that New York bankers with extensive international ties could easily transform those ties into policy. But exports have traditionally played a far smaller role in the American economy than in any other advanced capitalist society. Those economic groups that support exports and foreign loans have always had to fight a rearguard action against the great majority of Americans who have few ties to, and little interest in, the rest of the world. As Parker Gilbert bluntly and accurately warned the British, "The mere existence of [American] investments in Europe would not suffice to keep alive any beneficent interest in European affairs. Their loss would affect a couple of hundred thousand bondholders only and would cause a great outcry; but what would continue to interest the broad mass of American opinion would be the regular collection of [war] debts from the European Governments, which would affect the millions of taxpayers."[25]

German problems in dealing with the United States were compounded by the fact that Gilbert, as the one American who was really interested in the German loans and who came to dominate American policy, represented the very ideals that were most unsympathetic to Germany's political-economic weakness. He had made his reputation in the American government in the early postwar years by organizing the systematic repayment of American war loans—a policy he pursued without pause during the sharp depression of 1920–21. By late 1927, Gilbert had become convinced that German deficit spending was undermining the Dawes Plan and creating a trade deficit that prevented Germany from meeting its reparations obligations. His faith in orthodox economic theory and his conviction that the Germans were acting irresponsibly led Gilbert to pressure American bankers to reduce their loans and to demand that the German government produce the budget surpluses called for by the Dawes Plan.[26]

In late 1927, Gilbert's objections brought long-term lending to Germany to a near halt. Soon thereafter, changes in American financial markets would deal German hopes their final blow. As profits on the New York stock market began their spectacular climb, smart money moved out of foreign loans and into the stock market. By the middle of 1928, Germans found it hard to compete for American long-term money. While they continued to find some short-term funds, the heyday of the first cycle of American international investing was coming to an end, and the Germans found themselves in a new and devastating crisis. Their old fear had been that foreign lenders would control the German economy. The new reality was that their failure to find lenders would force a brutal retrenchment in German spending and investment.

Germans learned the lesson in the late 1920s and early 1930s that most heavy borrowers on the international market have had to relearn again and again: The market operates in response to short-term influences. American expectations that Germans would practice fiscal responsibility while paying above-market interest rates had made German loans attractive from 1926 to 1928. But, in 1928–29, as the risk premium fell on German loans and the American stock market offered higher returns to American investors, German bonds began to go begging. German governments and industries that had quickly grown accustomed to foreign loans found themselves even more quickly overextended in 1929–30.

The introduction of international lending to the domestic fiscal equation was transforming the way in which governments managed their spending and taxing policies. In the late 1920s, no one had any experience in how the international market would work, and even a critic of German spending such as Parker Gilbert expected that loans to Germany would remain a long-term fixture of international finance.[27] As Germans sent their monetary demands out into the foreign money markets, they had little reason to expect that the market would soon be sending powerful, contractionary signals back to Germany.

Germans would also be the first to learn that to the extent that bankers are able to influence American policy, they tend to support the

American government's attempts to impose orthodox fiscal policies on borrower states.

In 1925–26, Germans had initially tried to avoid heavy international borrowing. But as domestic pressures forced them to accept deficit spending and pay for it via foreign loans, they consoled themselves in the belief that American bankers would defend their loans by forcing the allies to reduce their reparation demands on Germany. Instead, the American assumption, correct as it turns out, was that if Germany reduced its government spending, it would reduce national income, which in turn would reduce the volume of imports purchased abroad. This, finally, would create a trade surplus and generate the gold and foreign currency needed to repay both the foreign debts and reparations. American policymakers ever since have applied the same logic to all international debtors, save the United States itself. From the outside, the needs of the international market take precedence without regard for the internal costs of falling income and rising unemployment caused by retrenchment policies. This is a far more subtle form of political intervention than old-fashioned gunboat diplomacy, but if government spending is a critical tool in social stabilization —as it has in fact become in the modern world—it can be just as traumatic.

Parker Gilbert understood that a balanced budget could help produce a trade surplus.[28] What he did not understand and what historians writing even today tend to ignore are the social-political costs of these monetary and fiscal policies.[29]

The fiscal deficits run up by the German government in the late twenties in an attempt to preserve political stability became fatal liabilities in the late 1920s. Unable to find any domestic support for further deficits (even many Social Democrats had become convinced that the deficits had to end) and running out of foreign loans to pay for them, German governments began a rigorous retrenchment. As German governments strove to balance their budgets from 1929 to 1931, they drove the economy deeper and deeper into depression and helped destroy the very stability the fiscal spending had originally been meant to preserve. German leaders may not have been terribly sophisticated in their economic thinking, but they had learned in 1925–26 that fiscal surpluses could help cause a depression, and a depression would allow Germany to generate a trade surplus and pay reparations.[30] But, by 1929, they no longer had effective control over their domestic or foreign policy options.

By late 1929, the Social Democratic government of Herman Müller found itself trapped by Germany's dependence on foreign loans. In the face of growing fiscal deficits, the reluctance of American bankers to make new foreign loans, and mounting pressure both at home and abroad to reduce government spending, the Social Democrats began the fiscal retrenchment that helped make the German depression one of the worst in the world. Under Müller's successor, Heinrich Brüning, this deflationary option was raised to high policy. Brüning thought, correctly, that if Germany drove itself into a crisis through deflationary policies, it could win worldwide support for an end to reparations. Of course, he also completed the burial of the Weimar democracy and took a giant step toward bringing Hitler and the National Socialists to power.

By 1929, the Weimar democracy found itself trapped by a system that made the government dependent on two masters. To win elections and ensure a minimum of social peace, the government had been forced to expand the size of the state and its welfare spending. This had included expensive infusions to all the major interest groups: agriculture, business and labor. But the political peace purchased with these subsidies was paid for by international loans. This in turn put Germany under the international financial pressure that was so important in reversing the expansionary fiscal policies. The attempt to solve the domestic political conflict between powerful and competing interest groups had led to dependence on the foreign loans and ultimately to the loss of control over both foreign and domestic economic policy.

It is worth emphasizing that this story is a tragedy and not a morality play. It is about the transformation of economic-political relationships and the problems faced by those caught in the middle of this systemic evolution. Looking back from the vantage point of six decades, we could argue that there were better choices available to both German and American officials. Responsible German fiscal policy combined with a willingness on the part of the United States to make a long-term, steady supply of money available to Germany might have dampened the German business cycle and helped stabilize the Weimar political system. But neither nation had the political institutions or the economic theory available on which to base such policies.

Germany remained in the midst of an unresolved political revolution throughout the 1920s. The issues at stake were always as much about who controlled the economy as about how fiscal policy should be conducted. German leaders had neither the social consensus nor the Keynesian economic theory which would have opened up more attractive options to them. It would only be in the aftermath of the depression, Nazism, the Second World War and the Cold War that Germany and the United States could digest the implications of the catastrophe of the 1920s. The almost pathological determination of the West German government to preserve a balanced budget after the Second World War grew directly out of the lessons of the inflation and debts of the twenties. And American decisions to make massive funds available to Europe in the form of the Marshall Plan reflected a remarkable learning curve as we came to understand that we could neither ignore the economic problems of the rest of the world nor leave the provision of investment funds in the hands of private bankers and the free market, as we had done in the twenties. To expect either German or American policymakers in the twenties to have acted otherwise than they did is to ask them to escape from the historical moment in which they lived.

The emerging interconnectedness of foreign and domestic economics brought with it new costs that no one in the 1920s could have been expected to understand. Even now, with over half a century of experience with these issues, the United States has not come to terms with its international obligations. New systems take time to assimilate, and that time can be extraordinarily costly. For Germany, failure to adjust to the new international economic system became a major ingredient in the destruction of the Weimar Republic.

Notes

1. Calculated from U.S. Department of Commerce, Bureau of the Census, *Historical Statistics of the United States; Colonial Times to 1970* (Washington D.C., 1975) p. 887 and *Statistical Abstracts of the United States, 1990* (Washington D.C., 1990) pp. 426 and 790.

2. For discussion of some implications of this process see, I.M. Destler, *Making Foreign Economic Policy* (Washington D.C.: Brookings Institution, 1980); Robert O. Koehane and Joseph S. Nye Jr., *Power and Interdependence* (Boston: Little, Brown, 1977); John Ruggie, "International Regimes, Transactions and Change: Embedded Liberalism in the Postwar Economic Order", *International Organization*, 36, no. 2 (Spring 1982); Peter Katzenstein ed., *Between Power and Plenty* (Madison: University of Wisconsin prsss, 1978) especially the introduction and the chapters by Stephen Krasner and Stephen Blank; Stephen Krasner, *Defending the National Interest* (Princeton: Princeton University Press, 1978) and Robert Keohane, *After Hegemony* (Princeton: Princeton University Press, 1984).

3. The history of efforts to revalue the debts is told in Michael Hughes, *Paying for the German Inflation* (Chapel Hill: University of North Carolina Press, 1988)

4. This argument is made most forcefully by Edward R. Tufte, *Political control of the Economy* (Princeton: Princeton Univesity Press, 1978) and confirmed by Douglas A. Hibbs Jr., *The Political Economy of Industrial Democracies* (Cambridge, Mass.: Harvard University Press, 1987) especially

p.9 and 117–118. Hibbs observes that election booms are not a "systemic feature" of American politics (p.151) but adds that presidents who have pumped up the economy prior to their reelection have won (Nixon in 1972 and Regan in 1984) while those facing election or reelections during a recession have lost (Nixon 1960, Ford 1976, Carter 1980, and Bush 1992) pp. 151 and 166. Hibbs also finds that since the early 1970s, economics had become the principle electoral issue in Britain and France (pp.224–5 and 259).

5. Robert Grathwol, *Stresemann and the DNVP: Reconciliation or Revenge in German Foreign Policy, 1924–1928* (Lawrence, Kansas: University of Kansas Press, 1980) and Stephen Schuker, *The End of French Predominance in Europe* (Chapel Hill: University of North Carolina Press, 1978) pp.264–5.

6. These expectations are set out most clearly in a memorandum by the Foreign Ministry's reparations expert, Karl Ritter, "Endsumme" written 26 or 27 August, 1927 in Politisches Archiv des Auswartigen Amtes (hereafter cited AA), RM 5, Vol. 20, also available in Bundes Archiv Koblenz, (hereafter cited as BA) R43I/42. Foreign Minister Gustav Stresemann spelled out German expectations in his speech to the Central Committee of the DVP, 6 July 1924 in BA R45II/39, pp.285,297–299 and 309.

7. Frank Costigliola, "The United States and the Reconstruction of Germany in the 1920's" *Business History Review* (Winter 1976) and Melvyn Leffler, *The Elusive Quest: America's Pursuit of European Stability and French Security, 1919–1933* (Chapel Hill: University of North Carolina Press, 1979).

8. William McNeil, "Could Germany Pay? Another look at the Reparations Problem of the 1920s" in Gerald D. Feldman et al eds. *Konsequenzen der Inflation* (Berlin: Colloquium Verlag, 1989).

9. William McNeil, *American Money and the Weimar Republic* (New York: Columbia University Press, 1986) pp. 48–54.

10. Quoted in Hermann Dietrich-Troeltsch, "Kommunalkredit, Reparationen und foederalistisches Prinzip" dissertation, Mainz 1970, p.589.

11. See Simon's extensive report that outlines the range of German Reparations policy options dated 11 January 1927 in AA SS-C, vol. 12.

12. German Embassy Washington to Berlin, 26 January 1926 in AA Botschaft Washington, Reparations, Dawes-Plan, vol.4.

13. BA R2/2000, Reichs Finance Ministry expert's report, 16 October 1924.

14. BA R43I/877 p.68, Sitzung des Reichsministeriums, 22 July 1925.

15. BA R43I/1135 p.99.

16. *Vierteljahrshefte zur Statistik des deutschen Reichs*, 36 Jahrgang, erstes Heft, p.185.

17. Fritz Blaich, *Die Wirtschaftskrise 1925/26 und die Reichsregierung* (Kalmuenz: Michael Lassleben, 1977) pp. 108–139, and more recently in English, William McNeil, *American Money*, pp. 112–133; and Harold James, *The German Slump* (Oxford: Oxford University Press, 1986).

18. BA R2/2001, note on the discussion on financing the work creation projects, 21 July 1926, and BA R43I/2031, p.227.

19. McNeil, *American Money*, p.169–170.

20. BA NL Koch-Weser 37, p. 127, Koch-Weser note, 15 March 1928.

21. BA R43I/2030. pp. 243 and 157.

22. Henry Kissinger, *White House Years* (Boston: Little, Brown, 1979) p.954.

23. AA WR-FV allg. 14 Am., vol.11, Kiep (Washington) to AA no. 763, 24 July 1927.

24. Federal Reserve Bank of New York (hereafter cited FRBNY) Strong papers 1012.2, Strong to Gilbert, 14 July 1928.

25. *Documents on British Foreign Policy*, Series IA, 5:80.

26. Gilbert's position was spelled out in extraordinary detail in a biting memorandum to the German government which was published in the *New York Times*, 6 November, 1927. This same attitude shaped bankers' responses to the British banking crisis of 1931. See Diane B. Kunz *The Battle for Britain's Gold Standard* in 1931 (London: Croom Helm, 1987).

27. For a general evaluation of financial conditions in late 1927, see Hoesch (Paris) to Berlin #1325, 22 December 1927 in AA SS-C, vol. 13. On Gilbert's expectations see Schubert's conversation with Gilbert 18 August 1928 in AA SS-Ggil, 1:174. The issue is also discussed in Werner Link, *Die amerikanische Stabilisierungspolitik in Deutschland, 1921–32* (Dusseldorf: Droste, 1970) pp. 416–433 and Leffler, p. 183..

28. See his *Report of the Agent General for Reparations Payments*, 10 June 1927, p.47; letter Gilbert to Strong, 8 September 1927, FRBNY, Strong Papers 1012.2; Sir R. Lindsay to Sir A. Chamberlain, 24 October 1927, *Documents on British Foreign Policy*, Series I A 4:57; and most fully, Gilbert's memorandum to the German government published in full in the *New York Times*, 6 November 1927, pp. 1 and 24.

29. There is an extensive literature on reparations with the modern view originally set out by Bertil Ohlin and Jacques Rueff in articles in *The Economic Journal*, June and September 1929. Also Fritz Machlup in "Foreign Debts, Reparations and the Transfer Problem" written in 1928 but available in his collection, *International Payments, Debts and Gold* (New York: Schribner's, 1964). Modern views are represented in Sally Marks, "Reparations Reconsidered: A Reminder," *Central European History*, (December, 1969); Stephen A. Schuker, *The End of French Predominance in Europe*; and Charles S. Maier, Recasting Bourgeois Europe, (Princeton: Princeton University Press, 1975), especially pages 252–253, and "The Truth about the Treaties," *Journal of Modern History* 51 (1979). The one strong dissenting voice is Peter Kruger, "Das Reparationsproblem der Weimarer Republik in Fragwurdiger Sicht," *Vierteljahrshefte fur Zeitgeschichte*, 1 Heft 29 (January 1981).

30. Minutes of the Reichsbank President's report, 20 January 1928 in BA R43I/635; Schaffer to Claussen, 24 February 1928 and 1 May 1929 (afternoon), Schaffer-Claussen Schriftswechsel, Institut fur Zeitgeschichte, Munich; Stresemann telegram to German embassies in London, Paris, etc., 3 January 1929, AA RM5, vol.24.

9

Hitler's Tripolar Strategy for World Conquest

Randall L. Schweller

In the summer of 1942, the empire of Adolf Hitler had reached its greatest extent, enslaving four hundred million people and stretching from the Mediterranean to the Arctic, from the English Channel to the Black Sea and almost to the Caspian. Between the Ukrainian steppes and the Pyrenees only one other state, Switzerland, had retained its sovereignty. Far from the turmoil in Europe, Hitler's U-boats were carrying the Nazi offensive to the New World, engaging enemy forces off the Atlantic coast of North America and in the Caribbean Sea.

The clarity of Hitler's aims for world dominion had by this time given rise to a countercoalition of world powers with the singular aim of defeating Germany and its partners. All that was asked of any available ally was that it should share faithfully this one major purpose. Among the members of the Allied coalition, however, only the Soviet Union, which had already suffered serious losses the year before, was actively fighting German land forces in Europe. And unlike in 1941, when the *Wehrmacht* had stalled in the snow outside Moscow and Leningrad, the renewed German offensive of 1942 had carried the spearheads of Hitler's panzer armies to Stalingrad and deep into the Caucasus, where they threatened Russia's richest oil field and, by extension, the Red Army's ability to continue the struggle against Germany.[1]

In short, by mid-1942, Hitler's Germany had mounted a serious challenge to the very survival of the modern state system, and it appeared to be winning the war. Never before or since has the existence of the international system been so seriously in doubt. How have historians and political scientists explained this unprecedented systemic disequilibrium?

Ironically, scholars rarely associate structural factors with the outbreak of the Second World War. Instead, the standard historical accounts of World War II evoke a tragic drama driven by a unique cast of villains (Hitler, Stalin, Mussolini, and company) and sinners (Chamberlain, Daladier, Beck, among others).[2]

Most students of international relations also employ a villain/sinner image to explain the origins of World War II. The father of neorealism himself, Kenneth Waltz, at least partially endorses it:

> A small-number system can always be disrupted by the actions of a Hitler and the reactions of a Chamberlain. . . . One may lament Churchill's failure to gain control of the British government in the 1930s, for he knew what actions were required to maintain a balance of power.[3]

Likewise, prominent game theorists such as Emerson Niou and Peter Ordeshook "sympathize . . . with the analyses that interpret Hitler's personality . . . as critical to the outbreak of World War II rather than some breakdown in traditional balance-of-power forces."[4] John Mueller argues that Hitler alone caused World War II, since "it almost seems that after World War I the only person left in Europe who was willing to risk another total war was Adolf Hitler."[5]

Several recent studies of the Second World War have focused on systemic-level, rather than unit-level, variables.[6] The problem with these studies is that they merely posit a multipolar interwar system containing five or more poles (their causal variable) without first establishing criteria for distinguishing between a pole and a middle power and then measuring the distribution of capabilities among the great powers to reveal the actual polarity of the system. When these tasks are performed, as the present study shows, the international system in 1938 is shown to be tripolar, not multipolar, with the poles being Germany, the Soviet Union, and the United States. This unique tripolar structure, I argue, explains a good deal about how the war unfolded, particularly Hitler's strategy for world conquest and why it ultimately failed.

One reason that multipolar explanations have dominated the systemic-level literature on World War II is that the most influential systems theory of world politics, Kenneth Waltz's *Theory of International Politics*, distinguishes between only two types of international systems: bipolar and multipolar. Declares Waltz, "Until 1945 the nation-state system was multipolar, and always with five or more powers. In all of modern history the structure of international politics has changed but once. We have only two systems to observe."[7]

Waltz's extraordinary book recasts classical realism in a more rigorous and deductive mold and addresses broad questions: why balances recurrently form after their disruption; what degree of stability is to be expected of international systems of varying structures; how the constraining effects of structure reduce the variety of behaviors and outcomes so that balancing behavior results even when no state seeks balance as an end.

Waltz's ideas have been both the intellectual springboard for important research within the structural-realist paradigm[8] and the main target of the detractors of neorealism.[9] Some critics of Waltz's theory charge that in its sacrifice of richness for rigor, structural realism winds up being a caricature of classical realism rather than a model of it.[10] Others admire the power and elegance of Waltz's theory but complain that as a systemic-level theory, it is too abstract to generate useful hypotheses about specific foreign-policy behavior, as Waltz readily admits.[11] By sacrificing some of Waltz's parsimony, the present study seeks to turn his theory of international politics into one of foreign policy.

The aims of this chapter, then, are twofold: to offer a new structural interpretation for the origins of World War II and to devise a systems theory that yields determinate balance-of-power predictions. The study opens with two modifications of Waltz's theory: (1) the distribution of capabilities is measured not only by the number of great powers but also by their relative size, and (2) states are identified as either status quo or revisionist powers. The theory is then applied to analysis of tripolar dynamics and to an explanation of Hitler's diplomatic and military strategy to achieve German world dominion. The essay concludes by suggesting the implications of the analysis for the post-cold-war world, which, I argue, is tripolar.

Two Modifications of Waltz's Systems Theory

The Distribution of Capabilities

Waltz offers a tripartite theoretical definition of system structure: (1) the ordering principle, either anarchy or hierarchy; (2) the functional differentiation of units; and (3) the distribution of capabilities. He claims that because international politics takes place within an anarchic realm and "as long as anarchy endures, states remain like units," international systems differ only along the third dimension, the distribution of capabilities.[12] Waltz operationalizes this dimension by simply counting the number of great powers in the system; the total number of great powers defines the polarity of the system.

Historically, however, the resources of the great powers have varied considerably, and these imbalances often prove decisive in explaining their individual foreign-policy strategies.[13] The key question is, Does it matter that Waltz abstracts considerably from reality?

For Waltz, the answer is clearly no; his theory pertains to the properties of systems, not individual states. But for those who would use his theory to explain foreign policy,[14] it does pose a problem, as Christensen and Snyder correctly point out.[15] If we are to turn Waltz's ideas into a theory of foreign policy, the descriptive accuracy of the theory must be improved to account for power inequalities among the major actors.

Not surprisingly, recent attempts to apply Waltz's theory to analysis of the post-cold-war system have focused on power asymmetries among the great powers. For instance, Mearsheimer states: "Both [bipolar and multipolar] systems are more peaceful when equality is greatest among the poles."[16] Many analysts, however, strongly disagree with this proposition.[17] Niou and Ordeshook conclude that system stability does not require "either a uniform or a highly asymmetric resource distribution."[18] And Wagner and Niou, Ordeshook, and Rose maintain that the most "peaceful distribution" is one in which one actor is "near-predominant"—it controls exactly half of the system's resources.[19]

To specify more fully the distribution of capabilities, I employ a two-step process. First, each great power is weighted according to its relative share of the total resources of the major-power subsystem. This measure captures the relative power disparities among the great powers, and it drives the analysis. By itself, however, it is too unwieldly to be useful as a way to classify different types of systems. To solve this problem, I further divide the great powers into two tiers: poles and second-ranking great powers (hereafter called middle powers). To qualify as a pole, a state must have greater than half the resources of the most powerful state in the system; all other great powers are classed as middle powers. This conception of polarity accords with the commonsense notion that poles must be great powers of the first rank. Middle powers can play important roles as kingmakers or stabilizers, but the behavior of the poles, due to their size, has the greatest effect on the system.

The Character of the Units: State Interest

Waltz describes the units as "unitary rational actors, who, at a minimum, seek their own preservation and, at a maximum, drive for universal domination."[20] While acknowledging that states do not always seek to maximize their power, Waltz does not incorporate this variance as a model-based feature—it simply washes out of the analysis. This is important for two reasons. First, as Jack Snyder crisply observes in the introduction to this volume, "The workings of [Waltz's] balance-of-power system are set in motion precisely by states who seek to conquer the world, or a substantial part of it." But because "Waltz makes no claim to be able to predict the extent of a state's goals from its structural position in the international system," Snyder argues, "the fundamental dynamic of Waltz's theory is driven by inputs from outside the boundaries of the system, as he defines those boundaries" (p. 9).

Second, Waltz's theory assumes that systems of the same polarity behave similarly despite differences in the power interests of the units. Stephen Walt convincingly shows, however, that states ally to balance against threats rather than against power alone.[21] Thus, changes in unit interests alone can drastically alter system dynamics and stability.

For these reasons, I treat the power preferences of the actors as a model-based feature that both differentiates the units of the system and, as a result, systems of the same structure. For the sake of parsimony, the continuous concept of state interest will be reduced to a dichotomous variable; units are identified as either status quo or revisionist.

Status quo powers are usually those states that won the last major-power war and created a new world order in accordance with their interests by redistributing territory and prestige.[22] As satiated powers, status quo states seek primarily to keep, not increase, their resources. For these states, the costs of war exceed the gains.

By contrast, revisionist states—variously called imperialist, expansive, revolutionary, have-not, aggressor, or unsatiated powers—are those states that seek to increase, not just keep, their resources.[23] For these states, the gains from war exceed the costs. Revisionist states are often those states that have increased their power "after the existing international order was fully established and the benefits were already allocated."[24] Thus, they often share a common desire to overturn the status quo order—the prestige, resources, and principles of the system.

Revisionist states are not always actively engaged in overturning the status quo; they may be temporarily passive because they lack the relative economic, military, and/or political capabilities needed to challenge the protector(s) of the status quo (e.g., the Soviet Union, 1919–39; Germany, 1919–36; and Japan, 1919–

31). Buzan points out, "Even the most rabid revisionist state cannot pursue its larger objectives if it cannot secure its home base."[25] It should also be noted that revisionist states need not be predatory powers; they may oppose the status quo for defensive reasons. As Schuman comments, revisionist states typically "feel humiliated, hampered, and oppressed by the *status quo*" and thus "demand changes, rectifications of frontiers, a revision of treaties, a redistribution of territory and power" to modify it.[26]

By elevating the concept of state interest to a position as prominent as that occupied by the distribution of capabilities, the model more accurately reflects the twin-pillared aspect of traditional realist theory—its equal focus on both the power and interests of states. Unlike Waltz's theory, which is all structure and no units, the revised theory contains complex unit-structure interactions such that predictions are codetermined by the power and interests of the units and the structures within which they are embedded.

Other factors, such as geography, military technology, and misperception of structure might be added to the theory.[27] I mention these elements when necessary, but space limitations prevent their full incorporation within the model. It is my contention, however, that these factors are generally less important than the power and interests of the units—without which geography and military technology provide only partial answers.

The next step is to link unit-structure interactions to expected outcomes, i.e., system stability, alliance patterns, individual foreign-policy strategies. The theory's two independent variables combine to produce many permutations, each of which must be analyzed according to its own systemic properties. For this reason, it is not possible to make quick deductions for all types of systems, let alone tests for all classes of cases. The discussion will therefore be limited to tripolarity and the Second World War, arguably the two most misunderstood cases.

Tripolar Systems

Given the definitional requirement that the weakest pole must have greater than half the resources of the strongest pole, there are four possible tripolar power configurations:

(1) $A = B = C$
(2) $A > B = C, A < B + C$
(3) $A < B = C$
(4) $A > B > C, A < B + C$

Definitions

(1) Revisionist powers: states that seek to increase their resources.

(2) Status quo powers: states that seek only to keep their resources.

(3) To qualify as a pole, a state must have greater than half the resources of the most powerful state in the system; all other great powers are classed as middle powers.

(4) Resources = military power potential.

(5) System stability means that no actor in the system is eliminated.

Assumptions

(1) Wars are costly; for revisionist states, the gains from war exceed the costs; for status quo states they do not.

(2) The alternatives among which the members of the triad may choose are (a) do nothing; (b) align with another member to block an attack; (c) align with another member to eliminate the third member; (d) wage a lone attack to eliminate one or both members of the triad.

(3) A stronger member or coalition defeats a weaker member or coalition.

(4) The strength of a coalition equals the combined total resources of its members: If $A = 3$ and $B = 2$, then $AB = 5$.

(5) In a coalition attack, the resources of the victim are divided proportionately among the winning coalition members. In a lone attack, they are absorbed in total by the victor.

(6) Resources are increased only by eliminating a member of the triad. States do not voluntarily cede resources.

Type 1. The Equilateral Tripolar System: $A = B = C$

This is the most unstable of all power configurations because it cannot be balanced by external means (alliances). While this is true of any odd-numbered system composed of equal units, the imbalance is proportionally greatest in this triad, where A and B combined possess 66 percent of the total resources as against C's 33 percent share.[28]

Composed of three equally sized units, this system is particularly prone to what Jervis calls "indirect effects"—systemic outcomes that do not correspond to the intentions of the actors.[29] For instance, an increase in either bilateral cooperation or friction between any two poles heightens the incentive to gang up against one of the poles, regardless of the intentions of the actors. Why increased hostility between two poles should result in instability requires no explanation. The connection between the increased cooperation of two poles and instability is not as obvious, however, because the outcome (system instability) is typically an indirect effect.

Suppose each pole earmarks half of its unreserved forces against each of the other two poles. Now, imagine that poles *A* and *B* reciprocally reserve or demobilize all or some substantial part of the forces that each has been deploying against the other. They now have more forces or resources to target against *C*. Consequently, *C*'s defense has been made less secure with respect to both *A* and *B*, whether or not the action was designed to have this effect.[30] Arther Lee Burns states the axiom thusly: "The closer the alliance between any two or more Powers, the greater the increase of opposition or 'pressure' (other things being equal) between any one of the two and any third Power or group of Powers."[31]

In general terms, this means that an equilateral tripolar system has a greater chance of maintaining stability when bilateral contacts between the poles are of low frequency and intensity. At the very least, each pole must prevent the formation of a hostile two-against-one coalition. This in turn depends upon the specific mix of revisionist and status quo poles within the triad.

One Revisionist Pole. Given only one revisionist pole, a stable system should result. Potential aggression will likely take the form of the lone revisionist pole attacking the nearest status quo pole. But such an attack is improbable because individual aggression in tripolarity tends to be self-defeating. On the one hand, if a stalemate results (and this is most likely among equally powerful poles), both combatants are weakened in relation to the neutral third, who obviously has no incentive to join the fray. On the other hand, if the revisionist pole appears to be winning, the neutral third must join the status quo pole to ensure its own survival. Consequently, war is unlikely because the revisionist attacker can expect only a war of attrition or certain defeat.

A geographically distanced pole may assume one of four roles: (1) *tertius gaudens*, (2) the abettor, (3) the eyewitness, or (4) the mediator. The first two are likely to be played by a revisionist pole, the latter two by a status quo pole. As *tertius gaudens* (the enjoying third), the remote pole turns the dissension of the two geographically proximate poles to its own advantage by asking an exploitative price for its support. As the abettor, it instigates conflict between the other members of the triad for its own purposes. In the role of eyewitness, it does nothing and seeks nothing from the conflict. In the mediator role, it declares neutrality toward the conflict and works to stabilize the triad.[32]

Two Revisionist Poles. A tripolar system composed of two revisionist poles is typically unstable because both power maximizers are highly motivated to augment their resources at the expense of the lone status quo pole. As a result, the two revisionist poles can be expected to put aside their competition temporarily so as to make substantial gains. And because the winning coalition consists of two equally powerful partners, each member can expect to gain half the spoils, so neither pole will be left vulnerable to the other after the war. Hence, there is little to prevent the partitioning of the isolated status quo state. Eliminating a member of the triad transforms the system into a relatively stable but competitive bipolar system because the two remaining poles (both power maximizers seeking gains at the other's expense) are expected to resume their rivalry.

A favorable geographic position may temporarily protect the lone status quo pole, but it will not appreciably stabilize this type of tripolar system. Suppose that the two revisionist poles are in close geographical proximity and the status quo pole is distanced from them. The triad contains, in effect, two subsystems: one bipolar, the other unipolar, wherein the rivalry between the two revisionist poles protects the remote status quo pole by preventing them from ganging up against it. The status quo power may assume the role of either "the enjoying third" or the "abettor." In either case, it remains on the sidelines, hoping that the two revisionist poles will bleed each other to death.

But this is a dangerous strategy for the status quo power because one of the revisionist poles may be able to defeat the other by either forming a winning alliance with one or more revisionist powers or by devouring weaker states until enough additional resources are acquired to defeat the nearest pole. Once this is accomplished, the victorious revisionist pole would be in control of at least twice as many resources as the lone status quo pole. (The case study discusses Hitler's use of this strategy and why it failed.)

Three Revisionist Poles. In this case, in which all three members are of equal strength and are revisionist powers, any possible coalition—*AB, BC,* and *AC*—is equally likely, making for an extremely volatile situation. All three members seek coalition since isolation means extinction. But the structure of this type of tripolar system prohibits external "balancing" behavior (alliances for the purpose of counterbalancing a stronger or more threatening power or alliance) because any coalition easily *defeats* the isolated third member. In addition, since all three members are revisionist powers, each pole must always be suspicious of the other two and none can enjoy true long-term security. Consequently, this system should exhibit the tendency to evolve into a stable bipolar system because two poles will be tempted to destroy the isolated third to gain lasting security. Eliminating one pole through partitioning should not present major difficulties because each member of the winning coalition is of equal strength and is therefore entitled to an equal share of the spoils.

Three Status Quo Poles. This, of course, is the most stable tripolar system because the interests of the actors are not strictly opposed to each other. In this system, in which no pole seeks the elimination of any other, the integrity of all three actors is virtually assured. Continued systemic stability simply requires the poles to make their intentions known, avoid provocative acts, and coordinate and consult with the others about their individual foreign policies. Their tacit agreement not to attack other poles in the system may be formalized by mutual nonaggression pacts between all dyads and/or a collective security agreement wherein each pole promises to come to the aid of any attacked pole.

Type 2. The Paradox of Power: $A > B = C$ but $A < B + C$

In this type of tripolar system, A is slightly stronger than B and C, who are of equal strength. All three members strive for a coalition because any combination defeats the isolated member. Paradoxically, when A is a revisionist pole, its strength proves to be a handicap since both B and C find A less attractive as a coalition partner than each other. This is true because in either an AB or AC alliance, A would be in control of its weaker partner. Consequently, A, in a coalition with either B or C, would be expected to gain at least an equal share of the rewards, and probably the lion's share—further disadvantaging the weaker ally, who must receive the bulk of the reward to gain security. Alternatively, a BC coalition (in which both B and C are of equal strength) secures an equal distribution of the reward and does not threaten either member.

Conversely, when A is a status quo pole, either B or C may align with it against the isolated third. Such an alignment is especially likely if either B or C is a status quo state, in which case an overpowering status quo coalition will form to oppose the lone revisionist member of the triad. Finally, when all three poles are status quo states, no coalition is predicted because there is no threat.

(This "no-coalition" prediction holds for any system composed of all status quo units).

Type 3. The Partitioned Third and the Balancer: A < B = C

The Partitioned Third. When both B and C are revisionist, A cannot align with either because once the coalition has partitioned the isolated member of the triad, A will be destroyed by its stronger ally. The only remaining alliance, therefore, is BC, which can safely partition A because its members are of equal strength. Indeed, for security reasons alone, B and C should partition A: B must block AC and C must prevent AB. Therefore, the most likely scenario is the formation of a BC coalition for the purpose of partitioning A and achieving an equal balance between B and C.

The Balancer. However, if B and C are mutually hostile, then it is clearly in A's interest to prolong their rivalry by acting as a balancer, gaining at the expense of the other two poles. The role of balancer, however, is a dangerous one for the weakest pole in the system to play because it must guarantee through skillful diplomacy that the two warring poles do not temporarily set aside their differences to gang up against it. This is no easy task, for by playing the role of balancer and continually frustrating the desires of B and C, A cultivates—through the years—a certain amount of bitterness from both B and C. Thus, one would expect that typically the balancer role would be played by a state that was stronger than the other two combined, not by the weakest triadic member.

Type 4. The Unbalanced Tripolar System: A > B > C but A < B + C

Although the logic is counterintuitive, a tripolar system is most likely to exhibit stability when at least some of the poles are of unequal weights. Consider, for instance, a tripolar system in which the power ratio among the three poles is $A = 5$, $B = 4$, $C = 3$. Let us further assume that all members of the triad are revisionist powers. At first glance, this system appears to be extremely unstable (i.e., one of the actors will be eliminated) and warprone, since any contest between two actors is decisive and any coalition is a winning coalition. Yet, it proves to be a very simple and stable form of a balance-of-power system.

First, consider an isolated attack within this triad. In such a situation, it is immediately obvious to the third power that it must block the efforts of the attacker by joining the weaker side, or else be dominated by the victor. The attacker knows not only that the third power must resist its efforts to destroy the initial victim but also that it has no hope of prevailing against such a coalition. Thus, a stronger member of the triad will not be tempted to attack a weaker power; the dynamics of the system discourage offensive actions.

Now let us consider an attack by a coalition against an isolated third pole. Although every coalition is a winning coalition, all pairings in a 5-4-3 triad are unbalanced—they consist of a stronger and a weaker member. Thus, if any coalition formed, went to war, and won as expected, the system would be transformed into a dyad with the weaker pole at the mercy of its stronger partner. The weaker ally will be imperiled even if the spoils of victory are divided equally rather than according to each member's proportionate resources.[33]

In summary, given the dynamics of this system, any pairing will inevitably result in only one remaining actor; since this is obvious to all three poles, no coalition will form in the first place. Although all actors are power maximizers and every pairing forms a winning coalition, what Jervis calls the "perverse effects" of the system virtually assure the continued integrity of all the actors and the absence of war among them. This is true for all mixes of revisionist and status quo states except a mix containing two status quo poles.

Ironically, when there are two status quo poles, the system is potentially unstable. In this situation, the status quo poles may be motivated, for defensive purposes, to wage a preventive war to destroy the revisionist pole, which poses a latent, if not immediate, threat to their individual security.

The Case Study: World War II

Operationalizing the Variables

Capabilities. Data from the Correlates of War (COW) project is used to measure the relative capabilities of the major powers.[34] COW capability scores reflect three distinct measures of national power: (1) military (existing forces), (2) industrial (war potential), and (3) demographic (staying power and war-augmenting capability). Each component is divided into two subcomponents. The military dimension consists of the number of military personnel and military expenditures; the industrial component is measured by production of pig iron (pre-1900) or ingot steel (post-1900) and fuel consumption; and the demographic component is divided into urban and total population. The composite power index is the sum of each state's mean score for the six measures as a percentage of all scores within the great-power subset.

TABLE 9.1   COW Percentage Share Distribution of Great-Power
Capabilities, 1938

U.S.S.R.	U.S.	Germany	U.K.	Japan	France	Italy
25.0	22.7	20.2	10.4	9.4	6.9	4.9

Source: Compiled using the "Correlates of War Capability Data-Set Printout, December 1987" made available through the Inter-University Consortium for Political and Social Research at the University of Michigan.

As Table 9.1 indicates, by 1938 the international system was tripolar, with Germany, the United States, and the Soviet Union being the three poles. Britain and France had fallen from the first tier, joining Japan and Italy as middle powers.

Interests. A state will be coded "revisionist" if (1) it expressed bitter dissatisfaction with the territorial changes, treaty revisions, or reparations that resulted from the last major-power war (whether it was on the winning or losing side), or (2) it grew to full power after the new order was established and complained that its increased power entitled it to greater benefits (territorial or prestige). All states that do not fall into at least one of these categories will be labeled "status quo."

If we apply these criteria to the interwar period, Britain, France, and the U.S. won the last major-power war, established the new order, and thus were sated status quo powers. By contrast, Germany and Russia[35] were both defeated in the First World War and saw the map of Europe redrawn largely at their expense. (Austria-Hungary was the biggest loser, of course.) Germany also suffered the loss of its colonies, huge reparation payments, and severe limitations on the size and equipment of its armed forces. Italy and Japan, though technically victors in the First World War, felt so betrayed by the Versailles peace settlement that they could not be relied upon to defend the new order.[36] By the 1930s, both states had substantially increased their military power and sought to expand beyond their existing territorial borders. As expected, Rome and Tokyo pursued naked revisionist aims: Mussolini tried to create a second Roman Empire, while imperial Japan strove for hegemony over East Asia (the so-called Co-Prosperity Sphere, which it announced in 1938). In fact, these two middle powers unleashed the initial blows against the status quo order.[37]

Table 9.2 converts the COW numbers into ratios and specifies the interests of the states:

TABLE 9.2   The Capabilities and Interests of the Major Powers, 1938

	Type	*Power*	*Interest*
U.S.S.R.	pole	5.0	revisionist
U.S.	pole	4.5	status quo
Germany	pole	4.0	revisionist
Britain	middle	2.1	status quo
Japan	middle	1.9	revisionist
France	middle	1.4	status quo
Italy	middle	1.0	revisionist

A. W. Deporte's discussion of this period nicely summarizes the essence of what Table 9.2 shows:

> Two things are sure: first, that both Germany and Russia were profoundly anti-status quo, and second, that the sum of their potential power was much greater than the sum of the power of those European countries that were pro-status quo (assuming the continued political abstention of the United States). . . . We may conclude, then, that in the long run the status quo was bound to be changed, but when, how, and to whose advantage were less certain.[38]

Table 9.2 also suggests that whether a state is revisionist or status quo is not an endogenous function of the distribution of capabilities, as some realist, Marxist, and geopolitical theories posit: Two of three poles were revisionist and half of the second-ranking great powers supported the status quo. Perhaps it is fair to conclude that for some reason the history of nations supports what the French characterized by the *bon mot* "l'appétit vient en mangeant," translated by Shakespeare as "the appetite grows by what it feeds on."[39]

Hitler's Assessment of the Balance of Power

Aside from its blatant racial cast, Hitler's expansionist grand strategy differed little from late nineteenth-century formulations for *Mitteleuropa*. Its foundation rested on the same encirclement fears that had motivated German geopoliticians and elites prior to the First World War. But unlike in the nineteenth century, Hitler's strategy and discussions of the balance of power suggest that he viewed the international system in tripolar, not multipolar, terms. Britain and France were now decaying powers; Germany, under his leadership, was poised for a continental grab. Germany had only two rivals, the Soviet Union and the United States. The continued growth of these two upstart, continent-spanning powers threatened the very survival of Germany, and all of Europe for that matter.

The tripolar image of Europe's vitality withering under the shadows cast by the growth in American and Russian power surfaces throughout Hitler's writings and those of his leading geopolitician, Karl Haushofer. Haushofer consistently warned of the force inherent in vast spaces, which made Russia and America the twin threats posing the greatest danger to European civilization:

> The threat to the world is precisely the growth of the space-colossi and the economic giants, like the realm of the Soviets, descendant of white Czarism, and the United States, heir of British colonial tradition; viz., encompassing and transgressing as far as their economic- political claws can reach.[40]

Only a united Europe under German leadership could prevent world domination by the North American and/or Asian (under Bolshevik leadership) continents. Accordingly, Hitler often argued that Germany did not fight merely for its own sake but to ensure the independence of Europe.

Hitler's propaganda of defending European civilization against alien barbarism by uniting the Continent under German rule attracted adherents from all parts of Europe to the Nazi cause. The crusade to create a united Europe "appealed to . . . young men from Holland, Belgium, and Scandinavia, who joined the Waffen SS to save Europe from Asiatic barbarism, by which they meant the Soviet Union."[41] In 1967 a book of interviews with former Waffen SS soldiers recruited in Holland was published. One of the soldiers, an Amsterdam bank clerk, says: "We no longer saw Holland, Germany, or France as contradictory forces, but we saw the creation of a New Europe! That's what we were fighting for! I met some Flemish Belgians in the train to Hamburg. They had the same ideas. And besides, a greater Europe would release them from the Walloons." Another former recruit exclaims: "I have sincerely believed in a united Europe through National Socialism. That didn't happen. I still believe we will have a united Europe, but not with this democracy. Democracy cannot bind us together." Still another opines: "The division of Europe in independent nations had probably come to an end. Units grew larger all the time. Only Germany was able to achieve this in Europe. Only Germany was powerful enough to ensure that Europe played the important leading role in the world."[42]

The American Threat

In *Mein Kampf* (1925), Hitler makes several references to the awesome power of the United States. At one point, he touts American power to emphasize the superiority of continental growth as opposed to colonial expansion as a method for power accretion:

> Many European States today are comparable to pyramids standing on their points. Their European territory is ridiculously small as compared with their burden of colonies, foreign trade, etc. One may say, the point is in Europe, the base in the whole world; in comparison with the American Union, which still has its bases in its own continent and touches the remaining part of the world only with its points. From this results, however, the unheard-of strength of this State and the weakness of most of the European colonial powers.[43]

In his second book (1928), Hitler argued that Europe's privileged place in the world order was endangered by the "threatening world hegemony of the North American Continent."[44] "With the American Union, a new power of such dimensions has come into being as threatens to upset the whole former power and orders of rank of the states."[45] Continuing on this theme, Hitler writes:

> That this danger threatens all of Europe has, after all, already been perceived by some today. Only few of them wish to understand what it means for Germany. Our people, if it lives with the same thoughtlessness in the future as in the past, will have to renounce its claim to world importance. . . . As a state in the future order of world states, [Germany] will at best be like that which Switzerland and Holland have been in Europe up to now.[46]

Similarly, returning from a visit to the United States in 1938, Major General Dr. Karl Haushofer, Hitler's leading geopolitical strategist, declared, "Potentially, the United States is the world's foremost political and economic power, predestined to dominate the world once it puts its heart into power politics."[47]

Indeed, of all the great powers, Hitler most feared the war potential of the United States. As early as 1937, Hitler and Göring, the head of Germany's air force, had authorized the development of bombers to strike at New York and other East Coast cities; and, as Gerhard Weinberg puts it, "if nothing much eventually came of these projects, it was not for lack of trying."[48] By January 1939, Hitler's statements indicated an obsession with America's shadow on the European scene. "From that time on," John Lukacs asserts, "he began to consider Roosevelt as his principal enemy—a conviction that Hitler held to the end."[49] Of the American danger to Germany, Hitler commented, "Confronted with America, the best we can do is to hold out against her to the end."[50]

The Soviet Threat

In contrast to the threat posed by America's political and economic mastery, the Soviet Union endangered "the freedom of the world" through "an inundation by disease bacilli [international Jewry] which at the moment have their breeding ground in Russia."[51] Hitler argued that the Jews had controlled Russia since the Bolshevik Revolution, and that a global Jewish conspiracy radiating outward from Soviet Russia threatened the continued survival of the Aryan race and its German core. Thus Hitler's Continental strategy—defeating the Soviet Union and thereby achieving German hegemony over Europe— became inextricably linked with the extermination of the Jews.[52]

Stalin's purges caused Hitler to lower his opinion of Soviet military strength. For instance, on April 29, 1939, the premier of Hungary, Count Pál Teleki, told Hitler that he had received a "warning" from the American minister to "be careful" not to align with Germany. The American had also predicted that Britain would "overthrow" Italy as well as Germany if Mussolini decided to honor the Pact of Steel with the reich. Hitler replied that "the Americans were mixing up the present situation with that of 1914." He went on to explain how the balance of power had shifted since then:

> In contrast to then he pointed to the forces of today, referred to the colossal power of Russia in 1914 as compared with a weak Russia today, referred to France's comparatively much greater military power then than now and added that, at present, France's population was very low. Four French age groups meant 450,000 soldiers and four German age groups meant over 2 million soldiers. . . . Our air superiority was tremendous. French policy was mad but the military, who after all could see the relative strengths, advocated peace. . . . Reverting to Russia, he said that according to our information this State had recently butchered four thousand high-ranking officers. Such a country could not wage war.[53]

Russia's weakened position afforded Germany a window of opportunity: Germany, Hitler believed, could now confidently wage a preventive war against the Soviet Union to eliminate this colossal menace to the East and gain supremacy on the Continent.

The minutes of the Hitler-Teleki conversation also reveal that the führer held British capabilities in equally low regard:

Today we dominated the Mediterranean, Central Europe and the Far East. Britain was in no position to render help, but was running around everywhere looking for help. Before, and even after Munich, Britain had constantly given guarantees. Britain did not impress the Führer.[54]

Hitler went on to say, "A change in England's strength was scarcely to be expected in the next two years. Even now she had no more steel and wanted to buy from us. With us it was different, for we were at the peak of our war production. If England really meant to encircle us then the Führer would strike first."[55] Similarly, Joachim von Ribbentrop declared in a conversation with M. Cincar-Markovic, the Yugoslav foreign minister, "Let there be no doubt about it, Germany could face calmly any combination of enemies."[56]

But by 1941 Hitler had reassessed Soviet military strength. Justifying the timing of the German attack on the Soviet Union, he asserted:

A few days before our entry into Russia, I told Goering that we were facing the severest test in our existence. . . . What confirmed me in my decision to attack without delay was the information . . . that a single Russian factory was producing by itself more tanks than all our factories. . . . if someone had told me that the Russians had ten thousand tanks, I'd have answered: 'You're completely mad!'[57]

As the German-Soviet war dragged on, Hitler grew more convinced that he had made the right decision to attack Russia when he had:

The more we see of conditions in Russia, the more thankful we must be that we struck in time. In another ten years there would have sprung up in Russia a mass of industrial centres, inaccessible to attack, which would have produced armaments on an inexhaustible scale, while the rest of Europe would have degenerated into a defenceless plaything of Soviet policy.[58]

In sum, the two titans posing the greatest obstacle to Germany's achieving world-power status were no longer France and Britain but rather America and the Soviet Union. Thus, according to Hitler, Soviet Russia had to be neutralized or else within a few decades, Germany and the rest of Europe would be engulfed, as by the prior Asiatic hordes, by the new Bolshevik menace to the East. Similarly, the growing strength of the American continent threatened all European great powers and their colonial possessions.

Because of its remote geographic location, the United States could not be defeated in the near future. But the other polar power, the

Soviet Union, could be destroyed if Germany sufficiently augmented its power resources prior to the "life and death" struggle for Continental hegemony. Thus, as will be discussed, conquest of France and the rest of Western Europe became a necessary sideshow to provide Germany with the additional resources required for victory in the ultimate battle against the Soviet Union.

The key for German success was to avoid a two-front war. Hitler thought he could achieve this by quickly defeating France; with its only ally out of the war, Britain would then sue for peace and accept German supremacy on the Continent. In other words, England would fall under the spell of Nazi dynamism and thus bandwagon with, rather than challenge or try to disrupt, the ascendant power of Germany and its European empire. Together, Britain and Germany would first eliminate the Bolshevik menace to the East and then defeat the American continent. Of the latter task, Hitler said: "I rejoice on behalf of the German people at the idea that one day we will see England and Germany marching together against America."[59]

Hitler's Tripolar Strategy

As early as the 1920s, Hitler planned a three-fold program to achieve world hegemony. The first step was to establish a Greater Germany through the *Anschluss* with Austria and the absorption of Czechoslovakia and adjacent areas in Poland occupied by German-speaking people. These lightening wars would cement German economic and political hegemony over central Europe and secure the additional strategic resources and military power (i.e., the 35 Czech divisions) needed for the next military campaign, the swing westward. The *Wehrmacht* would then smash Belgium, Holland, and France, neutralizing the Western flank and gaining direct control over the raw materials, food supplies, and labor reserves of Western Europe—all of which would serve to keep the German war economy afloat.[60]

Having brought Hungary, Yugoslavia, and Rumania firmly into the German economic sphere of influence and having secured through conquest free access to the resources of Poland, Denmark, Norway, the Low Countries, and France, Nazi Germany would finally be ready to engage in the inevitable titantic war against the Soviet Union, the success of which would determine the fate of Hitler's ultimate goal of *Lebensraum* (living space in the East, particularly the Soviet Ukraine). Under Hitler's grand design, "What India was for England, the territories of Russia will be for us."[61]

During the 1930s, Hitler added the United States to his master plan. In the drive for world domination, Germany first required hegemony over the Eurasian landmass. With these resources in hand, Germany would be able to favorably wage the final war against the U.S. (the third pole). Gerhard Weinberg explains:

> The Americans were the real threat to German predominance in the world. Hitler's deduction from this analysis was simple: only a Eurasian empire under German domination could successfully cope with this menace. A third war was now added to the original two. After the first two wars had enabled it to construct a continental empire from the Atlantic to the Urals, Germany would take on the United States. One of the major tasks to be performed by the National Socialist movement, therefore, must be the preparation of Germany for this conflict.[62]

Emphasizing demographics, Hitler viewed German Continental hegemony as a prerequisite for the ultimate war with the U.S.: "It is ridiculous to think of a world policy as long as one does not control the Continent. . . . A hundred and thirty million people in the Reich, ninety in the Ukraine. Add to these the other States of the New Europe, and we'll be four hundred millions, compared with the hundred and thirty million Americans."[63]

In sum, Hitler's grand strategy consisted of a series of isolated wars of escalating magnitude. First, Germany would win easily obtainable objectives in short and decisive campaigns in the east. Next, Germany would defeat France and coerce the British into an alliance against Russia and America. Finally, Germany would be ready to unleash successive polar wars against the Soviet Union and then the United States.

Hitler planned to overturn the tripolar system by initially devouring small and middle powers and then defeating quickly the nearest polar power (the Soviet Union) before the other pole (the U.S.) could intervene (see earlier discussion of equilateral tripolarity). German Continental hegemony would transform the tripolar system into a bipolar one, pitting the stronger European continent against the weaker American continent (Hitler believed that the U.S. would annex Canada). The final war would then convert the international system from bipolarity to hegemony under German rule.

According to the führer, the British Empire was also endangered by America's inexorable economic, military, and naval growth: "[Roosevelt] wants to run the world and rob us all of a place in the sun. He says he wants to save England but he means he wants to be ruler and heir of the British Empire."[64] Given his misguided notion of an underlying Anglo-American rivalry, the reich chancellor confidently expected Britain to join a German-led European coalition against the North American continent.[65]

But just in case the "thick-headed" British failed to see where their true interests lay, Hitler went to great lengths to convince Britain that Germany sought only freedom of action on the Continent and had no intention of threatening Britain's naval supremacy or empire. In the Anglo-German naval treaty (1935), whereby Hitler agreed to a proportional naval strength of 35:100, "Germany took the initiative in the negotiations in the spirit of making a gesture in Great Britain's interest; the German proposals themselves were clearly aimed at reassuring [Britain] on the question of German naval rivalry."[66]

Having made several generous offers to gain an Anglo-German alliance without success, the führer grew disillusioned with the British. He could not understand why the British refused to see that Germany, unlike France and the United States, sought only European hegemony and would gladly allow Britain to maintain her world ambitions. How could the British resist German friendship, he wondered, in the face of the obvious common threats posed by America and the Bolshevik menace? Was it not obvious that Germany's security had been severely compromised by the Franco-Russian alliance and that Russia was, in Hitler's words, "now the greatest power in the whole of Europe"?[67] Surely, this made an Anglo-German combination the most natural of alliances.[68]

Unable to gain an Anglo-German alliance, Hitler turned to the Soviet Union. In accordance with the prior discussion of tripolarity with two revisionist poles, to overturn the tripolar system, Hitler needed to augment German resources by waging a series of offensive wars against small and middle powers. This depended on cooperation with the revisionist pole, the USSR. At the very least, Hitler had to prevent the formation of a hostile Anglo-Franco-Russian coalition, as had occurred in 1914. Without the Nazi-Soviet pact, Germany could not have attacked Poland and France.

After taking care of France and Britain, Germany would turn around and attack its penultimate target, the Soviet Union. That Hitler planned this strategy prior to signing the Nazi-Soviet pact is made clear in his statement to the high commissioner of the United Nations, Carl J. Burckhardt, on August 11, 1939, in which the führer decried what he believed was the West's stupidity in not coming to terms with Germany: "Everything that I undertake is directed against Russia; if the West is too stupid and too blind to understand this, then I will be forced to reach an understanding with the Russians, smash the West, and then turn all my concentrated strength against the Soviet Union."[69] The prophesy about Russia shows that the Soviet pact did not signal a change in Hitler's ultimate goal to destroy the Soviet Union; rather, it was nothing more than an expedient to avoid a two-front war —a necessary short-term act of pure power politics.

The "power" side of the model predicts a Nazi-Soviet alliance, but only one in which the Soviets actively participate in the fighting and are assured of receiving along with Germany an equal share of the spoils. (See discussion of equilateral tripolar system with two revisionist poles.) By joining Germany to divide Poland, Stalin behaved according to the "partitioned third" version of tripolarity. True, Poland was not a pole; but the power configuration of Poland, Germany, and the Soviet Union was $A < B = C$, and so the logic of what I call a Type 3 tripolar system still applies. In carving up Eastern Europe, the territory that lay between the two revisionist poles was divided equally between them so that neither side made relative gains vis-à-vis the other.

Conversely, by encouraging Germany to attack westward by itself, Stalin acted contrary to the logic of the "power" side of the model. Stalin's "major blunder," as Isaac Deutscher correctly points out, was that "he expected Britain and France to hold their ground against Germany for a long time; . . . he overrated France's military strength; and he underrated Germany's striking power."[70] Consistent with these observations, in 1939 Stalin stated that "democratic states . . . are without doubt stronger than the fascist ones both militarily and economically."[71] Thus, Stalin calculated that the oncoming war between the fascist and democratic coalitions "would be a protracted one that would result in their mutual weakening or exhaustion while Soviet Russia was at peace and rebuilding its own strength."[72]

It is reasonable to assume that had Stalin realized that the system was no longer multipolar but instead tripolar (and by extension that the combined strength of the two middle powers, France and Britain, therefore did not equal that of Germany) he would have balanced against Germany—a rival revisionist pole. Indeed, in a conversation after the Second World War, Voroshilov said, "We in spite of it all thought that if Germany attacked Britain and France, it would bog down there for a long time. Who could have known that France would collapse in two weeks?"[73]

Given his misperception of the power distribution, Stalin had good reasons to seek a deal with Hitler. A nonaggression pact with Germany would destroy the status quo, afford easy spoils in Eastern Europe and Finland, and instigate a war of attrition among the capitalist powers. Better still, the Soviet Union enjoyed the role of kingmaker; both Germany and the democratic powers needed it to form a winning coalition. Thus, Germany would be made to pay heavily for Soviet assistance in a war from which Russia could safely abstain. Stalin used his bargaining power to prolong the Anglo-Franco-Soviet negotiations just long enough to extract additional concessions from Hitler, in exchange for which the Soviet leader put his signature to the pact with Germany that he desperately wanted anyway. It appeared that Stalin had succeeded in the role of abettor: Germany was deflected to the west while the Soviets comfortably looked on from the sidelines, gaining at the others' expense.[74]

Speaking of the pact, Stalin commented: "Of course it's all a game to see who can fool whom. I know what Hitler's up to. He thinks he's outsmarted me, but actually it's I who have tricked him."[75] Events would soon prove otherwise: Hitler had instead duped Stalin. With the September 1 deadline for the Polish attack only a week away, Hitler was willing to give the Soviet dictator whatever he wanted to secure Soviet neutrality and thereby deter Britain from honoring its pledge to Poland. Indeed, the führer seemed to be in an especially giving mood, confident that he would attack and crush Russia in the near future, taking back all he had given and more.[76]

In retrospect, we know that it would have been far better for the Soviets to have balanced against, rather than bandwagoned with, Germany. In that case, Stalin would have presented Hitler with the prospect of a two-front war, seriously undermining the führer's strategy and perhaps causing its abandonment. But because he mistakenly believed that Europe was structurally a tripolar, not a bipolar, system with France and Britain constituting a third pole, Stalin expected a war of attrition in the West. The fall of France abruptly ended Stalin's dream of easy conquests in a postwar period when the rest of Europe would be exhausted.

After the defeat of France, Hitler again felt optimistic about his chances of negotiating an end to the war with Britain. Together, Britain and Germany would first eliminate the Soviet Union and then turn their energies against the American continent. Backed by U.S. material assistance, however, Britain chose to fight rather than jump on the Nazi bandwagon. London's decision for war was eased by progress in its civil and air defense systems that greatly moderated the public's fear of a German "knockout blow."

Hitler's earlier naval concessions proved costly in the Battle of Britain; as late as September 1939, the German navy was woefully unprepared for a naval war with Britain.[77] Then, in early 1940, the German fleet suffered heavy losses in the Norwegian campaign that seriously impaired its ability to support an invasion of Britain four months later. Confronted by the prospect of a war of attrition with Britain that risked prematurely bringing the U.S. into the conflict, Hitler decided that the better gamble was to turn Germany's attention to the defeat of his primary target, the Soviet Union. If Russia could be knocked out of the war, Britain would lose its last potential Continental ally and would, Hitler believed, sue for peace. More important, in control of the European continent, Germany could then wage the final hegemonic war against North America.

Up until the German attack against Russia, the essentials of the strategies of the United States and the Soviet Union paralleled one another. Both countries were unprepared, militarily and psychologically, for war. Both nations viewed the defeat of Hitler's Germany as a vital national security interest, and yet neither state declared war on Germany. Both America and Russia entered the war against Hitler after being attacked. And both states, prior to being attacked, looked to the countries of Western Europe, primarily Britain, to do their fighting for them.[78]

As the lone status quo pole in an equilateral tripolar system, the United States seemed to be the most likely target of a hostile two-against-one coalition. America's enviable geographical position, however, enabled it to play a variety of roles—the eyewitness, the mediator, *tertius gaudens*, and the abettor—within the polar triad. Removed from the struggle over Europe, the U.S. had time to watch events unfold and change roles to suit the situation.

At a very high level of abstraction, the theory accurately predicts American foreign policy. The U.S. was compelled to enter the war when one of the two revisionist poles appeared to be defeating the other. Prior to that time, America stayed on the sidelines, reluctantly providing material support first to Britain and then to the Soviet Union.

But once Germany marched against the Soviet Union, the U.S. could no longer safely adhere to its posture of twilight belligerence; it had to actively participate in the war in order to prevent a "winner-take-all" outcome in the polar war between the two revisionist powers. (See discussion of equilateral tripolar system with two revisionist poles.) A victory by either the Soviet Union or Germany while the U.S. remained on the sidelines would have left one of the two revisionist poles in control of the rest of the Eurasian landmass. Had the U.S. allowed this to occur, it would have faced a revisionist pole of colossal size, against which the U.S. could not expect to defend itself or its allies.

That Roosevelt feared this scenario is evidenced by his adoption of a "Germany-first" strategy in mid-1941. Although America's entry into the war is usually attributed to the Japanese attack on Pearl Harbor, the Atlantic Charter—arranged prior to the Japanese attack on the U.S. but after the German attack on the USSR—indicates that the Roosevelt administration was preparing for war and was principally concerned with defeating Germany.

Both President Roosevelt and Harry Hopkins realized that little American aid would reach the Russians until after the 1941 campaign had been decided. Thus, the security of the United States depended on the Red Army's withstanding the initial German assault. Happily for the U.S., Germany's blitzkrieg strategy was foiled by the vast expanse of the Soviet Union, which allowed the Red Army to trade space for time. Germany might have won its gamble and defeated Russia in 1941, Hitler thought, if not for Mussolini's "idiotic intervention" in Greece.[79] Rescuing Italy cost Germany precious time and resources needed for the Russian campaign.

The failure of the *Wehrmacht*'s great offensive in 1941 gave the U.S. time to mobilize its enormous war machine and join the Soviet Union in an overwhelmingly powerful two-against-one winning coalition. "As Hitler's observations imply, once the United States and Russia gathered and combined their vast resources, Germany's fate would be sealed."[80] Had Hitler's victory come in a hurry, the tripolar system would have been transformed into a bipolar one, pitting the Eurasian continent against the weaker American continent (Hitler believed that the U.S. would annex Canada). The final war would then have converted the international system from bipolarity to hegemony under German rule.

Fortunately, the *Wehrmacht* stalled in 1941 and the U.S. and the Soviet Union went on to defeat and partition Germany. This transformed the volatile tripolar system into a stable bipolar one and finally eliminated the "German problem" that had caused two world wars in twenty-five years.

Implications for the Post-Cold-War World

Over the course of the past two years the unprecedented rate of global change has made the task of political forecasting as difficult as trying to paint a moving train. Yet there are clear signs that the emerging post-cold-war world is again becoming tripolar with the United States, Germany, and Japan as the poles—each in control of a sizable regional bloc.

Supporting this view, Walter Mead envisions a world made up of three rival blocs—Europe, East Asia, and the Americas—with the

U.S. heading the "weakest and most troubled" of the three.[81]
Similarly, Leonard Silk posits that the post-cold-war world

> has become "tripolar" economically, with the United States, Japan and
> Germany (or, in regional terms, North America, the Pacific Rim and the
> European Community) bound together in a complex relationship, both
> rivalrous and interdependent like a tempestuous marriage.
>   Depending on the way the ménage à trois behaves, the
> relationship may split apart or strengthen and mature. Threesomes are
> inherently unstable, however; the immediate danger, the Japanese
> believe, is that the Americans and Europeans will gang up on them.[82]

Likewise, Lester Thurow states, "In 1992 there is one military
superpower, the United States, standing alone, and three economic
superpowers, the United States, Japan, and Europe, centered on
Germany, jousting for economic supremacy. Without a pause, the
contest has shifted from being a military contest to being an economic
contest."[83]

The significance of economic tripolarity has heightened "now that
geoeconomics is turning geopolitics and all warfare into a provincial
phenomenon."[84] Today more than ever, scholars, leaders, and citizens
alike appreciate the links between security and economic issues and
conceive of political power more in terms of its economic than its
military dimension. Typifying this new awareness of the interactions
between economic and security concerns, Leslie Gelb points out that "in
the absence of the Soviet military threat, the Americans, West
Europeans and Japanese have lost incentives to set aside economic
differences. As a result, economic conflicts have become the most
pronounced source of tension between nations, and disputes are becoming
more difficult to resolve."[85]

The political balance is also becoming tripolar. Witness Germany's
decision to recognize Slovenia and Croatia against the objections of the
United States, the European Community, and the United Nations,
demonstrating that it is no longer an economic giant and a political
dwarf.[86] Some even argue that the "new Germany, like its
predecessors, has proved that it is a revisionist power, intent on
reshaping Europe."[87] Anthony Lewis agrees and warns that the "newly
reunited Germany is the big player in Europe, and its powerful
economy is going to make it ever bigger. At a time when angry
nationalism is flaring up in so many places, it is in everyone's urgent
interest to knit Germany into a larger Europe."[88]

Like Germany, Japan is beginning to assert political power more in
accordance with its status as an economic superpower. In the first U.S.-

Japanese bilateral negotiations since the collapse of the Soviet Union, the two countries pledged to share responsibility for maintaining peace and prosperity in the region. Yet, the competitive atmosphere at the Tokyo summit prompted *The Economist* to view it as a turning point in U.S.-Japanese relations: "From valued ally, Japan is being cast increasingly as a dangerous competitor, more of a threat than an opportunity."[89] Indeed, fifty years after Pearl Harbor, many Americans and Europeans are suggesting that Japan is in the process of creating its "Greater East Asian Co-Prosperity Sphere."[90]

Noting the similar tripolar structure of the interwar period and the emerging post-cold-war system, might we soon find ourselves longing for the 'good old days' of strategic bipolarity? For two reasons, I think not.

First, the post-cold-war world revolves around a tripolar economic, not military, competition. True, the three poles are engaged in a fierce, zero-sum game to gain supremacy in seven key industries— microelectronics, biotechnology, the new materials-science industries, telecommunications, civilian aviation, robotics plus machine tools, and computers plus software. But, as Thurow argues,

> No one gets killed; vast resources don't have to be devoted to negative-sum activities. The winner builds the world's best products and enjoys the world's highest standard of living. The loser gets to buy some of those best products—but not as many as the winner. Relative to the military confrontations of the past century, both the winners and the losers are winners in the economic game ahead. Being aggressively invaded by well-made Japanese or German products from firms that intend to conquer American markets is not at all equivalent to the threat of a military invasion from the Soviet Union or mainland China. Nor does it hark back to the German and Japanese military invasions of World War II.[91]

Second, as I have argued elsewhere, the huge increase in the number of democratic states and the fact that, unlike in the interwar system, all three poles of the post-cold-war system are democratic should serve to greatly mitigate the destabilizing effects associated with a tripolar structure.[92] In territorial terms, all three poles are status quo powers, and so the theory presented here predicts that military warfare will not occur among them.

Notes

1. Chester Wilmot, *The Struggle For Europe* (New York: Harper & Brothers, 1952), p. 17.

2. See Reinhard Meyers quoted in J. L. Richardson, "New Perspectives on Appeasement: Some Implications for International Relations," *World Politics*, Vol. 40, No. 3 (April 1988), p. 305.

3. Kenneth Waltz, *Theory of International Politics* (Reading, Mass.: Addison-Wesley, 1979), pp. 175–176.

4. Emerson M. S. Niou and Peter C. Ordeshook, "Stability in Anarchic International Systems," *American Political Science Review*, Vol. 84, No. 4 (December 1990), p. 1231.

5. John Mueller, "The Essential Irrelevance of Nuclear Weapons: Stability in the Postwar World," *International Security*, Vol. 13, No. 2 (Fall 1988), p. 75.

6. For multipolar accounts of World War II, see Waltz, *Theory of International Politics*; Barry Posen, *The Sources of Military Doctrine: France, Britain, and Germany Between the World Wars* (Ithaca and London: Cornell University Press, 1984); Thomas J. Christensen and Jack L. Snyder, "Chain Gangs and Passed Bucks: Predicting Alliance Patterns in Multipolarity," *International Organization*, Vol. 44, No. 2 (Spring 1990), pp. 137–169.

7. Waltz, Theory of International Politics, p. 163.

8. Joseph Grieco, "Anarchy and the Limits of Cooperation: A Realist Critique of the Newest Liberal Institutionalism," *International Organization*, Vol. 42, No. 3 (Summer 1988), pp. 485–507; John Mearsheimer, "Back to the Future: Instability in Europe After the Cold War, " *International Security*, Vol. 15, No. 1 (Summer 1990), pp. 5–56; Christensen and Snyder, "Chain Gangs and Passed Bucks;" Posen, *The Sources of Military Doctrine*; Stephen Walt, *The Origins of Alliances* (Ithaca, N.Y.: Cornell University Press, 1987).

9. Helen Milner, "The Assumption of Anarchy in International Relations Theory: A Critique," *Review of International Studies*, Vol. 17, No. 1 (January 1991), pp. 67–85; David Dessler, "What's At Stake in the Agent-Structure Debate?" *International Organization*, Vol. 43, No. 3 (Summer 1989), pp. 441–473; Alexander Wendt, "The Agent-Structure Problem in International Relations Theory," *International Organization*, Vol. 41, No. 3 (Summer 1987), pp. 335–70; Robert O. Keohane, ed., *Neorealism and Its Critics* (New York: Columbia University Press, 1986); Richard Rosecrance, "International Theory Revisited" *International Organization*, Vol. 35, No. 4 (Autumn 1981), pp. 691–713; and Morton A. Kaplan, *Towards Professionalism in International Theory: Macrosystem Analysis* (New York: Free Press, 1979), pp. 1–89.

10. See Richard Ashley, "The Poverty of Neorealism," *International Organization*, Vol. 38, No. 2 (Spring 1984), pp. 225–286. Snyder raises similar concerns in his critique of Walt's *The Origins of Alliances* and Emerson M. S. Niou, Peter C. Ordeshook, and Gregory F. Rose, *The Balance of Power: Stability in International Systems* (New York: Cambridge University Press, 1989). See Glenn H. Snyder, "Alliances, Balance, and Stability," *International Organization*, Vol. 45, No. 1 (Winter 1991), pp. 121–142, esp. pp. 124, 138.

11. Christensen and Snyder, "Chain Gangs and Passed Bucks," pp. 137–147; Joseph S. Nye, "Neorealism and Neoliberalism," *World Politics*, Vol. 40, No. 2 (January 1988), p. 245; Robert O. Keohane, "Theory of World Politics: Structural Realism and Beyond," in Ada W. Finifter, ed., *Political Science: The*

State of the Discipline (Washington, D.C.: American Political Science Association, 1983), pp. 512–527; John Gerard Ruggie, "Continuity and Transformation in the World Polity: Toward a Neorealist Synthesis," *World Politics*, Vol. 35, No. 2 (January 1983), pp. 267–268.

12. Waltz, Theory of International Politics, p. 93.

13. Of this inequality, Robert Tucker writes: "The history of the international system is a history of inequality par excellence....It is understandable that the natural inequalities of states should impress the observer of state relations. In their physical extent, population, natural resources, and geographic position, states are, as it were, born unequal; so much so, indeed, that by comparison the natural inequalities among individuals appear almost marginal." Robert W. Tucker, *The Inequality of Nations* (New York: Basic Books, 1977), p. 3.

14. See, for example, Mearsheimer, "Back to the Future;" Posen, *The Sources of Military Doctrine*; Walt, *The Origins of Alliances*.

15. Christensen and Snyder, "Chain Gangs and Passed Bucks," p. 138.

16. Mearsheimer, "Back to the Future," p. 18.

17. Niou, Ordeshook, and Rose, *The Balance of Power*; Niou and Ordeshook, "Stability in Anarchic International Systems;" A. F. K. Organski, *World Politics* (New York: Knopf, 1958), pp. 271–338; A. F. K. Organski and Jacek Kugler, *The War Ledger* (Chicago: University of Chicago Press, 1980), pp. 13–63; R. Harrison Wagner, "The Theory of Games and the Balance of Power," *World Politics*, Vol. 38, No. 4 (July 1986), pp. 546–576.

18. Niou and Ordeshook, "Stability in Anarchic International Systems," p. 1230.

19. Wagner, "The Theory of Games," p. 575; Niou, Ordeshook, and Rose, *The Balance of Power*.

20. Waltz, Theory of International Politics, p. 118.

21. Walt, *Origins of Alliances*.

22. For discussions of the terms status quo and revisionist, see Arnold Wolfers, *Discord and Collaboration: Essays on International Politics* (Baltimore: Johns Hopkins Press, 1962), pp. 18, 84–86; Barry Buzan, *People, States, and Fear: The National Security Problem in International Relations* (Chapel Hill: The University of North Carolina Press, 1983), pp. 175–186; and Paul Seabury, "The Idea of the Status Quo," in Seabury, ed., *Balance of Power* (San Francisco: Chandler, 1965), chap. 22.

23. See Hans J. Morgenthau, *Politics Among Nations: The Struggle For Power and Peace*, 1st ed. (New York: Alfred A. Knopf, 1948), p. 21; Frederick L. Schuman, *International Politics: The Destiny of the Western State System*, 4th ed. (New York: MacGraw-Hill, 1948), pp. 377–380; Max Weber, *From Max Weber: Essays in Sociology* translated and edited by H. H. Gerth and C. Wright Mills (New York: Oxford University Press, 1946), chap. 6; Henry A. Kissinger, *A World Restored: Castlereagh, Metternich, and the Problem of Peace, 1812–22* (Boston: Houghton Mifflin, 1957); and Johannes Mattern, *Geopolitics: Doctrine of National Self-Sufficiency and Empire* (Baltimore: Johns Hopkins University Press, 1942). Morgenthau divides the world into

imperialist and status quo powers; Schuman employs the terms satiated and unsatiated powers; Weber distinquishes between isolationist and expansive powers; Kissinger refers to revolutionary and status quo states; and Mattern, like other geopoliticians, differentiates between "have" and "have-not" states.

24. Organski and Kugler, *The War Ledger*, p. 19.

25. Buzan, *People, States, and Fear*, p. 177.

26. Schuman, *International Politics*, p. 378.

27. For analyses of system stability and alliance dynamics based on perceived offensive/defensive advantage and geography, see Robert Jervis, "Cooperation Under the Security Dilemma," *World Politics*, Vol. 30, No. 2 (January 1978), pp. 167–214; Christensen and Snyder, "Chain Gangs and Passed Bucks;" and Ted Hopf, "Polarity, the Offense-Defense Balance, and War," *American Political Science Review*, Vol. 85, No. 2 (June 1991), pp. 475–493. For an analysis of the impact of actors' misperceptions of structure on the origins of the First World War, see William C. Wohlforth, "The Perception of Power: Russia in the Pre-1914 Balance," *World Politics*, Vol. 39, No. 3 (April 1987), pp. 353–381.

28. For similar views of tripolar instability, see Theodore Caplow, *Two Against One: Coalitions in Triads* (New Jersey: Prentice-Hall, 1968); Lowell Dittmer, "The Strategic Triangle: An Elementary Game-Theoretical Analysis," *World Politics*, Vol. 33, No. 4 (July 1981), pp. 485–515; Brian Healy and Arthur Stein, "The Balance of Power in International History: Theory and Reality," *Journal of Conflict Resolution*, Vol. 17, No. 1 (March 1973), pp. 33–61; Waltz, *Theory of International Politics*, p. 163; Morton A. Kaplan, *System and Process in International Politics* (New York: John Wiley & Sons, 1957), p. 34; and Morton A. Kaplan, Arthur Lee Burns, and Richard E. Quandt, "Theoretical Analysis of the 'Balance of Power,'" *Behavioral Science*, Vol. 5, No. 3 (July 1960), p. 244. For theorists who find three-actor games the most stable of all systems, see David Garnham, "The Causes of War: Systemic Findings," in Alan Ned Sabrosky, ed., *Polarity and War: The Changing Structure of International Conflict* (Boulder, Col.: Westview, 1985), p. 20; Charles W. Ostrom, Jr. and John H. Aldrich, "The Relationship Between Size and Stability in the Major Power International System," *American Journal of Political Science*, Vol. 22, No. 4 (November 1978), p. 766; Niou, Ordeshook, and Rose, *The Balance of Power*, p. 95; and Wagner, "The Theory of Games," p. 575.

29. For his discussion of indirect effects, see Robert Jervis, "Systems and Interaction Effects," in Jervis and Snyder, *Coping With Complexity in the International System*, pp. 31–32.

30. This analysis is drawn from Arthur Lee Burns, "From Balance to Deterrence: A Theoretical Analysis," *World Politics*, Vol. 9, No. 4 (July 1957), pp. 494–499.

31. *Ibid.*, p. 497.

32. I have borrowed the terms "abettor" and "eyewitness" from George Liska, *Nations In Alliance: The Limits of Interdependence* (Baltimore: The Johns Hopkins Press, 1962) pp. 163–164; "*tertius gaudens*" and "the mediator" are taken from Caplow, *Two Against One*, p. 20; who, in turn, borrowed them

from Georg Simmel, *The Sociology of Georg Simmel*, trans. Kurt H. Wolff (New York: Free Press, 1950), pp. 148–149.

33. Even supposing that the stronger member promises in advance to turn over the lion's share of the spoils to its weaker partner, the latter must still reject the offer. This is because, after the initially targeted pole has been vanquished, the stronger pole no longer has any incentive (and it cannot be coerced) to comply with the agreement.

34. The COW capability index provides a reasonably accurate picture of the power bases held by the major actors with respect to their relative fighting capabilities. Originally a skeptic myself, I arrived at this view after having constructed my own "capability-index formula" (data available upon request) to test the validity and reliability of the COW numbers for the period 1938–40. My formula consists of ten separate power indices—eight of which are not used in the COW capability index—which attempt to measure the critical mass (population and territory), economic war potential, and military capabilities of the Great Powers. The result of this mini-experiment was that the Great-Power capability shares yielded by my index and the COW index were virtually identical.

35. For the Soviet Union as a "revisionist" power, see Michael Mandelbaum, *The Fate of Nations: The Search for National Security in the Nineteenth and Twentieth Centuries* (New York: Cambridge University Press, 1988), p. 104; Jiri Hochman, *The Soviet Union and the Failure of Collective Security, 1934–1938* (London and Ithaca, N.Y.: Cornell University Press, 1984); Sir Nevile Henderson, *Failure of a Mission: Berlin 1937–1939* (New York: G. P. Putnam's Sons, 1940), p. 258; Louis Fischer, *Russia's Road From Peace to War: Soviet Foreign Relations, 1917–1941* (New York: Harper & Row, 1969), p. 349; Anton W. DePorte, *Europe Between the Superpowers: The Enduring Balance*, 2nd ed. (New Haven and London: Yale University Press, 1979), pp. 31–32, 40; Edward Hallett Carr, *German-Soviet Relations Between the Two World Wars, 1919–1939* (New York: Harper & Row, 1951), p. 123ff. Whether motivated by security or predatory desires, Stalin's post-Munich foreign policy sought changes in the status quo. The USSR is thus coded revisionist.

36. At Versailles, Italy resented the way the allies concluded the Sykes-Picot Agreement behind its back and was further upset when Yugoslavia (largely comprised of Croats and Slovenes from the former enemy, the Austro-Hungarian empire) was accorded preferential treatment over Italy, *viz.*, the treaty assigned Fiume to Croatia. On May 25, 1919, the Italian Prime Minister told the British:

> I cannot look forward without grave apprehensions to the future of continental Europe; the German longing for revenge must be considered in conjunction with the Russian position. We can thus see even now that the settlement to be arrived at will lack the assent of more than half the population of the European continent. If we detach from the block on which the new European system will have to rely for support forty million Italians, and force them into the ranks of the malcontents, do you think that the new order will rest on a firm basis?

Quoted in Charles L. Mowat, ed., *The New Modern Cambridge History*, Vol. XII, *The Shifting Balance of World Forces, 1898–1945* (Cambridge: Cambridge University Press, 1968), p. 226. The danger of which the Italian Prime Minister warned eventually came to pass: Dissatisfied with the Versailles status quo, Germany, Soviet Russia, and Italy moved into the ranks of the European revisionist powers.

37. For a discussion of Japan and Italy as "challengers" against the status quo, see Kennedy, *The Rise and Fall of the Great Powers*, pp. 291–343. For authoritative works on Japan's drive to achieve autarky by means of territorial expansion in East Asia, see Michael A. Barnhart, *Japan Prepares For Total War: The Search for Economic Security, 1919–1941* (Ithaca and London: Cornell University Press, 1987); James B. Crowley, *Japan's Quest for Autonomy* (Princeton: Princeton University Press, 1966); and Saburo Ienaga, *The Pacific War, 1931–1945* (New York: Pantheon Books, 1978), chap. 8.

38. Deporte, *Europe Between the Superpowers*, pp. 30–31.

39. Quoted in Mattern, *Geopolitics*, p. 59.

40. Karl Haushofer, *Der nationalsozialistische Gedanke in der Welt* (München: Callwey, 1933), pp. 29–30. Quoted in Derwent Whittlesey, Charles C. Colby, and Richard Hartshorne, *German Strategy of World Conquest* (New York and Toronto: Farrar & Rinehart, 1942), p. 162.

41. Ian Buruma, "The Europeans: The risks—and promise—of the newest superpower," *The New Republic* (August 5, 1991), p. 22.

42. All responses quoted in *ibid.*

43. Adolf Hitler, *Mein Kampf* (New York: Reynal and Hitchcock, [1925] 1941), p. 180.

44. Adolf Hitler, *Hitler's Secret Book* trans. Salvator Attanasio, intro., Telford Taylor (New York: Grove Press, [1928] 1961), p. 103.

45. *Ibid.*, p. 83.

46. *Ibid.*, p. 103; see also p. 158.

47. Haushofer, quoted in Robert Strausz-Hupé, *Geopolitics: The Struggle for Space and Power* (New York: G. P. Putnam's Sons, 1942), p. 67.

48. Gerhard L. Weinberg, *World in the Balance: Behind the Scenes of World War II* (Hanover and London: University Press of New England, 1981), p. xiii.

49. John Lukacs, "The Coming of the Second World War," *Foreign Affairs*, Vol. 68, No. 4 (Fall 1989), p. 172.

50. Hitler in Hugh R. Trevor-Roper, ed., *Hitler's Table Talk, 1941–1944*, trans. Norman Cameron and R. H. Stevens (London: Weidenfeld and Nicolson, 1953), p. 199.

51. Hitler, *Hitler's Secret Book*, p. 104. See also Andreas Hillgruber, *Germany and the Two World Wars*, trans. William C. Kirby (Cambridge, Mass.: Harvard University Press, 1981), pp. 50–51.

52. Hillgruber, *Germany and the Two World Wars*, p. 51.

53. Conversation, Hitler-Teleki, April 29, 1939, in *Documents on German Foreign Policy* (hereafter *DGFP*), Series D, Vol. VI (Washington, D.C.: United States Government Printing Office, 1956), pp. 377–378.

54. *Ibid.*, p. 378.

55. *Ibid.*, pp. 379–80.

56. Conversation, Ribbentrop-Cincar-Markovik, April 25, 1939, *DGFP*, Series D, Vol. VI, p. 326. See also Conversation, Ribbentrop-Teleki and Csaky, April 30, 1939, *DGFP*, Series D, Vol. VI, p. 372, wherein Ribbentrop says, "If . . . Britain and France wanted such a trial of strength, they could have it any day."

57. Hitler, in Trevor-Roper, *Hitler's Table Talk*, p. 182.

58. Hitler in *ibid*, pp. 586–7; See also *ibid.*, p. 182.

59. Hitler quoted in *ibid.*, p. 26.

60. William Carr, *Hitler: A Study in Personality and Politics* (London: Edward Arnold, 1978), p. 87.

61. Hitler in Trevor-Roper, ed., *Hitler's Table Talk*, p. 24.

62. Gerhard L. Weinberg, "Hitler's Image of the United States," *The American Historical Review* Vol. 69, No. 4 (July 1964), p. 1009.

63. Trevor-Roper, ed., *Hitler's Table Talk*, p. 93.

64. Adolf Hitler, quoted in John Toland, *Adolf Hitler* (New York: Doubleday, 1976), p. 693.

65. For Hitler's thoughts on an Anglo-American rivalry and an eventual war between the U.S. and an Anglo-German coalition, see Conversation, Hitler-Ciano, October 25, 1941, in *DGFP*, Series D, Vol. XIII, p. 693; Trevor-Roper, *Hitler's Table Talk*, pp. 14, 26, 186, 188; and Conversation, Hitler-Mussolini, June 3, 1941, in *DGFP*, Series D, Vol. XII, p. 946.

66. F. H. Hinsley, *Hitler's Strategy* (Cambridge: Cambridge University Press, 1951), pp. 6–7.

67. Esmonde M. Robertson, *Hitler's Pre-War Policy and Military Plans, 1933–1939* (London: Longmans, 1963), p. 54.

68. For an excellent and concise presentation of Hitler's obsession to gain an Anglo-German alliance, see David Calleo, *The German Problem Reconsidered: Germany and the World Order, 1870 to the Present* (Cambridge: Cambridge University Press, 1978), pp. 95–115. For Hitler's initial thoughts on this matter, see Adolf Hitler, *Mein Kampf* (New York: Reynal and Hitchcock, [1925] 1941), pp. 181–185, 892–965. See, also, Toland, *Adolf Hitler*, pp. 536–537, 614–16, 692–4; Conversation, Göring-Welles, March 4, 1940, *DGFP*, Series D, Vol. VIII, p. 852; Henderson, *Failure of a Mission*, pp. 279–80.

69. Andreas Hillgruber, *Germany and the Two World Wars*, trans. William C. Kirby (Cambridge, Mass.: Harvard University Press, 1981), p. 69.

70. Isaac Deutscher, *Stalin: A Political Biography*, 2nd ed. (New York: Oxford University Press), p. 441. For Stalin's overestimation of Anglo-French strength, see Adam B. Ulam, *Expansion and Coexistence: Soviet Foreign Policy, 1917–73*, 2nd ed. (New York: Holt, Rinehart and Winston, 1974), pp. 227, 229, 264.

71. Statement by Stalin before the Eighteenth Congress of the CPSU on March 10, 1939, as quoted in Ulam, *Expansion and Coexistence*, p. 264.

72. Robert C. Tucker, *Stalin in Power: The Revolution From Above, 1928–1941* (New York and London: W. W. Norton, 1990), pp. 587, 592.

73. Voroshilov quoted in Tucker, *Stalin in Power*, p. 592.

74. Ironically, Stalin accused the Western democracies of engaging in an "abettor" strategy, which he himself would employ: "The [democracies'] policy of non-intervention reveals an eagerness, a desire...not to hinder Germany, say, from enmeshing herself in European affairs, from embroiling herself in a war with the Soviet Union; to allow all the belligerents to sink deeply into the mire of war, to encourage them surreptitiously in this; and then, when they have become weak enough, to appear on the scene with fresh strength, to appear, of course, 'in the interest of peace,' and to dictate conditions to the enfeebled belligerents." Stalin, quoted in James E. McSherry, *Stalin, Hitler, and Europe: The Origins of World War II, 1933–1939, Vol. I* (Cleveland and New York: The World Publishing Co., 1968), pp. 120–121.

75. Stalin quoted in Tucker, *Stalin in Power*, pp. 597–598.

76. Though debate exists on this point, Barry Leach argues that Hitler never wavered in his belief that war with the Soviet Union was inevitable. See Barry A. Leach, *German Strategy Against Russia, 1939–1941* (Oxford: Clarendon Press, 1973), chaps. 2 and 3. For the preventive-war aspects of Hitler's strategy, see Norman Rich, *Hitler's War Aims: Ideology, the Nazi State, and the Course of Expansion* (New York and London: W. W. Norton & Co., 1973), chaps. 9, 14, 15, and 18. For the propensity of authoritarian regimes to wage preventive war, see Randall L. Schweller, "Domestic Structure and Preventive War: Are Democracies More Pacific?" *World Politics*, Vol. 44, No. 2 (January 1992), pp. 235–269.

77. See Hinsley, *Hitler's Strategy*, pp. 6–7.

78. Warren F. Kimball, *The Juggler: Franklin Roosevelt as Wartime Statesman* (Princeton: Princeton University Press, 1991), pp. 21–22.

79. Calleo, The German Problem Reconsidered, p. 108.

80. *Ibid.*, p. 108.

81. Walter Russell Mead, "On the Road to Ruin," in Charles W. Kegley, Jr. and Eugene R. Wittkopf, eds., *The Future of American Foreign Policy* (New York: St. Martin's Press, 1992), p. 335.

82. Leonard Silk, "Some Things Are More Vital Than Money When It Comes to Creating the World Anew," *New York Times*, September 22, 1991, Section 4, p. 2.

83. Lester Thurow, *Head to Head: The Coming Economic Battle Among Japan, Europe, and America* (New York: William Morrow, 1992), p. 14.

84. Edward Luttwak, "Obsession," *The New Republic*, February 24, 1992, p. 13. See, also, Richard Rosecrance, *The Rise of the Trading State: Commerce and Conquest in the Modern World* (New York: Basic Books, 1986); and Theodore H. Moran, "International Economics and U.S. National Security," in Kegley and Wittkopf, *The Future of American Foreign Policy*, pp. 307–318.

85. Leslie H. Gelb, "Fresh Face," *New York Times*, December 8, 1991, Section 6, p. 54.

86. See John Tagliabue, "Bold New Germany: No Longer a Political 'Dwarf'," *New York Times*, December 16, 1991, p. A12; and "EC and Yugoslavia: Countdown to Recognition," *The Economist*, Vol. 321, No. 7738 (December 21, 1991– January 3, 1992), p. 57.

87. Michael Lind, "Recognize the Power of the New Germany," *New York Times*, December 27, 1991, p. A33.

88. Anthony Lewis, "Still Little England?" *New York Times*, December 16, 1991, p. A19.

89. "A Poor Match in Tokyo," *The Economist*, Vol. 322, No. 7741 (January 11–17, 1992), pp. 51–52 at p. 52.

90. See David E. Sanger, "Power of the Yen Winning Asia: New 'Co-Prosperity' is Displacing U.S.," *New York Times*, December 5, 1991, pp. D1 and D22.

91. Thurow, *Head to Head*, p. 23.

92. Schweller, "Domestic Structure and Preventive War," p. 268.

10

Interdependence and Instability

Anne Uchitel

Today, the international system is becoming increasingly complex and interdependent. Conventional wisdom holds that interdependence enhances systemic stability by increasing the costs of war and expanding the benefits of peace.[1] Kenneth Waltz, however, argues that interdependence reduces systemic stability by increasing the opportunities for conflict because states in an anarchic, self-help system "worry about securing that which they depend on."[2]

In fact, each of these positions captures only part of the truth. As Robert Jervis argues in this volume, systems are complex, and systems effects can be indirect, varied, and unexpected. In this chapter I elaborate the Waltzian position and claim that some kinds of dependence, specifically dependence on foreign supplies of strategic materials, create an incentive for states to adopt expansionist policies and offensive military strategies. Dependence on imported strategic goods decreases systemic stability for two reasons: (1) states need to expand to achieve military autarky, and (2) states must win initial wars of expansion quickly before exhausting their strategic supplies. The cases of Nazi Germany and imperial Japan support these hypotheses. Conversely, the case of interwar Britain demonstrates that not all dependence leads to destabilizing policies.

Interdependence is defined as mutual dependence or mutual vulnerability.[3] It is characterized by international trade or capital flows that are costly to forgo.[4] Interdependence may connote dependence on foreign sources of strategic goods and resources (those necessary to make war), or dependence on export markets. With respect to the hypotheses in this chapter, dependence need not necessarily be mutual, but it must indicate a reliance on foreign sources of strategic materials. If the dependence is reciprocal, then both states within the interdependent relationship will have an incentive to adopt destabilizing policies; if the dependence is unilateral, then only one state will have such incentives.

States that are dependent on foreign supplies of strategic materials have three options. First, they can remain dependent and accept the inherent vulnerability of this position. Small, weak powers often choose this option by default since the opportunities to ameliorate their situation are severely limited. Middle powers, however, are tempted to use their greater resources to escape military dependency and vulnerability. For these states, a second option is to seek military autarky by substituting indigenously produced synthetics in place of imported strategic goods. Such substitution, however, is usually economically inefficient as well as militarily inadequate. A final option, then, is to expand through negotiation or military aggression in order to acquire the resources necessary to achieve military self-sufficiency.

Strategic interdependence is therefore directly destabilizing because it creates an incentive for states to expand. It is also indirectly destabilizing because it creates an imperative for states to adopt offensive military strategies to ensure rapid victory. States that are dependent on foreign supplies of strategic goods are vulnerable to having that trade disrupted and cannot, therefore, fight over the long term. These states, can, of course, make war over the short term by stockpiling essential materials and capitalizing on this fleeting advantage. They must plan for short wars by adopting strategies for achieving rapid, decisive victories. Short-war strategies are necessarily offensive since it is impossible to win a war quickly by standing on the defensive, or by relying on attrition.[5]

Offensive strategies are systemically destabilizing.[6] They create incentives to strike first in a crisis, and they make security-conscious states indistinguishable from aggressors. Any suspicion that the other side is preparing to attack may cause decisionmakers to launch an attack for fear of being preempted. When offensive strategies predominate, "Wars may be easy to start and they may be very intense."[7]

These points are illustrated below by three cases that examine the causes of World War II. Both Nazi Germany and imperial Japan adopted short-war, offensive military strategies and expansionist policies to redress the vulnerability created by their dependence on foreign supplies of strategic materials. In contrast, Great Britain was dependent on foreign markets to generate the revenue necessary to ensure its ability to fight over the long term. In conclusion, I suggest policy options designed to avoid the systemically destabilizing effects of strategic dependence.

Nazi Germany and the Need for Lebensraum

The origins of World War II are often summed up in just one word: Hitler. Hitler's motivations and the actions of Nazi Germany are far too complex, however, to be so easily condensed. It is therefore inaccurate to focus only on Hitler's racism, or the German people's desire to release themselves from the Versailles diktat as a way of understanding the policies which led to war. Instead, a more complete understanding rests on the exploration of the economic conditions and perceptions of vulnerability which contributed to Germany's destabilizing expansionist policies and military strategies.

Hitler came to power with the promise of ameliorating the economic and military legacy of defeat embodied in the Versailles Treaty of 1919. The dual goals of economic efficiency and military autarky soon came into conflict, resulting in failure to obtain either objective. Hitler began by trying to achieve military self-sufficiency, with only limited success. He was soon forced by economic reality to turn to trade and consequent vulnerability.

Shortly after his rise to power, Hitler pursued military autarky, substituting synthetic products for those raw materials that Germany lacked.[8] He was supported in this goal by the influential industrialist I.G. Farben, who had been promoting synthetic fuel and coal production since the German experience with blockade in World War I. In December of 1933 the Nazi government reached an accord with Farben's company. The Feder-Bosch agreement stipulated that in return for specifying fixed prices and markets for fuel produced through hydrogenation, I.G. Farben would guarantee to increase annual production to a maximum of 350,000 tons within two years.[9]

The domestic production of other synthetic goods such as rubber was so costly that it engendered serious resistance from senior government officials, including Hjalmar Schacht, the minister of economics, and the commander-in-chief of the Wehrmacht, Werner von Blomberg.[10] By 1936, Hitler's desire for military autarky at the cost of economic efficiency contributed to the deterioration of the German economy. Hitler was nevertheless firm in his commitment to the domestic production of strategic goods and decided on government intervention to ensure its progress.[11]

It quickly became apparent that the cost of pursuing military autarky was economic inefficiency not only with respect to consumer goods but also with respect to military procurement. For example, the Germans were capable of producing iron ore indigenously, but the product was of substantially weaker quality than that of imported ore. Swedish iron ore produced almost twice as much pig iron as

German ore, demonstrating the inefficiency of reliance on domestic raw materials.[12] Similarly, synthetic production of oil and rubber was not cost effective. Hitler continued to emphasize domestic production "as far as possible,"[13] but by 1937 Germany was forced to import the majority of its strategic goods, becoming susceptible to supply interruption, especially during war: "All in all, German dependence on foreign sources of raw materials and the vulnerability of those sources to blockade presented German economic and strategic planners with a most depressing picture."[14]

Germany's vulnerability to strategic trade disruption reinforced Hitler's expansionist tendencies. The führer's aggressive intentions had been nurtured since his incarceration in the 1920s, when he wrote *Mein Kampf* and outlined his plans for German hegemony in Europe. Once Hitler was firmly established in power, and as his bold initiatives, including the remilitarization of the Rhineland and the Austrian *Anschluss*, were accepted by the rest of Europe, Hitler was able to elaborate his general plans for German expansion.

The substance of Hitler's grand strategy has been debated by scholars. Conventional wisdom endorses the view that not only did Germany plan a blitzkrieg military strategy in the event of war, but it had been Hitler's intention from the beginning to pursue such a policy. This view is supported by evidence which suggests that Hitler's economic policy during the interwar years was geared to advance such a military strategy.[15] Newer evidence, discussed below, suggests that it was actually Germany's economic position, and the resultant military vulnerability, which necessitated a resort to a blitzkrieg military strategy when war began sooner than anticipated by the Germans.[16] Hitler's general plan involved a multistep process by which Germany would acquire additional territories in the East one by one. This was to be accomplished, if possible, without armed conflict, through trade and peaceful annexation. Thus prepared, Germany would turn toward the Soviet Union and general war.[17] Hitler's strategy, then, was first to establish a "military-economic core" for the new reich to include Germany, Austria, Czechoslovakia, and parts of Poland. Then, Hitler planned to use this core to "provide the resources of the autarkic economy," from which he would wage the war to expand the reich even further east.[18]

Hitler was encouraged in his belief that Germany could acquire its "military-economic core" in Eastern Europe by the appeasement policies of France and particularly Britain.[19] The Rhineland, Austria, and portions of Czechoslovakia were secured without resort to arms. Hitler was prepared to fight for these territories if necessary, but only if the war was limited. Hitler did not intend to fight the major war of expansion for Soviet territory until Germany had acquired sufficient resources to fight a war of attrition: "The only possible course, taken by Hitler, was to build German forces up as rapidly as possible and then, with that short-term military advantage, conquer the raw material and financial base for a long war."[20] Prior to the acquisition of this material and financial base, German strategic vulnerability required that its wars of expansion be short. This requirement in turn necessitated the adoption of short-war, offensive, destabilizing military strategies.

Hitler planned for a long war with the Soviets, but at some point in the future. In May of 1939, Hitler declared that "the government must be prepared for a war of ten to fifteen years' duration."[21] By 1939, however, Hitler was forced because of Germany's dependence on imported strategic goods to adopt short-war, offensive military strategies. Moreover, and again because of the military vulnerability caused by Germany's trade relationships, Hitler was compelled to take advantage of his "short-term military advantage" when war became probable because of Germany's policies. Following Germany's attack on Poland, and the Allies' declaration of war, Hitler urged his generals to attack quickly in the West because "the danger in case of a prolonged war lies in the difficulty of securing [supplies] from a limited food and raw-material base for a population while at the same time securing the means for the prosecution of the war."[22]

Hitler would have preferred to avoid war with the West altogether. Hitler's immediate plans to redress German military vulnerability did not include westward expansion. It was not his intention at this point to become violently involved with the United Kingdom, France, or the United States. Hitler felt that the kaiser's most significant error before and during the Great War had been his attempt to establish hegemony in Europe while simultaneously offering a direct challenge to Great Britain.[23] Hitler wanted the United Kingdom to remain neutral throughout Germany's multistep expansion process. Toward this end, Hitler signed a naval treaty with Britain in 1935 that limited Germany's naval capacity to 35 percent that of Britain's. This treaty stood in contrast to the kaiser's strategy prior to World War I, which included a naval arms race between the German and British navies. Hitler diverged from the kaiser's strategy and wanted to indicate that Germany would not pose any threat to the United Kingdom.[24] Hitler thus avoided competing with Great Britain while simultaneously offering incentives for Britain to become a German ally, or at least a tacit participant in the execution of the plans for a greater Germany.[25]

Unfortunately for Hitler, Germany's eastward expansion plans conflicted with the goal of establishing and maintaining a friendship with Great Britain. Hitler was aware of this conflict, and while his preference was to avoid a confrontation with the West, his priority was the founding of the new autarkic German reich.[26] Britain's distrust and dissatisfaction with Germany significantly increased after Hitler revealed his desire to expand into Poland, despite the Munich agreement of 1938, which gave the Czechoslovakian Sudetenland to Germany in exchange for "peace in our time." Hitler came to believe that war with the West might be unavoidable. In a speech on May 23, 1939, Hitler speculated, "If it is not certain that a German-Polish conflict will not lead to war in the West, then the fight must be primarily against England and France."[27] Hitler elaborated this sentiment when he said, "It is our task to isolate Poland. . . . An attack on Poland will only be successful if the West does not intervene.[If the West does intervene, and an attack is necessary], it must be our aim to start with a shattering blow . . . but this is only possible if we do not slither through Poland into war with England."[28] This shattering blow was embodied in the von Manstein variant of the German *Fall Gelb* (Yellow Plan).[29] The aim of this plan was to bloody the Allies enough to encourage them to sue for a negotiated peace.[30]

Germany's strategic vulnerability for strategic goods not only required a "shattering blow," it also narrowed the window of opportunity available for the attack. If war with the West could not be avoided, it was necessary to go to war sooner rather than later because, as Hitler believed, time was on the side of the Allies. The conquest of Poland, and the possibility of victorious war with the West, in turn, would be feasible only if Germany's eastern frontier was secure. This was achieved with the Nazi-Soviet pact of August 1939. It was this pact that convinced Hitler that war against Poland and the consequent conflict with France and Great Britain would be short, and therefore practical.[31]

Hitler decided to attack Poland in April of 1939, despite the British guarantee to Poland on March 31.[32] He confirmed this decision in a speech on May 23, 1939. Given that Hitler believed time to be against Germany, he estimated that if the now-inevitable war must come, it must come soon because "should we not act until 1943-45, then any year could bring about the food crisis. . . . Over and above that, the world will anticipate our actions and increase countermeasures yearly . . . [and] we shall decrease in relative power."[33] In a speech on August 22, Hitler stated, "We have nothing to lose, we can only gain. Our economic situation is such that we cannot hold out more than a few years. We have no other choice, we must act. . . . The initiative cannot be allowed to pass to others. . . . We must accept the risk with reckless resolution. . . . We are facing the alternative of striking now or being destroyed with certainty sooner or later."[34] If the initiative was allowed to pass to others, the result would most likely be a long war and certain defeat.[35]

In a memo dated October 9, 1939, Hitler delineated the danger to Germany of a long war. A long war would heighten the probability that allies would defect, or that potential neutrals would turn against Germany. More important, though, was "the difficulty, owing to the limited supplies of food and raw material . . . of finding the means for carrying on the war."[36] Germany needed to win the war before its resources were depleted. Moreover, the longer the war lasted, "the more difficult would be the preservation of German air superiority," resulting in the further vulnerability of German war production. If Germany lost air superiority,

> from this moment the Ruhr, as an active factor in the German war economy, would either drop out or at least be crippled. There is no means of replacing it. But as this weakness is recognized just as clearly by England and France as by ourselves, the Anglo-French conduct of war, aiming at the utter destruction of Germany, would strive to reach this goal at all costs. Indeed, the less hope England and France have of being able to destroy the German Armed Forces in a series of actual battles, the more they will try to create the conditions for an effective long, drawn-out war of attrition and annihilation, the more certain does it become that they will terminate Belgian-Dutch neutrality. . . . Germany's possession of this area would be one of the few factors which would be any help to Germany in a long war.[37]

Hitler was thus clearly aware of his strategic vulnerability and the need to avoid a long war before Germany's resource base was strengthened.

Hitler was also correct when he predicted that British strategy would focus on denying Germany a short war. The British and French staff delegations drafted a memo in 1939 on the "broad strategic policy for the conduct of the war." In this memo, the Allies determined that "we should be faced by enemies who would be more fully prepared than ourselves for war on a national scale, would have superiority in air and land forces, but would be inferior at sea and in general economic strength. In these circumstances, we must be prepared to face a major offensive directed against either France or Great Britain or both. To defeat such an offensive, we should have to concentrate our initial efforts, and during this time our major strategy would be defensive. . . . During these stages, the steady and vigorous application of economic pressure would be reducing the powers of resistance of our enemies."[38]

It was this attitude on the part of Germany's opponents that forced Germany to consider the early invasion of Norway and Denmark; the Germans knew that these areas would be prime targets of Allied attention. Norway was an essential transport link for Swedish iron ore, vital to the German war effort.[39] The Germans, anxious to protect their sources and lines of supply, further expanded the scope of the already burgeoning war.[40]

Unwilling to accept its dependent position, Germany first tried to achieve autarky through the domestic production of synthetic substitutes. When economic efficiency forced Germany to import its strategic materials, the resultant vulnerability contributed to Hitler's expansionist tendencies. To expand, in turn, Germany adopted destabilizing offensive military strategies and thus promoted systemic instability both directly and indirectly.

Japan and the Greater East Asian Coprosperity Sphere

The policies of imperial Japan were quite similar to those of Nazi Germany. Like Germany, Japan entered into interdependent relationships for the purpose of economic efficiency only to find that it had thus made itself strategically vulnerable. This vulnerability contributed to its adopting systemically destabilizing policies which culminated in the expansionism that led to World War II. During the interwar years, Japan, like Germany, was confronted with an impossible choice between efficiency and autarky. Japan tried to become militarily self-sufficient by indigenously producing synthetics but found the economic cost prohibitively high. Imperial Japan concluded that it needed to expand its resource base by acquiring territory, and to reduce its strategic vulnerability by adopting short-war, offensive military strategies. This desire to expand incurred the enmity of the West, including the United Kingdom and the United States, and led to total war.

Japan had a small economy relative to the other great powers; its share of total world output in 1938 was only one third that of Germany's, for example. In an interdependent system, Japan was relatively dependent, particularly on imported strategic materials such as oil and metals. On the eve of war, Japan imported 83.3 percent of its iron ore; 37.8 percent of steel; 59.4 percent of aluminum; almost 80 percent of its crude oil; and 68.7 percent of its salt. Further, while Japan mined over 90 percent of its coal domestically, it produced none of the coking coal necessary for steel production.[41]

Japan's economy could sustain only a very short campaign against opponents with larger war potentials such as the United States or the United Kingdom.[42] Japanese strategy, therefore, was designed to quickly win the kind of war that would enhance Japan's resource base by acquiring territory to decrease Japan's dependence on foreign sources of supply.

Japan's strategy during the interwar years was similar to that of Nazi Germany. Japan wanted to create a "greater East Asian coprosperity sphere" which would include Thailand, Indonesia, the Philippines, and the nearer islands in the Pacific.[43] By acquiring these territories, either through foreign annexation or informal empire, Japan would increase its supplies of iron ore, manganese ore, nickel ore, copper, bauxite, crude rubber, industrial salt and rice. With these supplies Japan would have the essential commodities to fight a war of defense or expansion.[44]

Like the Germans, the Japanese recognized that their plans for expansion would probably generate foreign opposition, from their neighbors as well as from abroad. A number of officers within the Japanese military prepared for this. The so-called total-war officers of the Imperial Japanese Army, those men who believed in long-term economic planning in order to wage a future total war, began increasingly to control Japanese military and economic policies beginning in the early 1930s. For these officers, "the thing to be most feared is that future wars will be prolonged."[45] It was the dominant belief among Japanese policymakers that "future wars would be fought not only with guns, but with the entire resources of nations."[46] To prepare for such a war, Japan, like Germany, needed to expand its resource base so as to redress the strategic vulnerability resulting from its trading relationships.

As early as 1927, the Japanese government established the Cabinet Resources Bureau. This bureau basically functioned as a central planning committee to manage rapid mobilization in the event of war. This agency was given broad powers of control; the bureau staged exercises wherein the government declared a state of war and then executed mobilization plans for ten days. These exercises created a baseline standard from which to determine the deficiencies in the economy and to chart progress.[47] As a result of these exercises, the government quickly realized that national economic mobilization was insufficient to wage war of any kind. The indigenous resources of the country were inadequate to achieve military security. Japan needed to expand its resource base immediately. It could do so by substituting synthetic products, acquiring territory, or both.

The "logical starting point" for this expansion was Manchuria, because acquiring Manchuria achieved both objectives.[48] Manchuria had an important rail system as well as synthetic petroleum factories.[49] Oil was a crucial commodity to Japan's war effort; the Japanese navy relied on oil to fuel its ships, and Japan's oil reserves were minimal. The only known Japanese oil reserves, about 100,000 tons annually, were located in North Sakhalin. Because of a 1925 treaty with the United States, however, Japan had access to only half of Sakhalin's oil. North Sakhalin oil available to Japan was insufficient to meet the needs of the navy, much less the other branches of the armed services.[50]

Japan acquired Manchuria in 1932 and renamed it Manchukuo. In addition to having resources and transport facilities, Manchukuo was an important buffer between Japan and the Soviet Union. With this strategic position secure, North China became Japan's next target. North China offered supplies of iron ore, cotton, and other strategic goods. Japan's goal in this region was to create an autonomous political unit nominally tied to China but independent of the Chinese government. These Japanese ambitions eventually culminated in the China Incident, and eventual tragedy for Japan.

By July of 1937, Japan's desires to expand into North China had created serious opposition from China. The Japanese government anticipated that the ensuing conflict, the China Incident, would be minor; The Japanese predicted a three-month confrontation requiring no more than three divisions at a cost of 100 million yen.[51] Over a year later, the inaccuracy of these estimates was apparent as the hostilities continued and the monetary and human costs mounted.

Japan's determination to expand next into southeast Asia eventually generated opposition from that region, and from the United States and Great Britain: "The Japanese-American war was brought about by Japan's decision to extend control over southeast Asia, and by America's determination to prevent it."[52] The United States resolved to maintain the status quo in Asia, and to preserve British and French colonial interests there. After 1938, the Americans increasingly believed that events in Europe and Asia were intricately related.[53] Japan's expansionist aims were perceived as strategically threatening, as well as morally pernicious. The total-war officers of the Japanese military were not surprised; they had anticipated Western intervention, particularly American intervention, after the China Incident.

Policymakers in Japan were also aware of the potential conflict between their plans for a greater East Asian coprosperity sphere and the Western desire to preserve the status quo. Just as Hitler would have preferred to expand eastward without armed interference by the West but was willing to risk limited war in 1939 to achieve essential objectives, so the Japanese attempted to avert war with the West but would not sacrifice their security-driven expansion. From the Japanese perspective, expansion was the only solution to trade-induced vulnerability:

> Southern advance was a basic Japanese policy after 1938. Partly, this was a military move, an aspect of the new definition of national security. The military had explained their acts in Manchuria and China as an attempt to create an economically self-sufficient and militarily impregnable "defense state." The bloc embracing Japan, Manchukuo, and China was obviously far from being self-sufficient. From this point of view there was a logical necessity to include southeast Asia, with its rich mineral and vegetable resources, in the Japanese empire. Such a new order would help reduce Japan's dependence on American supplies of oil, iron, and other materials. *Thus, from a military standpoint, the new order was often conceived of as an alternative to Japanese-American trade. The Navy in particular, with its absolute need for fuel oil, came to view a southern advance as an inevitable choice forced upon Japan by America's policy.*[54]

In 1941, it became clear to the Japanese that the United States, with its ever-present threat of military reprisals, would absolutely oppose Japan's southern expansion. Japan felt compelled to resolve the problem. The Japanese knew that any extended conflict with the United States would end in defeat for Japan because the American resource base was so much larger than that of Japan. Thus, on December 7, 1941, the Japanese attacked Pearl Harbor in an effort to demonstrate Japanese resolve and to dissuade the United States from engaging the Japanese. These objectives were never achieved, and Japan became perhaps the biggest loser in the ensuing conflict.[55]

The Splendid Security of Great Britain

Unlike Nazi Germany and imperial Japan, British interdependence did not cause Britain to adopt short-war, offensive strategies or expansionist designs. Great Britain's dependence on export markets instead of imported strategic goods and resources influenced Britain's choice of less destabilizing policies and strategies. During the interwar years, Great Britain perceived itself to be militarily self-sufficient because of the resources of the empire and the Commonwealth, coupled with British command of the seas. Britain relied heavily on its extended resource base for its security. The United Kingdom saw the wealth of its empire and dominions as "supplementary sources from which to draw labor and materials on favorable terms."[56] Secure in their supply of strategic goods, the British directed their attention toward maintaining their financial ability to pay for their war-fighting effort. During the 1930s, the British sought to deter war by threatening their potential opponents with the prospect of a long conflict. Maintaining the economic health of the kingdom was crucial to the credibility of this threat. Toward this end, Britain planned to keep defense expenditures low during peacetime and to mobilize fully only when and if deterrence failed.

Whereas the Germans and Japanese were more concerned about their abilities to access strategic materials, then, the British were more concerned with their ability to pay for the supplies available to them: "Unlike the Germans, the British had access, both in times of peace and more importantly in war to the raw materials required by the massive production effort of war in the industrial age. . . . The British faced the problem of how to pay for imports of raw materials."[57] The British were unwilling to risk economic weakness for the sake of defense expenditure. "Throughout the late 1930s worries over the state of the British economy and the possibility that overexpenditure on defense might lead to economic catastrophe dominated arguments over rearmament policies at the highest level."[58]

Until the late 1930s, then, Britain maintained its defense expenditures at the lowest possible level. This policy was consistent with British security because a strong economy was seen as vital to effective defense. The minister for the coordination of defense, Sir Thomas Inskip, stated in February of 1938 that "nothing operates more strongly to deter a potential aggressor from attacking this country than our stability, but if other countries were to detect in us serious signs of strain, this deterrent would at once be lost."[59] Inskip recommended a ceiling on defense expenditure predicated upon the assumptions of finite commitments and limited adversaries.

Other ministers, notably First Lord of the Admiralty Alfred Duff Cooper and Home Secretary Sir Samuel Hoare, argued against setting a monetary restriction on the defense of the nation. This group contended that Germany, Italy, and Japan were better prepared for war in the near future.[60] These men maintained that Britain's potential adversaries (primarily Germany) did not set limits on their own defense expenditure, and that these nations were currently mobilizing a more substantial portion of their war potential. They noted that when and if war came, price would not be a factor in Britain's rearmament. This was a minority view, however, and the majority of the cabinet agreed with Inskip that mobilization during peacetime should be restrained in favor of maintaining Britain's economic stability.[61]

Trying to rearm while maintaining economic stability, Inskip recommended the following guidelines for armed services program planners in December of 1937:

> In considering whether we can afford this or that programme, the first question asked is how much the program will cost . . . the fact that the problem is considered in terms of money, must not be allowed to obscure the fact that our real resources consist not of money, i.e., paper pounds which are nothing more than a symbol, but of our manpower and productive capacity, our power to maintain our credit, and the general balance of our trade.
>
> The maintenance of our credit facilities and our general balance of trade are of vital importance, not merely from the point of view of our strength in peacetime, but equally for purposes of war. This country cannot hope to win a war against a major Power by a sudden knock-out blow; on the contrary, for success we must contemplate a long war, in the course of which we should have to mobilize all our resources. . . . This is no new conception. The reports of the Chiefs of Staff Sub-Committee on Planning for a war with Germany . . . was based on the general conception that Germany is likely to be the aggressor and will "endeavor to exploit her superior preparedness by trying to knock out Great Britain rapidly, or knock out France rapidly, since she is not well placed for a long war in which the Sea Powers, as in the past, are likely to have the advantage." We must therefore confront our potential enemies with the risks of a long war, which they cannot face. If we are to emerge victoriously from such a war, it is essential that we should enter it with sufficient economic strength to enable us to make the fullest use of resources overseas, and to withstand the strain.
>
> While, therefore, it is true that the extent of our [economic] resources imposes limitations on the size of the defense programmes which we are able to undertake, this is only one aspect of the matter. Seen in its true perspective, the maintenance of our economic stability would be more accurately described as an essential element in defensive strength: one which can properly be regarded as the fourth arm of defense, alongside the Defense Services, without which purely military effort would be of no avail.[62]

In February 1938, shortly after Inskip issued these guidelines, the cabinet agreed to spend 1,650 million pounds over five years (1937–41) on defense. This sum represented an increase of 150 million pounds over the original figures. Inskip warned that even this increase, while necessary, would place a strain on the British economy. Inskip speculated that such an increase might result in financial disorganization, which would in turn diminish the nation's ability to successfully defend itself when and if war came.[63]

Following the Sudetenland crisis in September 1938, the possibility of war became more urgent. Munich forced Great Britain to reconsider its policy of defense planning based on fixed financial limits. It was now necessary to risk financial vulnerability for the sake of military security. The cabinet decided to expand its defense expenditure. On October 26, 1938, the government established a committee, under the direction of Inskip, to "consider the proposals for extending the scope of the Defense Programmes and measures designed to accelerate production."[64]

The proposed expansion of defense production and expenditure differed from earlier efforts in that the government was no longer specifying monetary limits. The new criterion was necessity, not affordability. This is not to imply that the government was advocating rearmament at any cost. Instead, the maintenance of economic stability remained an important element of defense, but within a broader concern for more traditional means of military preparation. On October 6, the chancellor remarked that "the Air Ministry's Programme is, therefore, so costly as to raise serious doubts whether it can be financed beyond 1939–40 without the gravest danger to the country's stability. The damage which I apprehend is not of the sort which can be got over by calling for 'sacrifices'; it would consist in such a weakening of our economic and financial strength as . . . we should have lost the means of carrying on a long struggle altogether. I do not for a moment claim that purely financial considerations can have priority over urgent and definite needs for material defense. The two things have to be considered together."[65]

Given the fact that Britain had just emerged from a major depression, it was difficult to find the correct balance between economic and military security. Further, if economic stability was really the "fourth arm of defense," it made little sense to put that stability at risk to satisfy the other three arms. All four were vital, and therefore it was necessary to achieve a sensible compromise. As Inskip had stated in March of 1936, "Remember that we depend on the resources of finance for the successful fighting of a war as much as upon the production of munitions."[66] The compromise between economic stability and military security required a military strategy that allowed the United Kingdom to mobilize as little of its war potential during peacetime as possible.

A dependence on foreign markets contributed toward Britain's adoption of a defensive military strategy which depended heavily on economic attrition. The British were therefore determined to avoid the kinds of bloody, costly land battles that had characterized the western front during the Great War.[67] Instead, the British were to rely on a defensive strategy, which had been added to the threat of a long war, based upon the mighty financial reserves of Great Britain to deter potential opponents. Britain intended to outproduce the enemy by using its superior resource base. Without economic stability, such a threat would have been empty.

Before 1937, Britain used the menace of a long war of attrition as a deterrent.[68] Unsure of where the war would start, and fearful of the risk to *all* of its far-flung empire, Britain was reluctant to commit to any one theater. The British felt threatened by Germany, Japan, and Italy but recognized the impossibility of attacking all simultaneously.[69] Unwilling to accept fully the prospect of war, decisionmakers within the government placed excessive confidence in deterrence without paying sufficient attention to the possibility that deterrence might fail: "To deter her adversaries Britain had to rely on the threat of somehow defeating them with the imperial resources that she could ultimately mobilize. In order for her adversaries to be persuaded that Britain would mobilize these resources, these adversaries also had to be persuaded of her ability to deflect a knock-out blow."[70]

Should deterrence fail, and war start, Britain realized that the country would need to defend itself against the first attacks. Toward this end, then, the government relied upon the Royal Air Force, the only branch of the armed services to receive any significant funding during most of the 1930s.[71] This badly integrated two-pronged strategy of excessive deterrence and insufficient defense continued until 1937.

Britain adopted the defensive element of its strategy two years prior to the outbreak of World War II: "The key element in Western strategy would lie in the ability of the Allied economic, diplomatic and military measures to disrupt and unbalance the German war economy."[72] The British assumed that the Germans would aim for a short war, and a short war was precisely what Britain needed to deny Germany.

British naval policy reflected this strategy. The goal was to protect British resources while prolonging the war with Germany. Britain would deploy the main fleet "where it would give covering protection to British shipping against attack by fleets of the enemy."[73] This meant deployment primarily in the Atlantic shipping lanes and the western approaches. The threat to these lifelines would come from both surface ships and submarines. However, Britain had failed to produce a sufficient number of escort vessels, a notable deficiency in terms of Britain's desire to hold out over the long term.[74]

Naval operations focused on a strategy of slow attrition, disrupting the enemy's sources of supply: "Economic blockade was the main offensive weapon of British sea power, and it was a slow-acting one."[75] Because close blockade had been abandoned prior to the First World War, the remaining option was strategic blockade coupled with an elaborate and extensive system of contraband control. This system had irritated the neutral powers (particularly the United States) during World War I, but it was the most effective weapon available to Great Britain. Plans for this system of contraband control were already in place prior to the outbreak of the Second World War and consisted of control bases and naval patrols.[76] Thus, Britain prepared to protect itself and defeat Germany.

These policies of defense and deterrence were predicated, in large part, on the economic position of Great Britain. Britain was dependent on export markets as opposed to imported strategic goods and resources.[77] Because of the nature of its vulnerability, Britain, unlike Nazi Germany and imperial Japan, was free to adopt less destabilizing military strategies and policies.

Conclusions

Unfortunately, the benefits and costs of interdependence are not equally distributed. Analysts often fail to recognize the hidden dangers inherent in a complex interdependent system resulting from this inequity. The cases of Nazi Germany and imperial Japan, where states dependent on imported strategic materials adopted short-war, offensive military strategies and expansionist policies, illustrate the potential dangers of some kinds of interdependence. The case of interwar Britain, a nation dependent on export markets rather than strategic resources, demonstrates that not all forms of dependence are destabilizing.

Currently, opportunities for trade and dependence abound. The evolving new world order is characterized by a proliferation of states whose freedom to associate economically is virtually unlimited. The Union of Soviet Socialist Republics has disintegrated into separate republics, most of which are eager to interact, particularly economically, with the West and each other. Former Soviet satellite states such as Poland and Czechoslovakia have already become attractive targets of economic opportunity for Western entrepreneurs. The nations of Western Europe are rapidly moving toward economic federation distinguished by porous borders and intricate relationships. Consequently, the level of international economic interdependence will most likely escalate significantly.

To many theorists, interdependence is a force for peace; the complex international system predicted for the future would therefore be a cause for optimism.[78] This conclusion rests on two foundations: first, that interdependence entails absolute gains for all participating states. Thus, nations are more likely to be satisfied with the status quo, believing that they are achieving as much as they can. Second, interdependence is a force for peace because, on an absolute scale, interdependence increases the costs of war. Armed conflict becomes that much more expensive for all concerned when states must forgo the benefits of trade. Therefore, when nations are engaged in interdependent relationships, according to this logic, they have less incentive to go to war and less ability to fight.

The unintended consequences of interdependence, then, while potentially hazardous, should not condemn the entire phenomenon. Indeed, it would be most unlikely, as well as undesirable, for the states within the international system to revert to the isolationism characteristic of the years following World War I, for instance. Instead, there are policy options available to decisionmakers that might mitigate the destabilizing effects of interdependence.

A number of policies could prevent the undesirable outcomes sometimes associated with interdependence. First, policymakers from both individual nations and international organizations could monitor the distribution of strategic goods and resources, as well as trade in these materials, particularly to would-be regional or global hegemons. Such monitoring would be accomplished in much the same way as is supervision of commerce in arms and nuclear materials. Through such supervision, potentially dangerous situations where some nations become dependent on imported strategic goods and might therefore resort to destabilizing policies could be recognized and rectified if necessary. Second, indigenous production of substitute resources such as synthetic oil and rubber could be encouraged among nations that currently lack the capability. Such production could be encouraged through foreign aid by individual nations or through financial incentives offered by international organizations like the World Bank and the International Monetary Fund. In this way, nations that cannot afford both military autarky and economic efficiency could reconcile these goals and refrain from adopting destabilizing strategies and policies to redress perceived vulnerability. Third, collective security agencies like the United Nations could redefine aggression to include the adoption of destabilizing short-war, offensive military strategies and could sanction offenders. Rather than responding with reciprocal accumulation to the arms buildup and stockpiling that often accompany a country's adopting an offensive military strategy, other countries could apply economic sanctions.[79] Instead of waiting for a state to execute an offensive strategy and start a war, collective security agencies could use sanctions to modify the strategy itself and avert armed conflict. Fourth, Robert Jervis has suggested that "in order to protect their possessions, states often seek to control resources or land outside their own territory. Countries that are not self-sufficient must try to assure that the necessary supplies will continue to flow in wartime. . . . If there were an international authority that could guarantee access, the motive for control would disappear."[80] This would require the creation of a new kind of international organization that could fairly acquire and distribute such resources and goods. Alternatively, a fifth option would be to formalize specific trade agreements among nations which would legally guarantee the flow of goods during wartime. Nations that participate in mutual defense treaties wherein the signatories pledge their support to each other in time of war could include such an economic component in the agreement and explicitly undertake to continue supplying strategic materials during wartime. Such treaties would have to include nations whose borders are traversed during transport between the exporter and the importer of strategic goods. But such treaties would also legally bind the signatories to behavior which could avert the destabilizing consequences of interdependence without relying on an international authority.

There are, then, ways to enhance cooperation, defined here as a national willingness to enter into dependent relationships so as to accrue the benefits inherent in an interdependent system. Interdependence is a complex phenomenon involving intricate and nonadditive relationships among members of the international state system. A more sophisticated understanding of interdependence reveals that the consequences of interdependence are variable rather than constant. These consequences can either enhance or diminish systemic stability. Recognizing those consequences that pose a threat to systemic stability and preventing them can help to ensure that the system will enjoy the benefits of interdependence while averting its possible hazards.

Notes

1. Systemic stability is defined as the ease with which a system (a set of interacting units) deviates from a state of equilibrium. It is, then, the ease with which a system moves from peace to war which characterizes it stability.

On the stabilizing characteristics of interdependence, see, Robert O. Keohane and Joseph S. Nye, *Power and Interdependence: World Politics in Transition* (Boston and Toronto: Little, Brown, and Co., Inc., 1977).

I am grateful to the editors and authors of this volume, as well as to the workshop participants who contributed to the theoretical development of my ideas. I am particularly indebted to Tami L. Stukey, Bruce Cronin, James MacAllister, and Patricia Weitsman for their comments and criticisms. I also want to express my deepest appreciation to Warner R. Schilling and George J. Kuk for their much-needed support and assistance, without which this chapter would not have been completed.

2. Kenneth N. Waltz, *Theory of International Politics* (Reading, Massachusetts: Addison-Wesley Publishing Co., 1979), pp. 106, 138.
See also Kenneth N. Waltz, "The Myth of Interdependence," in Charles P. Kindleberger, ed. *The International Corporation* (Cambridge, Massachusetts and London, England: The M.I.T. Press, 1970), p. 205.

3. For an extended discussion of the definitions of interdependence see David A. Baldwin, "Interdependence and Power: A Conceptual Analysis," chap. in *Paradoxes of Power* (New York: Basil Blackwell, Inc., 1989); Richard N. Cooper, "Economic Interdependence and Foreign Policy in the Seventies," *World Politics*, Vol. 24, No. 2 (January 1972), p. 159; Keohane and Nye, *Power and Interdependence*, p. 9.

4. Waltz, "The Myth of Interdependence," p. 207; Karl W. Deutsch and Alexander Eckstein, "National Industrialization and the Declining Share of the International Economic Sector," *World Politics*, Vol. 13, No. 2 (January 1961), p. 272; Keohane and Nye, *Power and Interdependence*, pp. 9–13.

5. Carl von Clausewitz, *On War*, Michael Howard and Peter Paret, eds. (Princeton, New Jersey: Princeton University Press, 1976), pp. 128, 357.

6. Robert Jervis, "Cooperation Under the Security Dilemma," *World Politics*, Vol. 30, No. 2 (January 1978), pp. 186–206, and pp. 211–214; Jack Levy, "The Offensive/Defensive Balance of Military Technology: A Theoretical and Historical Analysis," *International Studies Quarterly*, Vol. 28, No. 2 (June 1984), pp. 219–238; Barry R. Posen, *The Sources of Military Doctrine: France, Britain, and Germany Between the World Wars* (Ithaca and London: Cornell University Press, 1984), pp. 16–24.

7. Posen, The Sources of Military Doctrine, p. 20.

8. William Carr, *Arms, Autarky, and Aggression: A Study in German Foreign Policy 1933–39* (New York: W.W. Norton and Company, Inc., 1972), p. 51.

9. Ibid., p. 52.

10. Ibid., pp. 52–53.

11. Ibid., pp. 54–57.

12. Williamson Murray, *The Change in the European Balance of Power, 1938–39: The Path to Ruin* (Princeton, New Jersey: Princeton University Press, 1984), p. 8.

13. Carr, Arms, Autarky and Aggression, p. 58

14. Murray, The Change in the European Balance of Power, pp. 10–11.

15. See Alan S. Milward, *War, Economy and Society* (Berkeley and Los Angeles: University of California Press, 1977), p. 29.

16. See R.J. Overy, "Hitler's War and the German Economy: A Reinterpretation," Economic Historical Review, Vol. 35, No. 2 (May 1982), pp. 272–276.

17. In addition to the acquisition of significant portions of the Soviet Union and Eastern Europe, Hitler made vague reference to eventual world domination, or to the inherently inimical relationship between Germany and countries such as the United States and Great Britain. These ambitions were clearly to be realized in the distant future, and were never discussed in any concrete manner. See Carr, *Arms, Autarky and Aggression*, p. 10; also, Overy, "Hitler's War," pp. 276–277.

18. Overy, "Hitler's War," p. 276.

19. Ibid., p. 275.

20. Murray, The Change in the European Balance of Power, p. 27.

21. Quoted in Overy, "Hitler's War," p. 274.

22. Murray, The Change in the European Balance of Power, p. 332.

23. F.H. Hinsley, *Hitler's Strategy* (Cambridge: Cambridge University Press, 1951), p. 9.

24. Ibid., p. 8.

25. Ibid., p. 6.

26. Carr, Arms, Autarky and Aggression, p. 115.

27. Hinsley, *Hitler's Strategy*, pp. 23–24.

28. Ibid., pp. 22–23.

29. J.F.C. Fuller, *Military History of the Western World*, vol. III (New York: Da Capo Press, Inc., 1957), pp. 388–391; also Telford Taylor, *The March of Conquest* (New York: Simon and Schuster, 1958), p. 220.

30. Taylor, *The March of Conquest*, pp. 255–261.

31. Carr, Arms, Autarky and Aggression, pp. 114–116.

32. Murray, The Change in the European Balance of Power, pp. 289–294.

33. Hinsley, *Hitler's Strategy*, p. 21.

34. Quoted in Hinsley, *Hitler's War*, pp. 24–25.

35. Ibid., p. 41.

36. Ibid., p. 40.

37. Hinsley, *Hitler's Strategy*, pp. 40–41.

38. J.R.M. Butler, *Grand Strategy*, Vol. II, *September 1939–June 1941*, in *History of the Second World War*, United Kingdom Military Series (London: Her Majesty's Stationary Office, 1957), pp. 10–11.

39. Murray, The Change in the European Balance of Power, pp. 329–330.

40. Hinsley, *Hitler's Strategy*, p. 49.

41. Milward, War Economy and Society, p. 31.

42. Ibid., p. 34.

43. Ibid., p. 35.

44. Ibid., p. 33.

45. Michael A. Barnhart, *Japan Prepares for Total War: The Search for Economic Security 1919–1941* (Ithaca and London: Cornell University Press, 1987), p. 42.

46. Ibid., p. 18.

47. Ibid., pp. 25–26.

48. Ibid., p. 27.

49. Ibid., p. 28.

50. Ibid., p. 29.

51. Ibid., p. 91.

52. Akira Iriye, *Across the Pacific: An Inner History of American-East Asian Relations* (New York: Harcourt, Brace and World, Inc., 1967), p. 201.

53. Ibid., pp. 202–203.

54. Ibid., pp. 207–208.

55. See John Mueller, "Pearl Harbor: Military Inconvenience, Political Disaster," *International Security*, Vol. 16, No. 3 (Winter 1991/92), pp. 172–203.

56. Milward, War, Economy and Society, p. 41.

57. Murray, The Change in the European Balance of Power, p. 52.

58. Ibid.

59. N.H. Gibbs, *Grand Strategy*, Vol. I, *Rearmament Policy*, in *History of the Second World War*, United Kingdom Military Series (London: Her Majesty's Stationary Office, 1976), p. 289.

60. Murray, The Change in the European Balance of Power, p. 62.

61. Gibbs, *Grand Strategy*, pp. 293–294.

62. Ibid. pp. 282–284.

63. Ibid., pp. 294–295.

64. Ibid., p. 297.

65. Ibid., pp. 297–298.

66. Ibid., pp. 301–302.

67. Murray, *The Change in the European Balance of Power*, p. 50.

68. Posen, *The Sources of Military Doctrine*, p. 141.

69. Murray, *The Change in the European Balance of Power*, pp. 62–63.

70. Posen, *The Sources of Military Doctrine*, p. 153.

71. Ibid., pp. 142–143.

72. Murray, The Change in the European Balance of Power, p. 311.

73. Gibbs, *Grand Strategy*, pp. 431–34.

74. Ibid.

75. Ibid., pp. 434–435.

76. Ibid.

77. Once war started, Briain discovered that it was not militarily autarkic, despite the available resources of the Empire; Britain needed the supplies received from the United States. Prior to the outbreak of war, however, The United Kingdom perceived itself to be self-sufficient, and it was this perception which governed its choice of policies.

78. See Keohane and Nye, *Power and Interdependence*, pp. 23–39; Jacob Viner, "Peace as an Economic Problem," chap. in *International Economics: Studies by Jacob Viner* (Illinois: The Free Press, 1947), pp. 258–267; Cooper, "Economic Interdependence and Foreign Policy in the Seventies," pp. 159–181; Edward Meade Earle, "Adam Smith, Alexander Hamilton, and Friedrich List: The Economic Foundations of Military Power," chap. in *Makers of Modern Strategy* (Princeton, New Jersey: Princeton University Press, 1971), pp. 120–124. See Jean de Bloch, *The Future of War in its Technical, Economic, and Political Relations* (London and Boston, 1899), cited in Michael Howard, "Men Against Fire," International Security, Vol. 9, No. 1 (Summer 1984), pp.

41–57; John Mueller, *Retreat From Doomsday: The Obsolescence of Major War* (New York: Basic Books, 1989); and Carl Kaysen, "Is War Obsolete?" International Security, Vol. 14, No. 4 (Spring 1990), pp. 42–64.

79. On the merits of economic sanctions, see David A. Baldwin, *Economic Statecraft* (Princeton, New Jersey: Princeton University Press, 1985).

80. Jervis, "Cooperation Under the Security Dilemma," p. 168.

11

Systems of Peace as Causes of War? Collective Security, Arms Control, and the New Europe

Richard K. Betts

Promotion of the idea of collective security has created a psychological situation in which the United States cannot turn its back on the concept, not because of what collective security can accomplish . . . but because of what millions of people . . . believe it may accomplish in time. Collective security has come to be the chief symbol of hope that . . . a community of nations will develop in which there will be no more war.

—Arnold Wolfers
Discord and Collaboration

The achievement of orthodox status is very often fatal to the integrity of a concept. When it becomes popular and respectable . . . men are strongly tempted to proclaim their belief in it whether or not they genuinely understand its meaning or fully accept its implications. If the tension between their urge to believe in it and their disinclination to believe that it is valid becomes too strong, they tend to resolve the difficulty by altering its meaning, packing into the terminological box a content that they can more readily accept.

—Inis L. Claude, Jr.
Swords into Plowshares

Collective security is an old idea whose time keeps coming.[1] The term has been resurrected and revised in three generations of this century, once after each world war (the First, the Second, and the Cold War), and has been used to refer to (1) the Wilsonian or ideal concept associated with the Fourteen Points and League of Nations; (2) the Rio Pact, the United Nations, and anticommunist alliances of the U.N. Command in Korea, NATO, the U.S.-Japan Mutual Security Treaty, SEATO, the Baghdad Pact, and CENTO,[2] and (3) current proposals for organizations to codify peace in Europe.[3]

The protean character of collective security reflects the fact that many who endorse it squirm when the terms are specified or applied to awkward cases. This has occurred with all incarnations of the idea.[4] The main problem is the gap between the instinctive appeal of the idea in liberal cultures as they settle epochal conflicts and the concept's inherent defects when it is applied to relations among independent states as they move from peace toward war. When particular cases make the defects obtrusive, the idea is revised rather than jettisoned. When revisions vitiate what essentially distinguishes the idea from traditional concepts it is supposed to replace, the urge to salvage the idea confuses strategic judgment. That is harmless only as long as strategy is not needed.

Among those who like the idea of collective security, negotiation of arms limitations among states is also popular. Many proponents of the League of Nations linked it closely to plans for general disarmament. That linking contributed to the association of Wilsonian collective security with utopian visions. In the second half of the Cold War the shift from pursuit of complete disarmament to limitations aimed at fixing the distribution of military power in stable configurations made the arms control enterprise more serious; indeed it became institutionalized after the 1960s.

Arms control treaties designed to stabilize military relationships, however, are vestiges of the Cold War. They make sense between adversaries, not friends, and the Russians are on our side now. This may not last, but the size and identity of coalitions that would be arrayed in a new strategic competition—information essential for prescribing the regulation of military balances—cannot yet be known. Bureaucracies and peace strategists nevertheless continue to lobby for arms control as a means to reinforce the current amity. Although constituencies for collective security and arms control overlap, there is at best little connection between the logic of the two goals, and at worst a contradiction. This allows potentially dangerous miscalculations.

The main argument in this essay is that reborn enthusiasm for collective security is fueled by confusion about which is the cause and which is the effect in the relation between collective security and peace, and by conflation of *present* security *conditions* (absence of a threat) with *future* security *functions* (coping with a threat). This conceptual confusion raises doubts about the congruence of form and function in a collective security system. Is the system designed in a form that will work in conditions where it is needed, or does the form reflect conditions where it is not needed? If changes in conditions prevent the system from functioning according to its design, the system will not make war less likely and will thus make coping with threats harder than if alternate security mechanisms had been developed.

The second possible danger is that instead of failing to perform according to design, collective security or arms control would succeed but would *worsen* military instability. Implementing collective commitments could turn minor wars into major ones, and equalizing military power of individual states through arms control without reference to their prospective alignment in war will yield unequal forces when alignments congeal. The usual criticism of collective security and arms control is that they will not work; the other is that if they do work, we may wish they hadn't.

Yes, these are opposite arguments. Moreover, not all the other criticisms I make of collective security or arms control proposals are mutually consistent. This would be dirty pool if the aim were to discredit the ideas with a contrary prediction of my own. My own view of the future, however, is agnostic. Various potential defects in ambitious proposals for systemic reform are listed not because they will go together, and not to stack the deck of argument, but simply to make the case that a wide range of possibilities is not foreclosed. That simple point precludes confidence in predicting whether or how institutions of collective security or arms control would work.

Security Systems

The function of a security system is to produce security, and the system should be judged by how it does so rather than by other things associated with it. This also means that a system designed in good times to cope with bad times should be judged in terms of the bad times rather than the good times. By my reading, many current proposals for collective security do not fully share these assumptions. To judge the efficacy of the idea and the potential for perverse effects, we need to clarify what the system is supposed to do and how and when it is supposed to do it.

For reasons argued below, the definition of collective security that we should use as a reference point is the classic Wilsonian ideal. Some charge that criticizing the ideal type prevents appreciation of more limited and realistic variants. We find on closer consideration, however, that most of the qualifications applied in current proposals make collective security more realistic by making it less collective and less automatic—and thus hard to differentiate from the traditional balance-of-power standards it is supposed to replace.

The essential element in the Wilsonian concept is the *rejection of alliances*, the commitment of all members of the system to oppose any attack against another: all for one, one for all. Peace is indivisible. Alliances for defense are mandated only if collective security fails (in the same way that a threatened citizen may rely on her own gun if the police fail to answer her call). Instead of planning against an identified adversary, security policy consists of the guarantee of united reaction against whoever might transgress. No grievance warrants resort to force to overturn the status quo; military force is legitimate only to resist attack, not to initiate it. States are to be legally accountable for starting wars. In contrast to traditional international relations, protection according to the Wilsonian concept comes not from balance of power but from preponderance of power against any renegade, guaranteed by universal treaty obligation to enforce peace whether doing so happens to be in a state's immediate interest or not. Community of power replaces balance of power.[5] The penalty for aggression is to be automatic economic or military sanctions.[6]

What Kind of System?

A collective security system is a *mechanism* to guard the sovereignty of its members, one *designed* to function according to certain norms.[7] Since it is not oriented to deterring a specific adversary, it does not function continuously in peacetime. It is an emergency safety mechanism sitting on the shelf unless activated by emergence of a challenger to the staus quo; in a sense it is comparable to the emergency backup system in a nuclear power plant, which functions only in the highly unlikely event that normal operation goes awry.

If we are to judge the effectiveness of an emergency system, it is useful to distinguish whether its most essential elements are automatic or volitional. That is, are the safety switches tripped by the alarm, or does the machine depend on ad hoc human choices to start it up and keep it going? If a set of conscious choices are required to run the machine, how many are real choices? Are there good reasons that those responsible might decide deliberately not to flip the switches necessary to keep the machine performing according to design? Are the "rules" for how the system works primarily empirical or normative? That is, do they describe how the linked components *do* work, in terms of laws of physics or evidence from experience, or prescribe how they *should* work or how they would work *if* the operators make the choices stipulated by the designers?

As Jervis and Perrow[8] make clear, the interactions in a complex system based on automatic switches may not be fully predictable. They should be far more predictable, however, than the outputs of a system which depends on a combination of existential choices. In the latter, the probability of unanticipated interactions of components is potentially doubled because mechanical uncertainties are compounded by decisional ones. The problem of predictability is further complicated by the strategic quality of decisions in a security system— statesmen trying not just to second-guess machines but to outwit each other. These differences are of course what makes action in any system of politics harder to predict than in one of physics.

Realist theories of balance-of-power systems are both empirical and normative, but primarily the former. Just as automobiles should drive on the right side of the road because they must do so to avoid a crash, states *should* seek power because they *must*.[9] The starkest versions of realism imply that precious little real choice is even available. The deterministic aspect of realism emphasizes automatic qualities of power-balancing in the international system more than do idealists who focus on cooperation or moral choices. Extreme realists see the rules of balance of power as almost a cybernetic process of constant adjustment to maintain equilibrium. If one state or coalition begins to dominate the system, the others, like thermostats, move to coalesce and right the balance.

A collective security system depends more on volition and normative rules. The design of collective security rests on the norm that states must subordinate their own immediate interests to general or remote ones. While there is disagreement about how thoroughly the theory and practice of balance-of-power systems have coincided in history, few claim that the case for collective security has yet been confirmed by experience. (As I will argue, the Concert of Europe is not a good example.) Indeed, the main theoretical argument against collective security is that its normative rules have been discredited by the empirically validated rules of balance of power.[10]

All of this highlights the question of congruence between form and function. Will the system's performance correspond to the rules in its design? If not, will the design be just superfluous, or counterproductive? Or will it ever have to perform at all? The test of a security system is how it functions when a challenge to security arises. If it is never tested, its function is only symbolic, not substantive.

Testing, however, poses two problems. One is that the first test may kill the system if the design is flawed—if empirical rules contradict normative ones, and form does not govern function. There are no simulations or dry runs in international conflict comparable to what can be done with real machines. Another problem is that we may not know when a test occurs. As with deterrence in general, if the design is so good that a would-be challenger does not even dare to try, the system has worked, but no one can prove that it has because there is no certainty that the challenge would have been made otherwise.

Forecasting and System Assessment

Since an emergency system functions only when the normal environment or operating condition breaks down, its design depends on assumptions about hypothetical and improbable futures. The implication of this point is not quite so obvious that it should insult a reader's intelligence.

First, many people naturally do think of a security system as one that functions from day to day, in normal times. This is true when normal times are conflictual, as they were in Europe during most of the lifetimes of anyone contemplating the question. Cooperation modified the East-West competition occasionally, but the term Cold *War* meant that reliable peace did not exist. Clarity of alignments enabled contingency planning and targeting of strategy against identified threats to develop as ongoing activities. NATO and the Warsaw Pact, high defense budgets and peacetime military readiness, episodic combat in the so-called Third World, and arms control negotiations all went with a security system for an insecure world. Under collective security, in contrast, everyone is supposed to be willing to act against anyone, so highly developed strategic preparation is circumscribed.

Enthusiasm for collective security emerges from the end of the Cold War, as it did for a while after 1918 and 1945, because the end of an epochal conflict makes peace appear normal. It should not be surprising, however, if people remain psychologically disposed to think of any security system, as they thought of NATO, as a machine whirring along from day to day, keeping threats under control. The renewed *appeal* of the idea of collective security flows directly from the present, the happy shock of liberalism's transcontinental triumph which shows that radical optimism is not naive after all. The *relevance* of the idea, in contrast, lies in a less happy future where other surprising rather than likely changes have occurred.

Second, while the design of an emergency system depends on forecasting the emergencies with which it might have to cope, there are no practical grounds for faith in political forecasts. While everyone will accept the bromide that no one knows what the future will bring, what does one do when asked to predict? The most common approach (and the one that tends to gain more support because other approaches evoke more skeptical reactions) is to extrapolate, to project the future as a trajectory from present trends. This reinforces any disposition to think of a collective security system as a constantly functioning one like an alliance. This approach is also conducive to relaxed specifications for the system's design because interest in the solution is highest when worry that it might have to be implemented is lowest.

Basing plans for a security system on extrapolation from current trends makes the problem easy. All the great powers are on the same side now, and all the discernible sources of violence are internal score-settling between national groups within states, or between states that are minor powers. To base plans on anything *other* than extrapolation seems arbitrary. Unless one of the great powers goes bad, or the small scraps in Eastern Europe metastasize, the nature of the international mechanism for preserving security is not terribly important. For either of the malign developments to occur, we have to imagine a sequence of changes in the present trend creating a nasty scenario—and discussion in terms of scenarios has an air of unreality. It is as easy for optimists to reject such approaches as "worst-case" alarmism as it is for pessimists to warn of the complacency in projecting the future from the present.

The problem for security policy is to predict threats and to devise means for coping with them, yet it is especially reckless at the moment to invest confidence in any estimate of why, how, and when things will go wrong. Major discontinuities in international relations are seldom predicted. Who would not have been derided and dismissed in 1988 for predicting that within a mere three years Eastern Europe would be liberated, the Communist Party of the Soviet Union deposed, and the USSR itself on the ash heap of history? Yet it is hard to believe that the probability of equally revolutionary negative developments, of economic crisis and ideological disillusionment, of instability leading to miscalculation, escalation, and war several years from now is lower than the probability of the current peace seemed then.

With unusually low confidence in the identity of future threats, flexibility and adaptability to unforeseen contingencies are unusually important. This is not a truism. To increase flexibility for various contingencies precludes optimizing preparations for any particular contingency.[11] Flexibility and power are traded off against each other. Flexibility aims to maximize freedom of choice, which varies inversely with the number of independent actors who must concur with a decision to act. Power, on the other hand, varies directly with the number of actors deciding to join forces.

What does this imply for mechanisms to produce security? *Unilateral* measures (or what Waltz calls "internal balancing") are the most flexible; they can be directed against any country and depend least on the cooperation of others. The price of maximal flexibility is a lower limit on the maximum amount of deployable power. *Alliances* combine reduced flexibility with increased power; any member's policy choices are more circumscribed than if it operates independently, but the grouping pools resources for agreed purposes. *Collective security* (if it is to function according to design) is the least flexible because it requires the most extensive cooperation among independent states, according to the most rigid rules, but it offers the greatest potential power (everyone in the system against any defector).

Alliances should offer the best compromise between unilateralism's weakness and collective action's rigidity. An alliance without a respectable adversary to give it life, however, is bound for dessication. NATO will endure because popular organizations can survive for a long time from inertia. The longer peace lasts, however, the more NATO will become a shell—not hollow, and replete with parades, committee meetings, and rhetorical affirmations, but bereft of serious strategic activity. Shells are far from useless—they can maintain the base from which remobilization and coordination can be accomplished in a shorter time than if they had to be accomplished from scratch—but they do not provide the animation or originality that revolutionary political changes seem to mandate. So collective security generates interest more by default than by its own merits: unilateralism seems ineffective or illegitimate, and alliance without an adversary seems anachronistic and empty.

Collective Security as a Norm

If we cannot test the mechanism before putting it into use, as we might test a nuclear power plant safety system, a heavier burden necessarily falls on deduction, and comparison with cases where security systems have indeed been tested, to validate the logic in the design. Therefore it is not pedantic to take current discussions of collective security to task for imprecision or ambivalence in defining the concept and prescribing functions.

Those who identified the concept with the regional anti-Communist alliance organizations spawned in the first decade of the Cold War were stretching the idea to cover arrangements really more consistent with traditional strategy. Dignifying regional coalitions like NATO as collective security organs helped to brand Communist states as outlaws and confirm the moralism in American policy, but the fact remained that they were alliances playing the power-balancing game. Many current proponents of collective security, in contrast, trim the concept to cover less than either the Wilsonian or Cold War variants by allowing big exemptions from the obligation to discipline countries who resort to force. These variants evade what distinguished collective security from either traditional alliances or military isolation. If a collective institution is really to function as a security system rather than a slogan, the elements that are conceptually unique rather than those that are shared with other constructs should set the standard for assessing the idea. What most differentiate collective security from balance of power are the principles of automaticity and universality.

Many who now claim to endorse collective security demur on the ironclad obligation to join in countering any and all aggression. This vitiates the concept. *Unless collective security requires states to act on the basis of the legal principle rather than their specific interests in the case at issue, and unless it forbids neutrality in the face of aggression, the concept adds nothing to traditional conventions of collective defense* based on alliances and balance of power.[12] Nevertheless, in the generations after Wilson many felt the need to endorse collective security while defining it in ways that overlapped significantly with traditional arrangements. They did so because they recognized that weakness of the League of Nations and the U.N. had embarrassed the pure concept as naive, yet they still resisted the argument that balance-of-power politics cannot be transcended.

What's Wrong with Collective Security?

Before confronting attempts to salvage the principle by softening it, we should note the reasons that so many have rejected it altogether. The main criticism has been that collective security does not work because states fail to honor commitments to automatic action. In the background of the many reasons that they renege is the problem that the animating motive for *constructing* a collective security system ("no more war") is in tension with the imperative required to make the system function when challenged ("no more aggression"); the former reflects abhorrence of war, but the latter requires going to war where immediate self-interest would not. This reduces the odds that parties to the system will feel the same way about the principle when it comes to cases.

A second objection is that the collective security principle's legalism is too rigidly conservative since it requires honoring the status quo ante irrespective of its merits.[13] As Elihu Root complained about Article 10 of the League Covenant:

> If perpetual, it would be an attempt to preserve for all time unchanged the distribution of power and territory made in accordance with the views and exigencies of the Allies in this present juncture of affairs. . . . It would not only be futile; it would be mischievous. Change and growth are the law of life, and no generation can impose its will in regard to the growth of nations and the distribution of power, upon succeeding generations.[14]

This is especially problematic because third parties often do not agree about which side in a war is the aggressor. The closest thing to a criterion that is both general and neutral would be "whoever strikes first across a national border," but this would never be universally accepted. For example, this criterion would have required members of a collective security system to act against the British and Russians in World War II for occupying Iran, against Israel for preempting in June 1967, and against the United States in the 1980s for invading Grenada and Panama. "The problem is not, as the Wilsonians imagined, one of suppressing an infrequent case of diabolism. . . . To determine the aggressor is really to decide which is a bad nation. And a general law can never do this."[15]

Insensitivity to this ambiguity among liberals arose in part because, from the establishment of the League of Nations through the war in Korea, "aggressors" were ideologically repugnant states; for democracies "it was natural . . . to assume that committing themselves to deter or punish 'any aggressor anywhere' meant in fact committing themselves to oppose nondemocratic aggressors who were their national enemies anyway." Not until the Suez expedition of 1956 did assigning guilt become awkward.[16]

A third standard objection is that in practice, organizing according to the principle of collective responsibility undermines preparations to balance the power of troublesome states. Potent alliances cannot be developed with a snap of the finger when innocent states suddenly lose faith in the collective guarantee. "No arrangement would be more likely to create conditions in which one nation can dominate," wrote Kissinger of the Wilsonian dream. "For if everybody is allied with everybody, nobody has a special relationship with anybody. It is the ideal situation for the most ruthless seeking to isolate potential victims."[17] Or the responsibility to counter every aggressor can endanger a threatened coalition, as when the League considered the obligation of resisting the Soviet attack on Finland after Britain and France were already at war with Germany.[18]

A fourth, more general criticism is the structural realist argument that collective security requires centralization, which conflicts with independence:

> States cannot entrust managerial powers to a central agency unless that agency is able to protect its client states. The more powerful the clients and the more the power of each of them appears as a threat to the others, the greater the power lodged in the center must be. The greater the power of the center, the stronger the incentive for states to engage in a struggle to control it.
>
> States, like people, are insecure in proportion to the extent of their freedom. If freedom is wanted, insecurity must be accepted. Organizations that establish relations of authority and control may increase security as they decrease freedom. If might does not make right, whether among people or states, then some institution or agency has intervened to lift them out of nature's realm.[19]

The main reason that liberals lost interest in collective security in earlier generations was that it did not work, and the challenge to it had to be met with traditional means. The League Covenant and Kellogg-Briand Pact neither deterred nor defeated Fascist aggressions in the 1930s because the volitional elements of the system faltered; when principle came to practice, leaders chose not to honor the commitment of the covenant to united action, not to flip the switches on the collective security machine.

Conservative realists, however, do not just fear that the principle would not work; to them it can be awful if it *does* work. Their criticism is that if abstract commitments are honored, the system inevitably turns small conflicts into big ones by requiring states to get involved when it is not in their interest to do so. This was the main reason that realists like Morgenthau and Kennan fell out with liberal hawks over the Vietnam War. The Cold War redefinition of collective security as the global coalition against Communist aggression, in rhetoric from Dean Acheson to Dean Rusk, fed the domino theory: South Vietnam was important not in itself but as a matter of principle. Fighting in Vietnam meant avoiding the mistakes of the 1930s in not fighting in Manchuria or Ethiopia. As Morgenthau posed the counterproductive effect of the principle:

> [I]t is the supreme paradox of collective security that any attempt to make it work with less than ideal perfection will have the opposite effect

from what it is supposed to achieve. . . . If an appreciable number of nations are opposed to the status quo . . . the distribution of power will take on the aspects of a balance of power. . . . The attempt to put collective security into effect under such conditions . . . will not preserve peace, but will make war inevitable. . . . It will also make localized wars impossible and thus make war universal. For under the regime of collective security as it actually works under contemporary conditions, if A attacks B, then C, D, E, and F might honor their collective obligations and come to the aid of B, while G and H might try to stand aside and I, J, and K might support A's aggression. . . . By the very logic of its assumptions, the diplomacy of collective security must aim at transforming all local conflicts into world conflicts. . . . Since peace is supposed to be indivisible. . . . Thus a device intent on making war impossible ends by making war universal.[20]

Another argument for the counterproductive effect of collective security norms cites the case of efforts to punish Italy for its aggression against Ethiopia. Where proponents of the norm see those efforts as feeble, conservative realists charge that they helped push Italy into the axis alliance. This argument also goes against current proposals for "limited" collective security as an alternative to the unrealistic demands of the ideal type. The problem in the 1930s was precisely the limitation of the concept, a compromise response; either extreme would have been preferable. Had *pure* collective security been applied, the Fascist powers could have been crushed early, *or* had pure balance-of-power strategy been applied, Italy might have been kept in the allied camp by ignoring its depredations in Africa. Falling between the stools, however, truncated collective security and left France and Britain with the worst of both worlds.

Realist arguments against a collective security system for Europe rest on both fears—that it would not work when needed, or would work when it should not. If commitments falter in a crunch, defense against a rogue power will be weaker than if the regular NATO alliance had remained the guarantor of security. If it does work, however, it precludes denying protection to Eastern European countries against each other or a great power. This makes a crisis in that cauldron of instabilities more likely to escalate than to stew in its own juice. Concern with this implication of the classic scheme of collective security for involvement in the Balkans, embodied in Article 10 of the League Covenant (to "preserve as against external aggression the territorial integrity of all members"), was a specific reason for U.S. domestic opposition to joining that organization over seventy years ago.[21]

Why Does Collective Security Keep Coming Back?

The Wilsonian ideal of collective security was buffeted by history from all sides, in the 1930s and again after the anti-Fascist alliance split. Redefinitions in the first half of the Cold War were also driven from favor—for hawks, by disappointment with the development of the U.N. after Korea, and for doves, by disillusionment with the crusade in Vietnam. The renewed popularity of the term "collective security" does not come from a change of mind about the earlier disillusionments but from the apparent inadequacy of alternative constructs for adjusting to the outbreak of peace, and because some now define the concept in narrow ways that avoid troublesome implications. At the same time, there is no agreement on whether the most troublesome commitment would be to counter aggression by a great power or to pacify wars between Eastern European states over borders and ethnic minorities.

Many proponents of a collective security system for post-Cold War Europe are ambivalent or opposed outright to requiring intervention in a new generation of Balkan wars. Richard Ullman proclaims that "Europe's peace has become a divisible peace" yet endorses a European Security Organization (ESO) that would include "a generalized commitment to collective security. Each member state would commit itself . . . to come to the aid of any other if it is the victim of an armed attack." The obligation, however, would not extend to little victims. Eastern Europe is to be "a vast buffer zone between the Soviet Union and Germany." If cross-border violence erupts over national minorities in Kosovo or Transylvania, "the major powers would be unlikely to get involved to an extent greater than through diplomacy and perhaps economic pressure." Besides "walling off" local conflicts, the anticipated benefit of the buffer zone is to facilitate great-power confidence in a shift toward defensively oriented military doctrines.[22] Similarly, the Kupchans prescribe collective security yet at the same time make a gargantuan concession to traditional balance of power by endorsing tacit recognition of "areas of special interest" such as a Russian *droit du regard* in Eastern Europe.[23] These notions recognize the defects in the Wilsonian ideal type, and they may reassure the great powers about their security; but they certainly decollectivize European security.

Uncertainty about whether the system would cover Eastern Europe is crucial. There are two essential trends in Europe today: in the West, economic and political integration, consensus on borders, and congruence between nations and states; in the East, the reverse—disintegration and lack of consensus or congruence. Will the stability of the West be protected by holding the mess in the East at arm's length? Ullman believes the new collective system would handle misbehavior by one of the great powers, but not by small ones,[24] presumably because the stakes are higher. By the same token, however, the *costs* and risks (such as involvement of nuclear weapons) would be higher too, so the balance of costs and benefits does not obviously make pacification of small wars in Eastern Europe a less attractive objective.

It should hardly be as daunting for the system to settle a fight between Hungary and Rumania or between Ukraine and Poland as to confront one between Russia or Germany and the rest of the continent. At the same time, apparent sideshows in Eastern Europe may offer occasions for abrasions and misperceptions among the great powers if they disagree about intervention. One nightmare would be a Russian attack on Ukraine (far less fanciful than a Soviet attack on NATO ever was; Vice President Aleksandr Rutskoi already broached the issue of recovering the Crimea for Russia).[25] Under true collective security, members of the system would have to aid Ukraine—doing what NATO would not do for Hungary in 1956—thus evoking the danger of escalation and nuclear war. Under realist norms, the West should leave Ukraine to its fate—tragic for the Ukrainians, but safer for everyone else. If we prefer the latter course, why try to dress it up by associating it with collective security?

If one is genuinely interested in collective security as something different from traditional spheres of influence and alignments based on power and national interest, it is hard to write off responsibility for dealing with wars involving *either* great or small states; but if one is primarily interested in avoiding escalation of limited wars into large ones, it is hard to accept advance commitment to engage either sort of challenge before knowing exactly what it is. Since the collective security concept cannot be copyrighted, promoters have the right to amend it to accommodate standard criticisms. Confronted with questions about how the system would handle particular worrisome scenarios, however, some of the revisionists argue not just that the system should be exempted from responsibility for that type of conflict but that such problems will not arise.

Conceptual Confusion
and System Dysfunction

If revisions of the collective security idea are used to cover arrangements that fit better under other basic concepts like traditional alliance formation or are used to dignify an arrangement other than a functioning security system, they make it less likely that effects of the system can be predicted from its design. Since collective security is an emergency safety system and cannot be tested in peacetime the way a real machine can, dysfunctions due to confusions in design may not be evident until the time when the system is most needed.

Confusing Causes and Consequences

Since the collapse of communism it is not always clear whether the invocation of collective security is to enforce peace or to celebrate its existence. Less emphasis is usually placed on how the system would restore peace in the face of war than on why war (or at least war worthy of concern) will not arise:

> If one were to rely on the historical record of generalized commitments to collective security, one could not be hopeful. . . . But it is arguable that the conditions now emerging in Europe make the past a poor predictor. . . . No major state has revisionist ambitions that its leaders think they could satisfy by sending troops across borders. . . . A genuine congruence of interests and goals sharply distinguishes the present from previous eras. . . . *It is unlikely that the great powers will soon find their commitments to collective security put to the test of a large, searing, and escalating crisis.*[26]

Ullman does recognize that things could go bad and urges taking advantage of the current window of opportunity to get an ESO going so that the regime could buttress stability in fouler weather. Why collective security should work any better in the face of the many logical and historical criticisms noted earlier, however, remains unclear, apart from the idea that it can work because there will be no rampaging rogue states or because not all aggressions will have to be countered. Such hope may also deflect reservations about automatic commitment to combat unidentified future aggressors, but it implies that *peace is the premise of the system rather than the product, that peace will cause peace rather than that collective security will cause peace.* If we fasten on the import of the current calm, we muddle the difference between the current need for a security organization (which we can see is low) and the future efficacy of such an organization (which we should want to be high).[27]

One can argue that even if peace may be the cause rather than the consequence at the beginning, it can become the consequence as a regime, once established, promotes cooperation and takes on a life of its own. Speaking of the Concert of Europe, Jervis notes that the expectation that it "could continue to function helped maintain it through the operation of familiar self-fulfilling dynamics. . . . There were no 'runs on the bank'." Rules, reciprocity, and institutionalization reinforced opposition to attempts to change the status quo. Recently, the Kupchans argue, the norm of reciprocity is growing again, as reflected in mutual concessions such as Soviet and western troop withdrawals from Central Europe.[28] These examples are weak reeds.

First, while the nineteenth-century Concert of Europe "influenced the behavior of states in ways that made its continuation possible even after the initial conditions had become attenuated," when the conditions eroded, the regime's efficacy did too. By 1823, a mere eight years after the Napoleonic Wars, the concert was fraying.[29] The concert "worked" well only as long as the great powers' disagreements were minor; when the consensus cracked over the Crimea in 1854, and later in the century, so did the concert.

As to the second argument, the idea that growing reciprocity characterized East-West relations in recent years misreads the end of the Cold War. The peace settlement was no compromise, it was a series of outright victories for the West. The USSR surrendered in arms control negotiations, accepting NATO's terms, which required grossly asymmetrical reductions in both the Intermediate Range Nuclear Forces (INF) and Conventional Forces in Europe (CFE) treaties. Moscow gave up political control of Eastern Europe without a fight in 1989, getting nothing in return. Within a year the Warsaw Pact was defunct, but NATO lived on. The West did not reciprocate Soviet concessions, it just pocketed them. There was more reciprocity during the Cold War when both sides were bargaining with each other (as in SALT I and II or the Helsinki accords) than there was in the ending as the Russians rolled over belly-up.

Perhaps regimes can bootstrap themselves from consequences to causes, but in the realm of security systems we still lack robust and reassuring models. As to whether regimes can promote peace independent of prior peaceful conditions, why are the failures of the League of Nations or U.N. to do so not indicative? Indeed, few who think collective security can now work in a Europe of thirty-plus nations yet endorse it as viable for the world as a whole. Why not? If an ESO can guard peace, why not the U.N.? Presumably because the rest of the world has not progressed beyond violent contests and is still "mired in history."[30] When exceptions to the applicability of collective security are pointed out, few reasons are offered for continuing to believe in the idea that do not come back to citing peace, satisfaction with the status quo, and consensus on legitimate behavior as preconditions for their own enforcement. If Europe remains at peace it is likely to be not because a collective security system causes it, but because the nations and states of Europe are satisfied.

Few dare propose a pure collective security system. Most of the qualified versions suggested, however, are too far from the essential idea that distinguishes the concept to make the qualified versions meaningful rather than misleading. Some modify the collective security idea to make it more realistic. They admit that the modified version will not solve all security problems but argue that limited versions are at least more effective than traditional "balancing under anarchy."[31] Those who take this approach misunderstand the choice. Collective security commitments do not obviate international anarchy; only world government would. And if the job of salvaging the concept is completed by dispensing with the unrealistic requirements of universality and automaticity, what then is really left that is *not* consistent with traditional "balancing under anarchy," to which collective security is ostensibly opposed?

If we strip away the rhetoric of collective security, the actual results that seem to be envisioned by the more realistic proposals that invoke the term are (1) marginal peacekeeping functions comparable to what the U.N. has attempted in the Congo, Cyprus, Sinai and Gaza (until Nasser evicted the U.N. force just before the 1967 war), and Lebanon; (2) a collective security cachet on what really amounts to policing by a single dominant power, comparable to the U.N. actions in Korea and Kuwait, where many nations sent token forces but the preponderance of power was imposed by the United States; (3) a condominial system of great-power tutelage modeled on the nineteenth-century Concert of Europe; or (4) a *de jure* overlay of collective security norms on a *de facto unorganized* security system, comparable to the Rio Pact "system" in South America.

The limitations of the first of these are well recognized. Cases of U.N. peacekeeping have generally been modest monitoring and interposition operations,[32] not forthright defeat of aggression as supposed in the basic model of collective security (in large part because there was no international consensus on which sides were the aggressors). The U.N. missions intervened impartially to separate contending forces under truces which the contenders accepted. Peacekeeping is not peacemaking. Even the peacekeeping was dubious: when the contenders fell out forcibly again (as in the June 1967 war, the Greek Cypriot coup and Turkish invasion in 1974, or the Israeli invasion of Lebanon in 1982), the U.N. troops were brushed aside by the combatants.

U.N.-mandated action in the Korean War and against Iraq in 1991 came the closest to real collective security, and the symbolic value of the large number of nations sending combat units was indeed quite significant. In neither case, however, was the military participation of countries other than the United States vital to the outcome. In the recent war, for example, it is implausible that the anti-Iraq coalition forces could have liberated Kuwait without the Americans, or that the Americans could have failed to do so without the assistance of the other forces (although they would have needed the bases in Saudi Arabia). The principle of collective security, however, was indeed vital in motivating the American decision to attack Iraq.[33]

The third and fourth variants suggested above deserve more scrutiny. The relevance of the Concert of Europe model has been overestimated, and that of the unorganized system has been underestimated.

The Old Concert and the New Europe

If we had to find a reasonable hybrid version of collective security, the nineteenth-century Concert of Europe would be it. As a modification, the concert does not go so far as to become identical with eighteenth- or late nineteenth-century balance-of-power models. The concert departs from important aspects of the ideal definition, however, and it also rests on archaic ideological premises. These problems may not disable it as a model for twenty-first century collective security, but they do weaken it.

One discrepancy between ideal collective security and the concert is that the former sanctifies the security of all nations while the latter subordinates the sovereignty of the weak to the interests of the strong. Under the concert the great powers colluded to keep peace by keeping each other satisfied; the rights of a Poland were not in the same class as those of an Austria, Prussia, or Russia. The security nurtured by the concert was selectively collective.[34] (Consider that the United Nations in 1945 resembled a concert. The role of the Security Council apart from the General Assembly accorded special rights to the great powers, and Poland's prewar borders were changed to compensate the USSR.) Maintaining a balance of power (by cooperation rather than competition) remained an important object of the concert regime.

The moral glue of much of the concert (at least the Holy Alliance in the East) was monarchical conservatism and *opposition* to liberalism and nationalism. Yet liberalism and nationalism are precisely what most characterize the recent revolution in Europe. This fact weakens the proposition that the time for another concert is ripe because the underlying conditions "are once again present," and because burgeoning democracy is conducive to it.[35] Only if the fact of ideological consensus *per se* was all that mattered, irrespective of its content, would the argument for another concert be convincing. The liberal consensus in today's world, however, has different implications for the rights of great powers. Outside of academic hothouses, liberals are unlikely to rejoice in the pacifying effects of transcontinental democracy in one breath and endorse a two-class system of policymaking and security rights in the next. Liberals cannot easily promote both collective security for the big boys on the block and every-man-for-himself for benighted weak states in Eastern Europe. The point was clear in the statement by Czechoslovakia's foreign minister, Jiri Dienstbier, that "the core of any collective system of European security must be a treaty committing every party to provide assistance, including military assistance, in the event of an attack against any participant."[36] Can we imagine the western powers giving the back of their hand to the new heroes of the liberated zones? Maybe in whispered back alley conclaves, but not in the formal conferences that defined the concert system at its height. Even then, as Flynn and Scheffer note in dismissing the concert as a form of collective security, "No one is prepared to redraw the map of Europe for balance-of-power purposes. . . . International law has evolved substantially to protect the integrity of all states."[37] A concert today would have more trouble juggling two contradictory sets of values: national self-determination and the sanctity of existing state borders.

Nor can a collective security regime be shorn of ideology, because the essence of the concept is an assumption of legal order and moral obligation independent of immediate national interest. To ignore this is hardly feasible when the flush of enthusiasm for collective security comes mainly from teleological liberalism.[38] The mechanics of the system and the prediction of how it would function cannot be easily separated from the values that are integral to its design.

Is an Organized System Necessary?

Collective security is popular despite all the logical problems because it is hard to think of what else should replace the Cold War alliance system. It seems to go without saying that there must be a grand design and a formal regulatory structure. If the structure is not to be designed in terms of bipolar alliances like during the Cold War or multipolar alliances like in the classical balance of power, or in terms of a fully United Europe or American dominance, then collective security becomes appealing by default. Coupled with the celebration of peace, collective security is appealing as a talisman, a security blanket legitimizing relaxation, rather than as a serious action plan for collective war against yet unknown "aggressors." Analysts, however, should bite the bullet and ask what this means about the substance of the security order.

If what we are facing is really a durable condition of *natural security* in Europe, a post-Hobbesian pacific anarchy, why assume the need for an organized *functioning* security system of any sort? Why is strategic laissez-faire, ad hoc adaptation as we go along, unthinkable? What would be wrong if the organization of security on the European continent became like that in South America for the past half-century, where symbolic organs like the Rio Pact continue to exist without substantive import and states dispense with significant alliance arrangements because there is little concern with the prospect of major international war?[39] Instead of an ESO, why not a UPE (Unorganized Pacified Europe)? If something goes wrong, states could look for allies or other tried and true solutions when the time comes. If this is what ambivalent fans of collective security are implicitly getting at, then an ESO and a UPE could coexist: an ESO overlay of symbolic commitment in principle to collective security could exist and could be left sufficiently ambiguous to allow the evolution of traditional initiatives for self-protection in the underlying UPE. In Perrow's terms this would be a "loosely coupled" collective security system with more potential for adapting to unforeseen circumstances,[40] but its substantive significance would be low; sensible states would not count on it in a pinch.

Unorganized need not mean chaotic and unstable. In physics, equilibrium in thermodynamic systems is called disorganization.[41] Among satisfied states that recognize each other's satisfaction, the security dilemma is not automatically a problem. Here the symbolic value of a collective security organization might indeed take on a slight substantive function if the rituals of meetings and consultations reinforced mutual perceptions of innocent aims. As long as genuflection to collective security forms did not impede traditional strategic adaptation to changing circumstances, the forms would be helpful at best and harmless at worst.

Arms Control Without Alignment

Most enthusiasts for collective security also favor negotiated limitations on armament. Both collective security organizations and arms control treaties aim to establish legal orders that deter challenges to peace. The rationales behind them, however, are not consistent.

The two forms of regulation deal in different currencies. Collective security is based on commitments of *intent* (that states will act against aggressors). Arms control is based on constraint of *capabilities*. These could be complementary, but there is still a disjunction between the political logic of one and the military logic of the other. Arms control relies on balance of power, aiming to construct a military balance that in itself dissuades states from thinking that they can use force effectively for attack; moral status in disputes between the parties to arms control is irrelevant to a treaty's impact on the stability of deterrence. Collective security, in contrast, relies on *im*balance of power, preponderance of the law-abiding many against the law-breaking few; moral claims of the states involved are everything.

The impact of arms limitations on military stability depends in principle on beliefs about what would happen if the forces allowed under the agreement were to crash into each other in battle: stability implies that neither side could win by striking first. Thus a stable agreement would be evaluated according to force ratios calculated in terms of dyads. If there is any strategic logic to an arms treaty, it is based on assumed knowledge of who would be on whose side in event of war. It would be nonsensical for A, B, and C to agree to binding constraints of equal armament, forswearing options of unilateral military buildup, if they thought that in a pinch two of them were likely to combine against the third. There is nothing stable about a peacetime ratio of 1:1:1 if it translates into a wartime ratio of 2:1. A country expecting that it may have to fight alone will want the option to increase its power unilaterally and will not logically settle for limits that prohibit that option.

Whereas arms control logically depends on specifying prospective alignment, however, collective security depends explicitly on *not* doing so. It *assumes* that if one breaks the peace the others must join to overwhelm it—that is the whole point of the system. And if collective security rests on the guarantee that members of the system will act together against a renegade, then the individual levels of armament among the states in the system hardly matter as long as no single one develops as much power as the others combined. However, if the system cannot rely on the universal guarantee, and collective self-defense has to be substituted for collective security, then the identity of alignments is crucial for judging the stability of peacetime force configurations.

Military Criteria for Limitations

Few proposals address in detail what standards or formulas would mesh limits for armament with the logic of a collective security system. Those that embrace the treaty on Conventional Forces in

Europe (CFE) or endorse further reductions along its lines would base arms control on the old Cold War framework of bipolar alliances, which is already gone. Another proposal does attempt to supersede the old framework, but with dubious implications. It would establish a supranational "organization, to which all states belong, that regulates the conditions of military deployment for everyone."[42]

What would be the benchmarks for regulation? At one point it is suggested that "standardized criteria for setting force ceilings *would ensure that no state faced a decisive advantage against any other single state*, and the residual alliances would offer protection against the formation of aggressive coalitions." In the next breath, however, it is proposed that each state be allowed force levels proportional to the length of its borders. By the author's own estimates this proposal shows the old USSR with *more than double* the "offensive potential" of Germany and a far higher margin against any other European state; Turkey with nearly four times as much as its enemy Greece; and Germany with more than twice as much as either Poland or France. All of this contradicts the prior criterion of no decisive advantage between any two states,[43] and shows that the identification of coalitions would remain absolutely essential to assessing the stability of military relationships on the continent.

If the prior criterion was to take precedence, the arms control order should be denominated in terms of force-to-*force* ratios rather than force-to-space and should accord *absolutely* equal forces, battalion for battalion, to all states irrespective of their size, population, or other asymmetries—Belgium's forces would have to equal Germany's. The proposal does not recommend such equality because it seeks to endow the new military allotments with a technical character more favorable to defensive operations than to attack and because it assumes that defensive advantage is related to capacity to cover borders with satisfactory force-to-space ratios. To take that criterion seriously, however, contradicts the aim of significant reductions of forces, or for many of the countries in Europe, any reductions at all.

Ensuring a linear defense means maximizing the density of forces covering the line to prevent probing attacks from finding a gap or weak point that can be penetrated. Yet the Steinbruner proposal, although denominated in terms of force-to-space ratios, seeks to *reduce* density rather than maximize it. It aims at an allowance of one brigade per seventy-five kilometers of front, which is a mere *one-fifth* of the ratio considered adequate (and only a tenth of the optimum) in tactical doctrines of modern armies.[44] This allowance could conceivably be rationalized by compensating for thinner ground forces along the line with unusually large amounts of mobile firepower from air forces, yet the proposal seeks to reduce that dimension of capability as well, and to do so disproportionately (on grounds that it is offensive).[45] Low density on the ground, uncompensated by other sources of firepower, opens up much larger possibilities for offensive movement. (If total force levels were low enough on both sides, this would prevent penetrations from occupying much of the defender's territory, operations could degenerate into the raiding/counterraiding style of medieval warfare, and strategy would move from denial or conquest toward punishment; but all this would hardly be conducive to linear defense.)[46]

It is easier to have defense dominance with high numbers of troops and low technology than with low numbers of troops and low-technology.[47] If one really wants simultaneously to base operational doctrine on linear defense and force-to-space ratios, and to reduce mobile firepower available to defenders that can allow quick reinforcement of threatened sectors, the answer is to *increase* ground forces (while limiting their mobility), not to reduce them. Increased armament, however, is not a plausible response to the end of the Cold War.

Tactical complexities aside, endorsement in principle of technological and doctrinal "defense dominance" by proponents of collective security[48] is reasonable, but not unambiguously so. Compared with traditional strategic arrangements which usually develop war plans, deployments, and doctrine in regard to an identified enemy, collective security *delays* reaction to attack because the members of the system must react, mobilize, and coordinate responses ad hoc. Since preponderant power is not arrayed against an attacker before transgression occurs (if it were, the system would be an alliance, not collective security), and since strategic initiative can often negate tactical advantage,[49] defeat of aggression will usually have to rely on *counterattack* to take back lost territory, rather than on direct defense. In that case the tactical advantage of defense passes to the original aggressor, and the counterattack has to rely on its disproportionate strength or offensive ingenuity at the strategic level to succeed. This was indeed the case in the two international actions of the past half-century that came closest to the collective security model—responses to the North Korean attack in 1950 and to the Iraqi invasion of Kuwait.

Political Criteria for Limitations

The legalism of collective security, which establishes obligations in terms of hypothetical rather than actual enemies, is an apolitical guide to arms control. If no danger of war ever arose, the various potential dyadic power balances affected by treaty limits would not matter strategically, and the agreements' value would depend on how much they facilitated cuts in military expenditure. Nor would they matter much if a challenge to collective security did arise and all the members of the system honored the obligation to roll back the aggressor. If war was to break out more raggedly, however, with a great power or a set of states challenging the status quo while a number of the others stood aloof from combat, the balances established by apolitical criteria could be disastrous; having been decided without reference to the wartime lineups, it would be only fortuitous if the distribution of capabilities happened to favor the side with defensive objectives.

Worse, formal limitations, especially if they do not produce a relevant dyadic balance of power, could have more directly dangerous effects. Accords can provide advance warning of aggression, arms controllers claim, facilitating timely countermobilization. As the Kupchans write, "a significant military buildup would *automatically* be interpreted as a sign of aggressive intent, *triggering* a response."[50] If the agreement was violated in order to prepare to commit aggression, automatic reaction would be a good thing; if the violation was motivated by anxiety about military vulnerability, however, such reaction would be destabilizing, producing the stereotypical escalation of tension that "spiral" theorists worry about. It is quite plausible that anxious states facing an unfavorable balance of forces with emerging enemies might feel compelled to abrogate limitations on their own options imposed by prior apolitically designed arms control formulas. If legal constraints do not exist, their military buildups might seem more innocent or ambiguous, and response might be determined according to the merits of the balance of power rather than the legal order of allowed armament.

This is a particular problem if we have reason to worry about a future change in Russian attitudes toward traditional security. The USSR did not let the Warsaw Pact crumble simply because it had no choice; there is no reason to assume that laying down the law or using a little violence before November 1989 (as in East Germany in 1953, Hungary in 1956, Czechoslovakia in 1968, and as would have happened in Poland in 1981 had Wojciech Jaruzelski not imposed martial law) would not have kept Communist governments in power. Instead, Gorbachev adopted a liberal foreign policy, mouthing all the axioms about cooperation, trust, insanity of the arms race, and obsolescence of traditional concepts of security that we have always heard from doves in the West.[51] If we could unwind the coiled spring of mutual suspicion and tension, Gorbachev believed, we would jointly conquer not just the symptom but the cause of conflict. "New thinking" embraced collective security because the new thinkers, like many liberals in the West, believed security was an artificial problem more than a real one, that there was nothing to fear but fear itself.

The concessions that ended the Cold War, however, while wonderful for everyone else were a precipitous loss of security for Russia in the hoary terms of balance of power. The Reds may never come back, but what if the realists do? What if economic disaster, apparent failure of western liberal models, nasty maneuvers by newly free republics, oppression of Russian minorities in those areas, and an upsurge of populist and nationalist bitterness bring the principle of looking out for number one back into favor? Will noticing that the old subservient buffer of Eastern Europe is not only gone but aligned with the West spur no interest in rearmament? The limits in the CFE agreement, conceived in the context of two alliances, left the USSR a lower ratio of forces to its opponents if former allies' forces were counted as having shifted into the opposing camp. The problem is accentuated for Russia alone, since it is smaller than the old union, and since other former Soviet republics might be included in a western coalition. In a meaner world such military inferiority might seem less tolerable to Moscow than it does now, when it seems irrelevant.

Arms control made sense in the Cold War because the relevant alignments by which stable force ratios could be estimated seemed clear and durable. By the same token, limitations on individual nations' forces might be pernicious after the Cold War because there is no logical basis by which to determine the allowed ratios before new cleavages emerge and harden. Military balances that appear neutral under one pattern of alignment or lack of it can instantly become destabilizing when countries start lining up in a different pattern. As Fairbanks and Shulsky argue:

> Arms limitation agreements, which by their very nature involve precise ratios and numbers of arms permitted to each side, are far more specific than most treaties. *They thus lack the flexibility that enables most international agreements to bend with change and be infused with a new political content....* When the rigid structure of an arms limitation agreement can no longer contain changed political forces, it will snap apart. The cost may be heavy: after an arms limitation treaty not renewed, as after a divorce, one cannot return to the starting point.[52]

This potential does not matter as long as there is no antagonism that could raise the danger of war, but for the same reason, neither does arms control matter in those circumstances, except to save money. That would be a big exception, and a valuable one if technical stability of military relationships is unimportant. But would arms control necessarily produce lower expenditures than laissez-faire?

Other Perverse Effects

In the present atmosphere most governments will rush to cut military budgets unilaterally, and with less attention to the effects on arcane calculations of military stability than in the past. Negotiating on prospective legal regulations, however, necessarily fixes more attention on technical calculations and nuances of disparity. This will especially be a problem if countries seeking arms control *do* worry about how it will affect stability. The goal of arms control might produce ongoing negotiations that reach no conclusion but retard unilateral cuts. The parties "will strain to be sure that all dangers and contingencies are covered," Mueller writes. "Participants volunteer for such regulation only with extreme caution because once under regulation they are often unable to adjust subtly to unanticipated changes. . . . Arms *reduction* will proceed most expeditiously if each side feels free to reverse any reduction it later comes to regret."[53]

Cold War critics claimed that arms control stimulated military spending (or at least failed to constrain it), as when Kennedy's Limited Test Ban, Ford's Vladivostok Accord, or Carter's SALT II Treaty coincided with defense budget increases. More indicative for the post-Cold War world should be the 1922 Washington Naval Treaty, which fixed capital ship ratios among the great powers, since it was concluded in a period of minimal international tension and was multilateral rather than bipolar in construction. Britain responded to that agreement "with greater activity in naval building than at any time since the armistice."[54] That treaty is also sometimes charged with stimulating competition in unregulated dimensions of weaponry (for example, the "treaty race" in bigger and better cruisers, replacing the battleship race) and channeling innovation away from defensive developments (fortifications were prohibited in the western Pacific to secure Japanese agreement to the battleship ratio) and into weaponry of more offensive, destabilizing, "first-strike" capability (aircraft carriers).[55]

Finally, contrary to conventional wisdom, arms control designed in the context of peacetime could endanger crisis management. Collective security proponents usually claim that arms control will reinforce crisis stability because treaty provisions for monitoring and verification will create "transparency" and rules of the road that will reduce chances of accidental escalation in a crisis confrontation.[56] This argument means the most to those who worry about uncontrolled interactions of military forces operating in alert conditions as a more plausible cause of war than premeditated resort to force.

Positive reasons for such controls certainly exist.[57] Their relative importance after the Cold War, however, is oversold, while their potential negative consequences are overlooked. Primary concern with crisis interactions as an autonomous cause of war—the notion of "inadvertant" or "accidental" war—is inconsistent with faith in the durability of the current causes of peace. You cannot get hair-trigger alert operations like those in the crisis of October 1962, or mobilization spirals like those in the crisis of July 1914, without a crisis. Yet crisis presupposes conflict. You cannot get a crisis through a *deus ex machina*, without a prior clash of interests. A conflict serious enough to produce a military confrontation will mean that the premise of continental contentment has been shattered, in which case *that* problem looms much larger than the technical one of crisis instability due to communication breakdowns.

As others have often noted, it is hard to think of any case of a genuinely accidental war (that is, one due to causes beyond political authorities' control as distinct from one due to their miscalculations).[58] World War I, the favorite case for those who worry about the problem, does not qualify. Trachtenberg has shown clearly how strategic mythology over the past several decades grossly exaggerated the political "loss of control" in the July 1914 crisis, even if one rejects the Fischer thesis that German aggression caused the war.[59] To promote arms control measures in order to limit accidental escalation elevates the secondary to the essential. Focusing on the secondary was reasonable in the Cold War context when the essential problem endangering security—the ideological and power competition between East and West—was well recognized and addressed steadily through alliances and defense plans, but not now when the principal problem is to anticipate what basic conflict of interest could arise.

It is also shortsighted to assume that treaty arrangements for verification in peacetime will help defuse crises. Inspection regimes are unlikely to be operating, and "transparency" will probably have gone by the boards by the time a crisis erupts. Treaty obligations are usually abrogated before that point is reached. There are no bolts from the blue—wars do not explode at the instant a conflict of interest develops. Germany junked the arms control provisions of the Versailles Treaty long before 1939, and Japan renounced the 1922 Naval Treaty five years before Pearl Harbor. While abrogation may provide political warning of crisis, it is misguided to count on monitoring provisions of arms control agreements to provide strategic warning of war or tactical warning of attack.

If inspection regimes or other agreements oriented to crisis management did remain in place during the runup to crisis, they could just as easily have a counterproductive effect as a dampening one, since the effect of abrogating *during* the crisis could seem much more threatening. It is more likely then, in comparison to what would happen in normal peacetime, that an anxious state would rush to revoke apparent restraints on its options for self-defense, or intrusive inspections helpful to its adversary, and that such actions could be read by the adversary as preparations to strike first. "Transparency" can apply only to capabilities, not to intentions. If the value of such greater openness depends on the assumption that actions inconsistent with arms control agreements will be presumed evidence of aggressive intent, the regime can harm crisis management as much as help it.

Conclusion

If there is any time when establishing a collective security institution should be feasible, this is it—but collective security will hardly matter unless the present peace goes bad. If there is any time when negotiated arms control should *not* matter, this is it—but agreements achieved now would leave equations of power whose significance could be utterly different, and dangerous, if peace goes bad. Conservative realism, however, is too fatalistic a guide, since it underestimates the potential grounds for pacific anarchy in Europe. Anarchy, and the competition for power that it encourages, are necessary but not sufficient causes of war. They need a *casus belli* to push conflict over the edge.[60] The UPE described above is not markedly less conceivable than Mearsheimer's hyperrealist nightmare.[61] Either one, however, is more plausible than a *functioning* collective security system or a politically disembodied arms control regime.

Instituting a collective security organization might be a good thing, nevertheless, for its symbolic value. Despite the negative emphasis in the rest of this essay, I am not set against the idea, provided that it is not taken seriously enough in practice to bar parallel security arrangements that should be considered incompatible with it in principle. Similarly, serious and comprehensive arms regulation may never be achieved if leaders lose their sense of urgency and get wrapped up in more important problems while their bureaucracies get bogged down in technical questions. Also, arms control constraints that could prove destabilizing in a Europe riven by new alignments would probably be abandoned long before a crisis at the brink of war, so strategists should not fall on their swords to prevent such agreements. But we should beware of too much insouciance.

In another context Jack Snyder has argued that "neo-liberal institution-building will do great damage if it is attempted, but doesn't work."[62] The same is true in regard to pressures to transform old security institutions in Europe into a collective security organization or conclude new arms control agreements unless we are disingenuous enough to couple them with other initiatives that work in different directions. If collective security and arms control were important only as symbols, we could accept them as harmless or reject them as diversionary. But symbols can have substantive effects. The effects may be consistent with the symbol if it motivates leaders to conform with the value that it enshrines. This is what regime theorists hope collective security might do. Or the effects may be antagonistic to the symbol if it obscures reality and prevents properly adaptive action. This is what realists fear it might do.

This implies accepting an ESO without junking NATO (a combination accepted by many current fans of collective security) and encouraging a discreet concert of the United States, Britain, France, Germany, and Russia without formal meetings like the economic summits (were that model followed, membership of the concert would have to expand in response to pleas from other big states in the system). We might also want to accept arms control agreements as long as they are modest enough not to seriously confine freedom of adaptation (alliances according to emergent threats, decisions to refrain from intervention in wars between small states).

The risk in this recommendation is that it will sound either stupid (a mindless endorsement of anything in response to uncertainty about everything) or cynical (a deliberate commitment to institutions whose rationales contradict each other) and thus prove infeasible. If governments devote themselves symbolically to collective security in a way substantial enough to have any beneficial effects, we cannot count on them to be cynical enough to pursue divergent policies in an equally substantial way. If the happily pacific order of the new post-Cold War Europe goes bad, then, the process of traditional adaptation will probably be more hesitant and delayed than otherwise. That might leave us the worst of both worlds: a collective security organization that falters when the chips are down, and a hysterical scramble to establish a better balance of power in too much of a hurry to avoid precipitous aggravation of political tensions.

But what else should we do if not tread water by dabbling in several somewhat inconsistent solutions? While a UPE may be possible, at least for some period of time, it would be reckless to bank on it; while NATO may last, it may wither if nothing new and big is injected to replace the Marxist menace; and while a collective security commitment may capture imaginations, it could leave us in the lurch if we count on it. The problem is, we cannot prescribe a system (if we expect actual statesmen to make it work) based on a principle without reference to cases; *we cannot compose a definite new solution until we confront a definite new problem*. The current peace is not what makes some novel solution to security suddenly plausible, it is what makes it *harder* to settle on any formula, and what encourages the logically inconsistent policy of overlaying various schemes, regimes, or organizations on each other.

Inconsistency is reasonable if we do not yet know when and against whom we will once again need a functioning security system for Europe. Relying on any single scheme is too risky in the new world, where the current threat is uncertainty. Yes, the idea that post-Cold War strategy must define itself against "uncertainty" is becoming a tiresome and suspiciously facile cliché. That is unfortunate but cannot be helped, because it happens to be true.

Notes

1. The concept can be traced back at least to the last millenium, when French bishops in a council at Poitiers and a synod at Limoges declared war on war, decided to excommunicate princes who broke the peace, and planned to deploy troops under a religious bannner to use force against violators. Stefan T. Possony, "Peace Enforcement," *Yale Law Journal* 55, no. 5 (1946).

2. This was prevalent in official thinking in the first half of the Cold War. For example see John Foster Dulles, *War or Peace* (New York: Macmillan, 1950), pp. 89–95, 204–207, and Dean Rusk, as told to Richard Rusk, and Daniel Papp, ed., *As I Saw It* (New York: W. W. Norton, 1990), pp. 503–505.

3. For example, Richard Ullman, *Securing Europe* (Princeton: Princeton University Press, 1991); Gregory Flynn and David J. Scheffer, "Limited Collective Security," *Foreign Policy* no. 80 (Fall 1990); Charles A. Kupchan and Clifford A. Kupchan, "Concerts, Collective Security, and the Future of Europe," *International Security* 16, no. 1 (Summer 1991); Malcom Chalmers, "Beyond the Alliance System," *World Policy Journal* 7, no. 2 (Spring 1990); John Mueller, "A New Concert of Europe," *Foreign Policy* no. 77 (Winter 1988–90); James E. Goodby, "A New European Concert" and Harald Mueller, "A United Nations of Europe and North America," *Arms Control Today* 21, no. 1 (January/February 1991); John D. Steinbruner, "Revolution in Foreign Policy," in Henry Aaron, ed., *Setting National Priorities: Policy for the Nineties* (Washington, D.C.: Brookings Institution, 1990). (Steinbruner terms his overall vision "cooperative" rather than "collective" security, but the description is

similar to the Wilsonian conception: "a global alliance. . . . all countries are on the same side and their forces are not directed against each other. . . . there are no neutrals." Ibid., pp. 68, 74, 109.) For a mixed view of prospects see Stephen F. Szabo, "The New Europeans: Beyond the Balance of Power," in Nils H. Wessell, ed., *The New Europe*, Proceedings of the Academy of Political Science, Vol. 38, No. 1 (New York: Academy of Political Science, 1991).

4. "For while the transmutation of lead into gold would be no nearer if everyone in the world passionately desired it, it is undeniable that if everyone really desired . . . 'collective security' (and meant the same thing by those terms), it would be easily attained; and the student of international politics may be forgiven if he begins by supposing that his task is to make everyone desire it. It takes him some time to understand . . . the fact that few people do desire . . . 'collective security', and that those who think they desire it mean different and incompatible things by it." E. H. Carr, *The Twenty Years Crisis, 1919–1939*, 2d edition (London: Macmillan, 1946), pp. 9–10.

5. G. F. Hudson, "Collective Security and Military Alliances," in Herbert Butterfield and Martin Wight, eds., *Diplomatic Investigations* (Cambridge: Harvard University Press, 1968), pp. 175–176; Kenneth W. Thompson, "Collective Security," *International Encyclopedia of the Social Sciences* (New York: Free Press, 1968), pp. 565–566; Kenneth W. Thompson, "Collective Security Reexamined," *American Political Science Review* 47, no. 3 (September 1953), pp. 753–756; Wolfers, *Discord and Collaboration*, chaps. 11–12; Inis L. Claude, Jr., *Power and International Relations* (New York: Random House, 1962), chap. 4; Claude, *Swords Into Plowshares*, 4th edition (New York: Random House, 1971), chap. 12; Roland M. Stromberg, "The Idea of Collective Security," *Journal of the History of Ideas* 17, no. 2 (April 1956); Robert E. Osgood, "Woodrow Wilson, Collective Security, and the Lesson of History," *Confluence* 5, no. 4 (Winter 1957), p. 344; M. V. Naidu, *Collective Security and the United Nations* (Delhi: Macmillan, 1974), chap. 2; Frederick H. Hartmann, *The Conservation of Enemies* (Westport: Greenwood Press, 1982), chap. 13; Erich Hula, "Fundamentals of Collective Security," *Social Research* 24, no. 1 (Spring 1957). Some have argued that collective security is really just an extension of the balance of power system (e.g., Edward Vose Gulick, *Europe's Classical Balance of Power* [New York: W.W. Norton, 1967], pp. 307–308), but this makes little sense unless one is defining it empirically rather than normatively.

6. Some collective security schemes rely on economic sanctions. This helps to sell the idea to those skeptical of military entanglement. See for example James T. Shotwell, *War as an Instrument of National Policy* (New York: Harcourt, Brace, 1929), p. 221. To keep discussion manageable within space constraints my argument addresses the stronger form of the idea, which assumes military obligations.

7. To purists like Waltz, defining a system normatively, in terms of a product expected from it, may be illegitimate. Nor might collective security or arms control be considered systems in themselves. Together, however, they come closer, since collective security is an "ordering principle" of sorts, and arms control affects "the distribution of capabilities across the system's

units." See Kenneth N. Waltz, *Theory of International Politics* (Reading: Addison-Wesley, 1979), pp. 82, 97, and passim. I will recklessly use the term "system" anyway.

8. Robert Jervis' chapter in this volume; Charles Perrow, *Normal Accidents* (New York: Basic Books, 1984), chap. 3.

9. Since this paper rests more on realist theory than its alternatives, I should admit the troublesome circularity involved here. Idealist statesmen are criticized because failure to bow to necessity and obey the rules of balance of power threatens the security of their nations. Why? Because other states follow the rules and will run over them. But if *some* states do not do what they "must," then in principle there can be no iron law that others will, no strictly logical reason for denying that all states could act according to another norm. In theory, all states could decide to drive on the left. The realist answer would be that empirical evidence shows that most do not do that, so a decision to drive on the left will probably get you killed. Thoroughgoing realism is an insufficient guide to life after the Cold War, however, if only because it offers little to explain why the Cold War ended.

10. Collective security can be defined empirically. Ernst B. Haas does so in terms of patterns of U.N. peacekeeping actions. "Types of Collective Security: An Examination of Operational Concepts," *American Political Science Review* 49, no. 1 (March 1955). See also John Gerard Ruggie, "Contingencies, Constraints, and Collective Security: Perspectives on U.N. Involvement in International Disputes," *International Organization* 28, no. 3 (Summer 1974). To evaluate the concept as a model for the more important aim of preserving peace in Europe, however, it is more useful to address it in terms of the aim.

11. Perrow, *Normal Accidents*, pp. 86–94.

12. Collective security "presumably would add nothing to the protection that victims of aggression would have enjoyed under the old system unless such victims could now expect more military assistance than they would have received otherwise." To add to the strength of defense and deterrence, nations must be willing to fight in situations where, "if they had not been devoted to the principle of collective security, they would have remained neutral or fought on the side of the aggressor. Instead of being allowed to reserve their military strength for the exclusive task of balancing the power of countries considered a threat to themselves or their allies, nations committed to a policy of collective security must divert their strength to struggle in remote places or, worse still, take action against friends and allies." In the 1935 crisis over Ethiopia, "when faced with the choice of losing the support of Italy or else defaulting on collective security, France chose the latter course." Wolfers, *Discord and Collaboration*, pp. 167–169, 187.

13. John Herz, *International Politics in the Atomic Age* (New York: Columbia University Press, 1959), pp. 85, 90–91.

14. Quoted in Arthur S. Link, *Wilson the Diplomatist* (Baltimore: Johns Hopkins Press, 1957), p. 136. "The dilemma of collective security has been that its major proponents have been driven to oppose social change in the name of the sanctity of treaties." Thompson, "Collective Security Reexamined," p. 770.

15. Stromberg, "The Idea of Collective Security," pp. 255, 258.

16. Wolfers, Discord and Collaboration, pp. 185–186.

17. Henry A. Kissinger, "Germany, Neutrality and the 'Security System' Trap," *Washington Post*, April 15, 1990, p. D7.

18. "We still read that the path to Nazi aggression was made possible by the failure of the League to coerce Japan in 1931 and Italy in 1935. We have the absurdity, to which collective security is always being reduced, of saying that war in 1931 would have prevented war in 1941. It is implied that had the western states been fighting Japan in Asia they could have fought Germany better in Europe. The verdict of careful history might be that the ill-conceived effort to apply 'sanctions' against Italy in 1935 weakened, not strengthened, the front against Germany." Stromberg, "The Idea of Collective Security," p. 254.

19. Waltz, Theory of International Politics, p. 112.

20. Hans J. Morgenthau, *Politics Among Nations*, Fifth edition (New York: Knopf, 1973), pp. 411–412. Of course Morgenthau did not oppose all interventions, only those warranted by a general law in conflict with a specific interest. See also Stromberg, "The Idea of Collective Security," pp. 258–259.

21. Henry L. Stimson and McGeorge Bundy, *On Active Service in Peace and War* (New York: Harper, 1948), pp. 102–103.

22. Ullman, *Securing Europe*, pp. 28, 29, 68, 73–74, 78, 147.

23. Kupchan and Kupchan, "Concerts, Collective Security, and the Future of Europe," pp. 156–157.

24. Ullman *Securing Europe*, p. 68.

25. Celestine Bohlen, "Russian Vice President Wants to Redraw Borders," *New York Times*, January 31, 1992, p. A9.

26. Ullman, *Securing Europe*, p. 66 (emphasis added).

27. An analogous issue for nuclear power safety is suggested by the Nuclear Regulatory Commission's inability in the early 1980s to think of a way to deal with the potential problem of genetic damage from a plant accident. "If the risks of an accident are kept low enough, they said, there will be no problem with ignoring inter-generational effects. This conclusion answers the question about consequences of accidents by saying they will be trivial because there will be so few accidents." Perrow, *Normal Accidents*, p. 69, citing U.S. Nuclear Regulatory Commission, "Safety Goals for Nuclear Power Plants: A Discuission Paper," *NUREG* 0880 (Washington, D.C.: NRC, February 1982), p. 15.

28. Robert Jervis, "Security Regimes," in Stephen D. Krasner, ed., *International Regimes* (Ithaca: Cornell University Press, 1983), pp. 181–182; Richard N. Rosecrance, *Action and Reaction in World Politics* (Boston: Little, Brown, 1963), p. 56; Kupchan and Kupchan, "Concerts, Collective Security, and the Future of Europe," p. 130.

29. Jervis, "Security Regimes," p. 184.

30. Francis Fukuyama, "The End of History," *National Interest* no. 16, (Summer 1989), p. 15.

31. Kupchan and Kupchan, "Concerts, Collective Security, and the Future of Europe," p. 116.

32. See *The Blue Helmets: A Review of United Nations Peace-keeping* (New York: United Nations Department of Public Information, October 1985).

33. Once Saudi oil was guarded by the Desert *Shield* deployment, there was no crucial material interest requiring the United States to spend blood and treasure for tiny Kuwait. Nor was enthusiasm for democracy an explanation. After booting Iraq out, Bush handed Kuwait back to the Sabah family oligarchy that had suspended the country's reasonably democratic constitution (and then stood aside as Saddam Hussein slaughtered the Shiites and Kurds who rose against Baghdad). Opposition to aggression as a matter of principle is the primary explanation of the U.S. decision for war.

34. See Richard B. Elrod, "The Concert of Europe," *World Politics* 28, no. 2 (January 1976), pp. 163–165.

35. Kupchan and Kupchan, "Concerts, Collective Security, and the Future of Europe," pp. 116, 149. On achievments of the regime see Paul W. Schroeder, "The 19th-Century International System," *World Politics* 39, no. 1 (October 1986). It is true that in the West the Concert did accomodate the new forces, as in the creation of Belgium. British and French ideological disagreements with the eastern powers, however, reduced the Concert's unity. F.H. Hinsley, *Power and the Pursuit of Peace* (New York: Cambridge University Press, 1963), chaps. 9–10.

36. Quoted in Flynn and Scheffer, "Limited Collective Security," p. 88.

37. Flynn and Scheffer, "Limited Collective Security," p. 81.

38. For example: "There is an inherent logic to the emerging era. . . . the basis of security is being altered by a natural historical progression." Steinbruner, "Revolution in Foreign Policy," p. 66.

39. As in Europe there are exceptions to stability, such as the Beagle Channel dispute which has brought Argentina and Chile close to war (most recently at the end of the 1970s). Unlike Cyprus in 1974, however, such fault-lines have not burst open. Reasons for the impressive long peace in South America since the Chaco War (1932–35) are not obvious, and present a significant challenge to theories on the causes of war offered by both major traditions of international relations theory, realism and liberalism. See the forthcoming Columbia University Ph. D. dissertation by Felix Martin-Gonzalez.

40. Perrow, *Normal Accidents*, pp. 88–97.

41. "Organization or order is lost. . . . When complete equilibrium (disorganization) has been reached it is said that the maximum *entropy* for the system has been achieved." The problem is that entropy is possible only in closed systems, which hardly ever exist. Open systems can have steady states, but maintained by negative feedback mechanisms. Floyd H. Allport, *Theories of Perception and the Concept of Structure* (New York: Wiley, 1955), pp. 474–475, 484–485 (emphasis in original).

42. Steinbruner, "Revolution in Foreign Policy," pp. 108–109.

43. Steinbruner, "Revolution in Foreign Policy," pp. 74–76 (emphasis added). The estimates also include figures for "defensive potential," but the bar on the graph for the USSR's offensive potential is still longer than any of

the bars for other countries' defensive potential, and Germany's offensive bar is longer than the defensive ones for any other countries in the compilation except the USSR. (The USA and UK do not appear on the chart.) A better rationale for the figures is available, ironically, if we substitute assumed coalitions for the notion of "global alliance." This can be read into Steinbruner's mention of "residual alliances," although there is only one alliance of any sort on the continent anyway, since the Warsaw Pact dissolved and many of its former members would like to join NATO. Allotting Russia forces grossly superior to any other state in the region might bring the actual situation closer to balance if we assume that solitary Russia were to face a coalition of many of the others. Moreover, as Chalmers suggests ("Beyond the Alliance System", p. 245), an ESO would limit obligations to Europe, not guaranteeing Russia against security problems in Asia or challenges to southern borders, so Moscow would have another justification for a surplus of capability.

44. John J. Mearsheimer, *Conventional Deterrence* (Ithaca: Cornell University Press, 1983), pp. 181, 265n.

45. Steinbruner, "Revolution in Foreign Policy," p. 77. He argues that because "it is generally believed that a standard brigade would have to be concentrated in less than a five-kilometer segment of front . . . in order to overcome well-prepared, competently positioned defenses," overall reduction of force levels would require an attacker to concentrate a larger proportion of its ground units, thus exposing its own defense in other sectors to greater risk of counterattack (p. 75). This, however, appears to lose sight of the relativity of requirements. If the defender's line is much thinner than the standard norm, the concentration an attacker needs to penetrate will be lower as well.

46. See Archer Jones, *The Art of War in the Western World* (Urbana: University of Illinois Press, 1987), pp. 558–560, 652–653, 666–667. At one end of the continuum of force-to-space ratios would be the western front in World War I, where density was so high that sustained penetration proved impossible for most of the war. At the other end would be guerrilla wars, where the ratios are so low that governments cannot cover all points they need to defend, while rebels can concentrate at will to raid those left vulnerable. Force-to-space ratios are certainly not all-determining, especially given big differences between forces in equipment and tactical doctrines. For the most extensive survey of the question see Stephen D. Biddle, *et al., Defense at Low Force Levels: The Effect of Force to Space Ratios on Conventional Combat Dynamics*, IDA Paper P–2380 (Alexandria: Institute for Defense Analyses, August 1991).

47. This point must be belabored because the Steinbruner proposal uses the counterargument that high-tech defenses and surveillance, coupled with limits on advanced offensive weapons, allow forward defense with low force levels. This is dubious for two reasons. First, it implicitly assumes that defensive forces can move and reconcentrate instantly, in response to instant intelligence detection of concentration by the attacker. No reasons are suggested as to why the strategic initiative, and the prerogative of choosing

circumstances of weather and terrain, give the attacker no advantage in timing. Second, it is unrealistic about the strategic flexibility of combined arms operations, which blurs simple distinctions between dominantly defensive or offensive characteristics of weapons. For example, in October 1973 the Egyptians used surface-to-air missiles and precision-guided anti-tank munitions (both normally tagged as inherently defensive weapons) to screen the advance of armored forces into the Sinai; similarly, the Israelis used "offensive" attack aircraft to defend against the advancing Egyptian tanks. Had both sides been limited to the "defensive" elements of force-structure only, the Israelis might have held if they had manned the Suez Canal Bar-Lev Line with high force-to-space ratios, but the line was lightly manned.

48. In addition to Steinbruner see Kupchan and Kupchan, "Concerts, Collective Security and the Future of Europe," p. 136 and Ullman, *Securing Europe*, pp. 73–74.

49. See Carl von Clausewitz, *On War*, Michael Howard and Peter Paret, eds. and trans. (Princeton: Princeton University Press, 1976), pp. 363–364, 367; Richard K. Betts, *Surprise Attack* (Washington, D.C.: Brookings Institution, 1982), p. 15; and Betts, "Conventional Deterrence," *World Politics* 37, no. 2 (January 1985), pp. 163–172.

50. Kupchan and Kupchan, "Concerts, Collective Security, and the Future of Europe," p. 127 (emphasis added).

51. "Peace is movement toward globality and universality of civilization. Never before has the idea that peace is indivisible been as true as it is now. . . . at the end of the twentieth century force and arms will have to give way as a major instrument in world politics." In the West, words like this always used to strike hardheaded types as pacifist globaloney, but they were typical Gorbachev rhetoric. "Excerpts From Gorbachev's Speech: 'The Idea That Peace Is Indivisible,'" *New York Times*, June 6, 1991, p. A12.

52. Charles H. Fairbanks, Jr. and Abram N. Shulsky, "From 'Arms Control' to Arms Reductions: The Historical Experience," *Washington Quarterly* 10, no. 3 (Summer 1987), p. 68 (emphasis added).

53. Mueller,"A New Concert of Europe," pp. 6, 9.

54. Stephen Roskill, *Naval Policy Between the Wars* (London: Collins, 1968), p. 332, quoted in Fairbanks and Shulsky, "From 'Arms Control' to Arms Reductions," p. 65.

55. Fairbanks and Shulsky, "From 'Arms Control' to Arms Reductions," pp. 66–67. See also Robert Gordon Kaufman, *Arms Control During the Pre-Nuclear Era* (New York: Columbia Press, 1990).

56. Ullman, *Securing Europe*, pp. 141–142; Kupchan and Kupchan, "Concerts, Collective Security, and the Future of Europe," p. 131; Steinbruner, "Revolution in Foreign Policy," p. 75.

57. See Joseph F. Bouchard, *Command in Crisis* (New York: Columbia University Press, 1991); Scott D. Sagan, "Nuclear Alerts and Crisis Management," *International Security* 9, no. 4 (Spring 19885); Scott D. Sagan, "Rules of Engagement," *Security Studies* 1, no. 1 (Autumn 1991); Bruce G. Blair, "Alerting in Crisis and Conventional War," in Ashton B. Carter, John D.

Steinbruner, and Charles A. Zraket, eds., *Managing Nuclear Operations* (Washington, D.C.: Brookings Institution, 1987); Bruce G. Blair and John D. Steinbruner, "The Effects of Warning on Strategic Stability," Brookings Occasional Paper (Washington, D.C.: Brookings Institution, 1991); Kurt Gottfried and Bruce G. Blair, eds., *Crisis Stability and Nuclear War* (New York: Oxford University Press, 1988).

58. Alexander George defines *inadvertent* war as one "neither side wanted or expected at the outset of the crisis." "Findings and Recommendations," in George, ed., *Avoiding War: Problems of Crisis Management* (Boulder: Westview Press, 1991), p. 545. This is expansive enough to include deliberate decisions by political authorities to initiate combat, which are not the same as hypothetical cases where decentralization of authority could produce military operational activities that elude policymakers' control and provoke escalation autonomously. See Paul Bracken, *The Command and Control of Nuclear Forces* (New Haven: Yale University Press, 1983), pp. 48, 53, 231–232, or John D. Steinbruner, "An Assessment of Nuclear Crises," in Franklin Griffiths and John C. Polanyi, eds., *The Dangers of Nuclear War* (Toronto: University of Toronto Press, 1980), pp. 39–40. Geoffrey Blainey persuasively debunks the notion that accidental wars have occurred, but argues that if miscalculation is included in the definition, virtually all wars could be considered accidental. *The Causes of War*, 3d edition (New York: Free Press, 1988), chap. 9, especially pp. 144–145.

59. Marc Trachtenberg, *History and Strategy* (Princeton: Princeton University Press, 1991), chap. 2, especially pp. 54–60, 77–80, 84–87, 90–92, 97–98.

60. World War I is sometimes cited as a pure product of concern about power, but without imperialist ideologies, territorial disputes, and militarist romanticism it would have been much harder to get the war started. Blainey argues against viewing motives, grievances, or substantive aims as causes on grounds that they are only "varieties of power." (*The Causes of War*, chap. 10.) That definition, however, makes the argument practically tautologous.

61. John J. Mearsheimer, "Back to the Future: Instability in Europe After the Cold War," *International Security* 15, no. 1 (Spring 1990).

62. "Averting Anarchy in the New Europe," *International Security* 14, no. 4 (Spring 1990), p. 40.

12

Common Markets, Uncommon Currencies: Systems Effects and the European Community

Kathleen R. McNamara

The dissolution of the Soviet Union and the easing of tensions between the superpowers has turned our attention away from one of the central concerns of U.S. policymakers in the postwar era—how to achieve credible nuclear deterrence against the Soviet Union—to a multiplicity of other policy challenges. As the international system changes from a bipolar to a multipolar distribution of power, our theories and policies will have to address increasingly complex relationships among nations. Not only is this the result of a change in the number of great powers, but it is also due to the increasing importance of domestic, institutional, intellectual and economic issues in determining outcomes in the international arena. We cannot rely solely on parsimonious theories that focus on military security and balance-of-power systems but instead should explore a broadened definition of systems theory, such as the one Robert Jervis describes in Chapter 2, if we wish to fully capture the evolution of international politics.[1]

As we shift our focus from the comparatively static Cold War U.S.-Soviet relationship, a systems analysis of policymaking in the European Community (EC) may be helpful not only as a guide to understanding economic and political integration but as an illustration of how both cooperation and conflict can arise in complex systems. The existence and development of the European Community has long presented a challenge to theorists and policymakers that is similar to the one we now face in the context of the international system. Three factors that make the EC difficult to analyze also are evident in the new multipolar system: the interaction between domestic-, EC-, and international-level political systems; the large number of actors and groups involved; and the variety of issue areas—political, economic and military—important in EC policymaking. Therefore, in this chapter I will examine the interaction between European Community agricultural and exchange rate policies, a case that illustrates a number of systemic qualities and shows how these qualities can exacerbate the likelihood of perverse policy outcomes. More generally, I hope the case will indicate how a broadened systems approach might be valuable when applied to other cases in a multipolar world.

The interrelationship of agricultural programs and exchange rate policy in Europe is a good example of how separate subsystems can interact to produce unintended outcomes. The Common Agricultural Policy (CAP) was established in the early 1960s as a customs union and common price support program within the countries of the European Community. However, the goal of common prices was compromised because each European country retained its own currency, meaning that currency fluctuations could push prices out of line relative to other participating countries. The elaborate network of programs built up to deal with the clash between a common agricultural policy and individual currencies brought on a series of unanticipated side effects that distorted trade, inflated food prices, and stretched the EC budget. These issues are only likely to be resolved when the two subsystems (agriculture and money) become compatible with the introduction of a single common currency across Europe.

The case study also powerfully illustrates the interaction effects that occur when systems are nested within other, progressively wider, systems—in this case, domestic, EC and international systems. For example, domestic political concerns played a large part in the European Community's decision to create a compensatory mechanism to keep agricultural prices from changing suddenly in countries that experienced currency fluctuations. In turn, as this new EC mechanism became institutionalized, it began to have a "boomerang" effect back onto the domestic level, distorting trade patterns and changing the relative trade competitiveness of national farmers.

At the next level, the nesting of the EC's agricultural and monetary policies within the larger international system was crucial to the development of European institutions in both policy areas. As long as the international monetary system set up after World War II stabilized exchange rates, the CAP system and its "green money" pricing system functioned as planned. But as the international monetary system forged at Bretton Woods fell apart, the operation of the EC's agricultural programs was disrupted. In response, a series of European monetary institutions were set up by European Community policymakers, and these new European exchange rate institutions have had their own repercussions for the international monetary system.

After describing in more detail how a systemic view relates to the specific characteristics of the European case, I briefly review some previous accounts of the integration process and indicate how they differ from the approach taken here. To illustrate how a systems approach sheds light on conflict and cooperation in the context of complexity, I look at the case of systems effects across European agriculture and exchange rate policy. I conclude with some thoughts on other examples of systems effects in the European Community, including the possibility of more positive systems effects.

Systems Effects and European Integration

A systems approach, as described by Robert Jervis in this volume, is more a theoretical orientation than a single theory, a "sensitivity" to certain types of dynamics in politics and social life that provides the context for more specific theories.[2] It aims to provide insight into complex interactions and reveal the interconnections that exist in the realm of international politics. One of the major elements of Jervis's systems approach is the concept of indirect linkage: actions taken in one sphere can lead to consequences in other spheres that are not readily apparent because of the existence of multiple causal paths or feedback loops. In addition, systems effects often cannot be deduced from the qualities of the units but instead are nonadditive in nature, requiring an assessment of the interaction of the units. For policymakers, systems effects can make it difficult to predict the outcome of a particular decision, causing policies to have unintended or even perverse outcomes.

A systemic understanding of the world is particularly useful in analyzing the European Community because the EC is itself a system made up of subsystems (nation-states) and embedded within a larger system (the international system). Because the EC is a regional grouping of nation-states, the interaction between domestic- and international-level politics is magnified as another level, the EC, is added in.[3] While it might be argued that the European Community does not merit the analysis of international relations scholars because it is not a true nation-state, ignoring the presence of the EC level would seriously compromise any study of recent European politics or international interactions among the major powers. While this may be more true for political economy issues than for security affairs, the continued expansion of legal capabilities at the EC level,[4] the increasing presence of European Community officials at international negotiations, and the movement toward a more independent European defense capability may make such a distinction obsolete in the near future.[5]

A focus on the European case necessarily brings in many levels of analysis, but a strategy of "divide and conquer" that treats each level separately will not capture the nonadditive nature of the system. Analyses that proceed along linear paths at each level, while useful for other purposes, will not take account of the interaction of different levels of policymaking and their nonadditive qualities.[6]

Such interactive dynamics most obviously include the influence of domestic politics in EC decision-making. For example, the launching of the European Monetary System (EMS) in 1979 was unexpectedly delayed by the French government, a strong supporter of the EMS. The French government, constrained by the protests of French farmers over the effects of currency changes on farm prices, agreed to the EMS's launching only after extensive negotiations over agriculture. These negotiations eventually led to changes in EC rules that had the unforeseen effect of adding to the already perverse systemic effects of the European agricultural programs, some of which in fact decreased the competitiveness of French farmers.[7] Changes in domestic governments can also have a powerful effect on the operation of the system, as the election of a British Labour government in 1974 showed when the new Labour leaders delayed the accession of the British to the EC and forced a renegotiation of the terms of British entry and the EC agenda.

Developments at the international level can be just as significant as domestic changes: the breakdown of the Bretton Woods system and the instability of the dollar played a large part in the initial steps and subsequent progress toward European monetary integration, while the proposed single European currency that has come out of this integration will have important consequences vis-à-vis the current international monetary system, particularly in terms of the role of the dollar. The dissolution of the Soviet Union and the Warsaw Pact and the reunification of Germany are bound to have far-reaching effects on the evolution of the European Community. One negative effect on cohesion has already come to light: German domestic economic policies after reunification have put severe pressures on the European exchange rate system, and contributed to the currency crisis of September 1992. The extent of these influences would be missed by focusing solely on a one-way relationship between the two levels of analysis.

The sheer number of national actors involved in policymaking in the

European Community also makes a systemic approach appropriate. Robert Jervis points out that complexity mounts quickly as you go from bilateral to trilateral relations and that this can, in some cases, amplify systems effects.[8] The corollary of this is found in the logic behind Kenneth Waltz's proposition that bipolarity is the best guarantee of international stability because of the comparative simplicity of bipolar relations.[9] In contrast, the EC began with six members and has expanded to include twelve countries, with several more European Free Trade Area partners close to joining. Many view membership for the countries of Eastern Europe as inevitable, which would bring the future membership in the EC to around twenty-four, greatly increasing the potential for complex interactions.

While it can be argued in response that major European powers—Britain, France, Germany, and Italy—are the primary actors, events have shown repeatedly that it is imprudent to ignore the role of other EC members in influencing outcomes. One study of the negotiation process leading to two recent agreements on European car emission standards concluded that the positions of the largest member states do not account for the policy outcomes. Instead, it is crucial to understand the role that actors from small countries played in the policy process both as "nuisances" (Denmark held up the implementation of one of the emissions directives for two years) and as conceptual mediators (compromise on the implementation was eventually reached due to the efforts of a group of Dutch representatives).[10]

In addition, focus on the largest actors is made more problematic because traditional definitions of capabilities do not adequately describe the distribution of power in the European Community. For instance, Germany, the strongest economic country in the European Community, has no national nuclear force, but Britain, which has recently fallen behind Italy in terms of its gross national product, does. It seems more useful to determine a country's power by carefully considering the scope of its potential influence in any given situation than purely by its capabilities, because the emphasis on consensual decision-making in the EC means that one country can create a policy logjam.[11]

Finally, a systems approach may be more likely than others to catch some of the dynamics involved when policymaking spreads over a variety of issue areas such as trade, industrial, environmental, and security policy, as it does in the network of programs that make up the European Community. The connections between exchange rates and agriculture that I outline in the case below are one indication of the potential for subsystem interaction effects among seemingly unrelated programs.[12]

In contrast to the unintended consequences examined in this chapter, the systemic nature of the European Community also means that deliberate linkages can be created by policymakers sensitive to the potential for cross-issue bargaining. The European Community encompasses a wide variety of policy realms, making possible the trading of concessions in one issue area for gains in another, particularly at the European Council summits, where heads of government negotiate face-to-face.[13] Examples abound: in the ongoing debate over the direction of integration, Germany has linked its concessions in the area of monetary integration to the achievement of its goals on the issue of increased democratic accountability in the EC.

These three elements—interacting levels of analysis, multiple national actors, and the linkages across issue areas—make a case for a systems orientation when studying the European Community. How have previous approaches to European integration dealt with these factors?

Systems Theory and Neofunctionalism

A systems approach to the European Community is not entirely uncharted territory—the functionalists and neofunctionalists did map out some of the consequences of systemic interaction. While their accounts of the development of the European Community did capture the nonadditive nature of the European case, they frequently misread the consequences of interconnectivity among levels, actors and issues. The result was that they placed too much emphasis on a model of coherent, incremental integration that leads inevitably toward a fully integrated European Community instead of acknowledging the complex systems effects that drove integration in the case of agriculture and exchange rates examined in this chapter.

Functionalism, the theoretical approach used in the first wave of European integration studies, posited that the most important characteristic of government in the postwar era was its ability to fulfill the welfare needs of its citizens; it was less important for governments to develop mass support for a new supranational or federalist political entity.[14] Thus, argued the functionalists, for the European Community to succeed, it must meet practical needs. These were defined rather broadly "as the maintenance of adequate economic and social standards" for citizens who would gradually learn to depend on the new, functionally specific international organizations instead of exclusively on their own national governments.[15]

Neofunctionalism later revised and extended the functionalist account with less focus on the transfer of popular loyalties and more on the role that interest groups would play by seeking out the benefits of regional integration. The neofunctionalists also placed new emphasis on the expanding capabilities of international institutions and the elites that managed them in determining the success of the integration process.[16]

Both functionalism and neofunctionalism were grounded in the idea that an integrative process, once begun, could feed on itself—that integration could be a cause for further integration. The neofunctionalists made this process explicit in their discussions of "spillover," a concept that incorporates the notion of systems effects, although in their argument, the linkages are intended, unlike the systems effects observed throughout much of this volume. Spillovers would occur when the successful transfer of policy authority in one area engendered further integration in other functionally linked areas, which was seen as both a desired and an intended process. It was thought that integration would proceed because national actors and interest groups would become convinced that regional institutions could better address certain policy needs, and because it would become increasingly more difficult for governments to keep administering separate but functionally related programs at each national level. In addition, the continued interaction of national and EC bureaucrats and politicians would slowly build up confidence and support for EC solutions to technical, and increasingly more political, problems.[17]

The neofunctionalist focus on linkage as the dynamic force behind integration was later broadened by Joseph Nye to include negative spillover effects, a necessary modification in light of the increasing stagnation of the integration process in Europe. Nye also added the role of negotiated package deals in furthering integration.[18] This expansion of the terms of interconnectedness in the European Community brought neofunctionalism closer to a systemic approach by incorporating unintended effects and feedback loops. But the following case study of agricultural and exchange rate policy illustrates how a neofunctionalist explanation, by focusing on the logic of spillover effects, would not account for the mounting complexity and illogic that overcame the existing institutions and forced the creation of new, but still highly problematic, programs. The connections between policies within the European Community, and the nesting of the EC within both the international system and its members' own domestic political contexts, produced not the incremental integration and transfer of loyalties predicted in the neofunctionalist accounts but a morass of unintended system effects. However, the outcome in the case study is close to that expected by the neofunctionalists, as the systems effects eventually acted to drive forward European integration—even though the neofunctionalist account predicts an entirely different integrative process than the one which occurred.

Agriculture and Exchange Rates
in the European Community[19]

The Common Agricultural Policy (CAP) was developed in the early 1960s by national officials, European Community administrators and representatives of agriculture. Their goal was the creation of a European customs union in agricultural products. The centerpiece of the CAP was the standardization of prices for agricultural products across the European Community and mechanisms to support those prices, such as internal price subsidies, export subsidies, and external third-country tariffs. These mechanisms were financed out of the EC budget, to which all the members contributed. The stakes were high for the success of the CAP, for it was one of the only areas of integration that all members could agree to pursue in spite of the persistence of differences in reasons for supporting it.[20]

The architects of the European Community had recognized agriculture as an area of common concern in the Treaty of Rome, the EC's constitution. The CAP was a priority among European governments, spurred by memories of food shortages in the wake of two world wars, a growing European farm lobby, and the view that agriculture was the best candidate for progress toward European integration. Because agriculture was one area where there already was widespread national intervention, it seemed both natural and necessary that the national programs be replaced by EC-level programs if a unified Common Market was to operate effectively.[21]

However, a basic problem with the working of the CAP was caused by the incompatibility of a collective pricing system in the context of sovereign national economies, each with its own currency. Prices could be set at one point in time so as to be equal across all currencies but once the value of one currency moved up or down, the price would no longer be in line with the others, defeating the purpose of the collective program. To achieve a common pricing system among countries with different currencies, all the members needed to have a fixed exchange rate relative to one another, denominated in some common unit, in order to limit exchange rate turbulence. Thus, when drawing up the CAP, commission officials created a new EC instrument, called the agricultural unit of account, to fill this need; the values assigned to each of the national currencies in this account were called "green monies." Green money was not real currency but an accounting device, a separate exchange rate used for agricultural purposes.[22]

At its founding, the CAP pricing system operated within a larger, international fixed exchange rate regime, the Bretton Woods system, which provided the European currencies with a context of stable currency values and made the working of the CAP much easier. The Bretton Woods system, created by Britain and the United States after World War II, allowed each member currency to deviate by plus or minus one percent against the U.S. dollar, creating a band of two percent total possible variance, beyond which the country's central bank was required to intervene by buying or selling currency to support or weaken its value.[23] In practice, the European countries stayed within smaller margins of three-fourths of one percent (.75) on either side of the dollar.[24] When it came into operation, the accounting value of the agricultural unit of account was also fixed at 0.88867088 grams of fine gold, identical to the value of a U.S. dollar at the time.[25] Since the dollar was the basis for the Bretton Woods system, the green exchange rate would be the same, at least initially, as the regular, nonagricultural rates pegged to the dollar.

Indeed, for the first few years of the CAP, the green money exchange rate system worked smoothly and thus so did the EC-wide agricultural price support scheme. The CAP system of fixed green currency values was stabilized, as were the general European exchange rates, by the larger Bretton Woods system, which in turn rested on the economic and political strength of the United States and the administrative capacity of the International Monetary Fund.[26] As long as the larger monetary system remained stable, the agricultural programs functioned without any serious difficulties.

The first significant challenge to the CAP pricing system occurred when the French government, without consulting the other EC members, devalued the franc in August 1969. The value of the franc against gold, and thus against all the currencies in the Bretton Woods system, was decreased by 12.5 percent. The drop in value was too large to be smoothed over by allowing the green rate to remain the same, as had previously been the case for minor fluctuations which caused only a small gap between the green franc and the general franc value. If the EC devalued the "green franc" by the same amount, the common price of all agricultural commodities covered by the CAP agreement would automatically rise by 12.5 percent in terms of French francs.[27] But a large rise in food prices threatened to worsen an already undesirable level of inflation in France, and the French government received permission from the Council of Ministers to phase in the new, higher price level over two seasons, despite the French farm lobby's desire for a shorter transition period to higher prices. In effect, the result was that agricultural products were exempted from the overall economic policy changes the French government had put into effect with its initial devaluation.

However, the special status of French agricultural prices created unwanted effects throughout the European Community system. The gradual upward adjustment of French prices had the unintended result of giving the French an artificial trade advantage over the other CAP members during the time that French prices were below the common CAP price. Irving and Fearn show how with the example of French sugar exports to Germany after a French devaluation:

> The intervention price [the price guaranteed by the CAP agreement] of sugar in Germany was 849.20 DM and the effective intervention price in France was 1048.14 FF, ie. the pre-devaluation level. If, however, a French trader exported sugar to Germany and sold it there at the intervention price, he would receive 849.20 DM, for which his bank would give him 1179.15 FF (at the new market rate of exchange of 1 DM = 1.388548 FF)—some 131 FF more than he would have received from the French Intervention Agency.[28]

French traders quickly realized that this disparity gave them a strong incentive to export their sugar for the higher price, and they began to do so. The reverse effects were also true: German exports to France would cost 131 FF more than comparable French goods, making German agricultural products uncompetitive with the French. French speculation in sugar exports and non-French farmers' frustration over their disadvantaged position quickly brought these unintended effects to the attention of politicians and EC policymakers.

To adjust for the trade effects of the diverging green money rates, agricultural experts in the commission devised monetary compensatory amounts (MCAs) as a temporary measure to help smooth the systemic effects caused by the French desire to phase in green money changes and higher food prices. MCAs were an elaborate program of border levies and subsidies paid out of the EC budget that would bring French exports up to the EC-level prices (the levies) and lower the price of EC food imports into France (the subsidies). They also were used to standardize the prices of agricultural goods from third countries. In effect, MCAs were border controls that insulated the French agricultural market from the rest of the EC, keeping prices lower than they would have been in the wake of the devaluation of the franc.[29]

MCAs solved the immediate problem of speculation and arbitrage across European agricultural markets. But the MCAs reintroduced the very levies and subsidies that the European Common Market had been set up by the Treaty of Rome to do away with. The French MCAs set a precedent, allowing the suspension of free trade among EC members when nominal exchange rates changed—a step that ran contrary to the basic assumptions of European integration. They also set a precedent of allowing two sets of agricultural prices (one at the national level and one at the common price level) instead of forcing an immediate adjustment on the part of farmers and consumers when an overall exchange rate change was made.[30]

Within a few months, the CAP system was again challenged, this time by the upward revaluation of the German mark by 9.29 percent in October of 1969. The potential domestic price effects were the opposite of the French devaluation: CAP prices in terms of marks would fall, reducing the intervention prices paid to German farmers. Heeding the protests of its farm sector, Germany asked for the gradual lowering of the intervention prices until they reflected the new exchange rate, with the EC-funded MCAs again compensating for the trade effects. The clash of two differing goals—agricultural price stability and the need for overall national currency adjustment—would have increasing repercussions for the EC's budget and its institutions in the coming years.

Nested Systems and International Instability

The problems that currency realignments brought to the working of the CAP were minimized by the relative currency stability of the 1960s, which kept green rates roughly in line with general exchange rates. However, the breakdown of the Bretton Woods system in the 1970s had severe consequences for the working of the common agricultural policy and showed that a European food policy system developed in a time of fixed, stable exchange rates would not necessarily work when the larger system around it was transformed into a floating rate regime.[31]

In 1971, after months of instability, including the floating of the mark outside the Bretton Woods currency fluctuation margins, the United States halted the convertibility of the dollar into gold. Italy, Belgium, the Netherlands, and Luxembourg all floated their currencies in response. The green money exchange rates remained at their prefloating levels while the general exchange rates fluctuated, once more opening a gap between the two types of exchange rates. Monetary compensatory amounts were again used by the EC to offset the trade-distorting effects of the different rates. However, the variability of the floating rates introduced a new degree of complexity into the program because MCAs had to move along with exchange rates to be effective instead of being adjusted only when a realignment took place.[32] The commission experts created a system for calculating the degree of divergence between rates and the values of the necessary MCAs, still based on the European currency values against the U.S. dollar. Using this system, the EC assigned MCA levies and subsidies out of its budget any time the floating currency moved by more than one percent, no matter how frequent that might be.

At the end of 1971, the countries of the defunct Bretton Woods system met at the Smithsonian in Washington, D.C., to reestablish a fixed exchange rate regime based on the dollar, which the United States agreed to devalue. However, the allowable variance of member currencies in this new system would be plus or minus 2.25 percent, creating a band of 4.5 around the dollar, more than twice the 2 percent band previously allowed in the Bretton Woods system. The implications of this Smithsonian Agreement for the European Common Agricultural Policy were significant. Because under the new arrangement each European currency could vary up to 4.5 percent against the dollar, the possible variation, or net change, over a period of time between two European currencies was now 9 percent.[33]

There was widespread agreement among EC officials and agricultural representatives that this potential 9 percent fluctuation was too wide to work alongside the CAP pricing system, for it would require large and continual MCA adjustments. This need for increased exchange rate stability was reinforced by the belief among economists and business leaders that growing intra-European trade flows would be disrupted by the potentially wide variance in European exchange rates. Also, European leaders, particularly in France and Germany, were growing dissatisfied with American management of the international monetary system. In response to these pressures, the member governments of the European Community decided to set up a new monetary system within Europe itself.

The "Snake in the Tunnel"

The Council of Finance Ministers of the European Community agreed in March of 1972 to limit exchange rate fluctuations among the European currencies to plus or minus 1.123 percent relative to one another, thus setting up a purely European exchange rate system, the European Common Margins Agreement, or "Snake."[34] The Snake in the Tunnel moniker came from the image of the smaller band of 2.25 percent fluctuation for the European currencies (the Snake) within the larger 4.5 percent total allowable fluctuation band of the Smithsonian Agreement, which held for the rest of the world (the Tunnel). The European currencies would continue to fluctuate against the U.S. dollar and other non-European currencies within the wider Smithsonian Agreement band, but their intra-European fluctuations would be decreased. Variable MCAs would make up for any differences between the green rates and the Snake rates, but because of the limited margin of European fluctuations, they would be needed only sparingly.

However, the enlargement of the European Community and the subsequent entry of the British into the CAP system soon created new difficulties for the working of the common pricing programs. Britain had been unable to keep the pound within the Smithsonian exchange rates and thus had been floating its currency for more than six months. The floating rate of the pound soon began to diverge from the green pound agricultural rate assigned by the EC when Britain joined the CAP, provoking a new round of variable MCAs, import subsidies, and export levies that changed weekly depending on the movement of the pound.[35] Ireland and Italy soon followed in floating their currencies and relying on variable MCAs.

These mounting internal complexities were compounded by external pressures from the international system. The U.S. dollar continued to weaken and was finally devalued once again in February 1973. Shortly thereafter, Belgium, Denmark, France, Germany, Luxembourg, and the Netherlands all decided they could no longer keep their currencies within the Smithsonian band against the dollar and began a joint float. In this joint float, they maintained the Snake margins among themselves but floated against the U.S. dollar. As Irving and Fearn write:

> By this time the Community's MCA system was, not surprisingly, becoming intolerably complex and was straining even the highly competent and resourceful administrators of the Commission. Frequent changes in market rates of exchange necessitated equally frequent changes in the MCAs telexed from the Commission to the Member states and subsequently published in the Official Journal. Indeed, the heights of absurdity were reached when the information on MCAs transmitted to Member States required telegrams running 40 to 50 feet in length.[36]

Clearly some alternative system was needed.

A new CAP pricing system introduced by the commission in June 1973 kept the two rates of currency exchange, the green rate and the market rate, but made a fundamental shift from dependence on the value of the dollar. The revised CAP linked the European agricultural unit of account to the values of the jointly floating European currencies so that the exchange rates and the green rates moved together, with a fixed difference between them. This somewhat simplified the operation of the MCAs, although commission administrators still had to make extensive calculations to determine the appropriate MCA levels.[37]

However, the CAP countries who were floating independently (Italy, Britain, and Ireland) still presented problems because the MCAs had to be variable to compensate for those countries' exchange rate fluctuations. Trade with countries outside the CAP also remained subject to variable import levies and export subsidies to maintain the pricing system.

Once again, a series of exchange rate changes in 1973–74 on the part of the Germans, the Dutch, and the Italians necessitated MCA adjustments. In 1974, the French decided they could no longer maintain the franc in the Snake joint float and began to float independently, and variable MCAs were reintroduced for the French except for the eight months they reentered the Snake in 1975–76.

In sum, the interaction of the two policy subsystems, agriculture and exchange rates, had produced a series of unexpected systems effects. The monetary compensatory amounts, created to neutralize the unintended trade effects of exchange rate changes on European farmers, had brought further complications. First, the goal of the CAP—to provide common prices to farmers across the EC—was not being met, as the constant use of MCAs indicated. MCAs had the effect of allowing for deviance from the standard EC price, and what had started as a temporary device was now a permanent buffering mechanism.

Second, MCAs conflicted with the goal of free movement of goods across the Common Market because of their trade-distorting effects. In 1975, the commission recognized this and stated that "the re-establishment of a single market must continue to be a fundamental objective of the CAP" and that MCAs were only a "transitional instrument" in the move from the Bretton Woods system to reliance on the European joint float.[38] But the existing system remained in place until the next major attempt at exchange rate stability, the creation of the European Monetary System.

One More Try: The European Monetary System

Many of the same motives that were behind the launching of the Snake in the Tunnel in 1972 were present in the 1978 creation of the European Monetary System.[39] Giavazzi and Giovannini make the following argument:

The European Monetary System is simply a recent step in the historical quest for exchange rate stability in Europe. Europeans dislike exchange fluctuations for three reasons. First, they all live in relatively open countries. Second, many of them hold the floating rates of the 1920s and 1930s responsible for the ensuing collapse of national economies and of the international trading and monetary systems. Third, postwar European institutions—particularly the common agricultural market—depend for their survival on exchange rate stability.[40]

One of the major differences between the European Monetary System (EMS) and its predecessor, however, was that the exchange rate system was not linked to the value of the dollar but instead to the European Currency Unit (ECU). The ECU is a collective monetary unit or basket of European currencies with the weights of the currencies changing over time as their values fluctuate against each other.[41] It was created to serve as a central rate benchmark, or *numeraire*, for the currencies in the EMS.[42] All of the participating countries agreed to keep their currencies within plus or minus 2.25 percent of their assigned ECU central rates, creating an allowable fluctuation band of 4.5 percent. Italy was initially allowed a plus or minus 6 percent fluctuation (and therefore a band of 12 percent) because its economy was deemed too prone to inflation to keep within the narrower band. This exchange rate mechanism (ERM) of the EMS called for each country's central bank to intervene by buying or selling currency whenever parities between two currencies diverged from these limits.[43]

The European Monetary System was a feat of political willpower on the part of French president Valéry Giscard D'Estaing and German chancellor Helmut Schmidt, who managed to craft an agreement among the European states with the aid of commission president Roy Jenkins. But agreement was almost thwarted by the protests of French farmers, a group that Giscard D'Estaing feared had the power to increase the strength of his political opposition. French farmers had seen their competitive advantage in EC trade deteriorate during the 1970s while Germany's agricultural position improved, in part due to the perverse effects of the operation of the MCA program, a program that was created by the EC in response to the French government's concerns about inflation in the wake of a franc devaluation. The MCAs, originally designed by EC officials to offset the effects of currency fluctuations on agricultural prices, had begun to act as a subsidy to Germany and other strong-currency countries, as EC funds were used to keep the agricultural export prices of such countries artificially low after an upward currency revaluation, thus increasing their trade competitiveness. In addition, the increasing use of sophisticated farming techniques, including high-cost fertilizers and heavy equipment, also favored strong-currency countries, which could thus import these goods more cheaply.[44]

Concerned about the domestic political implications of the farm dispute, Giscard D'Estaing held up the agreement on the European Monetary System for several months in early 1979. However, the need for exchange rate stability and the fear that a collapse of the EMS would deal a critical blow to the EC's integration hopes brought the French leader to the EC negotiating table and allowed the new monetary system to begin in the spring of 1979. The French agricultural minister received only a vague commitment from the other member-state representatives that MCAs would be reduced eventually, but no action to discontinue MCAs was taken at that time.[45]

The success of the European Monetary System in reducing currency fluctuations and the reforms brought on by the use of the ECU reduced the complications associated with the operation of the Common Agricultural Policy pricing system. From the start of the EMS in March 1979 until March 1983, currency values were realigned by member governments at a rate of once every eight months, while in the mid-1980s, realignments slowed until there were none between 1987 and 1990.[46]

Despite the emerging exchange rate stability in the European Monetary System, over time the working of the monetary compensatory amounts had begun to show an unanticipated pattern. The changes in relative competitiveness among European farmers due to the MCAs that French farmers had protested at the founding of the EMS continued to increase in the 1980s and began to have further perverse effects on food production throughout the EC. MCAs have been more persistent in countries that tend to experience upward revaluations in their currencies, such as Germany and the Netherlands, than in countries with depreciating currencies, such as France and Italy. Giavazzi and Giovannini chart this persistent asymmetry in adjustment, showing that since an upward revaluation has the effect of nominally decreasing farm prices, farmers are reluctant to give up the supposedly transitional MCAs because they counteract the revaluation and keep prices higher relative to the rest of the domestic economy. "As a result," they state, "market prices in Germany and the Netherlands are higher, on average, than in the rest of Europe."[47] In contrast, in countries that devalue their currencies, adjustment back to current market rates occurs through price increases, creating an incentive for farmers to seek the dismantling of MCAs by pressuring their governments.

The higher prices assured farmers through MCAs in strong-currency countries encourage production, raise the average CAP price levels and thus provide an incentive for overproduction in Europe as a whole.[48]

Overproduction increases the burden of agricultural price supports on the European Community budget.[49] The budget is thus affected in two ways: directly through the cost of transferring MCA funds to the countries that have not adjusted to exchange rate changes, and indirectly through the systemic consequences of the "temporary" MCA price support system on production levels. The exchange rate fluctuations of the pre-EMS period and the creation of MCAs have helped increase the share of the EC budget devoted to agriculture from 50 percent in 1965 to 80 percent in 1978.[50]

Although commission administrators attempted to reform the MCA adjustment process in 1984, the problems of asymmetry and the persistence of MCAs have continued to tax the budget and increase distortions in the agricultural market. In fact, the new MCA rules, which were supposed to spread the effects of a revaluation over all CAP countries instead of assigning country-specific MCAs, made farmers throughout the European Community more active in pressuring their governments to seek currency realignments in the European Monetary System as a way to get higher prices for agricultural products, once more increasing the EC budget.[51]

It may not be an accident that the interaction of agriculture and exchange rate policies in the European Community produces programs that are beyond the comprehension of all but a few agricultural lobbyists and EC bureaucrats. The complexity of the CAP and green money ended up increasing the share that farmers received from the EC budget. This may lead one to question whether the increased subsidies were truly unintended systems effects or instead whether the opaqueness of the feedback loops existing between agriculture and exchange rates were deliberately exploited by farming groups.

However, there is no evidence that the systems effects were premeditated. While farmers did achieve some important policy goals along the way, in general, EC and national actors tended to stumble from each decision to the next, with their subsequent choices conditioned in part by the systems effects set off by their earlier decisions. While the working of the CAP pricing system proved to be a powerful motive for limiting exchange rate flexibility in Europe, the linkage between agriculture and monetary integration was revealed only gradually, in increments, to policymakers.

The connections between agricultural pricing policies and exchange rates have resulted in systems effects that reverberate throughout the two policy areas and ultimately will only be solved with the introduction of irrevocably fixed exchange rates, or their essential equivalent, a single European currency. The European Monetary Union (EMU) currently under discussion in Europe would restore the balance that was lost when a common market in agricultural prices was created without a matching common currency area. The alternative way to ensure a compatibility between the two subsystems—dismantling the Common Agricultural Program and reinstating country-specific policies to match the domestically delineated currencies—was never an option because the CAP was seen as an important building block in European integration. The only way for the two policy subsystems to become compatible is for the EC to adopt a single currency, yet the lack of public support for the Maastricht Treaty on European Union has left the fate of a single currency in doubt, while leaving intact the perverse systems effects that have accrued in this area of EC policymaking.

Epilogue: The 1992 Project

The passage of the Single European Act by the governments of the European Community in 1986 represents the revitalization of the drive toward integration.[52] The EC has almost met the mandate of the single-market legislation by adopting close to 300 proposals to increase the free movement of goods, services, people, and capital and to remove barriers to economic activity across the EC by December 31, 1992. The increased scope of EC policymaking and the heightened level of interaction among policy subsystems is likely to increase the potential for extensive indirect and unintended consequences. In fact, many European officials and business leaders believe that the wide-ranging policy measures laid out in the Single Act will serve to increase integration through such unforeseen systems effects.[53] An observation by a neofunctionalist theorist is highly relevant: "Of all issues and policy areas the commitment to create a common market is the most conducive to rapid regional integration and the maximization of a spillover," in contrast to the limited impact of technical programs, military alliances, or narrow economic organizations.[54] The Single Act program can be seen as one effort to deliberately provoke systems effects in the hope that the majority of the effects would serve to increase integration.

One linkage has already come to fruition: the dismantling of capital controls and the liberalization of capital markets that occurred in July of 1990 has placed pressure on policymakers to increase economic and monetary coordination and has given new urgency to calls for a full Economic and Monetary Union to alleviate currency instability.[55] The free movement of people throughout the EC has created pressures to develop a common immigration policy despite important differences among member states on that politically divisive issue. In addition, the increased powers of the European Court of Justice have resulted in precedent-setting decisions with unexpected repercussions.[56] One important example is the *Cassis de Dijon* case, unheralded when decided in the late 1970s, which paved the way for mutual recognition of national standards, increasing the potential for the free movement of goods and service across Europe.[57]

It is interesting to note that this view of systems effects goes against this volume's prevailing assumption that systems effects are destabilizing and thus undesirable: in terms of the 1992 program, the systems effects are promoted as a way to achieve the benefits of a free market in the European Community. The case study of agriculture and exchange rates suggests that systems effects have the best chance of producing positive results if the policies that arise from them share the same basic principles—like the dismantling of barriers to free markets or the creation of a common economic and monetary system.

Conclusion

Policymakers guiding the new Europe through its next phase of integration will need to be aware of the potential for systems effects as more and more policy areas become subject to EC-wide management. There may be some desirable effects from increased interaction as the European Community widens its membership and deepens its political mandate, such as those arising from the single-market program.

It will take careful planning and foresight by the European officials to separate desired systems effects from perverse ones, as well as attention to the consequences of enacting programs that are incompatible in their basic assumptions, be it free market versus managed economies or a common agricultural policy versus individual currencies. Now as much as ever, the importance of creating the conditions for a stable and prosperous Europe cannot be underestimated. An increased knowledge of the potential for systems effects can only be helpful in achieving those goals.

The evolution of EC policymaking studied here also illustrates more generally how conflicts arise and are resolved in complex systems. The European Community, with its web of different programs and numerous political actors, presents a challenge that is similar to the one we now face in the context of the international system. The case of agriculture and exchange rates has shown how the interaction among different levels of political systems, the large number of actors and groups involved, and the variety of issue areas influence the development of policy in the European Community. The current international system would likewise benefit from analysis that incorporates a broadened systems approach.

Notes

I am grateful for comments by Miriam Avins, J. Samuel Barkin, Theresa Pelton Johnson, Charlotte Kim, Martin Malin, Jack Snyder and Harrison White and would like to thank the Center for the Social Sciences at Columbia University for providing a collegial setting for the writing of this paper. I also thank the Eisenhower World Affairs Institute and the Council for European Studies for research support.

1. Jack Snyder makes this point particularly relevant by citing the importance of factors outside the military balance of power as important in fueling recent changes in the former Soviet Union and elsewhere. See his introduction to this volume, pp. 1–4.

2. This view is echoed in Anatol Rapoport's discussion of general systems theory in his "Systems Analysis," in David L. Sills, ed., *International Encyclopedia of the Social Sciences* (New York: Macmillan and the Free Press, 1968) vol. 15, p. 452. For the purpose of this paper, the broadest definition of a system is appropriate: a system can be defined as "an arrangement of certain components so interrelated as to form a whole;" George J. Klir, "The Polyphonic General Systems Theory," in Klir, ed., *Trends in General Systems Theory* (New York: Wiley-Interscience, 1972), p.1. Thanks go to Randall Schweller for suggesting this definition.

3. The challenge of understanding and explaining the interaction of domestic and international level causes has been addressed by Peter Gourevitch, *Politics in Hard Times* (Ithaca, NY: Cornell University Press, 1986) and "The Second Image Reversed: the International Sources of Domestic Politics," *International Organization* 32 (Autumn 1978):881–909; and Robert Putnam, "Diplomacy and Domestic Politics: the Logic of Two-level Games," *International Organization* (Summer 1988):427–460.

4. Stanley Hoffmann and Robert Keohane effectively argue that the legal structures of the European Community, such as the European Court of Justice and the increasing jurisdiction of the EC over Single Market issues, as well as the compliance rate of member states to its laws, make the EC very distinct from other international organizations. See Hoffmann and Keohane, "Institutional Change in Europe in the 1980s," in their edited volume, *The New European Community: Decisionmaking and Institutional Change* (Boulder, CO: Westview Press, 1991), ch. 1.

5. A picture on the front page of the *New York Times* in July 1991 illustrated this point. The photo showed the heads of state at the historic London Economic Summit, in which the Soviet Union had participated to ask the West for economic assistance. Smiling along with Messrs. Bush, Major, Gorbachev, et al., was Jacques Delors, President of the Commission of the European Community. The EC has encountered difficulties acting in concert in world affairs as evidenced in its inability to secure a cease fire in Yugoslavia, but this does not negate the importance of the EC as a level of analysis.

6. George Tsebelis has approached this problem within a game-theoretic context by developing a theory of "nested games," where games in one context must be understood as affecting and being affected by games in other

contexts. Tsebelis, *Nested Games: Rational Choice in Comparative Politics* (Berkeley: University of California Press, 1990).

7. See "Implementation of the EMS," *Europe* No. 2597 (January 15–16, 1979) p. 6; "Farm Price Agreement May Be A High Price" *The German Tribune* 25 March 1979; and Peter Ludlow, *The Making of the European Monetary System* (London: Butterworths, 1982), pp. 198–205.

8. Robert Jervis, "Systems and Interaction Effects," (ch.1, pp. 35–37). The important influence of non-state actors, such as interest groups, compounds this complexity.

9. Kenneth Waltz, *Theory of International Politics* (New York: Random House, 1979).

10. Charlotte J. Kim, "The Mouse that Roared and the Mouse that Didn't: Belgium, the Netherlands and European Community Environmental Policy," Senior Thesis, Department of Social Studies, Harvard-Radcliffe College, March 1991. Kim also finds that small states are influential as conceptual innovators, in addition to being potential nuisances or conceptual mediators.

11. This is despite efforts at increasing the use of qualified majority voting following the passage of the Single European Act in 1987.

12. Monetary issues seem to be particularly open to systems effects because of the technical complexity of exchange rate regimes and macroeconomic policy. The case study that follows is not unlike Charles Perrow's study of the functioning of a nuclear plant, where linkages among units in the system may not be readily apparent even to the designers of the system themselves. See Perrow, *Normal Accidents* (New York: Basic Books, 1984).

13. The European Council is made up of the heads of state and government of the member countries. The European Commission is the administrative and bureaucratic arm of the European Community, headquartered in Brussels. It is headed by an appointed official, formally known as the President of the Commission to the European Communities. Representatives from the member countries, elected by direct vote in their home countries, make up the European Parliament which has limited political and legal powers.

14. David Mitrany, *A Working Peace System* (London: Royal Institute for International Affairs, 1946) is the functionalist classic.

15. Paul Taylor, *The Limits of European Integration* (New York: Columbia University Press, 1983), p. 4.

16. The neofunctionalist literature is more complex and differentiated than the brief summary given here. Ernst Haas has contributed some of its central works: *The Uniting of Europe* (Stanford: Stanford University Press, 1958) and *Beyond the Nation State* (Stanford: Stanford University Press, 1964). For his critical review of neofunctionalism, see also Haas, *The Obsolescence of Regional Integration Theory* (Berkeley: Institute of International Studies, University of California, 1975). A further elaboration of neofunctionalism is Leon Lindberg and Stuart Scheingold, *Europe's Would-Be Polity* (Englewood Cliffs, NJ: Prentice-Hall, 1970). Reviews that critique this literature in the

context of later theories include Henry R. Nau, "From Integration to Interdependence: Gains, Losses, and Continuing Gaps," *International Organization* 33 (Winter 1979):119–147; and Robert Keohane and Joseph S. Nye, Jr., "International Interdependence and Integration," in Fred I. Greenstein and Nelson Polsby, eds., *International Politics, Handbook of Political Science* Vol. I (Reading, MA: Addison-Wesley, 1975), pp. 363–415.

17. See the chapters in Leon Lindberg and Stuart Scheingold, eds., "Regional Integration: Theory and Research," *International Organization* 24 (Autumn 1970) and published under the same title by Harvard University Press, 1971.

18. Joseph S. Nye, Jr., *Peace in Parts: Integration and Conflict in Regional Organization* (Boston: Little, Brown, 1971).

19. For the purposes of this case study, the international monetary system is the systemic environment; the European Community is a system which is open due to its nesting within the larger international monetary system and its incorporation of two subsystems, the Common Agricultural Policy and European exchange rate policy. The countries that make up the European Community are units within the EC system, with national-level actors the parts that constitute the units. This case study indicates that the European Community is an organized, tightly-linked system, at least in the areas considered, with a high degree of complexity and numerous feedback effects. For a discussion of these terms see Jack Snyder's introduction, pp. 6–13.

20. Joan Pearce notes that "France would have refused to join a Community that provided for free trade in industrial goods but not in agricultural goods, since this would have meant opening its market to German industrial goods without obtaining an adequate compensating benefit." The Germans, who were not competitive in agricultural products, went along with the idea so as to achieve their goal of political rehabilitation and to assure a free market for their competitive products. See "The Common Agricultural Policy: The Accumulation of Special Interests," in *Policy-Making in the European Community* 2nd ed. (London: John Wiley and Sons, 1983), pp. 143–175, quote p. 143. For a general overview of the economics of the CAP, see *The Common Agricultural Policy and the European Community*, IMF Occasional Paper No. 62 (Washington, D.C.: International Monetary Fund, 1988).

21. Pearce, "The Common Agricultural Policy," p. 143–147.

22. The prices of each specific agricultural product, fixed in terms of the unit of account, are decided by the national agricultural ministers at annual meetings. Initially, cereals were the only products covered, but the CAP later expanded to include a large variety of farm products.

23. The fixed value of the dollar was at the center of each currency's band.

24. Robert Solomon, *The International Monetary System, 1945–1981* (New York: Harper and Row, 1982), p. 29.

25. R.W. Irving and H.A. Fearn, "Green Money and the CAP," Centre for European Agricultural Studies, Occasional Paper No. 2 (Kent, England: Wye College, 1975), p. 3. Much of my discussion of the early years of the CAP follows this excellent account. For a more analytic overview of the issues, see

Francesco Giavazzi and Alberto Giovannini, *Limiting Exchange Rate Flexibility: the European Monetary System* (Cambridge, MA: The MIT Press, 1989), ch. 1.

26. For more on the U.S. role in the Bretton Woods system see Robert Gilpin, *The Political Economy of International Relations* (Princeton: Princeton University Press, 1987), ch. 4; and Robert Solomon, *The International Monetary System.*

27. Irving and Fearn, "Green Money and the CAP," p. 6. Generally, a currency devaluation makes imports more expensive to domestic buyers while making the devaluing country's exports cheaper in overseas markets. However, the EC-wide operation of the CAP made all agricultural products, even those produced in France, act like imported goods and rise in price, because the food prices are set on a uniform, external basis. Thus, a devaluation of a country's green rate causes domestic agricultural prices to rise, while a revaluation causes them to fall.

28. Irving and Fearn, "Green Money and the CAP," pp. 8–9.

29. The effect was to keep food prices lower in France than they would have been through the use of subsidies paid out of the jointly financed EC budget. For a concise history of MCAs, see Joan Pearce, *The Common Agricultural Policy*, Chatham House Papers no. 13 (London: RIIA/Routledge and Kegan Paul, 1981), pp. 37–45.

30. Irving and Fearn, "Green Money and the CAP," p. 10.

31. See Giavazzi and Giovannini, *Limiting Exchange Rate Flexibility*, pp. 19–24, for a discussion of Europe and the international monetary system.

32. In a floating exchange rate regime, the value of the currency does not remain inside a specified band of variance but can change dramatically. In a fixed rate regime, the currency value varies only slightly, within set limits. Large changes occur only when the government declares that the value is to be realigned and a new fluctuation band delineated.

33. This was a function of the maximum differences possible between two currencies pegged to a third currency, e.g. the difference between case 1: the mark at the top and the lira at the bottom of the 4.5 percent band; and case 2: the mark at the bottom and the lira at the top of the 4.5 percent band. Over time, the maximum excursion of bilateral exchange rates in the European Community was thus nine percent. See Giavazzi and Giovannini, *Limiting Exchange Rate Flexibility*, pp. 25–26. I thank Bart Turtelboom for help on this point.

34. The Snake exchange rate values applied to all currency transactions among its members. A separate green money rate for agriculture was continued, to insulate the agricultural programs from day-to-day fluctuations between the European currencies. For a detailed political history of the creation of the Snake, see Loukas Tsoukalis, *The Politics and Economics of European Monetary Integration* (London: George Allen and Unwin, 1977).

35. Irving and Fearn, "Green Money and the CAP," p. 15.

36. Ibid., p. 17.

326   *Kathleen R. McNamara*

37. Irving and Fearn, "Green Money and the CAP," pp. 20–26, discuss these calculations in some detail.

38. European Economic Community, "Newsletter on the CAP," No. 3, 1975.

39. On the operation of the EMS, see Horst Ungerer, et al., "The European Monetary System: Developments and Perspectives," *Occasional Paper* No. 73 (Washington, D.C.: The International Monetary Fund, 1990); for an excellent review of its development and functioning, see Daniel Gros and Niels Thygesen, *European Monetary Integration: From the European Monetary System towards Monetary Union* (London: Longman Press, forthcoming). Peter Ludlow, *The Making of the European Monetary System* (London: Butterworths, 1982), is the only political history of the creation of the EMS.

40. Giavazzi and Giovannini, *Limiting Exchange Rate Flexibility*, p. 1. See also Michael Tracy, *Agriculture in Western Europe* (London: Granada, 1982), ch. 14; and Yves de Silguy, "Le Système Agri-Monétaire depuis la Création du S.M.E.," in Jean Raux, ed., *Politique Agricole Commune et Construction Communautaire* (Paris: Economica, 1984), pp. 203–215.

41. The composition of the ECU is periodically reviewed to ensure that exchange rate changes do not move the currencies far away from their original weights, which were related to the economic size of each participating country.

42. The other functions of the ECU at its founding were to provide a reserve asset and settlement instrument for European Community central banks, and to be used for central bank intervention operations in the EMS.

43. At its founding, the ERM included all the EC members except Britain, which was strictly speaking a member of the European Monetary System but not the Exchange Rate Mechanism. It has subsequently been the practice to allow new EC members a larger fluctuation band, which eventually shrinks to the EMS standard.

44. Peter Ludlow, *The Making of the European Monetary System* (London: Butterworths, 1982), p. 204.

45. Ludlow writes that the details of this dispute are "virtually unintelligible . . . to all but those directly involved (a latter-day equivalent of the Schleswig-Holstein question, which reputedly drove those who could grasp its intricacies to madness, amnesia or death)". Even after close examination of the question, Ludlow was unable to say why the French agreed to give up the fight at this moment. Ludlow, *The Making of the European Monetary System*, quotation from p. 279, see also pp. 279–283.

46. Gros and Thygesen, *European Monetary Integration*, ch. 3. See also Ungerer, et al., "The European Monetary System."

47. Giavazzi and Giovannini, *Limiting Exchange Rate Flexibility*, p. 17.

48. The average intervention prices for agricultural goods are raised across Europe because the bias in the price system introduced by the strong-currency countries is not offset by matching lower prices in weak-currency countries. See Giavazzi and Giovannini on this asymmetric bias, pp. 17–18.

49. Ibid., p. 18.

50. Ibid., p. 27.

51. For an explanation of the highly technical linkages that produced this result, see "Doing the Green Currency Shuffle," *Financial Times* December 23, 1986. They are also discussed in IMF, *The Common Agricultural Policy and the European Community*, pp. 7–8.

52. See Hoffmann and Keohane, eds., *The New European Community*, for an assessment of changes in the wake of the Single Act; for an account of the events leading up to it, see Andrew Moravcsik, "Negotiating the Single European Act" in the same volume.

53. Interviews with author, London, England (September 1991), and Brussels, Belgium (October 1991).

54. Ernst Haas, "The Study of Regional Integration," in Lindberg and Scheingold, eds. *Regional Integration: Theory and Research*, p. 12. This is also discussed in Nau, "From Integration to Interdependence," p. 125–26.

55. This is described in Peter Norman, "Monetary Trade-off," *The Wall Street Journal*, September 23, 1988.

56. I would like to thank Michael Hodges for discussions on this point.

57. In this case, the Court prohibited Germany from blocking the import of French liqueur on the grounds that the French products did not meet German national standards for alcohol percentages.

13

Conclusion: System Stability and the Security of the Most Vulnerable Significant Actor

Thomas J. Christensen

A collaborative effort like this book rarely provides a single theoretical conclusion. The chapters offer various reconceptualizations of how systems dynamics operate in the international arena. The diversity of approaches is one of the volume's strengths. However, there are common strands that run throughout the book. The various contributions suggest solutions to two shortcomings of existing international relations systems theories: their low levels of explanatory determinacy and policy relevance. By considering how structural variables such as the international balance of power or distribution of wealth interact with nonstructural variables such as military technology, actor preferences, or domestic politics, the authors offer more complete explanations of systemic stability and instability than are provided by purely structural approaches. The study of these nonstructural intervening factors can help us better understand how abstract variables like international system structure affect observable systemwide outcomes such as great-power war or the collapse of international economic arrangements.

Moreover, by focusing on variables that are more manipulatable than system structure, the authors suggest practical remedies for system instability. Several chapters point in the direction of a new practical systems approach that addresses the economic and security concerns of the most vulnerable significant actors in the international system. The weakness of key actors can tempt expansionist powers and might lead the vulnerable actors themselves to adopt rash, all-or-nothing responses to otherwise mild challenges. Either outcome might send destabilizing shocks and ripples throughout the system, particularly in conditions of structural multipolarity. Buffering the most vulnerable important actors might stabilize the system by removing dangerous international temptations. By understanding the forces that can reduce the vulnerabilities of important actors, we might create countermeasures that reduce the likelihood of positive feedback spirals. Moreover, in the process of addressing the concerns of actors with the most complex vulnerabilities, new institutions and norms may arise that serve to soften a number of security dilemmas throughout the system.

Systems Theories and the Foreign Policy Connection

Because they emphasize parsimony and general applicability, systems theorists generally play down the foreign policy aspects of their arguments. But when they actually apply their theories to historical case studies, the foreign policies of significant actors provide the critical connection between systemic causes and systemic outcomes. In practice, systems theories often work something like what is shown in Figure 13.1, which outlines a standard structural systems

FIGURE 13.1   The Standard Systems Theory in Practice

Systems Variable	*Transmission Belt*	*Systems Variable*	*Outcome*
Independent Variable	Activator	Catalyst/ Buffer	Dependent Variable
Structure: number of great actors, distribution of wealth, balance of power	Foreign policy of great actors under systems pressures	Tightness of systems links, determinants of type and degree of feedback (e.g.,) geography, military technology patterns of economic interdependence	Stability or instability: war or peace, trade or protectionism

theory. The first box is familiar and usually explicit in the literature. The second box is generally only implicit in systems accounts: the foreign policy of individual states are "activators" in that they trigger system dynamics but do not themselves determine their nature. The third box includes systemwide factors such as geography, patterns of interdependence, and technology that affect the degree to which shocks in one part of the system reverberate throughout. Below I refer to these as nonstructural, systemwide variables. One might also include in this category beliefs that are widely held by leaders in a given international system. Such beliefs interact with structural constraints and incentives to influence observable outcomes (box 4). Both the structure of the system and these other systemic catalysts and buffers will determine the degree to which subsystemic perturbations spread.

One should also note that the arrow between the second and third boxes points in both directions. The same systemwide factors that determine feedback (box 3) can also affect the calculations of state leaders before they initiate positive and negative feedback loops. By exposing and analyzing the inputs and outputs of the second box, we can remedy some theoretical and practical shortcomings of current systems theories. More important, we might begin to work toward practical safeguards against systemic dangers.

The Limitations of Current International Relations Systems Theories

Current systems theories tend to suffer from two major ailments. First, in the search for parsimony, they often exhibit too high a degree of abstraction, which renders them difficult to apply across historical periods without significant additional variables. Even if not simply invalid, such abstract theories begin to resemble causal correlational hypotheses rather than theories since in different cases, extremely different causal roads lead us from system cause A to system outcome B. So, in practical application, scholars generally only use abstract systems theories as a first cut at understanding historical problems, adding additional systemic or subsystemic variables to the case-study recipe as needed.

For example, in his classic *Theory of International Politics* Kenneth Waltz claims that multipolar systems are less stable than bipolar ones.[1] In both multipolar worlds described by Waltz disaster indeed struck, but it did so for very different reasons. In pre–World War I multipolarity, small perturbations triggered chain-ganging alliance behavior and the amplification of tensions. Each ally felt that its own security hinged on the survival of its partners. So, when one ally went to war, the others followed in lockstep. In pre-World War II multipolarity just the opposite tendency led to disaster. Potential allies passed the buck, allowing a huge problem—Hitler—to go unchecked.[2] Each potential ally felt it could rely on the others to stop or at least slow Hitler's juggernaut before it needed to enter the fray.

Given the dissimilar nature of the two multipolar alliance ailments, it should not be surprising that Waltz's bipolar remedies to multipolar instabilities are themselves inconsistent. Waltz explains that superpowers do not chain themselves to reckless allies, because the smallish allies are relatively unimportant to them. But he also argues that they do not buckpass because they concern themselves actively with even small incidents on the periphery.[3] In Waltz's cases, structural causes correlate with the predicted outcomes, but not always for the same reasons. Multipolarity twice led to world war, but for two opposite reasons. The bipolar world avoided world war, but because of two opposite stabilizing logics.

In international political economy, hegemonic stability theory is more indeterminate.[4] One of three cases of structural hegemony (the United States in the 1930s) did not lead to free trade regimes, and one of two cases of hegemonic decline (U.S. decline in the 1970s) did not lead to trade regime collapse. Hegemonic stability theorists do not get nearly as far as Waltz. In two crucial cases the system structures do not even co-vary with the predicted outcomes. Thus, additional nonstructural variables must be employed in order to explain the outcomes fully.[5]

A second shortcoming of current systems theories is the tendency to focus on variables which, even if they could be clearly identified, could not be manipulated in the real world. What prescriptive analyses can be derived from Waltz's analysis of multipolarity or bipolarity, short of the absurd recommendation that we support bipolarity and oppose multipolarity? Similarly, one might ask what can be done to prevent the breakdown of trade and monetary exchange regimes if they depend on the health of hegemonic leadership.

Of course, Waltz does not "prescribe" superpower dominance; nor do hegemonic stability theorists "prescribe" continued American hegemony. But it is not surprising that frustrated scholars on the left, searching for methods of systemic transformation, attack these authors as apologists for the status quo. The systems theorists justifiably respond that no one can influence the historical forces that generate the most fundamental characteristics of the system.[6]

Perhaps the most ironic aspect of the debate between critical theorists and structural theorists is that the former accuse the latter of creating only "problem-solving theories."[7] Sadly, this is a crime to which systems theorists would often need to perjure themselves in order to plead guilty. The flagship structural theories are best at locating problems; they only rarely offer workable solutions.

The best systems theories can, however, prove extremely helpful in warning against foreign policies which are inconsistent with a state's position in the international system. For example, in 1967 the field's leading systems theorist, Kenneth Waltz, offered an elegant and timely explanation for why the United States should not have been so deeply involved in Vietnam, and why the Americans should have been in a better position to exploit the Sino-Soviet split. In the spirit of George Kennan's strongpoint containment strategy, Waltz criticized ideologically charged and wasteful superpower overreactions in peripheral areas of the globe.[8]

Resolving Underdeterminacy
and Searching for Prescriptions

The Addition of Nonstructural, Systemwide Variables

In recent years, authors have begun addressing some of these shortcomings in structural systems theories. Since the general structural theories suffer from underdeterminacy, authors have searched for additional systemwide variables that explain variation in similarly structured worlds. Various works explore how nonstructural, systemwide factors may determine how structural factors play out in the real world.[9] But these efforts generally only help us further understand the nettlesome problems threatening systems stability. Like the original structural theories that they augment and critique, they offer variables that are, at best, difficult to manipulate.

Nonstructural, supplementary variables have been employed widely in the security literature. Following the leads of Robert Jervis and George Quester, authors employ the variables of offensive/defensive military advantages and misperception about such advantages to determine how stability may vary in similarly structured systems.[10] Although these authors are "problem-solvers," it is not clear how practical the prescriptions derived from their theses might prove. For example, even if we fully understand the dangers of offensive doctrines for crisis management, arms racing, and chain-ganging alliance behavior, it would be difficult to manage regimes that prohibit offensive military doctrines throughout the system. It is impossible to "disinvent" effective offensive technologies. While arms control is possible, preventing proliferation and stealthy deployments of such weaponry often constitutes a mammoth management challenge. (It should, however, be easier to disabuse leaders of misperceptions about offensive potency in defense-dominant worlds and vice versa).

Even on theoretical grounds, the offense/defense problem is stickier than it is usually portrayed, as the evidence offered by Anne Uchitel in Chapter 10 suggests. Uchitel describes the potentially perverse effects of dependence on foreign suppliers for strategic resources in worlds perceived to be defense-dominant (prone to "long wars" in her terms). She portrays a 1930s Europe in which all leaders, even Hitler, understood the military advantages of defensive, attritional, long-war strategies. But Germany lacked sufficient strategic resources within its borders to fight and survive such a war. This compelled Hitler to adopt piecemeal offensives against the small, resource-rich nations that lay between Germany and the system's poles. Hitler's destabilizing offensive strategy resulted not from his inherent belief in the advantages of the offensive but in his somewhat paranoid belief that Germany would ultimately be destroyed by resource-rich powers like the Soviet Union, the United Kingdom, and the United States unless the reich built an autarkic empire in Central Europe.

Uchitel argues that Hitler initially saw no conflict of interest with Britain. He attacked only after London rejected a separate peace. Hitler's offensives against Britain were designed to knock the UK out of the war quickly, before it could mobilize its latent strength and before Germany exhausted the strategic stockpiles it was saving to assault its most threatening rival, the increasingly powerful Soviet Union. Belief in the efficacy of British and Soviet long-run defenses, rather than deterring Hitler, encouraged him to jump through others' windows of vulnerability using fierce offensive tactics.

Uchitel's account suggests the following thesis: in multipolar worlds, generally stabilizing defensive dominance might still prove destabilizing, not only because of potential buckpassing among status quo allies but because of an imbalance of autarky among great actors. The most vulnerable (or least autarkic) significant actor might have strong incentives to conquer the small and medium-size powers on which it relies for strategic resources. Since defensive tactics do not work for expansion, vulnerable actors design offensives anyway. Since initial offensive campaigns trigger responses by other great industrialized actors, the vulnerable state's paranoia only grows because those states are felt to be particularly threatening if they are given time to mobilize their latent resources into military capability. So the vulnerable state tries to deliver fierce knockout blows to whichever great states take exception to its early expansion. This creates a positive feedback loop of escalation that only guarantees wider war with a greater number of more highly mobilized powers.

This thesis would be strengthened if we could find less demonic examples than Hitler of actors trapped in this tragic spiral. Hitler was almost certainly paranoid, but he was also aggressive and expansionist. Even if we accept the dictator's Darwinian equation of defense with the annihilation of potential rivals, it is difficult to accept a portrayal of Hitler's aggression as ultimately defensive unless we believe he could not feel safe without conquering all of Europe, North Africa, and the United States. In such a scenario the theoretical distinction between offense and defense simply becomes meaningless. Still, the thesis derived from Uchitel's account is deductively logical, and Uchitel's history demonstrates well how the logic operated to make Hitler even more aggressive than he might otherwise have been. Hitler's adoption of offensive tactics in a world of perceived defense dominance supports Jervis's general observation that in human systems, ingenuity can defy straightforward forces for stability.[11] Highly motivated actors like Hitler—both aggressive and fearful of the status quo—can invent new destabilizing methods to overcome obstacles that preserve the status quo.

Randall Schweller's portrayal of interwar Europe in Chapter 9 shares certain features with Uchitel's account. By respecifying the structure of the system as tripolar (The United States, Germany, USSR), Schweller offers structural reasons for Hitler's concern about the Soviet Union, the only great power other than Germany in Europe. If it could be annihilated before the Americans entered the fray, Germany could dominate the entire continent.

As does Uchitel, Schweller portrays the German attack on Britain as a temporary and annoying sideshow for Hitler. Hitler expected Britain to cut a separate deal with the reich. When, instead, it guaranteed Poland and refused to make a separate peace after the fall of Belgium and France, Hitler decided to knock the UK out of the war quickly before it fully rearmed. By defeating Britain, Germany would completely isolate the Soviet Union. Hitler did not expect the United States to become a factor until the mid-1940s. By that time, Germany would have already defeated the USSR and gained control of the continent. The main difference between Uchitel's and Schweller's historical accounts lies in how they view Hitler's analysis of the potential strength of Germany and Britain. Uchitel portrays Hitler as fearful of Britain's latent war potential; Schweller claims that Hitler saw Britain as a smallish potential ally at best and as an annoying hostile middle power at worst.

Schweller's theory of tripolarity offers two general contributions to the field of international systems theory. First, by adding as an independent variable the distribution of status quo states and revisionist states, he makes more determinate predictions about systemic outcomes than starker balance-of-power arguments can provide.[12] As Schweller points out, tripolarity alone cannot tell us why World War II occurred. We must know whether key actors are power maximizers (revisionist states) or security maximizers (status quo states). This distinction leaves ample room for Hitler's megalomania. Given Hitler's revisionism and the tripolar structure of the system, Schweller's theory explains well the early course of the war and the alignments of medium-sized status quo and revisionist actors. Second, Schweller argues persuasively that it is not just the number of significant actors in the system but also the distribution of power among them that matters in analyzing alliance and balance-of-power systems. This theme, touched on by Uchitel and an earlier work by Paul Schroeder, is discussed further below.[13]

Elements of the work by Schweller and Uchitel might be melded with earlier analyses to explain World War II. Schweller identifies the need to consider explicitly Hitler's revisionism and the varying power distributions within structural sets (like bi-, tri- or multipolarity). Uchitel helps us understand why Hitler adopted offensives and knockout strategies against Central European powers, Britain, and France *despite* his belief in the general advantage of long-war attritional strategies. Combining findings by Schweller and Uchitel with earlier works on British strategy, we can explain why Britain did not do more to help France even after the fall of Czechoslovakia, when British leaders decided that French security was crucial to Britain's own. To some degree British leaders were hoping to ride free on the independent defensive efforts of French forces.[14] Finally, some recognition of the equalizing influence of Britain's unique, natural defensive advantage must be taken into account if we are to understand the UK's triumph in the Battle of Britain and Hitler's frustrating decision to turn East before its successful conclusion.

Nonstructural, Systemwide Variables in International Political Economy

Systems theorists in international political economy have also introduced nonstructural systems variables to improve explanations of stability in international trade and monetary regimes. Helen Milner, for example, argues that despite the decline of American hegemony, industrial countries have "resisted the protectionist temptations" of a multipolar, interdependent world. This resistance flows partly from the new nature of interdependence itself: large corporations now manufacture final products transnationally. This fact makes manipulated trade a double-edged sword for large, politically influential producers: high trade barriers protect their domestic markets, but they also increase the costs of imported parts used in domestic production and raise the price of imported final products produced by subsidiaries overseas. By explaining why the decline of American hegemony did not lead to the beggar-thy-neighbor tariff races of the 1930s, Milner offers an elegant key—transnational production—to resolve the underdeterminacy of hegemonic stability theory.[15]

But Milner's key variable is not one that lends itself to conscious manipulation. One cannot prescribe more international production; it is the product of lengthy historical developments. However, by understanding its impact we may become more sanguine about the future of international trade policy and, perhaps, avoid a series of preemptive regulatory measures that might complicate the problem of trade cooperation and trigger irrational nationalist backlashes in time of recession.

A closer look at the world of transnational production that Milner describes may also offer new solutions for the knotty problems of international monetary management. In Chapter 6, Jeffry Frieden portrays the rise and fall of monetary regimes as ascending and descending positive feedback loops. When monetary agreements begin to form, they encourage international capital flows and trade, which increase the incentives for newly integrated actors to join the regime. So regime growth encourages further regime growth. While positive feedback loops are generally seen as destabilizing, in this case positive feedback creates desirable dynamic outcomes (what Frieden calls a "dialectic" of monetary integration).

However, when recession strikes the international economy or key actors within it, powerful domestically oriented producers put pressure on the state to protect their markets from cheap imports. Currency devaluation, aside from tariffs, provides the best means of achieving this. It constitutes a subtle and inclusive method by which states can make imports more expensive on the domestic market and exports more competitive on international markets. Once one or two actors defect in this fashion, a wave of defections follows as affected actors abroad try to avoid the "sucker's payoff" of being the last to devalue. As actors bow out of the monetary regimes, international capital flows decline in importance to domestic economies, and positive incentives for maintaining the regime are also removed. Thus, we have destabilizing positive feedback on the downside of Frieden's cooperation bell curve.

New systemic forces might discourage competitive devaluations. First, as Frieden discusses, the international sectors of all economies are growing relative to domestic producers. Even in traditionally autarkic nations such as the United States and China, trade now constitutes a significant portion of GNP. So, to the degree that economic clout drives the political power of societal interest groups, the power of protectionist domestic-oriented business coalitions should be declining relative to internationalist coalitions. Frieden argues persuasively that all things being equal, internationally oriented actors will prefer stable exchange rates. Stable rates allow for a degree of predictability in international business that is preferable to the capriciousness of highly volatile exchange rate fluctuations or competitive devaluations.

But all things are not always equal. As Frieden has recently argued elsewhere, exporters and importers agree on stability, but not on the appropriate level of exchange rates.[16] Importers prefer more appreciated domestic currencies while exporters prefer weaker currencies. Export manufacturers pay their workers and domestic suppliers roughly the same amount of domestic dollars before and after devaluation, but after devaluation their products become more competitive on the international market because those dollars are easier to come by. Export manufacturers in each country may desire international monetary stability, but at exchange rates preferential to themselves. Since it is impossible to please exporting groups of every nationality simultaneously, destabilizing devaluation competitions may still occur. Borrowing from Mancur Olson, Jervis addresses this classic structural systems dilemma; in Chapter 2 he writes, "even if everyone wants the system to be stable, no one may have incentives to contribute to that end."[17]

Combining Frieden's recent insights we can still see a potential for competitive devaluation spirals. If a country's currency is highly valued in a fixed-rate system, and its international trade is divided cleanly between importers and exporters, then we might see a devaluation alliance between exporters and domestic producers. Such coalitional alliances within member nations could create monetary regime instability even in a world of increasing trade as a percentage of GNP.

But Helen Milner's insights about transnational production and multipolar trade regimes also suggests a solution to the large-n prisoner's dilemma of multipolar monetary regimes. If internationally oriented actors are not only international in their marketing but also in their production, it may be easy for trading nations to "resist the devaluation temptation." While purely domestic producers or low-input exporters (such as farmers) will continue to push for manipulated exchange rates and undervalued currencies, manufacturing exporters may no longer be so keen on them. If they import production machinery or parts for their final products, after devaluation they will be paying an artificially high price for their inputs. Since they must pass these costs along to their foreign customers, the advantages and temptations of devaluation will be mitigated strongly.

This phenomenon has occurred in countries like Korea, whose export manufacturers gained surprisingly little when Japan revalued the yen in the mid-1980s. Korean manufacturers and the Korean government were at the forefront in urging Japan to revalue. While in general a revalued yen should have made Korean exports more competitive on international markets in relation to Japanese products, the higher cost of Japanese machine imports to Korean manufacturers largely offset the price benefits and actually increased Korea's trade deficit with Japan.[18]

Combining Frieden's systems theory insights with Milner's, we can see why in the future, highly integrated, internationally oriented economies like Korea's are likely to support international monetary stability: first, in a world increasingly based on trade, a stable monetary regime provides a degree of certainty in the business environment that carries inherent value of its own. Second, the increasing tendency of export manufacturers to be both importers and exporters will reduce their incentives to ally with domestic producers in order to push for devalued currencies.

If these forces do currently work to keep exchange rate fluctuation within a healthy range, then more international regulations might only prove counterproductive; they would serve no positive function and, like unnecessary trade regulation, might only spark nationalist indignation during economic hard times. Like Waltz's approach, Milner's and Frieden's analyses suggest practical proscriptions against unneeded policy activity.

The Addition of Subsystemic Variables:
The Importance of Individual States in Systemic Stability

In the approaches discussed above, the adoption of additional nonstructural systems variables allow more determinate explanations for observed outcomes than the original structural theories themselves. But like the original structural variables, other systemwide variables—e.g., the offense-defense balance, the relative distribution of autarky across great actors, or transnational production—do not easily lend themselves to conscious manipulation. Like Waltz's pioneering efforts, these new approaches do provide practical counsel against policies that are either unnecesary or counterproductive. But the theories' policy relevance is limited to such general proscriptions. By integrating more manipulatable subsystemic variables into systems analysis, the practical value of the original theories grows quickly, even if in the process we lose much of their elegant parsimony.

Schweller's analysis of World War II underscores one important factor not considered by ultraparsimonious systems theories: what types of individual actors make up the system? Considering the chapters by William McNeil (Chapter 8), Susan Peterson (Chapter 5) and Jonathan Mercer (Chapter 7), we might add a conciliatory/ belligerent distinction to Schweller's status quo/revisionist categories. A focus on the potentially destabilizing effects of the rise of belligerent/revisionist actors and the fall of conciliatory/status quo actors is new for neorealist systems theory. While such actor distinctions are often implicit in neorealist accounts, the fear of "reductionism" prevents their elevation to the level of independent variables. But such a subsystemic focus is not novel for more general systems theories. Charles Perrow, for example, has considered "normal accidents" at both the subsystemic and systemic levels.[19] Perrow's criterion for including variables is whether changes in them (accidents) reverberate through normal systemic channels and have systemwide repercussions. I find no compelling practical reason to reject such an approach in international relations theory as long as we can trace how the subsystemic factors affect international systems dynamics. In international relations theorizing, as in a sport like hunting or fishing, sparseness of equipment does not solely determine the quality of the hunt. Parsimony has intrinsic value, but only to the degree that one can choose between two equally powerful explanatory theories of differing elegance. If parsimonious theories are not catching fish or bagging deer at all, then unsatisfied theorists should not shun more sophisticated tools.

Schweller is correct in pointing out that structure alone, whether it be multipolar or tripolar, does not suffice to explain World War II. His chapter offers additional variables which not only tell a better story but also provide some hope for prescriptive theory. The revisionist nature of the German regime and its vulnerable location between the other two poles are central elements in the inexorable and disastrous logic of heterogeneous tripolar worlds. Since we cannot "prescribe" a different German geography, any prescriptive solution to European problems of the 1930s would have to focus on the sources of German revisionism. The 1938–39 world seems hopeless, so we should look further back, at the Europe of the 1920s, and in particular at Weimar Germany, a liberal regime and the most vulnerable significant actor in world affairs.

Combining the contributions of McNeil and Schweller, one could argue that after World War I, the attempts of the world's great actors to keep Germany weak via reparations rendered untenable the position of the conciliatory/status quo Weimar state. As McNeil describes, even sincere Weimar leaders could not answer simultaneously the demands of domestic politics, foreign lenders, and international reparations agreements. The humiliating collapse of the Weimar state under international pressure left fertile ground for the rise of a revisionist xenophobe like Hitler.

McNeil argues that the Weimar Republic was overwhelmed by crosscutting and incompatible demands: domestic politics demanded government spending, economic growth necessitated more capital in the marketplace, and reparation agreements mandated that trade profits be transferred to World War I victors. The Dawes Plan bought the Weimar regime time in the form of capital investment and loans, but since Germany could not solve its domestic problems, the plan, like the republic itself, was doomed. Even dedicated German leaders fully expected the Dawes Plan to fail. They merely hoped to buy time through halfhearted compliance so that the failure would not be directly blamed on them.

A marriage of Schweller's and McNeil's theses suggests a systems account of World War II with sophisticated domestic-international linkages. The theorizing implicit in the new account is a complex version of the "second image reversed" employed by Peter Gourevitch in *Politics in Hard Times*.[20] International pressures influence domestic coalitions, which in turn affect international outcomes. International pressures destroyed a conciliatory status quo regime in the most vulnerable of the world's significant states. The replacement regime, the Third Reich, mobilized latent German strength and did so behind the xenophobic legitimacy provided by ill-conceived World War I peace agreements. So Germany became not only stronger but more hostile.

McNeil, focusing on the 1920s, provides a second-image-reversed explanation for America's stubborn insistence on German reparations. Forces in American domestic politics blocked practical proposals to save the German economy and the American investments in Germany (namely, the cancellation of reparations plus provision of additional loans). Because of America's long history of relative isolation from the international economy, American internationalist forces were still domestically weak in the 1920s; and since median voters benefited directly only from the repayment of European war debts, not from investment in the German economy, any proposal to cancel reparations was impossible to push through Congress. Internationalist coalitions were only able to extract further foreign loans for Germany. The logroll of the Dawes Plan, mixing loans with maintenance of reparations, was insufficient to answer Germany's fundamental needs. Instead, the plan merely strung the German economy along for several years.

The final blow to Weimar solvency came in the form of the Wall Street boom and bust of the late 1920s. The boom made Germany's much-needed foreign loans less attractive to investors than stocks, and then the 1929 bust annihilated any possibility of significant American capital flows. Despite impending depression, the largely foreign pressure for fiscal conservatism led the Social Democrats to tighten government spending in 1929. This further restricted Germany's money supply and exacerbated a positive feedback loop toward economic and political disaster. From this Keynesian nightmare rose Hitler.

McNeil's portrait of the interaction of domestic and international politics is a complex and fascinating one. He identifies several crucial elements that contributed to the end of the Weimar Republic and, indirectly, to the birth of the Third Reich. First, linear thinking about how to exploit a nation's defeat and limit a nation's strength counseled the victors of 1918 to extract reparations from defeated Germany. Second, once it was in place, the regime of German reparations created popular interest in its maintenance among key domestic coalitions outside of Germany. For example, in the United States the vast majority of American taxpayers benefited only from the collection of war debts. This majority consisted of domestic-oriented groups, the natural rivals of the international banking community on whose cooperation the German government had become increasingly dependent. Since the domestic-oriented coalitions were influential in a relatively autarkic and democratic America, they were able to block internationalist plans that might have saved the German government from the burden of reparation payments. Finally, the continued application of reparation obligations to a war-torn German economy left the Weimar government insufficient flexibility in economic policy. It exercised fiscal restraint at a time that called for financial pump-priming. The downward spiral to economic disaster undermined the legitimacy of Germany's fledgling democratic state and left fertile ground for Hitler's adroit manipulation of resurgent hypernationalism. With Hitler's rise to power came Germany's transformation from a status quo to a revisionist power. This change interacted with systems variables described by Schweller and Uchitel to create destabilizing positive feedback loops of increasing tension and belligerence.

Given the limits of the intellectual tools and information available to the actors of the 1920s, McNeil is correct to label his drama a tragedy rather than a morality play. Unaware of Keynesian economics and the shadow of the Third Reich, linear-thinking isolationists in American and French society viewed the world in short-term, myopic ways against which Jervis's systems approach warns. They encouraged suboptimal parasitic policies by their national leaders. These policies did more than just kill the host (Weimar Germany); they spawned a new species (Hitler) that would attempt to feed off the other great powers. Consistent with McNeil's coalitional account, the same shortsighted domestic-oriented American and French actors who sought easy tax relief by leaning on German taxpayers also refused to make prompt sacrifices when German resentment and power potential exploded to the surface in the mid-1930s. Because of foot-dragging by these unenlightened groups, the Nazi threat was properly addressed only after it was too late to counter cheaply.

There may be little practical value to be drawn from the study of classic tragedy. But McNeil's story is nonetheless more useful than classic tragedy. Unlike actors at the time, we can now understand the long-term costs of short-term exploitation of Germany's defeat. A more educated, internationally alert American public might have acted differently in regard to German war debt. Happily, the lesson was ultimately learned after World War II, when the United States created some of the most enlightened, system-sensitive programs in diplomatic history: the Marshall Plan and the rebuilding of Japan. America learned that assistance to status quo governments in vanquished countries was preferable to short-term gains at the long-term cost of resurgent xenophobia and authoritarianism. Creators of America's strongpoint defense strategy recognized the value of potential economic powerhouses like Japan and West Germany. Rather than trying to repress West German and Japanese economic dynamism, the United States assisted them in order to foster strong, status quo regimes.

McNeil's case demonstrates well how systemic and subsystemic factors interact and why systems theorists should concern themselves with the subsystemic vulnerabilities to which key state actors are subject, such as economic crises, state-society legitimacy crises, and ethnic strife. If we can take concrete steps to avert subsystemic accidents that carry divisive systemwide effects, we might ameliorate dangerous positive feedback loops by blocking them before they begin.

McNeil's insights about Weimar Germany may counsel present-day leaders to think long and hard about aid and debt relief to fledgling democracies in Russia and other former Soviet republics. While it is not yet clear how effective foreign aid might be in stabilizing those democracies, Western leaders should at least realize that it matters a great deal who governs significant actors in the system and that there is some potential for foreign action to influence political outcomes within nations. At the time of this writing a potentially historic debate is being waged in Washington between internationalists who want to assist Russian democrats through a multibillion dollar ruble stabilization program and resurgent isolationists on the right and left who want to put "America first" in economic hard times.[21] In support of Richard Nixon's plea for more aid now to prevent despotism in Russia later, William Safire writes: "If he's wrong, and the West spends $20 billion a year extending freedom, no harm done; but if he's right, and the New Despotism arrives, the U.S. alone will be spending 20 times that every year; no peace dividend and our children would live in fear of nuclear destruction."[22] For a positive analogy to demonstrate the potential efficacy of intervention on the side of democracy, internationalists in the debate can evoke the Marshall Plan; for a negative analogy about the dangers of American inaction, they might point to the interwar period and the fall of Weimar as portrayed by McNeil.

Chapter 5 by Susan Peterson offers additional theoretical insights into preserving conciliatory states. Because the replacement of conciliatory states with revisionist, hypernationalist ones can alter system dynamics, Peterson's two-level bargaining analysis contains insights for practical systems theory. Peterson argues that standard crisis strategies derived from deterrence theory fail to account for domestic coalitional alignments in the target country. Peterson argues that by adopting unnecessarily coercive stances a state might not only change the other side's beliefs but the other side's leadership. If one enters a crisis with a relatively conciliatory leadership, the standard "open tough" strategy advocated by deterrence theorists might do more than simply signal one's resolve; it might also lead to a change of government in the target country from a conciliatory to a coercive leadership. Such an outcome exacerbates spirals of tension and increases the likelihood of great-power conflict, as Peterson illustrates in the case of the Crimean War.

Here Peterson supplements Jervis's observation about deterrence strategies. Jervis writes:

> It is true that, all things being equal, increasing defense spending or becoming committed to standing firm will increase the chance that the other side will back down. But it can never be the case that "all things are equal," because a very important element is the other side's beliefs, which will be modified by the state's actions.

Jervis is concerned with the potentially negative impact of tough strategies on the other state's beliefs. Peterson warns that such strategies can also cause unwanted changes in the other state's leadership itself.

In Chapter 7, Jonathan Mercer further counsels against tough strategies designed to demonstrate resolve. Attacking deterrence theory's assumption of interdependence in decision-making, Mercer suggests that standing firm rarely leads adversaries to draw positive conclusions about the signaling state's resolve. Rather, they may simply reinforce adversaries' previously held impressions of that state's belligerence.

If we combine Peterson's and Mercer's conclusions, we can arrive at a full-tilt assault on the iterated game strategies suggested by deterrence theorists. Mercer claims that foreign elites rarely attribute reputations for resolve, so it is often useless to signal toughness. Peterson goes further, arguing that tough strategies can actually do harm; they can undercut the domestic legitimacy of conciliatory leaderships abroad and thus bring more aggressive, risk-acceptant leaders to the fore. Since, as Schweller points out, changes of domestic regimes can carry enormous systemic consequences, systems theorists should concern themselves with Peterson's and Mercer's findings about deterrent signaling in iterated games.

The Most Vulnerable Significant Actors: A Practical Lesson for Systems Theory

Several chapters of this volume point in the direction of a practical systems approach that centers on the security problems of the most vulnerable significant actors in the international system. We must first identify what constitutes a significant actor in the international system. In existing neorealist theories actors are states as wholes. To maintain parsimony and avoid "reductionism," neorealists have not considered the security concerns of actors within states such as national governments and their bureacratic organizations or within politically influential sectors of society such as industrial or farm lobbies. Using the neorealist standard of actor designation, a "significant actor" would be a state important enough to trigger a systemwide crisis by its behavior or demise. Its relative vulnerability would be determined by its economic or military capabilities and its geographical position compared to other significant actors. For example, in Uchitel's and Schweller's accounts of the interwar period, Germany is the most vulnerable state because of its geographic encirclement and because of its relative lack of resource independence.

But in suggesting interesting amendments to standard neorealist approaches, the chapters in this volume offer a more complicated actor designation for international systems theory. Contributors employ a less restricting standard for the concept of "significant actor," considering any actor whose behavior or demise creates systemwide ripple effects that travel through normal systems channels. Some authors discuss the significance and vulnerability of certain national governments (e.g., the Weimar Republic), as distinct from states (e.g., Germany), in their analyses of systemic stability or instability. Schweller, McNeil, Peterson, and Schroeder all consider the rise and fall of certain types of governments as factors that can create systemwide instability. In addition, McNeil (Chapter 8), Frieden (Chapter 6), and Kathleen McNamara (Chapter 12) consider pressures on important governmental and societal actors who influence system stability.

The Vulnerability of National Governments and System Stability

Above I outlined how exploitative treatment of the most vulnerable significant governmental actor in 1920s Europe—Weimar Germany— contributed to the rise of an irredentist, totalitarian, and highly mobilized replacement for the liberal Weimar regime. As Schweller and Uchitel outline, once a revisionist Hitler was in power, Germany's position as the most strategically vulnerable great pole led Hitler to devise blitzkrieg strategies, which further destabilized the system. Schweller argues that Hitler hoped to knock out the Soviets before the Americans could enter the war. Uchitel agrees but focuses on an additional German vulnerability: the lack of sufficient indigenous resources to survive a long war. These vulnerabilities created a positive feedback dynamic in which Hitler attacked first his resource-rich neighbors, and then any other state, such as Britain, that mobilized in response to Germany's initial expansionary efforts.

Hitler's vulnerabilities were beyond management. Germany's geographic and power position in the international system were not subject to direct manipulation. And as the world witnessed after Munich, given Hitler's revisionism, any plan to appease him by allowing him to gain key resources through moderate expansion would only have encouraged his aggression. By the time Hitler came to power, some version of World War II was inevitable.

But Hitler's rise to power itself does not seem inevitable. While interwar Germany was destined to be an unhappy country, foreign powers could have done much more to help a status quo German regime stay on its feet. Ironically, it was largely the foreign powers' recognition that Germany was a potential powerhouse that panicked them into shortsighted efforts to hold it down. With a less linear, more systems-oriented approach, they might have recognized that German power potential was an unalterable reality and that all that could be consciously altered was the political form that power potential would take.

The Americans recognized this truth in the late 1940s, allowing West Germany to industrialize and become the first line of defense against Soviet revisionism. As hegemonic stability theorists argue, such enlightened system management was facilitated greatly by the concentration of economic and military power in the hands of one great state. In a multipolar world, guaranteeing the security of individual states and encouraging stability and growth among vulnerable, potentially significant great actors is a knottier problem. Who pays the costs and whose ideas are applied to maintain such a system? The combination of intellectual complexity and collective goods problems make such regimes hard to manage and even more difficult to create in the first place.[23]

The chapter by Schroeder provides a fine guide to the creation of such regimes. Schroeder's history of late eighteenth- and early nineteenth-century Europe suggests that if sincere, intelligent, status quo leaders rule over the most vulnerable significant state within the system, those state leaders might raise the best proposals for international regimes that can stabilize the system as a whole. The farsighted, multifaceted arrangements that these vulnerable states advocate should solve not only their own local security dilemmas but related security dilemmas throughout the system. Regulatory regimes that secure their borders and their domestic political stability should also ameliorate similar, but less acute, problems throughout the system.

Best of all, when these new regimes become institutionalized, long-run diplomatic practices may be transformed, as William Daugherty points out in Chapter 4. Regime creation does more than provide a beneficial alternative to destabilizing, linear strategies in the present. Leaders may get into the habit of turning first to the international regime rather than to military force when confronted with potentially escalatory international disputes. Though initially created to meet the short-term needs of the most vulnerable significant actor, the regime creates beneficial positive feedbacks. At the time the regime is created, it serves to resolve intertwined domestic and international security dilemmas in far reaches of the international system. Over time, more actors become accustomed to turning to the regime first in time of international dispute. As with Frieden's positive feedback loop of monetary integration, such positive feedback loops are unusual in that they are not destabilizing (at least in the usual negative connotation of "destabilizing").

Richard Betts, however, questions the usefulness of some international regimes for promoting international stability. In Chapter 11 he correctly dismisses idealistic notions of universal collective security as utopian at best and as dangerously seductive at worst. But Betts's account leaves room for a limited great-power condominium like the Concert of Europe. Betts argues that of all arrangements on the spectrum from concert to collective security, concert systems are the most realistic. Schroeder and Daugherty concur; they point out that the concert worked because it was not an idealistic rejection of *realpolitik* but a great-power forum for clear explication of sophisticated systems dynamics. It did not seek to cancel international anarchy or individual great powers' ultimate recourse to force but rather provided an arena in which great powers could discuss common threats and proscribe simple, linear, destabilizing responses to them.

Betts is correct to caution that the 1815 concert was a council of despots, not a group of democratic great powers. I still find it plausible, however, to argue that it was ideological homogeneity, not despotism per se, that provided the common ground for the major actors in the concert.[24] As all monarchs in Europe gained from avoiding democratic revolution, all great power democracies will benefit from avoiding the rise of xenophobic despotism in member states such as Russia. A loose North Atlantic concert that includes a status quo Russia might serve the purpose of managing potentially destabilizing small-power conflicts in areas between the great powers (e.g., local Eastern European conflagrations), and managing financial assistance to the most domestically vulnerable concert member, Russia.

Paul Schroeder's historical account in Chapter 3 demonstrates that the best ideas for such regime creation and management need not come from a secure, hegemonic great power. Schroeder's research suggests that in a multipolar world it may be wiser to turn to the sages of besieged states for intellectual leadership. In light of the multipolar systems approach advocated here, it is not surprising that the ideas for the concert came from Leopold and Metternich, who ruled over

Austria, the significant state most hamstrung by geography, military limitations, and ethnic and class-based disturbances.

By linking domestic and international stability, these Austrians invented regimes that deterred domestic revolutionaries and foreign exploitation of them while simultaneously deterring foreign aggression. Aggression was deterred directly by concert policing mechanisms. Equally important was the growing acceptance throughout Europe of Leopold's and Metternich's complex systems logic, making explicit the connection between the destruction of a monarch's domestic legitimacy through invasion, encouragement of domestic revolution in the country attacked, and the precipitation of revolution everywhere through intellectual contagion. The Austrian arguments were convincing to all monarchs who were threatened to varying degrees by the same international and domestic forces and had learned over the past century that more traditional tactics of ensuring their security were painful and of limited effectiveness. Moreover, the fact that the most vulnerable state invented the concert meant that few destabilizing scenarios were ignored. The plethora of interwoven problems facing Austrian leaders not only made them reject linear thinking, it made them the best systems thinkers in Europe.

Schroeder's chapter provides further proof of my thesis that in conditions of multipolarity, the weakest rather than the strongest significant state should be expected to support the best system-informed proposals. Schroeder outlines the intellectual history of acceptance of concert ideas, and indeed, the more vulnerable the state, the earlier it accepted the logic of concert. Most Austrian leaders had learned concert thinking by 1801. Next on board, by 1807, were the relatively vulnerable Prussians, whose interests were threatened by Russia, France and to a degree by the German ally in Vienna. Following the Prussians were the Russians, relatively invulnerable to direct attack by other major powers but facing complex imperial challenges in an ethnically divided Eastern Europe and Balkan region. Finally, the internationally and domestically least vulnerable state, Britain, came on board only in 1813–14. So, the most secure state and hegemon-to-be was the last, not the first, to support a managed multipolar European system. Unlike nineteenth-century British trade and monetary regimes and both Cold War bloc arrangements, concert rules and norms were created in centers of weakness rather than strength. The most vulnerable state stepped forward with the most effective proposals. These proposals did not change the fundamental anarchic nature of the international system: the concert was not a government but a congress of systems thinkers furthering their own selfish interests through community efforts. It was the state with the most to lose through power politics that taught others their own long-term interests.

If in the 1920s states had recalled the lessons of 1815, they might have taken two crucial factors into account: (1) the Weimar Republic was *not* the same actor as Wilhelmine Germany, and placing strict reparations demands on it served only to destroy their own brainchild, the liberal republic itself; (2) the pleas of sincere Weimar officials for reparation relief should have been heeded not only because they were not the kaisers of the past but because they were not the Nazis of the future. A relaxed systems approach that takes distributions of vulnerability and the nature of national governments into account would have counseled a serious look at the economic and political needs of liberal elites in Germany.

Attempting to hold down Germany as a nation was an example either of linear thinking or of overly simple systems thinking by the victorious allies of World War I. It was linear in the sense that it attacked in the simplest way the most obvious threat of 1914, German power potential. It was poor systems thinking (if it was systems thinking at all) in that rather than manipulating systemic and subsystemic variables that lent themselves to adjustment, the world's major actors sought to remove a pole from the system.

Fortunately for Europe today, the most powerful elements in a resurgent Germany are liberal and pro-Western. This desirable outcome would have been unlikely if the victorious Allies had pursued a policy advocated by many after Germany's defeat: the forced suppression of postwar German industrialization. Instead Marshall and Acheson—extraordinary systems thinkers—decided to foster German and Japanese strength while ensuring that it would be employed by liberal leaders in the service of the Free World.

Societal Actors and System Stability

In Chapter 12 Kathleen McNamara offers an example of how important, vulnerable societal actors can affect system stability. The universal concern of European states with domestic farm lobbies led the European Community to create an ad hoc international regime—"green money"—designed to protect farmers from the vicissitudes of increasing international monetary integration. This protection was meant to address the economic concerns of farmers in each country who might otherwise form blocking coalitions in each country against increased European monetary and trade cooperation. But what was originally a limited buffer program to protect farmers generated major trade distortions when international monetary and trade relations became more complex and volatile in the 1970s. Moreover, the complexities of the two-tiered system may also tempt the most vulnerable actors, farmers, to manipulate the discrepancies in the European monetary system in order to gain additional rents; they can do so without easy detection because less directly affected economic groups have little incentive to learn the intricacies of the system.

McNamara's analysis of the concurrent development of European monetary and green money agreements demonstrates how straightforward strategies to solve systemic problems often create ironic and unanticipated problems. European monetary agreements were designed in large part to facilitate trade between European nations. But free trade arrangements threaten the security of farmers within European states. In order to keep member states committed to the integration process, the EC tried to mollify powerful domestic farm lobbies with ad hoc green money arrangements designed to prevent agricultural price discrepancies across borders. As fluctuations in exchange rates became more common and more pronounced after the collapse of Bretton Woods, the contradictions between the subsystem of green money and the more general European monetary system became greater. The distortions created by the green money subsystem began to affect the natural flow of goods between countries, thus reducing the trade benefits of the general monetary system itself.

While in the case of European monetary and trade integration, the influence of vulnerable societal groups threatened regime stability, important societal actors can also act as positive factors in international systems stability. In Helen Milner's account of trade regime stability, powerful international manufacturers are likely to oppose the adoption of destabilizing tariffs because they are both importers and exporters. The rise of international production might similarly preempt destabilizing devaluation alignments between exporters and farmers because exporters increasingly acquire machinery and parts abroad. By weakening devaluation alliances, new business group alignments within countries might lessen states' incentive to take the first step in Frieden's "vicious cycle" of defections from monetary regimes.

Protecting Vulnerable Actors: A Double-Edged Sword

Even if we can identify the most vulnerable significant state, governmental, or societal actors in the international system, it does not necessarily follow that buffering them from systemic vulnerabilities will stabilize the system. When designing such solutions we should remember the sobering analysis of Robert Jervis in Chapter 2. If there is one lesson of systems theorizing, it is that there are rarely simple panaceas to systemic instabilities. The strategy of buffering the most significant vulnerable actor in the international system is no exception to this cardinal rule. Regimes designed to protect vulnerable great powers can backfire for two reasons. First, status quo elites in such vulnerable states may feign weakness and instability in order to maximize foreign assistance. Second, believing themselves to be under the protection of foreign benefactors, they may adopt more provocative external policies than they would in a less secure environment. If the most vulnerable actors are not natural supporters of the status quo, then protecting them may only make them more adventurous.

For example, German guarantees of Austria-Hungary before 1914 probably made Vienna more aggressive toward its neighbors. As Laurence Lafore has argued, Austria-Hungary wanted a tough policy toward the Balkan states not only to preempt the contagion of ethnic nationalism within its borders but also to legitimize the existence of a united empire through an "active" foreign policy.[25] Given this Austro-Hungarian belligerence, less foreign protection might have had a more sobering effect.

A similar example is provided by the triangular relations between Taipei, Beijing, and Washington in the 1950s. While Chiang Kai-shek was not a significant international actor under the definition provided above, the growth of his belligerence during a period of protection is still instructive for our purposes. The American decision to block the Taiwan Straits in 1950 did more than just protect Chiang Kai-shek's regime from the Communists. It also convinced Chiang that he still had a chance to fulfill his irredentist claims on the mainland by dragging the United States into war with the Chinese Communists. Thus, Chiang might not have acted so provocatively in the Straits during the 1950s if he had not enjoyed American protection and had not harbored hopes that the United States might be coaxed into a war with Beijing.

When we design international agreements that buffer vulnerable actors, it is therefore imperative to determine whether the vulnerable actor in question is status quo or revisionist. While belligerence sometimes results from insecurity, it would be naive to assume that it always does. If an actor has expansionist or irredentist tendencies, those tendencies might only be amplified if the actor feels it no longer needs to concern itself with its own security.

Conclusion: Where to Look for Explanations of Systems Outcomes

The studies of eighteenth-, nineteenth- and twentieth-century Europe in this volume should shed light on the security problems in a multipolar post-Cold War world.[26] The earlier European cases provide examples of multipolar management problems not faced in the simpler world of bipolarity. But, as the contributions clearly indicate, understanding what new problems will arise will require much more than recognizing the structural shift.

The chapters in this volume supplement a new literature that recognizes dynamic variables missed by purely structural systems theories. Nonstructural systemwide variables that warrant consideration include offensive/defensive military advantage, patterns of economic interdependence and levels of transnational production, the distribution of status quo and revisionist states, and variations of power distribution within multipolar sets. The book's authors also consider a group of subsystemic factors within key states that can trigger systemic effects, including domestic regime stability or instability, and the relative power of various domestic economic and political coalitions. Since changes in these variables affect the likelihood that significant actors will take the first steps in destabilizing positive feedback loops, systems theories should consider them in their analyses.

Notes

1. Kenneth Waltz, *Theory of International Politics* (Reading, MA: Addison-Wesley, 1979).

2. For this critique of Waltz's theory, see Thomas J. Christensen and Jack Snyder, "Chain Gangs and Passed Bucks: Predicting Alliance Patterns in Multipolarity," *International Organization*, Vol. 44, No. 2 (Spring 1990), pp. 137–169.

3. For discussion of these contradictory virtues of superpowers, see Waltz, *Theory of International Politics*, pp. 169, and 171–172.

4. For some examples of hegemonic stability theory see Charles Kindleberger, *The World in Depression: 1929–1939* (Berkeley: University of California Press, 1973); Robert Gilpin, *War and Change in International Politics*, (Cambridge, UK: Cambridge University Press, 1981); Stephen Krasner, "State Power and the Structure of International Trade," *World Politics*, Vol. 28 (April 1976), pp. 317–347; Robert Keohane, "The Theory of Hegemonic Stability and Changes in International Economic Regimes," in Ole Holsti, et al. (eds.), *Change in the International System* (Boulder, Colo.: Westview, 1980). For critiques of hegemonic stability theory on theoretical and empirical grounds, see Keohane, *After Hegemony: Cooperation and Discord in the World Political Economy* (Princeton: Princeton University Press, 1984);

Duncan Snidal, "Limitations of Hegemonic Stability Theory," *International Organization*, Vol. 39, No. 4 (Autumn 1985), pp. 579–614; Bruce Russett, "The Mysterious Case of Vanishing Hegemony: or Is Mark Twain Really Dead?" *International Organization*, Vol. 39, No. 2 (Spring 1985), pp. 207–232; and Susan Strange, "Protectionism and World Politics," *International Organization*, Vol. 39, No. 2 (Spring 1985), pp. 233–260.

5. An excellent collaboration that addresses many of the shortcomings of purely structural theories of international political economy is G. John Ikenberry, David A. Lake, and Michael Mastundano, eds., *The State and American Foreign Economic Policy* (Ithaca, NY: Cornell University Press, 1988). In this volume, various scholars adopt a "state as pivot" approach, in which domestic and international forces combine to determine observed policy outcomes.

6. For the debate between critical theorists and neorealists see Robert Keohane, ed., *Neorealism and Its Critics* (New York: Columbia University Press, 1986).

7. I believe this label was first pinned on neo-realism in Robert W. Cox, "Social Forces, States and World Orders: Beyond International Relations Theory," in Keohane, ed., *Neorealism and Its Critics*, p. 208.

8. Kenneth Waltz, "The Politics of Peace," *International Studies Quarterly*, Vol. 11, No. 3 (September 1967), pp. 199–211. The early date of this astute analysis demonstrates the pragmatic value of Waltz's general approach.

9. Robert Jervis, "Cooperation Under the Security Dilemma," *World Politics*, Vol. 30, No. 2 (January 1978), pp. 167–214; Helen V. Milner, *Resisting Protectionism: Global Industries and the Politics of International Trade* (Princeton: Princeton University Press, 1988); John Gerard Ruggie, "International Regimes, Transactions and Change: Embedded Liberalism in the Post-War Economic Order," *International Organization*, Vol. 36, No. 2 (Spring 1982), pp. 379–415; Steven Van Evera, "Causes of War" (Ph.D. Dissertation, University of California at Berkeley, 1984); Stephen Van Evera, "The Cult of The Offensive and the Origins of the First World War," in Stephen E. Miller, ed., *Military Strategy and the Origins of the First World War*, (Princeton, NJ: Princeton University Press, 1985), pp. 58–107; Christensen and Snyder, "Chain Gangs and Passed Bucks."

10. For the pioneering works, see Jervis, "Cooperation Under the Security Dilemma"; and George Quester, *Offense and Defense in the International System* (New York: Wiley, 1977). In addition to the works by Van Evera and Christensen and Snyder cited in note 9, see Barry R. Posen, *The Sources of Military Doctrine* (Ithaca, NY: Cornell University Press, 1984); and Jack Snyder, "Civil-Military Relations and the Cult of the Offensive, 1914 and 1984," in Miller, ed. *Military Strategy*. For an excellent critique of the concepts of offense/defense balance in political science, see Jack S. Levy, "The Offense/Defense Balance of Military Technology," *International Studies Quarterly*, Vol. 28 (June 1984), pp. 219–238.

11. See Jervis, Chapter 2.

12. For another article by Schweller that analyzes the impact of differing domestic regimes on whether declining hegemony will lead to preventive war, see "Domestic Structure and Preventive War: Are Democracies More Pacific?" *World Politics*, Vol. 44, No. 2 (January 1992), pp. 235–269.

13. See Paul Schroeder, "The Neo-Realist Theory of International Politics: An Historian's View" (unpublished manuscript). In international political economy, David A. Lake has analyzed how differing distributions of economic capability within hegemonic and non-hegemonic international systems affect the likelihood of free trade. See his "International Economic Structures and American Foreign Economic Policy," *World Politics*, Vol. 35, No. 4 (July 1983), pp.517–43.

14. See Posen, *Sources of Military Doctrine*, ch. 5; and Christensen and Snyder, "Chain Gangs and Passed Bucks," pp. 162–165.

15. Milner, *Resisting Protectionism*; Milner, "Resisting the Protectionist Temptation: Industry and the Making of Trade Policy in France and the United States During the 1970s," *International Organization*, Vol. 41, No. 4 (Autumn 1987), pp. 639–665; and Milner, "Trading Places: Industries for Free Trade," *World Politics*, Vol. 40, No. 3 (April 1988), pp. 350–76.

16. Jeffry Frieden, "Invested Interests: The Politics of National Economic Policies in a World of Global Finance," *International Organization*, Vol. 45, No. 4 (Autumn 1991), pp. 425–451.

17. For the classic formulation, see Mancur Olson, *The Logic Of Collective Action: Public Goods and the Theory of Groups* (Cambridge, MA: Harvard University Press, 1965).

18. See Paul Ensor, "Caught in the Machine: Seoul Tries to Cut its Dependence on Tokyo," *Far Eastern Economic Review*, September 18, 1986, pp. 62–64.

19. Charles Perrow, *Normal Accidents* (New York: Basic Books, 1984).

20. For the original formulation see Peter Gourevitch, "The Second Image Reversed," *International Organization*, Vol. 32, No. 4 (Autumn 1987), pp. 881–912. The terms first, second, and third images were coined by Kenneth N. Waltz to refer to international relations theories that view human nature, domestic politics, and the international system, respectively, as the causes of international phenomena. See Waltz, *Man, The State and War: A Theoretical Analysis* (New York: Columbia University Press, 1954 and 1959). The "second image reversed" refers to theories that explain how international phenomena influence domestic political formations. My phrase "complex version of the second image reversed" refers to Gourevitch's argument that international pressures (crises) affect domestic coalitional alignments within countries, which in turn affect the subsequent foreign and domestic economic policies of those countries. See Gourevitch, *Politics in Hard Times: Comparative Responses to International Economic Crises* (Ithaca: Cornell University Press, 1986).

21. For an excellent discussion of the various policy options open to American and Western leaders in regard to the former Soviet Union, see Stephen Van Evera "Meeting the Eastern Crisis: Preventing War in the

Former Soviet Empire," forthcoming in *Security Studies*, Vol. 1, No. 3 (Spring 1992).

22. William Safire, "The New Despotism," *The New York Times*, March 12, 1992, p. A23.

23. For the classic discussion of collective goods problems in international politics, see Mancur Olson, Jr., and Richard Zeckhauser, "An Economic Theory of Alliances," *The Review of Economics and Statistics*, Vol. 48, No. 3 (August 1966), pp. 266–279. For an article that stresses how intellectual coordination (e.g., an international epistemic community) facilitates international cooperation, see G. John Ikenberry, "A World Economy Restored: Expert Consensus and the Anglo-American Post-War Settlement," *International Organization*, Vol. 46, No. 1 (Winter 1992), pp. 289–322.

24. This is the position taken by Charles A. Kupchan and Clifford A. Kupchan in "Concerts, Collective Security and the Future of Europe," *International Security*, Vol. 16, No. 1 (Summer 1991), pp. 114–161.

25. Laurence Lafore, *The Long Fuse: An Interpretation of the Origins of World War I*, 2nd ed. (New York: Lippincott, 1971), Chapters 5 and 6.

26. One might argue that the world is currently unipolar as does the recently leaked February 18, 1992, draft of the "Defense Planning Guidance for the Fiscal Years 1994–1999." See "Excerpts from Pentagon's Plan: 'Prevent the Re-Emergence of a New Rival'," *New York Times*, March 8, 1992. Despite Pentagon optimism, the future of American hegemony has a seemingly unsound foundation, resting as it does on continued American economic leadership, the perseverance of German and Japanese military weakness, and the long-term willingness of the American public to fund policing activities around the globe.

About the Book and Editors

Prevailing theories of the international system reflect the bygone era of the bipolar Cold War stalemate. Understanding the complex new multipolar era requires a fresh approach. In this volume, Jack Snyder and Robert Jervis show why ultra-parsimonious systems theories that focus on the balance of power among a few large states fail to capture the dynamics of today's highly interdependent, multipolar system. Taking issue with the accepted wisdom of the international studies field, Snyder argues that systems theories must address the interactions between international and domestic systems, and between military and economic systems.

Using Robert Jervis's seminal essay on unintended consequences in complex systems as their point of departure, the contributing authors explore case studies of past and present multipolar systems to present analyses that challenge current thinking in international security and economics.

Historical chapters show how understanding the workings of complex systems allowed statesmen to devise the Concert of Europe and how the collapse of the Concert in the Crimean War was triggered by the tsar's failure to comprehend the indirect impact his strategies would have on British public opinion. Another chapter highlights the feedback processes between domestic politics and the international monetary system that led to the rise and fall of the gold standard and to the creation of the European monetary system. The diplomacy of the Moroccan crisis of 1905 is used to show that conventional wisdom places unwarranted weight on a state's reputation for standing firm in the interconnected international system.

The discussions also explore the systemic causes of World War II: Contributors examine how the international financial system unwittingly helped destroy Weimar democracy and offer a challenging reinterpretation of the workings of the balance of power in the 1930s. Qualifying the view that interdependence promotes peace, we see how German and Japanese economic dependence led them to adopt offensive military strategies.

The contributing authors rebut currently popular arguments for collective security and trace the complex, unforeseen interactions between Europe's monetary system and its scheme for financing agricultural subsidies. The final chapter, tying all the case studies together, argues that the key to systemic stability is to provide security for the most vulnerable, important state in the system.

Jack Snyder and **Robert Jervis** are both professors of political science at the Institute of War and Peace Studies, Columbia University. Snyder has written several books on international security issues, including *Myths of Empire: Domestic Politics and International Ambition.* Jervis's most recent book is *The Meaning of the Nuclear Revolution.*

Index